History and Memory in African-American Culture

History and Memory in African-American Culture

Edited by

GENEVIÈVE FABRE
ROBERT O'MEALLY

New York Oxford
OXFORD UNIVERSITY PRESS
1994

Oxford University Press

Oxford New York Toronto
Delhi Bombay Calcutta Madras Karachi
Kuala Lumpur Singapore Hong Kong Tokyo
Nairobi Dar es Salaam Cape Town
Melbourne Auckland Madrid

and associated companies in
Berlin Ibadan

Published by Oxford University Press, Inc.,
200 Madison Avenue, New York, New York 10016

Library of Congress Cataloging-in-Publication Data
History and memory in African-American culture / edited by Geneviève Fabre, Robert O'Meally.
p. cm.
Includes index.
ISBN 0-19-508396-2; 0-19-508397-0 (pbk)
1. Afro-Americans—History. 2. Afro-Americans—Historiography.
3. Afro-American arts. 4. American literature—Afro-American authors. I. Fabre, Geneviève. II. O'Meally, Robert G., 1948–
E185.H546 1994
973'.0496073—dc20 93-37582

9 8 7 6 5 4 3 2 1

Printed in the United States of America
on acid-free paper

Permission to reprint the following selections is gratefully acknowledged:

"The Politics of Fiction, Anthropology, and the Folk: Zora Neale Hurston," by Hazel Carby, from *New Essays on "Their Eyes Were Watching God,"* ed. Michael Awkward © 1991 by Cambridge University Press. Reprinted by permission of Cambridge University Press.

" 'Of Plymouth Rock and Jamestown and Ellis Island'; Or, Ethnic Literature and Some Redefinitions of 'America,' " by Werner Sollors, from *Immigrants in Two Democracies: French and American Experience,* ed. Donald Horowitz and Gérard Noiriel © 1992 by New York University Press. Reprinted by permission of New York University Press.

"What One Cannot Remember Mistakenly," by Karen Fields © 1993 by Baylor University. Reprinted by permission of Baylor University.

"Between Memory and History: *Les Lieux de Mémoire,*" by Pierre Nora © 1989 by the Regents of the University of California. Reprinted from *Representations,* no. 26 (Spring 1989), pp. 7–25, by permission of the publisher.

Permission to quote from the following is gratefully acknowledged:

Invisible Man by Ralph Ellison. Copyright © 1947, 1948, 1952 by Ralph Ellison. Reprinted by permission of Random House, Inc.

Angle of Ascent, New and Selected Poems by Robert Hayden. Copyright © 1975 by Liveright Publishing Corporation. Reprinted by permission of Liveright Publishing Corporation.

Island: Poetry and History of Chinese Immigrants on Angel Island, 1910–1940, by Him Mark Lai, Genny Lim, and Judy Yng, Copyright 1980, History of Chinese Detained on Island Project. Reprinted with the permission of University of Washington Press.

Selected Poems by Langston Hughes. Copyright 1926 by Alfred A. Knopf, Inc. and renewed 1954 by Langston Hughes. Reprinted by permission of the publisher.

Beloved by Toni Morrison. Copyright © 1987 by Toni Morrison. Permission granted by International Creative Management, Inc.

"Joal" and Section III of "To New York" from *The Collected Poetry of Léopold Sédar Senghor,* translated by Melvin Dixon. Copyright 1991 by The University Press of Virginia. Reprinted by permission of the publisher.

Portions of "Dahomey" are reprinted from *The Black Unicorn: Poems* by Audre Lorde, by permission of W. W. Norton & Company, Inc. Copyright © 1978 by Audre Lorde.

" 'Mystery Boy' Looks for Kin in Nashville" is reprinted from *Angle of Ascent: New and Selected Poems* by Robert Hayden, by permission of Liveright Publishing Corporation. Copyright © 1975, 1972, 1970, 1966 by Robert Hayden.

"Heritage" by Countee Cullen. Copyrights held by the Amistad Research Center, Tulane University, La. Administered by JJKR Associated, New York, N.Y.

Acknowledgements

First of all, the editors and writers wish to thank Harvard University's W. E. B. Du Bois Institute for Afro-American Research for hosting our faculty working group and for supporting our explorations in black history and memory. Most especially we are grateful to the Institute's Randall Burkett, whose leadership was indispensable to the seminar's progress.

We thank the Ford Foundation for its generous funding of the seminar. We are particularly grateful for Sheila Biddle's supportive guidance.

Harvard was our seminar's home, but we also convened at the Center for the Study of Southern Culture at the University of Mississippi at Oxford. We are deeply indebted to the center's director, William Ferris, for his rich colleagueship. We are grateful for the welcome we received at Rust College in Holly Springs, Mississippi, where we attended an unforgettable blues and gospel festival.

We also met in New York City. We wish to extend our warmest thanks to Howard Dodson, chief of the Schomburg Center for Research in Black Culture of the New York Public Library. We offer thanks to James Hatch and Camille Billops for introducing us to the Hatch Billops Collection; and to Julia Hotton, who welcomed us at the Manhattan East Gallery.

For our final meeting, an international conference held at The Rockefeller Foundation Study and Conference Center in Bellagio, Italy, we thank The Rockefeller Foundation and all of our hosts at the center.

For their assistance in preparing the manuscript, we thank Soo Ji Min and Jeanne Marie Liggio, English majors at Barnard College. The project's friend in its final stages has been Sanda Lwin, a graduate student in English at Columbia University, whose skills as a researcher and writer helped make the book a reality. We are grateful to Barnard and Columbia for their sponsorship of these student workers.

Finally, we wish to thank Oxford's editors, Elizabeth McGuire, Elda Rotor, and Henry Krawitz, for their steadfastness and their excellent professionalism, and Patricia Perrier for the superb index.

Contents

History and Memory in African-American Culture

1

Introduction

ROBERT O'MEALLY AND GENEVIÈVE FABRE

> Ask your wife to take you around to the gin mills and the barber shops and the juke joints and the churches, Brother. Yes, and the beauty parlors on Saturdays when they're frying hair. A whole unrecorded history is spoken then, Brother.
>
> —Ralph Ellison, *Invisible Man*

> It was not a story to pass on. So they forgot her. Like an unpleasant dream during a troubling sleep. . . . They can touch it if they like, but don't, because they know things will never be the same if they do.
>
> —Toni Morrison, *Beloved*

The contemporary philosopher Cornel West has said that in this nation infamous for its brash will to historical forgetfulness, African Americans have been the ones who could not forget: They have been the Americans "who could not not know."[1] American whites, by contrast, could act as if by leaving the Old World they had escaped the burdens of the past in favor of a vigorously principled new place where only the vividness of the present and promise of the future really mattered. Blacks could not not know differently. The legacy of slavery and the serried workings of racism and prejudice have meant that even the most optimistic black Americans are, as the expression goes, "born knowing" that there is a wide gulf between America's promises and practices. For blacks this tragic consciousness has spelled a cautious and critical attitude toward unfolding experience—a stance toward history that is braced by the awareness that the past, as Faulkner put it, has never really *passed.* "Every shut eye ain't sleep, every good-bye ain't gone."[2]

This critical perspective coincides with that of the modern historian who knows that history is not so much a fixed, objective rendering of "the facts" as it is a process of constant rethinking and reworking in a world of chance and change. "History is always written wrong," declared Santayana in 1905, "and so always needs to be rewritten."[3] And so blacks and whites—historians as well as other professionals, along with front-porch observers—have been engaged in a struggle over what to say about America's past and how to say it.

Which parts of history matter most? Who makes history? Whose history will prevail? These are the thorniest of questions in an American scene where the stakes are high and where American history is being rewritten root, branch, and trunk—where (as one recent university conference poster announced) "the past ain't what it used to be."

For the time has long since passed when it would somehow suffice for historians just to amend "the master story" here and there, adding a black figure or two while keeping the same old narrative shapes and plot lines. As Nathan Huggins has stated, altering American history to account fully for the nation's black voices would change the tone and meaning—the frame and substance—of the entire story. Rather than a sort of *Pilgrim's Progress* tale of bold ascent and triumph, American history with the black parts told in full would be transmuted into an existential tragedy, closer, Huggins says, to Sartre's *No Exit* than to the vision of life in Bunyan[4]—or, perhaps, closer to the yes–no/sweet–bitter black American blues.

But what are the real implications of telling the true story? What does telling the full truth about black American history actually signify? Here one is confronted with the paradox that even as blacks have been excluded from most written accounts of American history (certainly until twenty-five years ago this was dramatically the case), they nonetheless have been indispensable makers and shapers of the American cultural and sociopolitical legacy. Though often invisible to history, they have played roles in it that have proved crucial. Paradoxically, the black American has served as a kind of barometer of what is most American about America. "The Negro is America's metaphor," wrote Richard Wright. "The history of the Negro in America is the history of America written in vivid and bloody terms; it is the history of Western Man writ small. It is the history of men who tried to adjust themselves to a world whose laws, customs, and instruments of force were leveled against them."[5] The state of the nation's commitment to its own promises of social justice could well be measured, says Wright, by how well or unwell U.S. blacks were faring in their American homeland.

Accordingly, Ralph Ellison has pronounced what he has called Ellison's law: *First something happens to us; and then, just wait, it happens to every other group in America.*[6] The black something that happens can be a new style of expression (like rock 'n' roll) or a problematic social circumstance (like drug abuse). Either way, just as whites were most sure they could ignore events that seemed not to involve them at all, they spread across the nation in a flash. Coming from the bottom of the American social ladder—and for so long rendered untouchable and invisible by slavery and segregation—blacks ironically have been relatively freer from the rules enforced by the official cultural monitors. As a group they tended to care the least about what, for instance, the black social dance called the Black Bottom looked like to the proctors at the local ballet class (be they white or black). Thus it is no surprise that blacks—who invented such definitively American forms as the spiritual, jazz music and dance, as well as expressions associated with the cultures of rags, blues, bebop, hip hop, and rap—have had such a potent impact on

America's cultural life and history. What would American culture be without their presence?[7]

According to Ellison, U.S. black-created forms can be "immediately recognized as what the American culture and society had instead of a sacred past." What there is of an indigenous American tradition "didn't come from across the water; it came from the land and it came from beneath the social hierarchy. . . . We provided the past."[8] If this is true at home, it has been just as true abroad. Referring to ragtime music, James Weldon Johnson wrote in 1912: "In Paris they call it American music."[9] For Americans at home and abroad, black Americans and their expression seemed to encapsulate something central about the nation's culture, something definitive about its history. Coda to Ellison: "We provided the past."

But, of course, blacks have been more than just markers and gauges for nonblack Americans seeking who they are (and, oddly, who they believe they are not). African Americans have "made history" in other senses as well. We refer here not just to the long tradition, stretching from George Washington Williams to the present, of black historians writing American history books as such. We also refer to those blacks who may not be professional historians but who nonetheless are a watchful people, a people who could not not know: a people of long memory.

In her essay "The Site of Memory," Toni Morrison has insisted upon the responsibility modern African–American fiction writers have toward the past, and upon the necessity of "ripping the veil" which has been drawn over certain facts of black experience. Examining her literary heritage—and, most important, slave narratives, "the print origins of black literature"—she became aware of the blanks left by those early authors, of the constraints under which they worked. "The act of imagination is bound up with memory," she writes, and the act of imagination may help fill the blanks, reveal unheeded or silenced aspects. Inventing a new literary tradition, in *Beloved* she herself tried to find and expose part of the truth about slave life, either by revealing "proceedings too terrible to relate," "unspeakable things unspoken," or by probing into "the private and interior life of people who did not write it."[10]

Which brings us to this book's key question of the past viewed through the twin matrices of history and memory. Both processes involve the retrieval of felt experience from the mix and jumble of the past, the bulk of which certainly is not to be passed on. Most of what happens (consider not just dull interludes but sicknesses and nightmares) is best forgotten.[11] At least until quite recently, many observers would agree that while history at its finest is a discipline (sometimes classified as a social science, sometimes as one of the liberal arts), memory is something else again, something less. Memory, these same observers might say, is by definition a personal activity, subject to the biases, quirks, and rhythms of the individual's mind. If a remembered event is expressed verbally, the remembrance is of course slanted by the teller's choice of words and by his or her sense of how to shape a tale. It is a created version of an event snatched from the chaos of the otherwise invisible world gone by.

History, according to this paradigm, is closer to a scientific field wherein the practitioners routinely insist on proofs and corroborating evidence to support balanced and sober modes of analysis. This is so even for the contemporary historian, who recognizes that historians are human beings (with their own biases, quirks, and rhythms of the mind) who use language, shape histories, and sometimes cite twice-told tales as part of the evidence. If history is an imperfect tale always open to revision, as Santayana said, the historian can still take pride in the fact that history is a tale to be revised with as much disinterested objectivity as can be humanly mustered. Compared with the helter-skelter and dreamy impressionism of human memory, history is closer to human knowledge, which can fall back on the stability of fact and reasoned truth.

And yet the writing—narrating—of history has not been the exclusive concern of historians; it has also been the province of artists and writers as well as other thoughtful and sometimes brilliant people. It is significant that in some languages (as in French) the word for "history" also means "story." The French word *histoire* designates history as it is lived and experienced, the discipline through which it is approached and grasped, and the narrative which relates it. We are thus reminded again that historians are storytellers after all, concerned with introducing characters and shaping their stories with some sense of the rhetoric needed to confront their audience's expectations and to bring the past to life. The first black American historians may have been the authors of slave narratives, those whose testimonies comprised not only eyewitness accounts of remembered experience but also a set of worldviews with interpretations, analyses, and historical judgments. At these points, and indeed at many points around the compass, memory and history come together.

Some French historians, like Jacques le Goff and Pierre Nora, have attempted to reexamine this complex interaction between history and memory.[12] At the same time, literary critics and philosophers (among them Paul Ricoeur) have studied the relationship between history and narrative as well as the configuration of time in historical or fictional narratives.[13] Thus, a more expansive and yet critical attitude toward both history and memory has evolved. Memory itself has become an object of concentrated scrutiny by historians studying its forms: written or oral; collective or individual; concrete or ephemeral; affective, analytic, or obedient to the rules of magic. Here the great questions have remained: When is memory a part of history? In what sense is what is remembered a crucial part of what is to be passed on to future generations? What is the true relation of art and history or of history and memory?

The present volume began as a set of faculty seminar papers questioning the stark dichotomy of memory and history and focusing on African-American culture as a locus for study.[14] Geneviève Fabre's idea was to use as a starting point and framework for the group's inquiries about African-American history and memory the concept of *lieux de mémoire,* or "sites of memory." The term was coined and the theory developed by the French historian Pierre Nora in his introduction to a seven-volume study of France's history and national memory called *Les Lieux de mémoire.*[15]

In this important landmark study in French historiography, Nora examines the polarization so often established between abstract, intellectual history and the affective stuff of memory—and declares his distrust for "dictatorial, tyrannical" memory. But what is most striking is Nora's yearning to discover ways in which history and memory can creatively interact. He argues that in our rapidly changing contemporary societies, our relation to the past has been radically altered. The swift forward pull of modern life instills a feeling of uprootedness and drift. We moderns have to confront the problem of no longer having "overarching ideological narratives . . . for example, The Triumph of Western Civilization . . . defining what is supposed to be memorable."[16] The desire to retrieve the past still endures. Threatened by a sense of discontinuity and forgetfulness, we seek new moorings and props, new means of reactivating the processes of remembrance as we reach toward a better sense of who we are and whence we have come.

As Nora describes his term, *lieux de mémoire* exist

> where memory crystallizes and secretes itself at a particular historical moment, a turning point where consciousness of a break with the past is bound up with the sense that memory has been torn—but torn in such a way as to pose the problem of the embodiment of memory in certain sites where a sense of historical continuity persists.[17]

In our modern pluralistic societies, the idea of a total history supported by a global memory has given way to decentered microhistories and to a multiplicity of memories. Spurred on by a will to remember—by a conscious effort to limit forgetfulness—*lieux de mémoire* are the products of this interaction between history and memory, of the interplay between the personal and the collective. To create *lieux de mémoire,* according to Nora, we "deliberately create archives, maintain anniversaries, organize celebrations, pronounce eulogies . . . [and exercise] commemorative vigilance."

Whether deliberately or not, individual or group memory selects certain landmarks of the past—places, artworks, dates; persons, public or private, well known or obscure, real or imagined—and invests them with symbolic and political significance. Thus a *lieu de mémoire* may be historical or legendary event or figure, a book or an era, a place or an idea; it can be "simple and ambiguous, natural and artificial, at once immediately available in sensuous experience and susceptible to the most abstract elaboration." Nonetheless it is "material, symbolic, and functional." *Lieux de mémoire* can prompt both the processes of imaginative recollection and the historical consciousness. Such *lieux de mémoire* as New Orleans, *The Souls of Black Folk,* the civil rights movement, or the tar baby tale are products of this highly energized interaction of history and memory and stand at the nexus of personal and collective memory.

Werner Sollors has reminded us that at times the very term *history* can imply motives of aggressively willful exclusion. For example, Hegel argued in his "Lectures on the Philosophy of History" that America and Africa had not entered the upper room of what he termed "the true theater of History."[18]

"For this reason," said Sollors, "what is called 'memory' (and Nora's *lieux de mémoire*) may become a form of counterhistory that challenges the false generalizations in exclusionary 'History.' " Nor do we need to accept a polarized view of history and memory which posits that the whites (or some other "advanced" group with power or privilege) had the history while the blacks (or some other "simple" group without power or privilege and thus relegated to what Lévi-Strauss calls the realm of "inculture")[19] were stuck with nothing but impulsive, affective memory. Black and white Americans, our group found, had both categories of recollection; neither one, history or memory, can be entirely disentangled from the other. And in America *lieux de mémoire*—"sites" that are "wrapped up" with "a heap of signifying"[20]—are objects of history and memory, keystone places worked over by the American imagination, by blacks and whites.

Our seminar began with terms and concepts invented in France to describe French historiography, but quickly we found that they nonetheless could offer rich possibilities for us as scholars of African Americana. Our application of the concept of *lieux de mémoire* to culture helped in our reconsideration of U.S. black identity as part of a historical process involving dynamic inventions and communications in books, art, and oral forms. Energized by Nora's cornerstone essay, and by the interdisciplinary work and play of the seminar, we set out to grasp new ways of conceiving our projects. And, indeed, many of us found that our essays were changed for the better by the cross-fertilizing experience.

Our task was to reconsider American history not only so that it better accounted for the works of black historians in the usual sense. Our larger purpose was to revise what was meant by this history as a process inclusive of "black and unknown bards," historians without portfolio, who inscribed their world with landmarks made significant because men and women remembered them so complexly and so well that somehow the traces of their memory survived to become history.

Our seminar's first job was to identify certain African-American *lieux de mémoire*. We did so from the perspectives of scholars in the fields of U.S. history, cultural history and anthropology, folklore, sociology, art history, and literary theory. Many of us worked in spaces between the disciplines; some of us presented our findings as writers of poetry and autobiography. Whatever our disciplinary foci, we paid careful attention to the manners in which significances of *lieux de mémoire* are conveyed—verbally, kinetically, visually—through the careful coining of signs, symbols, and icons. We looked with care at such monumental books as *The Souls of Black Folk* and *Invisible Man;* at such events as Juneteenth and other Emancipation celebrations; and at the blues, sounding through a hundred years of the music in a variety of forms and fashions.

Not that this identification of *lieux de mémoire* was a simple matter. We noted that certain sites of memory were sometimes constructed by one generation in one way and then reinterpreted by another. These sites may fall unexpectedly out of grace or be revisited suddenly, and brought back to life. We found that *lieux de mémoire* are constantly evolving new configurations of meaning, and that their constant revision makes them part of the dynamism of the historical process.

For us African Americanists perhaps the most significant aspect of the idea of *lieux de mémoire* was its capacity to suggest new categories of sources for the historian: new sets of sometimes very difficult readings. We considered, for example, how to read certain dances, paintings, buildings, journals, and oral forms of expression. More than ever, we saw novels, poems, slave narratives, autobiographies, and oral testimonies as crucial parts of the historical record. These varied repositories of individual memories, taken together, create a collective communal memory.

As a group looking at these complex forms of expression, we realized our responsibility to confront the issue of audiences: of those directly and indirectly addressed by these varied historical makers and markers, these *lieux de mémoire*. It is clear enough that audiences varying in ethnic affiliation, class, gender, and/or location in space or time—such different ones will receive sometimes widely different messages from the coded texts we were studying. And sometimes a line would be drawn or a battered curtain would fall. In the midst of an interview between the Italian scholar Alessandro Portelli and a black couple in Kentucky, Portelli was told:

> My grandma they, they—she was a daughter of—slaves. Her parents were slaves. And they used to sit around and tell things, you know, that happened when they were children and what they parents said. And I'll tell you what that will do for you: although you might not have done a thing in this world to me, but because you're white, of what my parents said. . . . *I don't trust you, you know*. . . .[21]

Nor have we taken the easy way of approaching African Americans as a monolith. Our studies paid close attention to divisions within this deeply varied group. Sometimes, we noted, interactions within the veil of African America have concerned constituencies that are intimately related; then again, they have involved groups that hardly acknowledge each other. Our studies of black "folk" and "elite" groups, for example, brought such divisions sharply into focus. Here again—in a sense following Nora's example—we have resisted the conventional wisdom of viewing orality and literacy as opposite cultural modalities; rather, we have seen them as parts of a tightly interwoven matrix of expression for a people who have nurtured a rich oral tradition and who at the same time have set literacy as a persistently sought ideal. Indeed, we have found ourselves at odds with the common Western assumption of the superiority of the written tradition. Our emphasis fell on the ways in which African Americans have idealized the mastery of both modes of expression. Both the word on the page and the word spoken in air can combine, we found, to create richly meaningful statements or "structures of feeling."[22]

The particular essays here were given at our meetings, which took place most often at Harvard University's Du Bois Institute, which hosted the seminar and supported it generously. We also held meetings at the Schomburg Center for Research in Black Culture in New York City and at the University of Mississippi at Oxford. Finally, we held an international conference at Bellagio, Italy, for an expanded meeting that involved participation by Americans who had not been in our group before and by scholars from Africa, Europe, and the West Indies. Our idea was to broaden the scope of our discussions as much as we could and to acknowledge formally the study of the culture of blacks in the United States as an important international endeavor. Doubtless Ellison's law has a counterpart that says: Watch out for the brother and sister in black; what they do may affect history and memory all over the world.

Our group in its varied configurations took on questions of history and memory and of *lieux de mémoire* not in a manner of "following" or "applying" Nora; each essay offers a critical engagement with the possibilities inherent in his argument for a reexploration of black history in an American context.

Melvin Dixon's essay takes direct aim at Nora's opposition of "history" and "memory," and at his biases in favor of recorded historical analysis when he considers non-Europeans. Dixon proposes the alternative of using *literary* evocations of memory to reconstitute wholeness. For him the tensions between history and memory are further enhanced by those between narrative and metaphor. Attentive to textual images, rhythms, and moods, Dixon sees striking differences in the poetic strategies of certain poets throughout the diaspora: strategies of remembering in Senghor, of disremembering in Hayden, of unremembering in Cullen.

In Dixon's analysis, a network of interconnections emerges between different geographical places—Harlem, with its distinctive history and topography; the South, that "very old place"; the French West Indies and the other islands; and Africa itself. Each conveys special intimations and ideas of creolization, *négritude,* and blackness. In the quest for identity and the assertion of birthright and ancestry, sites are anchors and frames. Geographical places and place-names map out bearings in space and time. Memory ultimately becomes the essential metaphor, a means to confront the troublesome past and the uncertain present.

Geography is a concern for Hazel Carby, too, as she reflects upon the canonization of Zora Neale Hurston's work on the rural "folk" in recent years. Why all the energy for the retrieval of this set of pastoral and romantic tropes, particularly this novel, *Their Eyes Were Watching God,* as a *lieu de mémoire* at this time? Does the great fascination for Hurston over the past decade parallel the interest in African Americans as representatives of the exotic and the primitive in the 1920s? As she raises such troubling queries, Carby makes us aware of the forces of myth and ideology at play in the arena of history and memory—especially when the highly charged figure of a powerful black woman stands at center stage. Focusing mainly on the crisis in representation and the way cultural responses are shaped, Carby analyzes Hurston's evidently contradictory position as one who was herself simultaneously part of the folk and of the elite. She takes Hurston to task for her choice to simplify the definition of African-American culture as essentially rural at a time when urban migration was bringing dramatic changes to black communities, north and south. Carby also makes clear that the process of remembering is tightly knit with that of forgetting. When *Their Eyes Were Watching God* makes its way to syllabi all over campus, what more pointedly political works get dropped?

In his essay David Blight is concerned in another way with history and memory as fields of contestation. He gives a detailed analysis of W. E. B. Du Bois's active scholarly work at struggling for American historical memory, especially in *Black Reconstruction.* Blight cites an essay by Du Bois, who described black American history as a "swarthy spectre sitting in its accustomed seat at the nation's feast"—like Banquo's ghost come to haunt the historians at the dining table.[23] Coupling a scientific approach with a poet's intuition and language, Du Bois developed an acute awareness of the conflicting memories. As Blight shows, he used new sources to tell "the American story" in a drivingly counterhistorical manner—in a way to threaten the positivists of his era with losing their bearings.

Certain categories of *lieux de mémoire* can change the very shape of the year. Geneviève Fabre's essay focuses on the multitude of freedom celebrations that constitute nothing less than a new way of organizing time, a black calendar. (And calendars, as Werner Sollors has observed, are themselves subtle *lieux de mémoire:* "[T]hey connect a present community to its political past.") Focusing on the antebellum era, Fabre shows that landmark dates like the Fourth of July could not have the same meaning for black and white America; the American Revolution could not be the same site of memory for those who were still held in bondage and for those who had set themselves free from colonial servitude.

Black freedom celebrations—which shifted from one date to another (from the first of January to the fifth of July to the first of August) as various steps were taken toward partial and gradual emancipation—were both a constant reminder of enduring inequalities and injustices as well as an anticipation of Freedom Day to come. Considered as historical gestus and as cultural performances, these festive events, conjuring and performing as they did a freedom which was at the same time presence and absence, blended indictment and hope; they combined memory with utopian desire and prophecy. They imagined a history where former Africans and slaves would become full-fledged American citizens. Here black culture is considered as part of an aggressively political and intellectual process in which blacks are scrutinizing their situation, resisting and rebelling against it when necessary, and making plans to turn things around. They are building an insurgent history and projecting a new vision of the future, a "memory of the future."

In his essay Werner Sollors also considers American landmarks and the fiercely debated stories that go with them: Plymouth Rock, Jamestown, and Ellis Island. These monumental metaphors function to symbolize certain views of America and its past. As sites of memory, they inspire us to remember, to forget, and even to fabricate untrue stories in support of our familial and national myths of what we wish had happened, the way we wish we were.

What one sees when one sees the Statue of Liberty depends, Sollors says, on who does the looking, when it is done, and the attitudes toward history that frame the vision. Seeing such *lieux de mémoire* inspires us to lie (to make up *histoires*) in directions that are most revealing.

Alexandre Dumas père, Henry Ossawa Tanner, and Josephine Baker are considered in the essay by Michel Fabre, who notes their identification by black American intellectuals as African-American *lieux de mémoire*—"beacons," as he calls them, shining out "France's" promise of a better day for blacks back in the United States. Here again it is clear that a *lieu de mémoire* may be such a personage as Dumas himself (considered a hero in the black American press of his era) or such a place as the Château d'If near Marseilles—famous only because of its description in Dumas's novel *The Count of Monte-Cristo*. Frederick Douglass took his wife to the Château d'If "because the genius of the Negro had woven around it such a network of enchantment." In turn, as Fabre observes, many black American writers who went to France as exiles soon became important legends and *lieux de mémoire* for the worldwide black community.

Angelika Krüger-Kahloula focuses on yet another kind of monument—the *lieux de mémoire* of U.S. graveyards and headstones memorializing the African-American dead. She notes that "the categories of caste and class that affect the residential patterns of the living also touch the homes of the dead," lain to rest in cemeteries whose grounds are as strictly segregated as the neighborhoods in which they lived. "Racism pervades the metropoles and the necropoles, biography and memory." In a twist of fate, Krüger-Kahloula's own essay changes the meaning of these sites—established to reinforce all patterns of segregation and white superiority—making them one of black irony and the struggle against white violence and hubris. They are reminders of a past to move beyond.

Karen Fields's essay turns on the challenges of her role as a social scientist who wants to get straight a set of stories told to her by Mrs. Mamie Garvin Fields, her grandmother, a southern black woman with her own sense of the etiquette of how to tell what happened. Here we have the spirited record of a sometimes heated dialogue between representatives of two generations who approach memory from two diverging perspectives and using different tools: fascinatingly, the exchanges force the younger Fields, the sociologist, to reconsider her craft and her scientific discipline.

According to her own sense of story, Mrs. Fields tells how the white city fathers in her southern town erected a statue of John C. Calhoun: "Blacks took that statue personally. . . . We used to carry something with us, if we knew we would be passing that way, in order to deface that statue—scratch up the coat, break the watch chain, try to knock off the nose." Here was a woman with a memory and a lesson of resistance—or, put in the language of this seminar: here was a community bent on deconstructing a subversive *lieu de mémoire* and now constructing another in the form of Mrs. Fields's self-authenticating, didactic narrative. Do we require proofs or photos to back up this woman's voice?

In somewhat the same vein, Alessandro Portelli examines the processes of "history-telling" by witnesses recounting their stories to an interviewer, in this case—as already noted—to one outside the witnesses' family and accustomed circle of conversationalists. Portelli explores the relation of literary "lines" to lines on a map as he witnesses the composition of history as a set of oral testimonies. He studies the witnesses' engagement with the interviewer (in significant switches of personal pronouns) and their imaginative reconstitution of causality into (often conficting and nonchronological) memories. Implicitly making the point that there is no such thing as raw data in a setting like this, Portelli addresses the complicated workings of memory when the teller realizes that his or her report will result in a product (a tape, a text, a book) that will in turn become part of history.

Susan Willis's essay raises important theoretical problems in characterizing the process whereby black cultural production is broadcast throughout the mass media and then rebounded to the black community (and everybody else who is tuned in) as part of a game whose motive is money. How can these black cultural forms possibly be as potently empowering for the community as "folk forms" of other eras seemed to have been? Have the blind forces of the marketplace so manipulated them that they are utterly dysfunctional? In other words, this essay addresses one of the questions that Zora Neale Hurston eluded: it looks at the inevitable transformation that mass (and mainly urban) culture is bringing to African-American culture, changes which are turning it into a commodity product and creating another major crisis in representation.

Taking a strong stand against Nora's archival conception of culture, Willis focuses her analysis on culture as process and practice rather than a body of data. She examines the way African Americans participate in the reinvention of the culture and the forging of new images. And she argues that certain figures, like Br'er Rabbit, can become mediators in the confrontation between folk culture and mass culture in the search for new icons. On this battleground, authentic images and faked stereotyped ones wage war, expressing all the historical complexities and ambivalence of racial representations. What can we make of such current *lieux de mémoire* as Mickey Mouse cartoons (with their echoes from blackface minstrelsy) or rap music (now used to push new products all over the television dial)? Whose stories do they tell?

VéVé Clark's study of the significance of African-American art in motion—black dancers and their dances—is also a theoretical "intervention" that is pointedly critical of Nora. Questioning Nora's view of memory and history as dissociated, Clark shows how Katherine Dunham, in her work as ethnographer–historian and choreographer, stressed instead memory and history's *continuities*. Like Hurston, Dunham is an intellectual–artist who offers interpretations of the folk memory: here again we find the tension and interplay between individual and collective, folk and elite.

Using the Caribbean and the American South as her fields of observation, and juxtaposing indigenous art forms with the styles of formal modern dance, Dunham creates a vitally cross-cultural mode—the Dunham technique. Such is perhaps her response to the growing creolization she discovered, and to the result of her sharp awareness of class and color antagonisms. Based on her observation of these conflicts and oppositions, the syntax of Dunham's choreography evolved out of both her research methods and her performance principles—of oxymoron and paradox. It comprises a critical reappraisal of the history of the British West Indies and the French West Indies, seen in their specificity but also in their close relation to the southern United States. In her dances, some of them boiling with political rage, Dunham expresses the contradictory history of New World acculturation: "the memory of difference."

It is important that this essay also contains Clark's forthright challenge to readers of complex texts across several mediums to develop their literacy when it comes to telling how dancing bodies achieve their meanings. Clark closely reads the *lieux de mémoire* of Dunham's dances in a way that might make the dance-illiterate among us want to get with it and do better.

Catherine Clinton's essay steps forward to contemplate the meaning of the rape of black women—a subject silenced in conventional histories but engraved on the memories of rape's victims and prevalent, too, in historical sources when we know where to find them. Rape, says Clinton, leaves the mark of an "ineradicable memory." Using voices from black literature as key witnesses, Clinton makes the case that there is a history to be written that hears black women and grapples with the significance of their trials in the American "penarchy." "The power of memory," says Clinton, "must draw us out of the novel and into the archives."

Like Clinton, Carby, and Dixon, Andrée-Anne Kekeh uses fiction as a prism through which to view issues of history and memory as they pertain to black women in particular. The fine reading by Kekeh of passages central to Williams's novel *Dessa Rose* demonstrates how themes of "history and descriptive power of memory" can be written into a work of art. The novel's central figure achieves her freedom by remembering her linkages with her community and its traditions. Kekeh considers the case of Dessa's memory of "Mammy" as a figure inspiring memory, a *lieu de mémoire*—"Mammy" the rebel who is also an agent of cultural remembrance. Her hands and her way of fixing Dessa's hair passed along a felt message of survival: "Mammy cornrowed our hair," recalls Dessa. "This is where I learned to listen right, between Mammy's thighs, where I first learned how to speak, from listening to grown people talk."

Visual and aural *lieux de mémoire* are considered in Richard J. Powell's essay. This art historian reads paintings and collages by African-American artists Aaron Douglas and Romare Bearden as stylized evocations of aspects of the African past and of the American black tradition of the blues. Powell evaluates the tonal and rhythmic play in paintings by blacks as what Albert Murray has termed "the visual equivalent of the blues." Here, as in the Kekeh essay, among others, the crucial issue of who makes and who writes history—so often raised in historiography—is central. For Powell the artist is a maker of traditions: a historian of the textures, shapes—and perhaps even the sounds—of "epochs" ("styles are epochs") gone by and yet vividly with us. Herein, suggests Powell, lay the seeds for a theory of African-American art and its efflorescent traditions.

Robert G. O'Meally's essay considers the blues, too, along with other African-American vernacular forms as sites of memory. Jangling blues, traditional tales, and other forms jar the heroes of Ralph Ellison's fiction to consciousness—by which term O'Meally means not just self-awareness but community awareness, a sense of history that spells a responsiblity to take meaningful action. Such vernacular *lieux de mémoire* inspire the Invisible Man, the main man in a work which is itself a *lieu de mémoire.* Here the suggestion is that storytellers (exalted "liars" of the southern black idiom) may be history makers, too. Certainly it is true that several generations of students, here and abroad, learn something about black life and times by doing the homework assignment calling for them to study the lying and signifying of a black boy whose once-upon-a-time tale starts, "I am an invisible man."

Nellie McKay's essay also considers literature as a text retrieving memory and making history. She seconds Pierre Nora's declaration that "dictatorial" history—which, in McKay's words "considered itself universal but represented only a segment of memory"—is undermined by *lieux de mémoire.* This latter idea of considering the past suggests, she says, that "the quest for history and the privilege of authenticating memory now belong to everyone." Accordingly, McKay turns to a *lieu de mémoire* in the form of the autobiographical journals of Charlotte L. Forten-Grimké, a keen observer of the troubled nineteenth-century world she knew. Forten-Grimké gives a particular view of the institution that has inspired national amnesia—slavery. Her journals and she herself are complex reminders, *lieux de mémoire* of might and signification. McKay's presentation of Forten-Grimké suggests a wide field of black autobiographical writings as historical sources not yet sufficiently tapped. There's a better, fuller history to be written, McKay's work says: a history textured with the reports of magnificent witnesses.

This collection concludes with a very personal essay by Robert Burns Stepto meant to balance the keynote essay by Melvin Dixon. It is a lyrical reminiscence of the writer's early years in Chicago. Now the literary historian and critic lays aside his scholarly armor and remembers the wonder and verve of times at the "Fifty-seven twenty-*two* Indiana Ave*nue*" home of Grandma and Grandpa Burns, as well as time spent with other relatives his parents stayed with before they got a place of their own. Stepto's anecdotal remembrances remind us of the mysterious processes of memory itself. He sees his family history through the lens of a man who has read a mountain of books and heard a great riverful of good-time talk and lies (some well told right here). Of course, all of his experiences shape what is remembered, and how the rememberer tells his life. Story cascades into story as Stepto marks the spaces of his youth—record store, barbershop, Chinese restaurant (who says a Chinese restaurant isn't part of a black memoir?)—all personal as well as communal sites of memory. Set up as the tale of young man on his way somewhere, these *lieux de mémoire* connect with larger scheme of heroics begetting (in the way that legendary heroes and tales do)[24] further legends and further heroic action.

We dedicate these essays to the memory of our dear friends Nathan Huggins—brilliant historian and man-of-letters and the inventor of the concept of a Black Studies faculty working group at Harvard—and Melvin Dixon—magnificent poet, novelist, critic, and translator—both of whom served as the group's intellectual guides and standard-bearers.

We also want to acknowledge the symbolic significance of the W. E. B. Du Bois Institute at Harvard for our work. What could we have accomplished without the wisdom, know-how, and high energy of Randall Burkett, the institute's assistant director? The institute, a marvelous place to exchange ideas and experience moments of true intellectual comradeship, is itself a splendid "site of memory."

Notes

1. West said this at a lecture at Wesleyan University in May 1988. See also Ellison, *Shadow and Act* (New York: Random House, 1964), p. 124.

2. African-American folk expression; quoted in Sterling A. Brown, Arthur P. Davis, and Ulysses Lee, eds., *Negro Caravan* (New York: Dryden Press, 1941), p. 423.

3. George Santayana, *The Life of Reason, Reason in Science* (New York: Scribner's, 1932), p. 45.

4. Nathan Huggins, "The Deforming Mirror of Truth," introduction to the 1990 edition of *Black Odyssey: The African-American Ordeal in Slavery* (New York: Vintage, 1990), p. xvii.

5. Richard Wright, *White Man, Listen!* (New York: Doubleday, 1957), p. 109.

6. Ralph Ellison, "On Being the Target of Discrimination," *New York Times* (special suppl.: "A World of Difference"), April 16, 1989, pp. 6–9.

7. This question is raised in an essay called "What America Would Be Like Without Blacks," included in Ellison's *Going to the Territory* (New York: Random House, 1987).

8. Quoted in "The Alain Locke Symposium—December 1, 1973," *Harvard Advocate* (special issue), (1974), 22.

9. James Weldon Johnson, *The Autobiography of an Ex-Coloured Man* (New York: Knopf, 1927), p. 87.

10. Quoted in William Zinsser, ed., *Inventing the Truth: The Art and Craft of Memoir* (Boston: Houghton Mifflin, 1987), pp. 103–24.

11. Santayana, *The Life of Reason,* p. 52.

12. See Jacques le Goff, *Histoire et mémoire* (Paris: Gallimard, 1988); Jacques le Goff and Pierre Nora, eds. *Faire de l'histoire,* 3 vols. (Paris: Gallimard, 1974).

13. Paul Ricoeur, *Temps et récit: le temps raconté* (Paris: Seuil, 1985).

14. Geneviève Fabre was the seminar's convener and Melvin Dixon was her co-chair. The theme was suggested to her by her reading of recent French historiography.

15. The introduction to his study is reprinted as the last chapter of the present volume.

16. Nora, *Les Lieux de mémoire,* p. 7. Here the sense of Nora's meaning derives from an early draft of Nellie McKay's essay, included in the present volume.

17. Ibid., p. 7. Subsequent quotations refer to the same source.

18. Georg Wilhelm Friedrich Hegel, *Lectures on the Philosophy of History: The Lectures of 1825–1826,* (Berkeley: University of California Press, 1990), p. 98.

19. Claude Lévi-Strauss, *Race et Histoire* (Paris: UNESCO, 1952).

20. Ralph Ellison, *Invisible Man* (New York: Random House, 1952), p. 379.

21. The emphasis is the editors'; see Portelli, this volume.

22. This phrase is from Raymond Williams, *The Long Revolution* (New York: Columbia University Press, 1961).

23. The Shakespearean allusion in this context is borrowed from Werner Sollors.

24. Here one has in mind Albert Murray's novel *Train Whistle Guitar* (New York; McGraw-Hill, 1974), a work which meditates brilliantly on this question of the interplay of history and memory.

2

The Black Writer's Use of Memory

MELVIN DIXON

This essay centers on my interest in the way geographic locations such as the American South and Africa have become important sites of memory in the construction of a viable African-American culture. In this connection, it is very significant that Pierre Nora's conception of memory-generating experiences rests on his assessment of major differences, if not stark ruptures, between history and memory.[1]

Nora sees history as static and memory as dynamic. He defines history loosely as "how our hopelessly forgetful modern societies, propelled by change, organize the past." He defines memory as an actual phenomenon, "open to the dialectic of remembering and forgetting" (p. 8). Where history, for Nora, is the reconstruction of what no longer exists, memory is life itself, vulnerable to the vicissitudes of our time, nourishing recollection, yet responsive to trends, including censorship. Whereas history calls for analysis and criticism, memory is almost sacred, absolute, concretely rooted in "spaces, gestures, images, objects" (p. 9). Here Nora appears to echo Joseph Campbell on the power of myth and Carl Jung on the prevalence of dream symbols and the power of the collective unconscious.

Although Nora emphasizes the analytic characteristic of history and the psychological aspects of memory, which interests those of us who, as writers, become critics of culture, he betrays something of a Eurocentric bias in favor of recorded historical analysis when he considers non-Europeans. He argues (much too disparagingly, for my taste) that "among the new nations, independence has swept into history societies newly awakened from their ethnological slumbers by colonial violation. Similarly, a process of interior decolonization has affected ethnic minorities, families and groups that until now have possessed reserves of memory but little or no historical capital" (p. 7).

Using Nora's own criteria for the recovery of the past, I intend to show that the presence in our culture of significant *lieux de mémoire* establishes the value of cultural memory and the very kind of history or historiography that is not dependent on written analysis or criticism but rather achieves an alternative record of critical discussion through the exercise of memory. Memory becomes a tool to regain and reconstruct not just the past but history itself. What is useful in Nora's argument is his broad recognition of how *lieux de mémoire* may contribute to the process of cultural recovery.

When particular places, gestures, images, or objects deliberately call us to remember, when they project a definite will to remember—such as firework displays on the Fourth of July, the Vietnam Veterans Memorial in Washington, D.C., the AIDS quilt pieced together from individual lost lives and displayed collectively in traveling exhibits nationwide, or the Macy's Thanksgiving Day Parade featuring cartoon characters as inflated giants of our childhood fantasies—when these events call us to remember, they become *lieux de mémoire,* sites of memory. In essence, Nora argues that "the quest for memory is the search for history."

"One disremembered time"

When I consider the abject exclusion of African Americans from the discourse of mainstream American history, culture, or society, and when I ponder the distinct rupture in black family genealogy, I look for what strategies of recollection have been used to transmit an Afrocentric wholeness in our heritage. I am reminded of one of my favorite poems by Robert Hayden, a major poet who died in 1981. Hayden's work includes classic historical meditations (such as his sonnet "Frederick Douglass" and his poem on the slave trade called "Middle Passage"). He also recounts in intimate, personal terms the psychological consequences of the loss of family and, by turns, memory and a name. His poem "Mystery Boy Looks for Kin in Nashville" goes like this:

> Puzzle faces in the dying elms
> promise him treats if he will stay.
> Sometimes they hiss and spit at him
> like varmits caught
> in a thicket of butterflies.
>
> A black doll,
> one disremembered time,
> came floating down to him
> through mimosa's fancywork leaves and blooms
> to be his hidden bride.
>
> From the road beyond the creepered walls
> they call to him now and then,
> and he'll take off in spite of the angry trees,
> hearing like the loudening of his heart
> the name he never can he never can repeat.
>
> And when he gets to where the voices were—
> Don't cry, his dollbaby wife implores;
> I know where they are, don't cry.

We'll go and find them, we'll go
and ask them for your name again.[2]

What is true for the psychological dislocation and disremembering in this poem becomes emblematic for the urgency of our recovery of cultural memory. And this reach exceeds the boundaries of national identity, those "creepered walls" and the cruel, taunting voices of mistaken heritage. In my reading of African-American literature I sense a movement of cumulative racial significance, from the particular to the global, from, say, Harlem, an urban district, to the South, a region of several states, and to Africa, a continent. These sites have been used by many African-American writers not only to evoke a sense of place but, more importantly, to enlarge the frame of cultural reference for the depiction of black experiences by anchoring that experience in memory—a memory that ultimately rewrites history.

Let me take you, for a moment, to the neighborhood where I now live, Harlem, in New York City. Entering my part of Manhattan from the Major Degan Thruway at the intersection of Lenox Avenue and 145th Street there are two nightclubs, one called the Zanzi-bar, the other called the Lagos Bar. Farther south Lenox Avenue becomes Malcolm X Boulevard. At the intersection of 125th Street and Malcolm X Boulevard street vendors have for many years kept an open-air market for fruits, vegetables, North Carolina pecans, cassette tapes, and dungarees. The street sign above this corner says AFRICAN MARKET SQUARE. A short walk in the vicinity brings you in contact with black people of every shade and texture, living on numbered streets and on streets that have changed their names to Frederick Douglass Boulevard, Johnny Hartman Plaza, Marcus Garvey Park, and Adam Clayton Powell Boulevard.

What you may gather from these names and places is a sense of changes within history, for these people were important in Harlem's past. But most important—especially to me, a relative newcomer to the area—is the fact that the people have taken charge of their lives and their identity as African Americans. Not only do these names celebrate and commemorate great figures in black culture, they provoke our active participation in that history. What was important yesterday becomes a landmark today. Invoking memory of that time or that person is the only way to orient oneself today. If you are lost in upper Manhattan, you must remember the people who lived there and those who continue to live there or you will never find your direction. This is the way some people have defined their community and themselves. This exercise and reification of cultural memory reconstructs a history of that region that never included blacks until 1915. Harlem, you recall, was not settled originally by blacks, nor was the great, spacious design of urban boulevards and vintage architecture designed for blacks, but for a wealthy white Euro-American population. Furthermore, the predominant presence of blacks in Harlem from 1915 onward simply represented a demographic shift in the population. Only later and through an affirmation of the lived experience of the people did changes in street names and urban character signal the revitalization of a community into an expression of cultural memory.

By calling themselves to remember Africa and/or the racial past, black Americans are actually re-membering, as in repopulating broad continuities within the African diaspora. This movement is nonlinear, and it disrupts our notions of chronology. If history were mere chronology, some might see Africa as the beginning of race consciousness—and racial origin—rather than the culmination or fulfillment of ancestry. Enslaved Africans were brought to the New World, mainly to the American South (only later did they migrate in great numbers to the North). But in much of the material centered in a construction of racial culture and identity, an ahistorical, cyclical, figurative movement emerges as the reverse. An investigation of Harlem as a northern urban community reveals direct ties—deliberate, crafted ties—to the American South and then to Africa. And these are not places but stages or sites on which the drama of self-acquisition is played. Take, for example, the scene in Ellison's *Invisible Man* when the nameless protagonist eats a yam purchased from a Harlem street vendor. He, of course, asserts his birthright in the delirium of his joy when he exclaims, "I yam what I am."[3] Most critics have reflected upon the affirmation of identity and cultural punning that occurs here. But further investigation reveals that with one delicious bite the protagonist is projected back to the South of his cultural conditioning and source of his present rebellion, and forward to a reassessment of racial "sites," events, or *lieux de mémoire.*

"Then you must be from South Car'lina," the vendor says with a grin. And the protagonist reponds, "South Carolina nothing, where I come from we really go for yams." The protagonist exchanges place specificity for a broader reference—gustatory, culinary, and otherwise. Yet just as soon as he delights in another discovery when he reflects: "Yet the freedom to eat yams on the street was far less than I had expected upon coming to the city" (p. 261), he ingests a bit of yam spoiled by frost. This moment of memory and revelation—almost akin to Proust's reverie with the tasty madeleine—is laden with Ellison's persistent irony in the novel, forcing the protagonist and the reader to rethink at every turn the most manifest expressions of a recaptured, remembered past. This scene of bittersweet birthright comes just before the invisible man happens upon the eviction of an elderly couple whose belongings include Free Papers and in whose defense the protagonist acts in such a way as to earn him a position with the Brotherhood. Ellison's boomeranging of expectations, a spiral of history and memory, fuels the novel. But Ellison's argument about ancestry and the validity of purely racial sources extends far back to the beginnings of African-American cultural expression.

A look at the names of black fraternal organizations, schools, and newspapers during the nineteenth century reveals a preponderance of references to Africa: The African Association for Mutual Relief (1827), the African Free School (1828) and, of course, the African Methodist Episcopal Church. These names serve two functions: (1) to acknowledge the fact of historical origin and (2) to remind members past and present of that historical origin. If family disruption and loss of precise genealogy distance black Americans from more solid, or literal, connections to an African identity, they nonetheless increase our predilection for the way figurative connections become charged with increasing symbolic importance. And here again memory rather than history becomes a fruitful strategy for the recovery of the past.

Memory as Metaphor: "I'm still in Luzana?"

The prose tradition in African-American literature, as seen in Ellison's *Invisible Man,* contributes to Nora's argument differentiating history and memory. The conflict for black writers is crucial, for it addresses the simple issue of control of the past as well as proper transmission of the past. The presence in our literature of such distinctive genres as the slave narrative, the autobiographical novel, and the poetics of blues music suggests the subversive lengths artists have gone to preserve the personal past and project distinctive voices into the whirlwind. Ernest Gaines's novel *The Autobiography of Miss Jane Pittman* instructs us about the gains that accrue from memory's revision of history. The protagonist, Miss Jane, is important. She is a *lieu de mémoire* ripe for the promulgation of cultural memory and African ancestry, as represented by her skill at oral rather than written transmission or analysis of her story, her history. The tension between conventional history—and even the recently valued technique of oral history—and memory here suggests that Miss Jane's exercise of memory makes her into a metaphor.

When the historian arrives to hear Miss Jane's story, his efforts are thwarted by Mary, Miss Jane's neighbor. The exchange between them is telling:

> "What you want to know about Miss Jane for?" Mary said.
> "I teach history," I said. "I'm sure her life's story can help me explain things to my students."
> "What's wrong with them books you already got?" Mary said.
> "Miss Jane's not in them," I said.[4]

The record of history contained in books contrasts sharply with Miss Jane's as yet unrecorded memory. As he listens and records her story, the historian learns that without ever leaving Luzana (itself a metaphorical rendering of what Louisiana really is in folk speech, and hence a place different from the state's geographical name), Miss Jane experiences all of history (slavery, emancipation, Reconstruction, Jim Crow segregation, and the civil rights movement, and a nascent period of black power). She contains that history, carries it in her memory. Her larger historical participation makes her a metaphor of the witness of the past. Secondly, the historian learns that orality and memory transmitted orally require communal expression. When Miss Jane would fall silent, "someone else would always pick up the narration." When the historian concludes his introductory remarks he affirms, "Miss Jane's story is all of their stories, and their stories are Miss Jane's." By remaining within Luzana and remaining faithful to her individual and collective memory, Miss Jane records a new history.

If history as story promotes narrative, then memory, which is often expressed episodically and through visceral imagery independent of chronology, very much like a dream, reveals itself often as metaphor. The tension between history and memory then can also be expressed as a tension between narrative and metaphor. If I can extend this argument into a consideration of race and gender, I want to note that the tension between the telling and receiving of Miss Jane's story owes something to the dynamic of the male historian confronting the black female memory, subject to the demands and release of a suppressed authority as a woman. I mention this aspect of the framework largely to call our attention to Gaines's fiction and to the persistent manner in which major novels by contemporary black woman writers have used similar strategies of reappropriation of the past. In Sherley Anne Williams's novel *Dessa Rose,* the memory of the slave woman must elude capture in the "history" of rebellion about to be written by Adam Nehemiah. When Dessa is able to preserve her name and her memory from further violation in history, she becomes a metaphor for the way a black woman's story remains her own.

More recently, Toni Morrison's novel *Beloved* argues for this same complexity when Sethe's narrative of infanticide is disrupted by the actual presence of memory in the form of her dead daughter's ghost. Morrison, like Ellison, enjoys the irony of memory associations and continuous haunting. When Morrison tells readers at the novel's close "It was not a story to pass on,"[5] we are reminded of the three-hundred-odd pages of the telling, the passing on. This is the novelist's effort to heal the psychological disruption of identity Robert Hayden spoke about. With Baldwinesque urgency, Morrison, speaking of Beloved, intones: "Everybody knew what she was called, but nobody anywhere knew her name. Disremembered and unaccounted for, she cannot be lost because no one is looking for her, and even if they were, how can they call her if they don't know her name?" (p. 274).

"What is Africa to me"

Tradition in black poetry, like its cousin in prose, observes the presence of racial ancestry and memory with considerable irony and surprise. If we overlook the most glaring clichés of the "African warrior o my beautiful black woman" poetry of the sixties, we learn that racial memory provoked poets as distant in time and sensibility as Phillis Wheatley, Countee Cullen, and Langston Hughes, and distantly beyond our shores to the *négritude* poetry of Aimé Césaire, Jacques Roumain, and Léopold Sédar Senghor. Here metaphor and remembrance occupy the charged terrain of cultural authority.

If Phillis Wheatley claims the moral authority that derives from African ancestry when she admonishes her Puritan audience that "Negroes black as cain / may be refined and join th'angelic train,"[6] why has there been such a reluctance among modern black poets to use cultural memory for reclamation rather than renunciation?

Poetic practice throughout tradition has charged the word *Africa* with meaning but not memory. And mere utterance of the word cannot endow us with the living phenomenon a *lieu de mémoire* requires. Perhaps we would do better if we examined the conflicting elements of race that appeared during the years of the Harlem Renaissance when such poets as Countee Cullen and Langston Hughes were battling over the poetic prizes of cultural memory. Cullen embraced book learning, Hughes experience. Cullen treasured the written text of history, Hughes the memory of active living. Compare, for example, Cullen's lines "Africa? A book one thumbs / Listlessly, till slumber comes"[7] with the compelling *lieux de mémoire* within an unnamed Africa in Hughes's active musings in "A Negro Speaks of Rivers," written before Hughes ever traveled to the continent: "I bathed in the Euphrates when dawns were young / I built my hut near the Congo and it lulled me to sleep."[8]

Cullen's poem "Heritage" remains an enigma of cultural memory without the masterful jousting and dueling between narrative and metaphor we find in selected prose. Although Cullen's poem vacillates between acceptance and rejection of ancestry, the speaker's ambivalence fails to affirm—even ironically—the complexity of a self discovered through the art of memory. Against the speaker's repeated claims of forgetfulness toward a "heathen" Africa, an imperative of ancestry emerges in the inescapable discovery of his racial nature, "one three centuries removed." He begins:

> What is Africa to me:
> Copper sun or scarlet sea,
> Jungle star or jungle track,
> Strong bronzed men, or regal black
> Women from whose loins I sprang
> When the birds of Eden sang?
>
> (p. 36)

Cullen attempts to counter these stereotypical and received images with the overwhelming urge to amnesia brought on by conversion to Christianity. "Unremembered are her bats / Circling through the night, her cats." Then nature intervenes to question the extent of the speaker's forgetting: "In an old remembered way / Rain works on me night and day" (p. 36). This brings the speaker face to face with the racial and religious conflicts behind his dilemma. Memory, even in its absence, is the poet's chief means of confronting a troublesome past and an uncertain present.

How the Senegalese poet Léopold Sédar Senghor recognized Cullen's poetics of racial amnesia only to subvert them reveals the distinctive strategies this African poet used to project metaphors of remembering. Senghor's recurring master trope is "the Kingdom of Childhood," that realm of personal past he reclaims from the prejudices of Europe and baptizes as *négritude,* which he defines as the sum total of cultural values in the black world. Memory, for Senghor, is a celebration of the self. And although he acknowledges a debt to Cullen, Senghor shouts his repeated "I remember" as a proclamation and embrace of ancestral joy rather than the "unremembering" in Cullen or the "disremembering" in Hayden. These points became clear to me as I began to translate Senghor's poetry. In his poem "Joal" Senghor celebrates his birthplace and, in so doing, celebrates himself:

> Joal!
> I remember.
>
> I remember the regal *signare* women under the green shade of verandas,
> Those mulatto women with eyes as surreal as moonlight on the shore.
>
> I remember the red glory of Sunset
> Koumba N'Dofene would weave into his royal cloak.
>
> I remember the funeral feasts fuming with the blood
> Of slaughtered cattle,
> The noise of quarrels, the rhapsodies of the griots.
>
> I remember the pagan voices singing the *Tantum Ergo,*
> The processions and the palm leaves and the triumphal arches.
> I remember the dance of nubile girls,
> The wrestling songs—Oh! the final dance of stout young men
> Poised so slender and tall
> And the women's pure shout of love—*Kor Siga!*
>
> I remember, I remember . . .
> My head swirling.
> What a weary walk through the long days of Europe
> Where sometimes an orphan jazz comes sobbing, sobbing, sobbing.[9]

Senghor's choice of "Je me rappelle" in the original French for "I remember" suggests an important act of self-creation in the exercise of memory. The reflexive verb can mean literally "I myself recall" or "I recall myself," thus bringing the self into being. Senghor also ponders the redemptive power of blackness when he observes Africanness in New York City in all its racial and spiritual dimensions:

> New York! I say New York, let black blood flow into your blood.
> Let it wash the rust from your steel joints, like an oil of life.
> Let it give your bridges the curve of hips and supple vines.
> . . . .
> Just open your eyes to the April rainbow
> And your ears, especially your ears, to God
> Who in one burst of saxophone laughter
> Created heaven and earth in six days,
> And on the seventh slept a deep Negro sleep.
>
> (p. 87)

Unlike Senghor, the Caribbean poet Derek Walcott adopts Cullen's strategy of rhetorical questioning as a way to provoke his own confrontation with memory and history. In "A Far Cry from Africa," however, Walcott affirms rather than rejects ancestral imperatives even when they force him to accept an uncomfortably dual racial heritage:

> I who have cursed
> The drunken officer of British rule, how choose

Between this Africa and the English tongue I love?
Betray them both, or give back what they give?
How can I face such slaughter and be cool?
How can I turn from Africa and live?[10]

Duality is also key to Audre Lorde's approach to affirming ancestry through gender and celebrating gender through ancestry. In her collection *The Black Unicorn,* Lorde's remembered women from Dahomey, Coniagui, and 125 Street achieve voice from the ancestral empowerment of gender; this occurs without Walcott's or Cullen's despair or Senghor's feminization of the past. In "Dahomey" she responds to Walcott's question about language as follows:

Bearing two drums on my head I speak
whatever language is needed
to sharpen the knives of my tongue
the snake is aware although sleeping
under my blood
since I am a woman whether or not
you are against me
I will braid my hair
even
in the seasons of rain.

Rain, for Lorde, is not an occasion for the surrender of ancestry, as it is for Cullen, but rather a moment for control, as when nature presents a challenge to such autonomy as suggested by braiding the hair.

Cullen, Senghor, Walcott, and Lorde represent cardinal points in the way poetry can orient the compass of memory. The differences in their strategies for meeting the imperatives of ancestry and the complexity of their affirmation of self through heritage form the basis of my analysis of the impact of memory and the use of memory by modern black poets. Such acts of recollection give shape to a literature in diaspora whose common racial ancestry cuts across boundaries of language, nationality, and gender.

Memory, whether acquired (through received images as in Cullen) or lived (recalled or recollected images in Senghor and Walcott) or mythologized (as in Lorde), is the poet's chief means of writing the self into the larger history of the race.

Memory and Me

In my own fiction and poetry I, too, have been haunted by the twin demons of history and memory. My book of poems *Change of Territory* revisits Europe and Africa through living on those charged continents and ruminating on the impact of place on my racial person. The four-part structure of the collection suggests changes in place or sites of recovery from historical dislocation as I experienced them in the American South, Europe, Africa, and during a return home.

In my novel *Trouble the Water* the protagonist is a black historian who forgets the painful aspects of his past only to suffer their sudden and potentially tragic consequences in his family's reconciliation.

Apart from uttering references to Africa or the South, I hope that my lived experiences there furnish the actual phenomena required to call memory into being and transmit the pride of cultural revalidation. My poem remembers the textures of "winter without snow (DaKar, Senegal)":

> Harmattan starts its December howling,
> hurling grit of the Sahara all around.
> Don't look to the sky for rescue.
> Breathe, and you fill up with sand.
>
> Run to the woods and the grass has dried.
> Those baobab trees are the squat arms
> of grandfathers poking from their graves,
> some hands waving us out to play, some
> holding back the brown fog from the blue.
>
> It's no trick, no delicate mirage.
> Screech like a hawk when your feet won't move,
> nobody hears you, and roaches big as thumbs
> come crumbing at your toes, the ants to dance.
> Stay where you are, grow round and down.
>
> Remember your father's cough, the hacking phlegm,
> your uncle's South brown teeth? Ever wonder
> why fingers crook where they come from?
> It's your turn to sun burn. Just don't let them
> catch you combing desert dust from your hair.

Notes

1. Unless otherwise noted, all quotations are from Pierre Nora, "Between Memory and History: *Les Lieux de Mémoire*," *Representations* 26(Spring 1989): 7–24.
2. Robert Hayden, "Mystery Boy Looks for Kin in Nashville," in *Angle of Ascent, New and Selected Poems* (New York: Liveright, 1975), p. 38.
3. Ralph Ellison, *Invisible Man* (New York: Vintage, 1952), p. 260.
4. Ernest Gaines, *The Autobiography of Miss Jane Pittman* (New York: Dial, 1971), p. viii.
5. Toni Morrison, *Beloved* (New York: Knopf, 1987), p. 274.
6. Phillis Wheatley, "On being brought from Africa to America," in *The Collected Works of Phillis Wheatley,* ed. John Shields (New York: Oxford University Press, 1988), p. 18.
7. Countee Cullen, "Heritage," in *Color* (New York: Harper, 1925), p. 37.
8. Langston Hughes, "A Negro Speaks of Rivers," in *The Weary Blues* (New York: Knopf, 1926), p. 51.
9. Léopold Sédar Senghor, *The Collected Poetry,* trans. Melvin Dixon (Charlottesville, Va.: University Press of Virginia, 1991), p. 7. This translation is based upon the French edition of Senghor's poetry published by Editions du Seuil (1964, 1990).
10. Derek Walcott, "A Far Cry from Africa," in *Selected Poems* (New York: Farrar, Straus, 1964), pp. 3–4.
11. Audre Lorde, "Dahomey," in *The Black Unicorn* (New York: W. W. Norton, 1978), pp. 10–11.

3

The Politics of Fiction, Anthropology, and the Folk: Zora Neale Hurston

HAZEL CARBY

The works of Zora Neale Hurston, in particular the novel *Their Eyes Were Watching God,* have been the object of more than a decade of critical attention. In addition to the critical consideration of Hurston's writings, her work has received the level of institutional support necessary for Hurston to enter the American literary mainstream. Two examples of this support would be the special Hurston seminar held at the Modern Language Association annual conference in 1975 and the awarding of two grants from the National Endowment for the Humanities to Robert Hemenway to write Hurston's biography.[1] Hurston's work has also received institutional support from publishers: the rights to reprint *Their Eyes Were Watching God* in a paperback edition were leased to Illinois University Press by Harper and Row, but the 1978 Illinois edition proved to be so profitable that Harper and Row (now HarperCollins) refused to renew leasing contracts and has reprinted *Their Eyes, Jonah's Gourd Vine, Mules and Men,* and *Tell My Horse* in a series, edited by Henry Louis Gates, Jr., that will eventually include all of Hurston's previously published books. During the years between Hemenway's biography and the new HarperCollins/Gates monopoly of Hurston there have been a variety of anthologies and collections of Hurston's essays and short stories, and, in 1984, a second edition of Hurston's autobiography, *Dust Tracks on a Road,* was published.[2]

As academics we are well aware that we work within institutions that police the boundaries of cultural acceptability and define what is and what is not "literature": our work as teachers and as critics creates, maintains, and sometimes challenges, those boundaries of acceptability. Graduate students tell me that they teach *Their Eyes Were Watching God* at least once a semester: it is a text that is common to a wide variety of courses, whether African-American studies, American studies, English, or Women's studies. It is frequently the case that undergraduates in the humanities may be taught the novel as many as four times, or at least once a year during their undergraduate careers. Traditions, of course, are temporal and are constantly being fought over and renegotiated. Clearly, a womanist- and feminist-inspired desire to recover the neglected cultural presence of Zora Neale Hurston initiated an interest in her work, but it is also clear that this original motivation has become transformed. Hurston is not only a secured presence in the academy, she is a veritable industry and an industry that is very profitable. The new Harper-Collins edition of *Their Eyes* sold its total print run of 75,000 in less than a month.[3] The *New York Times* of February 4, 1990, published an article on Hurston called "Renaissance for a Pioneer of Black Pride" in which it was announced that a play based on Hurston's life and entitled *Zora Neale Hurston: A Theatrical Biography* was opening in New York, and that another play, *Mule Bone,* a collaboration with Langston Hughes, was scheduled to open in the summer.[4] On February 14, 1990, PBS in its prestigious American Playhouse series broadcast "Zora Is My Name" starring Ruby Dee in a dramatization of selections from *Mules and Men* and *Dust Tracks.* It could be said, then, that Hurston has "arrived" as a contemporary, national, cultural presence; we need only a Hollywood movie of any one of her works to inscribe this presence into the realm of the transnational popular memory of the media conglomerates.

I am as interested in the contemporary cultural process of the inclusion of Hurston into the academy as I am interested in her writing. I wonder about the relation between the cultural meanings of her work in the twenties and thirties and the contemporary fascination with Hurston. How is she being reread, now, to produce cultural meanings that this society wants or needs to hear? Is there, indeed, an affinity between the two discrete histories of her work? Certainly, I can see parallels between the situation of black intellectuals in the twenties and thirties, described now as a "Renaissance," and the concerns of black humanists in the academy in the eighties and nineties. Literary histories could doubtless be written about the "renaissance" of black intellectual productivity within the walls of the academy in the post–civil rights era of the twentieth century.

Their Eyes Were Watching God now, of course, has a cultural existence outside of the realm of African-American studies and independent of scholars of the field. But how tenuous is this presence? Does the current fascination of the culture industry for the cultural production of black women parallel the white fascination for African-American peoples as representatives of the exotic and primitive in the twenties?[5] And will the current thirst for the cultural production of black women evaporate as easily? Will the economic crisis of the late eighties and early nineties be used, in a future literary history, to mark the demise of the black intellectual presence in the academy in the same way the 1929 stock market crash has been used by literary historians to mark the death of the Harlem Renaissance? If there is a fragile presence of black peoples in universities, is our cultural presence secure or only temporarily profitable? With or without reference to our contemporary economic conditions, it is startlingly obvious that current college enrollment figures reveal a sharp fall in the numbers of black graduate students—figures which would seem to confirm the tenuous nature of our critical presence. But what I find most intriguing is the relation between a crisis of representation that shaped cultural responses to black urban migration after World War I and the contemporary crisis of representation in African-American humanist intellectual work that determines our cultural and critical responses, or the lack of response, to the contemporary crisis of black urban America.[6]

However, let me make a theoretical intervention here. Edward Said has asserted that it is "now almost impossible . . . to remember a time when people were *not* talking about a crisis in representation," and he points to the enormous difficulties of uncertainty and undecidability that are a consequence of transformations "in our notions of formerly stable things such as authors, texts and objects."[7] In an attempt to be as specific as I can about the particular crisis of representation in black cultural production out of which, I am going to argue, Hurston's work emerges, I will try to define some terms.

The subaltern group that is the subject of Hurston's anthropological and fictional work is represented as the rural black folk. However, the process of defining and representing a subaltern group is always a contentious issue and is at the heart of the crisis of representation in black intellectual thought in both historical moments.[8] The dominant way of reading the cultural production of what is called the Harlem Renaissance is that black intellectuals assertively established a folk heritage as the source of, and inspiration for, authentic African-American art forms. In African-American studies the Harlem Renaissance has become a convention particularly for literary critics but it is, as is the case with all literary histories, an imagined or created historical perspective which privileges some cultural developments while rendering other cultural and political histories invisible. The dominance of this particular literary history in our work, as opposed to organizing a history around a Chicago Renaissance, for example, has uncritically reproduced at the center of its discourse the issue of an authentic folk heritage. The desire of the Harlem intellectuals to establish and re-present African-American cultural authenticity to a predominantly white audience was a mark of a change from, and confrontation with, what were seen by them to be externally imposed cultural representations of black people produced within, and supported by, a racialized social order. However, what was defined as authentic was a debate that was not easily resolved and involved confrontation between black intellectuals themselves. Alain Locke, for example, who attempted to signal a change or a break in conventions of representation by calling his collection of the work of some Harlem intellectuals *The New Negro,* assumed that the work of African-American intellectuals would be to raise the culture of the folk to the level of art.[9] Locke's position has been interpreted by contemporary critics as being very different from, if not antagonistic to, the dominant interpretation of the work of Hurston, who is thought to reconcile the division between "high and low culture by becoming Eatonville's esthetic representative to the Harlem Renaissance."[10]

In 1934, Hurston published an essay called "Spirituals and Neo-Spirituals" in which she argues that there had "never been a presentation of genuine

Negro spirituals to any audience anywhere." What was "being sung by the concert artists and glee clubs [were] the works of Negro composers or adaptors *based* on the spirituals. Glee clubs and concert singers put on their tuxedos, bow prettily to the audience, get the pitch and burst into magnificent song—but not *Negro* song. . . . Let no one imagine that they are the songs of the people, as sung by them."[11] Hurston was concerned to establish authenticity in the representation of popular forms of folk culture and to expose the disregard for the aesthetics of that culture through inappropriate forms of representation. She had no problem in using the term "the people" to register that she knew just who they were. But critics are incorrect to think that Hurston reconciled "high" and "low" forms of cultural production. Hurston's criticisms were not reserved for the elitist manner in which she thought the authentic culture of the people was reproduced. The people she wanted to represent she defined as a rural folk, and she measured them and their cultural forms against an urban, mass culture. She recognized that the people whose culture she rewrote were not the majority of the population and that the cultural forms she was most interested in reproducing were not being maintained. She complained bitterly about how "the bulk of the population now spends its leisure in the motion picture theatres or with the phonograph and its blues." To Hurston "race records" were nothing more than a commercialization of traditional forms of music, and she wanted nothing to do with them.[12]

Understanding these *two* aspects of Hurston's theory of folk culture is important. When Hurston complained about the ways in which intellectuals transformed folk culture by reproducing and reinterpreting it as high culture, she identified a class contradiction. Most African-American intellectuals were generations removed from the "folk" they tried to represent. Their dilemma was little different from debates over proletarian fiction in the Soviet Union, in Europe, in the Caribbean, and in North America: debates that raged over the question of how, and by whom, should "the people," the masses of ordinary people, be portrayed.[13] Hurston identified herself as both an intellectual and a representative figure from the folk culture she reproduced and made authentic in her work. However, asserting that she *was* both did not resolve the contradictions embedded in the social meanings of each category. When Hurston complained about "race records" and the commercialization of the blues, she failed to apply her own analysis of processes of cultural transformation. On the one hand, she could argue that forms of folk culture were constantly reworked and remade when she stated that "the folk tales [like] the spirituals are being made and forgotten every day."[14] But on the other hand Hurston did not take seriously the possibility that African-American culture was being transformed as African-American peoples migrated from rural to urban areas.

The creation of a discourse of the "folk" as a *rural* people in Hurston's work in the twenties and thirties displaces the migration of black people to cities. Her representation of African-American culture as primarily rural and oral is Hurston's particular response to the dramatic transformations within black culture. It is these two processes that I am going to refer to as Hurston's discursive displacement of contemporary social crises in her writing. Hurston could not entirely escape the intellectual practice which she so despised, a practice which reinterpreted and redefined a folk consciousness in its own elitist terms. Hurston may not have dressed the spirituals in tuxedos, but her attitude toward folk culture was not unmediated: she did have a clear framework of interpretation, a construct which enabled her particular representation of a black, rural consciousness.

Gayatri Spivak has pointed to an important dilemma in the issue of representing the subaltern. She sees "the radical intellectual in the West" as being caught either "in a deliberate choice of subalternity, granting to the oppressed . . . that very expressive subjectivity which s/he criticizes [in a post-structuralist theoretical world] or, instead, she faces the possibility of a total unrepresentability."[15] I don't know if the choice is always as bleak or is quite so simple and polarized. Langston Hughes, for example, in his use of the blues to structure poetry, represented a communal sensibility embedded in cultural forms and reproduced social meaning rather than individual subjectivity. In his blues poetry the reader has access to a social consciousness through the reconstruction and representation of nonliterary, contemporary, cultural forms that embodied the conditions of social transformation. Hurston, by contrast, assumed that she could obtain access to, and authenticate, an individualized social consciousness through a utopian reconstruction of the historical moment of her childhood in an attempt to stabilize and displace the social contradictions and disruption of her contemporary moment.

The issue of representing the subaltern, then, is not only one of the relation of the intellectual to the represented but of the relation of the intellectual to history. In Hurston's work the rural black folk became an aesthetic principle, a means by which to embody a rich oral culture. Hurston's representation of the folk is not only a discursive displacement of the historical and cultural transformations of migration but it is also a creation of a folk who are outside of history. Hurston aggressively asserted that she was not of the "sobbing school of negrohood," in particular to distinguish her work from that of Richard Wright, but she also places her version of authentic black cultural forms outside of the culture and history of contestation which informs his work. What the *New York Times* has called Hurston's "strong African-American sensiblity," and is generally agreed to be her positive, holistic celebration of black life, also needs to be seen as a representation of "Negroness" as an unchanging, essential entity, an essence so distilled it is an aesthetic position of blackness.

Hurston was a central figure in the cultural struggle among black intellectuals to define exactly who the people were that were going to become the representatives of the folk. Langston Hughes shaped his discursive category of the folk in direct response to the social conditions of transformation, including the newly forming urban working class and "socially dispossessed," whereas Hurston constructed a discourse of nostalgia for a rural community.[16] In her autobiographical writings, Hurston referenced the contradictory nature of the response of the black middle class and urban intellectuals to the presence of rural migrants to cities. In an extract written six months after completion of *Their Eyes Were Watching God,* Hurston describes this response:

> Say that a brown young woman, fresh from the classic halls of Barnard College and escorted by a black boy from Yale, enters the subway at 50th street. They are well-dressed, well-mannered and good to look at. . . .
>
> [T]he train pulls into 72nd street. Two scabby-looking Negroes come scrambling into the coach . . . but no matter how many vacant seats there are, no other place will do, except side by side with the Yale–Barnard couple. No, indeed! Being dirty and smelly, do they keep quiet otherwise? A thousand times, No! They woof, bookoo, broadcast. . . .
>
> Barnard and Yale sit there and dwindle and dwindle. They do not look around the coach to see what is in the faces of the white passengers. They know too well what is there. . . . "That's just like a Negro." Not just like *some* Negroes, mind you, no, like all. Only difference is some Negroes are better dressed. Feeling all of this like rock-salt under the skin, Yale and Barnard shake their heads and moan, "My People, My People!" . . .
>
> Certain of My People have come to dread railway day coaches for this same reason. They dread such scenes more than they do the dirty upholstery and other inconveniences of a Jim Crow coach. They detest the forced grouping. . . . So when sensitive souls are forced to travel that way they sit there numb and when some free soul takes off his shoes and socks, they mutter, "My race but not My taste." When somebody else eats fried fish, bananas, and a mess of peanuts and throws all the leavings on the floor, they gasp, "My skinfolks but not my kinfolks." And sadly over all, they keep sighing, "My People, My People!"[17]

This is a confrontation of class that signifies the division that the writer, as intellectual, has to recognize and bridge in the process of representing "the people." It is a confrontation that was not unique to Hurston as intellectual but it was one that she chose to displace in her decision to recreate Eatonville as the center of her representation of the rural folk.

The Eatonville of *Their Eyes Were Watching God* occupies a similar imaginative space to the mountain village of Banana Bottom in Claude McKay's novel of the same name published four years earlier.[18] McKay's Jamaican novel is set in the early 1900s and recreates the village where he grew up. Much of the argument of *Banana Bottom* emerges in the tension between attempts by missionaries to eradicate black cultural forms and the gentler forms of abuse present in white patronage of black culture. Against these forms of exploitation McKay reconstructs black culture as sustaining a whole way of life. But it is a way of life of the past, of his formative years, a place that the intellectual had to leave to become an intellectual and to which he does not return except in this utopian moment. Eatonville, likewise, is the place of Hurston's childhood, a place to which she returns as an anthropologist. As she states in her introduction to *Mules and Men,* she consciously returns to the familiar[19] and she recognizes that the stories she is going to collect, the ones she heard as a child, are a cultural form that is disapppearing.[20]

In returning to and recreating the moment of her childhood Hurston privileges the nostalgic and freezes it in time. Richard Wright, in his review of *Their Eyes Were Watching God,* accused Hurston of recreating minstrelsy. Though this remark is dismissed out of hand by contemporary critics, what it does register is Wright's reaction to what appears to him to be an outmoded form of historical consciousness. Whereas Wright attempted to explode the discursive category of the Negro as being formed, historically, in the culture of minstrelsy, and as being the product of a society structured in dominance through concepts of race, Hurston wanted to preserve the concept of Negroness, to negotiate and rewrite its cultural meanings, and, finally, to reclaim an aesthetically purified version of blackness. The consequences for the creation of subaltern subject positions in each of their work are dramatically different. The antagonism between them reveals Wright to be a modernist and leaves Hurston embedded in the politics of Negro identity.

Eatonville, as an anthropological and fictional space, appears in Hurston's work before her first anthropological expedition in 1927.[21] Not all the stories and anecdotes in *Mules and Men* originated from her research, and many appeared in different versions in different texts.[22] Rather than being primarily valued as a mode of scholarly inquiry, anthropology was important to Hurston because it enabled her to view the familiar and the known from a position of scientific objectivity, if not distance. She couldn't see her culture for wearing it, she said: "It was only when I was off in college, away from my native surroundings, that I could see myself like somebody else and stand off and look at my garment. Then I had to have the spy-glass of Anthropology to look through at that."[23] Anthropology, then, is seen by Hurston as providing a professional point of view. Ethnography becomes a tool in the creation of her discourse of the rural folk that displaces the antagonistic relations of cultural transformation.[24]

George Marcus and Michael Fischer have described the ways in which anthropology "developed the ethnographic paradigm" in the 1920s and 1930s. "Ethnographies as a genre," they argue, "had similarities with traveler and explorer accounts, in which the main narrative motif was the romantic discovery by the writer of people and places unkown to the reader."[25] Hurston shares this romantic and, it must be said, colonial imagination. Her representation of Eatonville in *Mules and Men* and in *Their Eyes Were Watching God* is both an attempt to make the unknown, known, and a nostalgic attempt to preserve a disappearing form of folk culture.[26] Marcus and Fischer argue that there are three dimensions to the criticism that ethnography offered of Western civilization:

> They—primitive man—have retained a respect for nature, and we have lost it (the ecological eden); they have sustained close, intimate, satisfying communal lives, and we have lost this way of life (the experience of community); and they have retained a sense of the sacred in everyday life, and we have lost this (spiritual vision).[27]

While the other students of Franz Boas, Margaret Mead and Ruth Benedict, turned to societies outside of Europe and North America to point to what the West had lost but the cultural "other" still retained, Hurston's anthropological work concentrated upon the cultural "other" that existed within the racist order of North America.

In 1935, Ruth Benedict published *Patterns of Culture,* in which she asserted that black Americans were an example of what happens "when entire peoples in a couple of generations shake off their traditional culture and put on the customs of the alien group. The culture of the American Negro in northern cities," she continued, "has come to approximate in detail that of the whites in the same cities."[28] With this emphasis in the school of anthropological thought that most influenced Hurston, anthropology provided her not only with a "spy-glass" but with a theoretical paradigm that directed her toward rural, not urban, black culture and folk forms of the past, not the present.

Hurston, like Benedict, was concerned with the relationships between the lives and cultures that she reconstructed, and with her own search for a construction of the self.[29] Hurston lived the contradictions of the various constructions of her social identity and rewrote them in *Their Eyes Were Watching God.* Her anthropological "spy-glass," which she trained on the society that produced her, allowed her to return to that society in the guise of listener and reporter. In her fictional return, Hurston represents the tensions inherent in her position as an intellectual, in particular as a writer, in antagonistic relation to her construction of the folk as community. It is in this sense that I think Hurston is as concerned with the production of sense of self as she is with the representation of a folk consciousness through its cultural forms. Both, I would argue, are the motivating forces behind the use of anthropological paradigms in Hurston's work. But it is the relation and tension between the two, particularly the intellectual consciousness and the consciousness of the folk, that is present in the fictional world of *Their Eyes Were Watching God,* which was written between her two books of anthropology, *Mules and Men* and *Tell My Horse.* In this novel, we can see how Hurston brings into being a folk consciousness that is actually in a contradictory relation to her sense of herself as an intellectual.

Throughout the thirties Hurston was in search of a variety of formal possibilities for the representation of black rural folk culture. She produced three musicals—*From Sun to Sun, The Great Day,* and *Singing Steel*—because she was convinced that folk culture should be dramatized. After a gap of six years, she returned to fiction when she wrote "The Gilded Six Bits" in 1933 and *Jonah's Gourd Vine,* published in 1934. Then Hurston seriously considered pursuing a Ph.D. at Columbia in anthropology and folklore. After finalizing all the arrangments for the publication of *Mules and Men,* however, Hurston accompanied Alan Lomax on a trip to collect folk music for the Library of Congress in 1935. That fall she joined the Federal Theatre Project and was prominent in organizing its Harlem unit as well as producing a one-act play, "The Fiery Chariot." Between 1936 and 1938, Hurston spent a major part of her time in the Caribbean collecting material on voodoo practices. She spent six months in Jamaica, and *Their*

Eyes Were Watching God was written while she was in Haiti.[30] In *Their Eyes* she reproduces Eatonville from a distance which is both geographic and metaphoric—a place that is politically inscribed with issues of gender and class. Hurston's work during this period, then, involves an intellectual's search for the appropriate forms in which to represent the folk as well as a decision to rewrite the geographic boundaries of representation by situating the southern, rural folk and patterns of migration in relation to the Caribbean rather than the northern states.

Henry Louis Gates, Jr., has explored in great detail matters of voice in *Their Eyes Were Watching God* in relation to a politics of identity by tracing Hurston's construction of a protagonist engaged in a search "to become a speaking black subject."[31] On the other hand, Mary Helen Washington and Robert Stepto have both raised intriguing questions about Janie's *lack* of voice in the text. Washington relates this silencing of a female protagonist to her reading of *Jonah's Gourd Vine,* and concludes that "Hurston was indeed ambivalent about giving a powerful voice to a woman like Janie who is already in rebellion against male authority and against the roles proscribed for women in a male dominated society."[32] However, both sides of this debate about the speaking or silent subject exist within the same paradigm of voice. I wish to introduce an alternative paradigm that suggests ways in which *Their Eyes Were Watching God* is a text concerned with the tensions arising from Hurston's position as writer in relation to the folk as community that she produces in her writing. In other words, rather than remain within critical paradigms that celebrate black identity, I want to concentrate upon the contradictions that arise in the relation between the writer, as woman and intellectual, and her construction of the subaltern subject.

The two chapters that frame the story of Janie's life and are central to arguments about the ways in which Hurston prepares the fictional space in which Janie can tell her own story actually detail the antagonistic relation between Janie, as a woman alone, and the folk as community. The community sits "in judgment" as the figure of Janie, the protagonist, walks through the town to her house. This walk can be seen as analogous to crossing a stage and "running the gauntlet." Oral language, as it was embodied in the folktale in *Mules and Men,* was a sign of an authentic culture that enabled a people to survive and even triumph, spiritually, over their oppression. In the opening chapter of *Their Eyes Were Watching God,* however, oral language is represented as a "weapon," a means for the destruction and fragmentation of the self rather than a cultural form which preserves a holistic personal and social identity. Questions become "burning statements" and laughs are "killing tools" (10). Janie has broken the boundaries of social convention and becomes the accused. She doesn't act appropriately for her age, which is "way past forty" (10, 12) (Hurston was forty-five at the time the text was written, but on various occasions she subtracted between seven and nineteen years off her age).[33] Also inappropriate are the class codes that Janie threatens in her behavior and in her dress: as a middle-class widow she should not have associated with the itinerant Tea Cake; and as a middle-class woman, her "faded shirt and muddy overalls" are a comforting sign to the folk as community who can ease their antagonism and resentment with thought that maybe she will "fall to their level someday" (11).

Hurston increases the tension between her protagonist and the community to which she returns through a series of binary oppositions between the intellect, or mind, and speech. The process of the analysis by the anthropological self in *Mules and Men* is reversed by the creator of fiction in *Their Eyes Were Watching God.* In the former the oral tale is a sign of a whole healthy culture and community, in the latter the individual functions of speaking are isolated and lack a center. Janie responds to her victimization through synecdoche. The community is indicted as a "Mouth Almighty," a powerful voice that lacks intellectual direction. Far from being spiritually whole, the folk who are gathered on the porch are reduced to their various body parts: in each an "envious heart makes a treacherous ear" (16).[34] This is the context that determines Janie's refusal to tell her story directly to the community, a refusal which distinguishes her story from the directly told and shared folktale. In the process of transmitting Janie's story, Hurston requires an instrument of mediation between her protagonist and the folk, and it is Janie's friend Phoeby who becomes this mediator. When Janie decides to tell her story through her friend—"mah tongue is in mah friend's mouf," she says—Hurston creates a figure for the form of the novel, a fictional world that can mediate and perhaps resolve the tension that exists in the difference between the socially constructed identities of "woman" and "intellectual" and the act of representing the folk (17).[35]

Hurston's particular form of mediation appears to be an alternative version of the anthropological "spy-glass" that she needed to create a professional point of view between her consciousness of self and the subjects she was reproducing. Janie's definite refusal to tell her tale directly, as in a folktale, distinguishes not only her story from other stories that are communally shared but also her position from that of the folk as community. Hurston's position as intellectual is reproduced as a relation of difference, as an antagonistic relationship between Janie and the folk. The deficiencies in the folk figures—the porch sitters' absence of mind or intellectual direction—are symbolically present when Janie mounts her own porch.

In *Mules and Men,* the porch is the site for the expression of the folktale as an evocation of an authentic black culture. In *Their Eyes Were Watching God,* the porch is split and transformed. While the anthropological self of *Mules and Men* is positioned on a figuratively unified porch, primarily as a listener and a recorder, in *Their Eyes Were Watching God* the anthropological role of listener is embedded in the folk as community and the role of recorder situated in the mediator—Pheoby/the text. In the novel, then, a listening *audience* is established for the narrative self, while in *Mules and Men* Hurston constructs a listening *anthropological subject.* It is Janie who can address and augment the lack in the folk as community, and Janie who can unify the division between mind and mouth. Janie, of course, is placed in the subject position of intellectual and has the desire to "sit down and tell [the folk] things." Janie, as intellectual, has traveled outside of the community and defines herself as "a delegate to de big 'ssociation of life"; her journey is the means by which knowledge can be brought into the community (18). As intellectual she creates subjects, grants individual consciousness, and produces understanding—the cultural meanings without which the tale is useless to the community—"taint no use in me telling you somethin' unless Ah give you de understandin' to go 'long wid it," Janie tells Phoeby. The conscious way in which subjectivity is shaped and directed is the act of mediation of the writer: it is in this sense that Phoeby becomes both Hurston's instrument of mediation and her text in an act of fictionalization.

The second part of the frame in the last chapter of *Their Eyes Were Watching God* opens with the resolution of the tension, division, and antagonism that is the subject of the opening chapter. The pattern of division of the first part of the frame is repeated: Janie is verbally condemned by the folk as community because she killed Tea Cake. The folk "lack" the understanding of the reasoning behind Janie's actions, but this deficiency is only compensated for through Janie's defense of herself in a court of law. The folk on the muck finally end their hostility to Janie when Sop explains that Tea Cake went crazy and Janie acted to protect herself. Reconciliation, then, between the position of intellectual and the folk as community takes place through acts of narration. The discursive unity that is maintained in the framing of the text prefigures the possibility for reconciliation between the position of Janie, as both intellectual and woman, and the folk as community when Phoeby provides them with the understanding of Janie's life through what will be another act of narration. *Their Eyes Were Watching God,* as such an act of narration itself, offers a resolution to the tension between Hurston, as intellectual, as writer, and the people she represents. In a paragraph that reproduces the tension in relation of the intellectual to the folk, Hurston specifies the source of antagonism between Janie and the Community as being a lack of knowledge.

> Now, Pheoby, don't feel too mean wid de rest of 'em 'cause dey's parched up from not knowin' things. Dem meatskins is *got* tuh rattle tuh make out they's alive. Let 'em consolate theyselves wid talk. 'Course, talkin' don't amount tuh uh hill uh beans when yuh can't do nothin' else. And listenin' tuh dat kind uh talk is jus' lak openin' yo' mouth and lettin' de moon shine down yo' throat. It's uh known fact, Pheoby, you got tuh *go* there tuh *know* there. Yo' papa and yo' mama and nobody else can't tell yuh and show yuh. Two things everybody's got tuh do fuh theyselves. They got tuh go tuh God, and they got tuh find out about livin' fuh theyselves. (285)

The passage that I have quoted here is the final paragraph in Janie's story. It gains authority from claiming the tone of the preacher and the pedagogue, and at the same time it evokes the dilemma of the intellectual. Hurston's journey away from the community that produced her and that she wants to reproduce has provided her with a vision of an alternative world. While it is not actually present in the text, the novel ends with the possibility that this history could be brought into the community and suggests that Phoeby/the text is the means for accomplishing the transformation necessary to reconcile difference. As a woman and as an intellectual, however, Hurston has to negotiate both gendered and classed constructions of social identity and subjectivities.

Critics often forget that Janie is a protagonist whose subject position is defined through class, that she can speak on a porch because she owns it. The contradictions between her appearance in overalls, a sign of material lack, and the possession of nine hundred dollars in the bank are important. Hurston's anthropological trips for *Mules and Men* were financed by a patron, Mrs. Osgood Mason, to whom she dedicates the text. The folklore material that Hurston had collected she could not freely utilize as she wished: Mason had made it abundantly clear that she claimed proprietary ownership of all that ethnographic material. Hurston traveled to Jamaica and Haiti on her own Guggenheim grant and when she was writing *Their Eyes* must have luxuriated in the pleasure that in this instance no one else could claim ownership of her words and her work. However, the problem is that providing her protagonist with the financial independence that Hurston herself must have found necessary in order to occupy a position from which to write reinforces the division between Janie and her community. The text echoes with Janie's grandmother's demand for a place like the white woman's, a place on high. The fact that Janie does indeed mount and purchase her porch enables the story, but also permeates it with a bourgeois discourse that differentiates her from the folk as community.

But this intellectual and property owner is also a woman, and thus the problem of representation here is also a question of how a woman can write her story within a site that is male-dominated and patriarchally defined. In *Mules and Men,* Hurston addresses the social constitution of gender roles in particular tales and through brief narratives that describe the relations among the tale-tellers on the porch, but she does not inscribe a concern with gender within the terms of the professional role of the anthropologist itself.[36] However, the role of listener had its limitations. Hurston's conscious reversal of the role of anthropologist reveals the contradictions inherent in the processes through which an intellectual, an intellectual who is also a woman, can instruct a community about what is outside of its social consciousness. This is the problem that frames the novel. The final metaphor of the horizon as a "great fish-net" with "so much of life in its meshes" that Janie pulls in and drapes around herself is an appropriate image for a writer who can re-create and re-present a social order in her narrative. But what this metaphor also confirms is the distance between the act of representation and the subjects produced through that act of representation. The assertion of autonomy implicit in this figuration of a discourse which exists only for the pleasure of the self displaces the folk as community utterly and irrevocably.

I have suggested ways in which the narrative strategies of *Mules and Men* and *Their Eyes Were Watching God* are different and yet similar in that they both evoke the romantic imagination so characteristic of ethnography in the thirties. If, as Marcus and Fischer suggest, the main narrative motif of ethnography is the "romantic discovery by the writer of people and places unknown to the reader," then *Mules and Men* both discovers the rural folk and acts to make known and preserve a form of culture that embodies a folk consciousness. The folk as community remain the "other," and exist principally as an aesthetic device, a means for creating an essential concept of blackness. The framing of that novel is the process of working out, or mapping, a way of writing and discovering the subject position of the intellectual, in relation to what she represents.

Hurston's journey to Jamaica and two trips to Haiti produced *Tell My Horse,* a book which Robert Hemenway has dismissed as Hurston's "poorest book." Hemenway argues that Hurston "was a novelist and folklorist, not a political analyst or traveloguist."[37] I would agree that Hurston's overtly political comments in *Tell My Horse* are usually reactionary, blindly patriotic, and, consequently, superficial. The dominant tendency in Hurston scholarship has been to ignore or dismiss as exceptional some of her more distasteful political opinions; but, as Marcus and Fischer have explained, the ethnology and travelogue share a romantic vision, and I would add a colonial or imperial vision, making *Tell My Horse* not an exception to Hurston's work at this moment in her life but an integral part of it. In the second chapter of part 2 of *Mules and Men,* the section on hoodoo, Hurston shifts away from a concern to record and preserve a particular form of black culture, the folktale, and toward a desire to create the boundaries of a cultural world in a relation of difference to the dominant culture. The geographical boundaries of Hurston's black folk are rural, but their southernness is not defined through a difference to northernness as much as it is related to cultural practices and beliefs of the Caribbean. This shift is clear when Hurston, the anthropologist, moves from Florida to New Orleans and seeks to become a pupil of a "hoodoo doctor."[38]

In her introduction to *Mules and Men,* Hurston explains that she chose Florida as a site for the collection of folklore not only because it was familiar but because she saw Florida as "a place that draws people . . . Negroes from every Southern state . . . and some from the North and West. So I knew it was possible for me to get a cross section of the Negro South in one state."[39] In the section of *Mules and Men* that is situated in Louisiana, we can see a shift in Hurston's work to a stress on a continuity of cultural beliefs and practices with beliefs and practices in the Caribbean. In *Their Eyes Were Watching God,* this system of reference is continued through the way in which Hurston discursively displaces the urban migration of black people in the continental United States. In her novel, as in *Mules and Men,* migration is from the southern states further south to Eatonville, Florida. Migration in a northerly direction is undertaken only by the Barbadians who join Janie and Tea Cake on the "muck." After the completion of her novel, Hurston continued her search for an appropriate vehicle for the expression of black culture in *Tell My Horse*—a first-person account of her travels in Jamaica and Haiti. Part 3 of *Tell My*

Horse completes the journey, initiated in *Mules and Men,* in search of the survival of voodoo ritual and practices.[40]

The geographic boundaries that enclose *Their Eyes Were Watching God* enlarge our understanding of the metaphoric boundaries of self and community. The discourse of the folk, which I have argued is irrevocably displaced in the figuration of a discourse of individualized autonomy existing only for the pleasure of the self, is dispersed and fragmented in a narrative of Hurston's personal initiation into African religious practices in the diaspora. Hurston does not return again to a romantic vision of the folk. Her next book, *Moses, Man of the Mountain,* is an extension of her interest in the relations between and across black cultures because it rewrites in fictional terms the worship of Moses and the worship of Damballah that had first interested her in Haiti.[41] This figuration of Moses/Damballah also transforms questions about the relation of the intellectual to the folk as community into an exploration of the nature of leaders and leadership. The intricate inquiry into the construction of subject positions, as writer, as woman, and as intellectual, is also not repeated. In *Dust Tracks on a Road,* an apparently autobiographical work, Hurston ignores her earlier attempts to represent the complexity of the relationship between public and private constructions of the self. She continues, however, to displace the discourse of a racist social order and maintains the exclusion of the black subject from history. This is the gesture that eventually wins her the recognition and admiration of the dominant culture in the form of the Anisfield-Wolf Award for the contribution of *Dust Tracks on a Road* to "the field of race relations."[42]

We need to return to the question of why, at this particular moment in our society, *Their Eyes Were Watching God* has become such a privileged text. Why is there a shared assumption that we should read the novel as a positive, holistic, celebration of black life? Why is it considered necessary that the novel produce cultural meanings of authenticity, and how does cultural authenticity come to be situated so exclusively in the rural folk?

I would like to suggest that, as cultural critics, we could begin to acknowledge the complexity of our own discursive displacement of contemporary conflict and cultural transformation in the search for black cultural authenticity. The privileging of Hurston, an attempt, you may say, to memorialize her, at a moment of intense urban crisis and conflict is perhaps a sign of that displacement: large parts of black urban America are under siege; the number of black males in jail in the eighties doubled; the news media have recently confirmed what has been obvious to many of us for a while that one in four young black males are in prison, on probation, on parole, or awaiting trial; and young black children face the prospect of little, or inadequate, or no health care. Has *Their Eyes Were Watching God* become the most frequently taught black novel because it acts as a mode of assurance that, really, the black folk are happy and healthy?

Richard Wright is now excluded from contemporary formations of the African-American canon because he brought into fictional consciousness the subjectivity of a *Native Son* created in conditions of aggression and antagonism,[43] but, perhaps, it is time that we should question the extent of our dependence upon our re-creations of particular aspects of the romantic imagination of Zora Neale Hurston to produce cultural meanings of ourselves as native daughters.

Notes

An earlier version of this essay appeared in Michael Awkward, ed. *New Essays on "Their Eyes Were Watching God"* (Cambridge: Cambridge University Press, 1990). I would like to thank all the members of the W. E. B. Du Bois Institute's seminar on "History and Memory in African American Culture, 1988–1990" for their insightful comments on an earlier version of this essay. In particular I would like to thank Robert O'Meally and VéVé Clark for providing me with additional material and information about Hurston. I am also very grateful to Richard Yarborough, who carefully read a draft of this essay and made supportive and insightful suggestions for its improvement.

1. Robert E. Hemenway, *Zora Neale Hurston: A Literary Biography* (Urbana: University of Illinois Press, 1977).

2. Zora Neale Hurston, *Their Eyes Were Watching God* (Urbana: University of Illinois Press, 1978); *Dust Tracks on a Road,* 2nd ed. (Urbana: University of Illinois Press, 1984); *Mules and Men: Negro Folktales and Voodoo Practices in the South* (New York: Harper & Row, 1970); *Tell My Horse* (Berkeley, Ca.: Turtle Island, 1980). All page references in this essay refer to these editions. The new editions include: *Jonah's Gourd Vine, Mules and Men, Their Eyes Were Watching God,* and *Tell My Horse* (New York: Harper & Row, 1990).

3. Personal communication from Henry Louis Gates, Jr., February 1990.

4. Rosemary L. Bray, "Renaissance for a Pioneer of Black Pride," *New York Times,* February 4, 1990, pp. H–17, 41.

5. A more detailed consideration of this parallel would need to examine what Nelson George calls "selling race." The ability of the record industry to market and make a profit from "black talent performing black music" in the twenties could be interestingly compared to the highly profitable publishing of the work of black women writers, the Book-of-the-Month-Club's distribution of Alice Walker's novel *The Color Purple* and the subsequent film of the same name, and the success of Spike Lee's *She's Gotta Have It* and *School Daze.* See Nelson George, *The Death of Rhythm and Blues* (New York: Pantheon, 1988), pp. 8–9.

6. Hazel V. Carby, *Reconstructing Womanhood: The Emergence of the Afro-American Woman Novelist* (New York: Oxford University Press, 1987), pp. 163–66.

7. Edward W. Said, "Representing the Colonized: Anthropology's Interlocutors," *Critical Inquiry* 15 (Winter 1989): 205–6.

8. See Gayatri Chakravorty Spivak, *In Other Words: Essays in Cultural Politics* (New York: Methuen, 1987), pp. 197–221. Spivak identifies and elaborates upon the concern of the work of subaltern studies with change as "confrontations rather than transition" and the marking of change through "function changes in sign systems." This rather awkward latter phrase becomes, in the process of Spivak's analysis, the somewhat shorter phrase "discursive displacements."

9. See for example, Hemenway, *Zora Neale Hurston,* p. 50.

10. Ibid., p. 56.

11. Zora Neale Hurston, "Spirituals and Neo-Spirituals," in *The Sanctified Church* (Berkeley, Ca.: Turtle Island, 1981), pp. 80–81.

12. Hemenway, *Zora Neale Hurston,* p. 92.

13. See Hazel V. Carby, "Proletarian or Revolutionary Literature: C. L. R. James and the Politics of the Trinidadian Renaissance," *South Atlantic Quarterly* 87 (Winter 1988): 39–52.

14. Hurston, "Spirituals and Neo-Spirituals," p. 79.

15. Spivak, *In Other Worlds,* p. 209.

16. See Ralph Ellison, "Recent Negro Fiction," *New Masses* 40 (August 1941): 22–26.

17. Hurston, *Dust Tracks on a Road,* pp. 292–94.

18. Claude McKay, *Banana Bottom* (New York: Harper & Row, 1933).

19. Hurston, *Mules and Men:,* pp. 17–19.

20. Ibid., p. 24.

21. See Zora Neale Hurston, "The Eatonville Anthology," *Messenger* 8 (Sept—Nov. 1926): 261–62, 297, 319, 332.

22. See Arnold Rampersad's comments in his introduction to the new edition of *Mules and Men* (New York: Harper & Row, 1990), pp. xxii–xxiii.

23. Hurston, *Mules and Men,* p. 17.

24. See Hemenway, *Zora Neale Hurston,* p. 221, who calls this reconstruction of Eatonville idealized but feels that Hurston chose to assert positive images "because she did not believe that white injustice had created a pathology in black behavior." I remain unconvinced by this argument because it simplifies to a level of binary oppositions between positive and negative images what are very complex processes of representation. It is interesting that Hemenway seems to realize this inadequacy in the next paragraph, when he raises but cannot resolve the problem of "professional colonialism" in Hurston's anthropological stance.

25. George E. Marcus and Michael E. Fischer, *Anthropology as Cultural Critique: An Experimental Moment in the Human Sciences* (Chicago: University of Chicago Press, 1986), pp. 129, 24.

26. Hurston's desire to make black people and culture known is evident in letters she wrote to James Weldon Johnson. See Zora Neale Hurston to James Weldon Johnson, January 22, 1934, in which she complains that the J. B. Lippincott Company "are not familiar with Negroes," and May 8, 1934, in which she comments about the review of *Jonah's Gourd Vine* in the *New York Times* that she "never saw such a lack of information about us." Both letters are in the James Weldon Johnson Collection, Beinecke Library, Yale University.

27. Marcus and Fischer, *Anthropology as Cultural Critique,* p. 129.

28. Ruth Benedict, *Patterns of Culture* (Boston: Houghton Mifflin, 1934), p. 13.

29. See Margaret Mead's introduction to the 1959 edition of *Patterns of Culture,* which was written in 1958 (Boston: Houghton Mifflin, 1959), p. ix.

30. Hemenway, *Zora Neale Hurston,* pp. 184–85, 202–27, 230.

31. Henry Louis Gates, Jr., *The Signifying Monkey: A Theory of Afro-American Literary Criticism* (New York: Oxford University Press, 1988), pp. 170–216.

32. Mary Helen Washington, *Invented Lives: Narratives of Black Women, 1860–1960* (New York: Doubleday, 1987), p. 245. Washington's rereading of *Their Eyes Were Watching God* is an admirable analysis of the ways in which this text has been romanticized and initiates the important work of comparative analysis across texts. It was this essay that first encouraged and inspired me to follow her lead and think seriously of the relations among Hurston's texts. Robert Stepto, *From Behind the Veil: A Study of Afro-American Narrative* (Urbana: University of Illinois Press, 1979), pp. 164–67.

33. See Hemenway's introduction to the second edition of *Dust Tracks on a Road,* p. xi.

34. I am grateful to Richard Yarborough for pointing out that this aphorism is itself drawn from oral tradition. My emphasis is that in its application at this point in the novel it stresses division.

35. I am implicitly arguing, therefore, that it is necessary to step outside of questions of voice and issues of third-person—as opposed to first-person—narration in order to understand why Hurston needs an instrument of mediation between the teller of the tale and the tale itself.

36. This may have been because other women, like Mead and Benedict, were also using the role of anthropologist as a position from which to accumulate knowledge that was both authoritative and scientific. But this is just a guess. The relations among these three anthropologists have not been explored, as far as I know, but a comparative examination of the nature of their work would seem to be an interesting area for future study.

37. Hemenway, *Zora Neale Hurston,* pp. 248–49.

38. Hurston, *Mules and Men,* p. 239.

39. Ibid., p. 17.

40. It would be fruitful to explore the relationship between Hurston's interest in and use of the Caribbean in these years with the cultural production of intellectuals who turned to the Caribbean—in particular, the island of Haiti—as a source for an alternative revolutionary black history. I am thinking here, among other works, of the following: the production of the play *Toussaint-Louverture* by C. L. R. James, which opened in London in March 1936 and starred Paul Robeson, and the publication in 1938 of *Black Jacobins;* Jacob Lawrence's series of paintings on Toussaint-Louverture, 1937–38; Langston Hughes's *Troubled Island,* written for but never produced by the Federal Theatre; and the New York Negro Federal Theatre 1936 production of *Macbeth* (often referred to as the "voodoo" *Macbeth*), directed by Orson Welles. Other black units in the Federal Theatre performed *Black Empire,* by Christine Ames and Clarke Painter, and *Haiti,* by William Du Bois, who was a journalist for the *New York Times.*

41. Hurston, *Tell My Horse,* pp. 139–40.

42. Hemenway, "Introduction," *Dust Tracks,* p. ix.

43. See Gates, *The Signifying Monkey,* pp. 118–20, 181–84.

4

W. E. B. Du Bois and the Struggle for American Historical Memory

DAVID W. BLIGHT

The greatest enemy of any one of our truths may be the rest of our truths.
—William James, "What Pragmatism Means" (1906)

Americans can be notoriously selective in the exercise of historical memory.
—Ralph Ellison, "Going to the Territory" (1979)

On February 23, 1968, marking the hundredth anniversary of W. E. B. Du Bois' birth, Martin Luther King, Jr., delivered one of his last major addresses at Carnegie Hall in New York City. In a year that would prove pivotal in African-American history, and that would bring such anguished events as King's own death, it is interesting and fitting to note how King chose to celebrate Du Bois' legacy. Above all, among Du Bois' scholarly and organizational achievements, King stressed his role as historian. Du Bois' "singular greatness," argued King, was his "unique zeal," which "rescued for all of us a heritage whose loss would have profoundly impoverished us." King especially emphasized Du Bois' work on Reconstruction, a period traditional historians had for three generations portrayed as a tragic mistake in American race relations, an era when blacks, incapable of honest political behavior and self-reliant economic activity, had been the principal cause of a sordid interlude in the progress of American history. King was no professional historian, but his own prophetic sense of history enabled him to grasp the social implications of historical understanding and debates. With all too much continuity, "the collective mind of America," declared King, "became poisoned with racism and stunted with myths." Traditional historians' treatment of the black experience, the civil rights leader argued, "was a conscious and deliberate manipulation of history and the *stakes* were high."[1] The question of the stakes involved in struggles over rival versions of history leads us not only to the political and social meanings of what historians do; it also provides an angle of understanding about the confluences of history and memory for intellectuals and for the larger society.

In her book *The Art of Memory,* Frances Yates has demonstrated how, throughout time, versions of historical memory have been employed in the service of ruling ideologies, philosophies, or states. Complex and ambivalent, his achievements sometimes stunted by a legendary arrogance, Du Bois was, nevertheless, a pioneer in illuminating this phenomenon in American culture with reference to history and race. He spent much of his career as a scholar and an artist trying to dislodge American history from its racist moorings. He was a self-conscious creator of black counter-memory. Du Bois was, "in the first place," said King, "a teacher . . . about our tasks of emancipation." Those tasks included an active confrontation with all of the force and power of traditional historiography about slavery and race, with scientific racism, with indifference, and with the mythology of the Lost Cause, which had become influential in American popular culture by the early twentieth century. In his essay "The Propaganda of History," representing the final chapter of *Black Reconstruction in America* (1935), Du Bois declared himself "aghast" at what American historians had done to the fields of Reconstruction and African-American history. The American historical community had not only subordinated the black experience but had rendered it virtually unknown. The state of popular historical misunderstanding in the first third of the twentieth century is what Du Bois sought so contentiously to overturn.[2] As this partial examination of Du Bois' work helps to demonstrate, the study of historical memory might therefore be defined as the study of cultural struggle, of contested truths, of moments, events, or even texts in history that thresh out rival versions of the past which are in turn put to the service of the present.

In Du Bois' large body of historical writing he was not merely crying foul at racist historians for leaving blacks out of the story of American history. He was trying to restore his people's history, while at the same time, he believed, enriching American history. He was very much interested in how multiple parts could make a new whole, how pluralism might be a new conceptual framework for American history. Du Bois helped spark a major historiographic turn in the study of Reconstruction and race among American historians. This turn that Du Bois initiated at least as early as the publication of *The Souls of Black Folk* in 1903 took many years to bear fruit (with major historiographic consequences in the 1960s and 1970s). Du Bois appreciated the political and social stakes of historical debates; he understood the power of historical images in shaping social policy and human interactions. In his historical writings, therefore, a tension developed between art, politics, and the pursuit of scientific truth. As Arnold Rampersad has shown, Du Bois made a gradual but persistent turn away from the scientific empiricism in which he was trained to the poetic sensibilities that characterized so much of his writing after he left Atlanta to edit the *Crisis* in 1910.[3] Du Bois' efforts to forge an African-American counter-memory should be understood in the context of this turn in his work from social science toward art.

Du Bois came of age and was trained during the era (1880s and 1890s) when history assumed the mantle of a "science." He was by any estimation a highly skilled and accomplished social scientist who, at Harvard, studied philosophy with William James, Josiah Royce, and George Santayana, and history with Albert Bushnell Hart. "It was James with his pragmatism and . . . Hart with his research method," Du Bois wrote in his autobiography, "that turned me back from the lovely but sterile land of philosophic speculation, to the social sciences as the field for gathering and interpreting that body of facts which would apply to my program for the Negro." Du Bois understood himself to be an emerging historical sociologist, though Harvard did not yet recognize the field. Although at times Du Bois' rhetoric can be overwrought, and his arguments exceedingly self-righteous or arrogant, he was committed to the sheer accumulation of the "body of fact" that might be thrust before an ignorant or contentious world. In an autobiographical piece written for Rayford Logan's *What the Negro Wants* in 1944, Du Bois admitted that he had "rationalized" his personal story into a "coherent unity" that masked some of the "hesitancies" and "graspings" of his life. Indeed, we would do well to use his autobiographical writings with caution. But Du Bois' self-assured claim that his early career had a singular aim is instructive. "*History* and the other social sciences," he wrote, "were to be my *weapons,* to be sharpened and applied by research and writing."[4] So, always the trained historian in search of verifiable evidence, he also came to use history as a *strategy* to confront and overcome traditional, often white supremacist versions of American history.

In his earliest writings one already finds the tensions between scientific truths and art, between data and politics, and between past and present.[5] In his bitterly ironic commencement address at Harvard in 1890, "Jefferson Davis as a Representative of Civilization," the twenty-two-year-old Du Bois offered Davis, the recently deceased former president of the Confederacy, as an American "Teutonic hero." Boldly, he used Davis as a symbol of the "type of civilization" (national and not merely southern) which had advanced itself by "murdering Indians," had created a culture "whose principle is the rise of one race on the ruins of another," and which was driven by an "overweening sense of the I and a consequent forgetting of the Thou." The veiled implication of Du Bois' speech was that America's quest for sectional reconciliation had led it not only to honor ex-Confederate leaders but to fashion a society where might made right, where unbridled individualism reigned, and where racism flourished. The "glamour of history," and therefore the rise of a nation, declared Du Bois, depended on strength and force. "The Anglo-Saxon loves a soldier," declared Du Bois." Jefferson Davis was an Anglo-Saxon, Jefferson Davis was a soldier." In his few minutes of commencement glory Du Bois urged his Harvard audience to make way for the rise of the quieter, creative, "submissive" culture of blacks, "the race of whose rights Jefferson Davis had not heard." Implicit in Du Bois' message was the notion (or the hope) that the day of Anglo-Saxon hegemony had passed, and the rise of the black race had commenced. Moreover, the speech was an anguished cry for justice, for inclusion, and for a new "standard" by which to judge civilization. While there were elements of nineteenth-century racialist thinking (claims of distinguishable racial characteristics) in the young Du Bois' rhetoric, and he too would one day exalt the soldier, at bottom, Du Bois' address was a direct appeal to the historical memory and moral imagination of his audience (Harvard and America). "You whose nation was founded on the loftiest ideals," challenged Du Bois, "and who many times forget those ideals with a strange forgetfulness, have more than a sentimental interest, more than a sentimental duty. You owe a debt to humanity for this Ethiopia of Out-stretched Arm, who has made her beauty, patience, and her grandeur law."[6] By addressing his audience so personally as *You*, Du Bois asserted that history had left a collective responsibility in America. Slavery and racism were everyone's legacy and everyone's problem. The link between Jefferson Davis, "civilization," and "You" was not only a brilliant stroke of irony for such a young orator but a clear indication that Du Bois had launched his lifelong project of contending against America's prevailing historical memory.

Du Bois' early conception of history as contending memories is further illustrated in *The Suppression of the African Slave Trade to the United States of America, 1638–1870,* his doctoral dissertation (1896), which became the first volume published in the Harvard Historical Monograph series. Reflecting his rigorous methodological training under Hart and during his two years in Germany studying economics, *Suppression* was primarily a legalistic analysis of the long effort to abolish the slave trade. But an ethical tone informs the volume and pervades its concluding chapter. Du Bois' moralism was relatively typical of American historiography during the 1890s.[7] Even under the new veneer of scientific analysis, most historians claimed the duty of teaching moral lessons; hence the final section of *Suppression* is entitled "The Lessons for Americans." But something deeper can be learned from a closer look at Du Bois' language in the final passages of *Suppression.* Du Bois was fully aware that by the mid-1890s American society was in the midst of a near crusade of sectional reconciliation, the celebration of the mutual heroism of North and South in the Civil War, and the quest for a present and a future that allowed people to forget slavery and racial conflict, a position now championed by the popular historian James Ford Rhodes. Moreover, as aloof as Du Bois could be, he could hardly have been completely detached from the poverty and oppression he had already witnessed in the South, or the racism he had encountered at Harvard, when he wrote of the enrichment of the western world "in just such proportion as Americans stole Negroes and worked them to death" in the eighteenth and nineteenth centuries.[8] His chastisement of the "moral apathy" of antebellum Americans, as one generation after another postponed the slavery problem, was no doubt spurred by the moral weaknesses of an era of lynching. As Du Bois' voice turns from description to moralizing in the final pages of *Suppression,* we see not only the doctoral candidate's attempt to attach an ethical conclusion to his monograph. Rather, we begin to see the turn toward art and polemicism in Du Bois' work about which Arnold Rampersad has written.[9]

We also see in this, his earliest formal work of history, an engagement with the oldest and most enduring conception of the American past: the providential view of America as a chosen nation, a people of progress who ultimately solve their problems, and offer the world a model of an omniscient society thriving above threat or conflict. Du Bois was one of the earliest historians, therefore, to challenge what Nathan Huggins has called the "master narrative" of American history. Whether in the 1890s or the 1990s, the "aggravating persistence" of racism in American society makes "challenging demands on the past," wrote Huggins, "demands that cannot be comprehended through the sanitized and innocent master narrative." Anticipating some of the historiography of his own generation and of the modern "consensus" school of the 1940s and 1950s, Du Bois challenged his readers to reflect from the heart as well as the head and to acknowledge contradiction and paradox:

> No American can study the connection of slavery with United States history, and not devoutly pray that his country may never have a similar social problem to solve, until it shows more capacity for such work than it has shown in the past. It is neither profitable nor in accordance with scientific truth to consider that whatever the constitutional fathers did was right, or that slavery was a plague sent from God and fated to be eliminated in due time. We must face the fact that this problem arose principally from the cupidity and carelessness of our ancestors.

The tone of Du Bois' language clearly reflects his awareness that he lived in a nation still unwilling to believe that the "growing evil" of slavery had opened "the highway that led straight to the Civil War." Americans, he maintained, lacked historical consciousness and, therefore, "moral foresight." They congratulated themselves "more on getting rid of a problem than on solving it."[10] The young Du Bois illuminated America's struggle in the 1890s to contend with the memory of slavery, racism, and the Civil War. He also quietly announced one of the principal aims of all of his future historical work: to forge a memory that might help solve or transcend the race problem, rather than simply getting rid of it.

From his most scientific studies of black and southern life (the Atlanta University studies) to his essays, fiction, and poetry, a sense of history informs nearly everything Du Bois wrote. From his earliest writings, and especially with the publication of his classic, *The Souls of Black Folk* (1903), Du Bois became a self-appointed sounder not only of America's peculiar "race concept" but of the full range of tragedy and possibility in American history. Indeed, as a student of race, and therefore of conflict, Du Bois was placed in an oppositional—and sometimes advantageous—position from which to comment on the struggle over contending memories in American society. The famous passage in *Souls* about "double consciousness," anguished as it is, nevertheless begins with the claim that "the Negro is a sort of seventh son, born with a veil, and gifted with a second-sight in this American world. . . ." The dilemma of "twoness" might have the potential to deny "true self-consciousness," but the black historian/artist, like all historical "outsiders," had a unique vantage point. As he would in various ways throughout the rest of his life, in *Souls* Du Bois asserted that the black experience stood at the center of national history, at least for those who cared to look at conflict rather than only continuity, at irony rather than pleasing myth. His image of the "swarthy spectre" sitting in its "accustomed seat at the nation's feast" stunningly frames his claim that "the nation has not yet found peace from its sins" in the fortieth year since emancipation.[11] Specters haunt, and American memory was haunted, Du Bois seemed to be saying; this country's collective memory awaited new voices, new scholars and storytellers whose "strivings" might liberate it from the past.

Indeed, the novelist John Edgar Wideman declared that if he were allowed only one book with which to teach post–Civil War American history it would be *The Souls of Black Folk.* Such a comment not only attests to the function of *Souls* as a work of historical importance, but Wideman also claimed that each time he teaches or reads the book, when he closes it, "beauty and pain linger." He finds himself transported to beautiful memories of the AME Zion church in which he was raised, a place of hope and sustenance; and then, he is also left with the message of pain, the "disquieting thought," the fear that "nothing has changed" about race in America through time. In Du Bois' own time many perceptive readers wondered about the somber tone of *Souls.* In 1906 William James wrote to Du Bois questioning the despair of the book. "You must not think I am personally wedded to the minor key," Du Bois answered. "On the contrary I am tuned to the most aggressive and unquenchable hopefulness. I wanted in this case simply to reveal fully the other side to the world."[12] One wonders if this response did not contain a bit of both bravado and insecurity in the face of a mentor's reading of the author's most important work. But Du Bois' answer to James reveals his sense of writing about the tragic "other side" of American experience. This endless dialectic between the beauty and the pain in American history is just what Du Bois sought to capture by bringing the black experience to the center of the story.

As time passed Du Bois would become even less shy of generalization about the place of blacks in the American story. By 1924 he made the bold claim that "dramatically, the Negro is the central thread of American history. The whole story turns on him whether we think of the dark and flying slave ship in the sixteenth century, the expanding plantations of the seventeenth, the swelling commerce of the eighteenth, or the fight for freedom in the nineteenth. It was the black man that raised the vision of democracy in America. . . ." Thus, early on, in such portentous prose Du Bois had anticipated and joined all of the black poets and scholars who would write from an oppositional mood, an inherently critical and, ironically for America liberating point of view. Among the many meanings in Du Bois' famous metaphor of the "veil," therefore, rests this duality in the oppositional mood: the veil can be the walls of a "prison house," forever stunting creativity and self-consciousness; or it can be the challenge and the source of "new points of view" that provide the thinker with the "chance to soar."[13] Make no mistake, the veil had to be lifted; but it first had to be remembered, analyzed, and understood.

Claiming the center as scholars, or singing from the margins as poets, writers about race in America have for generations fashioned a "counter-memory," a concept elucidated by Michel Foucault and several other theorists. In *Language, Counter-Memory, Practice* (1977), Foucault characterizes the history we write and learn as a continuous product of a "rancorous will to knowledge." One does not have to accept fully Foucault's notion of history as ceaseless "discontinuities" in a veritable moral vacuum (facts, evidence, and the ceaseless struggle for truths must remain our bedrock principles of inquiry) to see a certain wisdom in his discussion of contending memories. He reminds us that our obsession with "origins" can blind us to the "vicissitudes of history," to its "jolts, its surprises, its unsteady victories and unpalatable defeats." This admonition might especially be directed at proponents of a providential, transhistorical view of America, as well as at romantic, ethnically essentialist conceptions of the past. One is reminded here of Du Bois' plea for historical irony in *Black Reconstruction in America* (1935). "Nations reel and stagger on their way," wrote Du Bois, "they make hideous mistakes; they commit frightful wrongs; they do great and beautiful things. And shall we not best guide humanity by telling the truth about all this, so far as the truth is ascertainable?"[14]

Foucault is helpful, I think, in explaining the sheer passion and violence of cultural conflict over memory. Relying on Friedrich Nietzsche, Foucault characterizes such cultural struggle as a "hazardous play" of "endlessly repeated dominations." A domination (read: an interpretation of history or other mode of power) becomes "fixed, throughout its history," claims Foucault, "in rituals, in meticulous procedures that impose rights and obligations. It establishes marks of its power and engraves memories on things and even within bodies." According to Foucault, history "proceeds from domination to domination"; it develops as an endless cycle of contending wills and interpretations. In extreme, and perhaps cynical, form, Foucault nevertheless captures the fickle ways that social and historical memories are forged. Du Bois never gave up believing in an ethical basis for history, even after he embraced a more materialist, economic analysis in the 1930s. But he fully understood and eloquently warned against the problem of domination in historical memory. "With sufficient general agreement among the dominant classes," he declared in 1935, "the truth of history may be utterly distorted and contradicted and changed to any convenient fairy tale that the masters of men wish."[15] Hence, representing both the danger and the inspiration of much *re*vision of history it is power and persuasion that keep any version of social memory dominant. On the larger, social scale, the *stakes* in such "hazardous . . . play" between memories are, therefore, quite serious. They may include collective and personal identities, the fundamentals of school curricula, the objectives and justifications of major wars, the creation and survival of human rights, and even the rise and fall of governments. Memories rise and fall from dominance, sometimes through the force of armies and always, it seems, through the use of language. As intellectuals all over Eastern Europe, the Soviet Union, South Africa, or China are demonstrating in our own time, and as black writers have understood in America at least since the first slave narratives, the ownership of language—the liberation of words from debasement and control by the masters of plantations or states—can rescue the human spirit from totalitarian control. Words and, indeed, the images and myths they convey are the signposts of memory. And, as Peter Burke has argued, conflicts of memory are most acute in those societies most deeply embedded with "memories of conflict."[16]

As a historian, Du Bois was most concerned with social, and therefore collective, forms of memory. How groups remember and contend in the marketplaces of power and culture for hegemony is perhaps the central problem in the study of historical memory. In his pioneering study, *The Collective Memory* (1925), Maurice Halbwachs explained how individuals depend on other members of their own groups for independent confirmation of the content of their memories. The incessant human quest for identity and communion makes it such that culture itself could hardly exist without these social dimensions of memory. Collective memory is held together by the confidence derived from association. Yet we have also learned from the philosophy of history and from modern psychology that collective memory is a constructive and reconstructive process. Memories are not merely reproduced; they are *constructed* in all the various cultural forms: music, dance, fiction, poetry, and historical scholarship.[17] Hence, we create and recreate narratives in response to ever-changing political and social circumstances. In the hands of such a self-conscious historian–artist as Du Bois, the forms of those narratives become a mixture of the scholarly and literary dimensions of history, and such a combination may occur in historians' work more than we are willing to admit.

As Paul Ricoeur has demonstrated in *Time and Narrative* (1984), we can only begin to understand and mark time with memory; and we only really understand memory through narratives we construct to give it meaning and substance. We need stories, the "poetic act of emplotment," argues Ricoeur, to render the bewilderment of time and experience intelligible. Deep understanding is usually derived from the deepest memories, those that have somehow engaged the "soul" and elicited lasting narratives. "It is *in* the soul, hence as an impression," says Ricoeur, "that expectation and memory possess extension." Ricoeur leads us to an understanding, therefore, between memory (the past) and expectation (the future), the crucial philosophical elements in any consideration of the stakes of social memory. Passionate debates over the actual nature and meaning of the past—often involving claims of collective guilt or responsibility—are concerned, while they remain in the realm of reason at least, not with retribution but with anticipation. As Steven Knapp has argued, the "ethical relevance" of the past (any exercise of collective memory) derives from an "agent's imaginative relation to the future consequences of some contemplated action." In other words, we not only have art so that we will not die of reality; we have narratives as an authoritative means of negotiating between retribution and forgiveness, between ignorance and knowledge, between lies and enlightenment. In this context, I am reminded of Frederick Douglass' timeless definition of racism as a "diseased imagination."[18]

Certainly Du Bois understood the destructive and stultifying aspects of racism in the same manner. He also understood how deeply embedded the problem of racism was in American historical narratives, as well as how much those narratives continued to shape the future. He said as much many times, notably in *The World and Africa* (1947), where he charged that it is "the greatest indictment that can be brought against history as a science and against its teachers that we are usually indisposed to refer to history for the settlement of pressing problems." This was not merely another call for a usable history; it was a warning against selective, willfully narrow history, history that resulted from "certain suppressions in the historical record current in our day" and from "the habit, long fostered, of forgetting and detracting from the thought and acts of the people of Africa." Du Bois also had future consequences in mind in his moralizing about national "duty" in the final pages of *Suppression of the African Slave Trade.* Moreover, he clearly had present and future purposes in mind for the image of John Brown that he constructed in his polemical biography of the abolitionist in 1909. Du Bois' short historical synthesis of blacks throughout the African diaspora, *The Negro,* published in 1915, was intended in great part to historicize Africa in a world scrambling to colonize that continent's land and resources. And, finally, as Rampersad has argued, "duty" was itself the hero of Du Bois' essay on the Freedmen's Bureau, "Of the Dawn of Freedom," in *Souls,* a work filled with lessons for a turn-of-the-century world struggling with the problem of the color line.[19]

As for the problem of narratives that reflect deep memory, that engage the "soul," we need only look to the title and content of Du Bois' most famous book. In the "Forethought" of *Souls,* Du Bois addresses the "Gentle Reader" directly and invites him or her to see "buried" treasures, "things which if read with patience may show the meaning of being black" in America. With poetic sensibility, in these essays and one short story, Du Bois made an offering to the souls of Americans.[20] *Souls* was like a gift of narratives that might help mediate America's treacherous journey between memory and expectation about race.

Many scholars have stressed the importance of *aesthetic* appeal in the art of memory. The emotional power of a historical image or of an individual or collective memory is what renders it lasting. As Yates demonstrated, unforgettable images that inspired awe and a sense of sacred space were what gave meaning to the memory "wheels," "theaters," and "palaces" of the Italian Renaissance. Moreover, the eighteenth-century philosopher Giambattista Vico forged a conception of memory as the deep structure of knowledge, revealed only in poetic expression. The more profound the poetic imagery or the metaphoric association, the more lasting a memory might be in any culture. This could be true of oral as well as literary traditions, of spoken epics as well as printed texts. As Patrick Hutton has contended, even with the modern revolution that the printing press brought to the art of memory, the power of single, poetic images, events, or moments are what still gave substance to cultural memory. Even under the influence of highly individualized modern psychology, whether we believe in the collective unconscious or not, the memory palaces of our own time can be a single image conveyed in a novelist's metaphor or a historian's persuasive prose. We may be focused, introspectively, on the printed page instead of listening to the ancient storyteller's voice, but the object is the same: to invoke the emotional chords of memory through aesthetic sensibilities.[21]

Trained in the social sciences, influenced by William James' psychology, and devoted to a search for verifiable truth where possible, Du Bois was nevertheless deeply aware of this poetic level on which collective memory works. After all, if James' mentoring had any influence at all, Du Bois could never have sidestepped the spiritual elements of life and thought. Du Bois' early writing swayed between his commitments to empirical scholarship and an increasing appreciation of the power and necessity of aesthetic expression. Both Du Bois' historical writings (studded with fictionalized anecdotes and examples drawn from literature) and his historical novels revealed this tension; intellectually, and even spiritually, he lived a "double life." Du Bois' rigorous training in research served him well; he never gave up on his commitments to scholarship and his faith in mind as a social force. But Du Bois saw himself both as a scholar and as a nineteenth-century "gentleman of letters," as Rampersad has put it.[22] Moreover, as this gentleman of letters turned increasingly toward art and persuasion in his role as a race spokesman, the poetic energy in his writing exploded.

According to Rampersad, Du Bois' turn toward art came in 1897, after he first "experienced the goad of southern racism." That year the young scholar–teacher published the original version of "Of Our Spiritual Strivings," which became the first chapter of *Souls.* Therein Du Bois first constructed the metaphor of the "veil," and explored the psychological depths of African-American "double consciousness." Throughout the rest of *Souls,* what prompts repeated imagery of the veil and other metaphoric barriers are those moments when imagined freedom seems almost tangible but just beyond reach. In Du Bois' story "The Coming of John" (chapter 13 of *Souls*), "the veil that lay between him and the white world" is first revealed to a young black man as he becomes educated. Moreover, as John, full of zeal, returns to his sleepy southern hometown to help his people, he finds that he no longer speaks their language and that is was "so hard and strange to fit his old surroundings again." Utterly out of step with his fellow blacks, and about to be lynched by whites, John has a homecoming that is a tragic "waste of double aims."[23] For Du Bois, education and bitter experience had revealed the "veil." Only through some kind of dissenting imagination in history or fiction, therefore, could he confront and peer through such barriers. With the publication of *Souls* in 1903 and *John Brown* in 1909, and after breaking with the academy in 1910 when he left Atlanta University, Du Bois would never again write strictly descriptive, empirical history. He had not only turned toward art and polemicism, but he had turned toward the construction of a counter-memory in American history. To many in the historical profession, this would render his history suspect or even irrelevant; but like most self-conscious pioneers, though his conclusions would always remain debatable, he had begun to ask new and compelling questions.

In addition to the obvious ways in which Du Bois' literary style was the product of the time and place of his training, as well as of his temperament, we might also consider his conscious grasp of the art of memory as another explanation of his developing rhetorical style. Although *Souls* is on the surface a collection of essays, it is also a self-conscious attempt to write a historical epic. *Souls* might be considered a modern African-American "memory palace," a storehouse of unforgettable images conveyed with such aesthetic power that readers and writers might return to it, generation after generation, for historical understanding and inspiration. No text ought to be valorized beyond its merits, but in my experience whenever young students initially encounter *Souls,* they are first struck by the power of the prose. The work seems to defy students' traditional categories; they have entered a memory theater (via the printed page), and they find themselves both instructed and moved by the performance.

In *Souls* Du Bois takes his reader on many journeys to sacred *places* of memory, similar, at least imaginatively, to what Pierre Nora has called *lieux de mémoire.* In his ironic autobiographical tale, "Of the Meaning of Progress" (chapter 4 of *Souls*), Du Bois the schoolteacher ushers us, "once upon a time," to a remote, segregated hill town in eastern Tennessee, where a bright but poverty-ridden young black woman named Josie dreams of an education. Du Bois tries to engage the reader's senses—on as many emotional levels as possible—as we hear the music thunder from two black churches, enter a makeshift and "sad-colored schoolhouse," and listen to the "dark fatalism" of the freedmen and freedmen's sons and daughters. But this is no romantic tale set amidst the humble poor and the blue Appalachians. It is a tragic narrative of human struggle, crushed hope, and death. It is also a historian's challenge to the theory of progress in America, told by a narrator who must ride a Jim Crow car in and out of this "little world" that Du Bois seeks to plant in American memory.[24]

Moreover, in "Of the Black Belt" (chapter 7 of *Souls*), Du Bois takes us, again by Jim Crow car, on a revealing journey to the "crimson soil of Georgia." In vivid imagery he describes a "monotonous" quality of the landscape of the former Cotton Kingdom, yet he "did not nod, nor weary of the scene; for this is *historic ground.*" Here is Du Bois the artist–scholar combining rich descriptions of nature with the social history of the legions of sharecroppers. Here is a more believable Georgia than that of Margaret Mitchell; here is a landscape and a society truly "gone with the wind," where only the "black tenant remains," and the "shadow-hand of the master's grand nephew or cousin or creditor stretches out of the gray distance to collect the rack-rent remorselessly." Remnants of the big houses, the "parks and palaces of the Cotton Kingdom," remain, but that "merry past" now lies in "silence . . . , ashes, and tangled weeds." Here is even the beginning of a challenge to the southern historian Ulrich B. Phillips' depiction of the benign world of masters and slaves in his classic *American Negro Slavery.* Du Bois depicts this "Egypt of the Confederacy" as a society built by the blood and toil of generations of blacks, and as a "cause lost long before 1861."

On every level, Du Bois' journey through Georgia is an imaginative way to dissent from the traditional image and history of slavery and the South. He frequently allows the voices of the freedmen themselves to tell the story. In a scene framed by the "bare ruin of some master's home," an old ex-slave says:

"I've seen niggers drop dead in the furrow, but they were kicked aside, and the plow never stopped. Down in the guard house, there's where the blood ran." In his "Of the Black Belt" Du Bois combined the beauty and power of nature, the sweep of history in epic proportions, and the painful ruck of the freedmen's daily lives to forge an indelible memory, a memory that countered the romance of the Lost Cause and national reunion. There are no happy darkies in the Black Belt; race relations have not been better off left to the South's own devices. And finally he described a prison farm (a metaphor for the whole landscape and for the collective despair of black debtors) where the present is so full of the past that the tenses become blurred. "It is a depressing place," wrote Du Bois, "bare, unshaded, with no charm of past association, only a memory of forced toil—now, then, and before the war. They are not happy, these men whom we meet throughout this region." In effect, slavery has transcended time in Du Bois' imagery. Neoslavery had emerged by the turn of the century, and two generations of black tenants bore their burdens with a combination of hope and gloom.[25]

Examples abound in *Souls* of Du Bois' attempt to revise history, both with evidence and with aesthetic appeal. In his essay on the Freedmen's Bureau, "Of the Dawn of Freedom" (chapter 2), Du Bois presents a logical case for viewing the agency in a more positive historical light rather than as a villain in the tragedy of Reconstruction. Du Bois offers a sympathetic portrayal of the "tremendous undertaking" that the Freedmen's Bureau represented in its all too short life: its charge to provide for refugees, create schools, administer abandoned lands, and extend political rights and justice to the freedmen. He does not ignore the flaws and failings of the bureau, nor of its agents. But this is an essay designed to create a new framework of history in which the plight of the freedmen might be more easily understood. At bottom this is a fin-de-siècle probing for legacies. The essay begins and ends with the same sentence: "The problem of the twentieth century is the problem of the color-line." In this case, history must be explored and felt in order to know the responsibilities of the present. It must be seen and heard, and like the voice of a prophet, Du Bois tried to provide the necessary imagery. First, he urges the reader to cast his/her vision to the rear of the grim parade of history. He suggests three images in the procession of Sherman's march across Georgia: "The Conqueror, the Conquered, and the Negro." "Some see all significance in the grim front of the destroyer," writes Du Bois, "and some in the bitter sufferers of the Lost Cause. But to me neither soldier nor fugitive speaks with so deep a meaning as that dark human cloud that clung like remorse on the rear of those swift columns. . . . In vain they were ordered back . . . , on they trudged and writhed and surged until they rolled into Savannah a starved and naked horde of tens of thousands."[26] Here are the nameless freedmen, inexorably both liberated and self-liberated in a terrible war, given equal billing in this memory theater with the tragic planters and the awesome William Tecumseh Sherman.

Moreover, in a brilliant passage about passion in the South after the war, Du Bois suggested "two figures" that typified the era of Reconstruction and demonstrated the power of its legacy,

> the one a gray-haired gentleman, whose fathers had quit themselves like men, whose sons lay in nameless graves; who bowed to the evil of slavery because its abolition threatened untold ill to all; who stood at last, in the evening of life, a . . . ruined form, with hate in his eyes;—and the other a form hovering dark and mother-like, her awful face black with the mists of centuries, had aforetime quailed at that white master's command, had bent in love over the cradles of his sons and daughters, and closed in death the sunken eyes of his wife,—aye, too, at his behest had laid herself low to his lust, and borne a tawny man-child to the world, only to see her dark boy's limbs scattered to the winds by midnight marauders riding after "damned niggers." These were the saddest sights of that woeful day; and no man clasped the hands of these passing figures of the present-past; but hating, they went to their long home, and hating their children's children live today.[27]

Past and present met in this imagery with frightful intensity and authentic tragedy. Here were not the clichéd "forms" of old soldiers who had met in battle and could now clasp hands in mutual respect. Here were the veterans of an even deeper conflict, and perhaps a deeper tragedy. Here was the image of an old male slaveholder, the broken symbol of power and sexual domination, and an old black woman, representing "Mammy," mother, and survivor. The heritage of slavery lived on in these "two passing figures of the present-past." Or, in other words, the problems of slavery lived on in the problem of the freedmen, and the problem of the freedmen lived on in the problem of the color line. But more important still, no racial reconciliation could ever match the vaunted sectional reconciliation without a serious confrontation with the hostility rooted in sexual abuse, lynching, and racism. Du Bois used gender here to render his imagery all the more meaningful. As essay on the Freedmen's Bureau had been converted into a telling statement about the most persistent evils of slavery and racism. Du Bois could have chosen no starker example than white male sexual abuse of black women. As he would later write in 1920, Du Bois could forgive the white South almost anything: "its slavery, for slavery is a world-old habit . . . its fighting for a well-lost cause, and for remembering that struggle with tender tears." But he would never forgive the "persistent insulting of black womanhood which in [the white South] sought and seeks to prostitute to its lust."[28] Deep memory, Du Bois had exhibited in his writing, was rooted in stark imagery and its conflicts were never easily reconciled.

Black Reconstruction in America (1935), a project Du Bois had worked on intermittently for more than twenty-five years, is his most direct and complicated confrontation with the meaning of historical memory. Du Bois assumes the posture of an empiricist, but in the preface he acknowledges the dual function of the historian: "to tell and interpret." It is especially interesting that in a one-page preface Du Bois believed it necessary to "say frankly in advance" that his most basic assumption was that blacks were "ordinary human beings," that he sought to refute any theory of Negro inferiority, and that he understood that this might curtail his audience. The weight of traditional interpretations of slavery and the Civil War and Reconstruction both inspired and haunted this long book. Du Bois conceded that he would not convert any diehard racists, but that he would no longer allow emancipation and black enfranchisement after the war to be so easily dismissed as "gestures against nature." *Black Reconstruction* would, therefore, be more than what we are accustomed to calling revisionist history, just another point of view or interpretation. It would be a bold effort to retell what Du Bois considered "the most dramatic episode in American history. . . . the sudden move to free four million black slaves in an effort to stop a great civil war, to end forty-years of bitter controversy, and to appease the moral sense of civilization."[29] It would be the construction of counter-arguments and counter-memories, all in an effort to dislodge and replace the customary historical image of the situation of black people in America.

The first chapter of *Black Reconstruction,* "The Black Worker," is a meditation on the meaning of slavery in American history. Coupled with the final chapter, "The Propaganda of History," these two essays independently serve as a primer for the field of African-American history as it has developed since the 1930s. Although Du Bois' tone was unquestionably polemical, he did strive for some balanced perspective. He acknowledged that slaveholders were not unremittingly evil people, and even that the institution of slavery was "not usually a deliberately cruel and oppressive system." He allowed that slaves may have been reasonably housed and fed. But looking back upon the historiography of slavery, as well as at popular attitudes toward the Old South as they stood in the 1930s, Du Bois declared inconceivable "the idyllic picture of a patriarchal state with cultured and humane masters under whom slaves were as children, guided and trained in work and play, given each such mental training as was for their good." Instead, he offered a picture of a labor system bent on the "ultimate degradation of man," and the "psychological" disorientation of individuals. Such a picture anticipated the future work of Stanley Elkins and critiqued the earlier work of U. B. Phillips at the same time. Moreover, Du Bois' conception of slavery as ultimately a violent and debilitating system directly challenged Booker T. Washington's famous characterization in 1901 of slavery as a "school" for blacks.[30]

To Du Bois the broadest significance of slavery lay in its definition of the limits of American democracy. As long as labor, freedom, and constitutional rights were defined in racial terms, America's historical self-definition would always be stunted. Du Bois quoted at great length from Frederick Douglass' famous Fourth of July oration in 1852 to underscore the fundamental irony and dishonesty at the core of American history. Du Bois called Douglass the voice of the exploited "black worker," vaguely setting up his subsequent Marxist analysis of Reconstruction. But more importantly, he appropriated Douglass' scorching phrases to the long-term aim of an alternative history, one not characterized by "deception, impiety, and hypocrisy—a thin veil to cover up crimes." He used the fiery former slave, in some of his angriest rhetoric, to expose that American history where the "ten thousand wrongs of the American slave" were kept in "the strictest silence," and where he who would reveal them was considered an "enemy of the nation" for daring to "make those wrongs the subject of public discourse."[31] The heroes of the slavery era, Du Bois contended, were the fugitive slaves who constantly tested the power of slavery by their escapes and their witness. Indeed, fugitive slaves like Douglass not only provided leadership but also furnished a "text for the abolition idealists." Such "texts" (the slave narratives), as many historians and critics have argued in recent years, provided the foundation of African-American literary and political history. Moreover, if the black worker, as Du Bois contended, was the "founding stone" of the antebellum economic system that tumbled into civil war, then the slave narrative—the entire abolitionist literature—was the "founding stone" of an alternative American history. Near the end of *Black Reconstruction,* Du Bois returns to Douglass as he continues to explore the meaning of slavery. "No one can read that first thin autobiography of Frederick Douglass," Du Bois declares, "and have left many illusions about slavery. And if truth is our object, no amount of flowery romance and personal reminiscences of its protected beneficiaries can keep the world from knowing that slavery was a cruel, dirty, costly, and inexcusable anachronism, which nearly ruined the world's greatest experiment in democracy." Writing at the very time the WPA slave narratives were being collected, and well before any serious rediscovery of Douglass or the other antebellum black writers, Du Bois made an important claim about black sources and black history: some of the best witnesses had never been asked, the very notion of a source needed redefinition, and an entire history was yet to be told. In what may have been an ironic reference to Booker Washington, Du Bois insisted that black history did not begin with emancipation: "*Up from this slavery* gradually climbed the Free Negro with clearer, modern expression and more definite aim long before the emancipation of 1863."[32]

Du Bois' "Propaganda of History" is an indictment of American historiography and a probing statement of the meaning of race in American historical memory. If the stakes in *Souls of Black Folk* were the spiritual and psychological well-being of blacks in the age of segregation—the creation of a counter-memory to that forged by white popular literature and by Booker Washington—then the stakes in *Black Reconstruction* were collective *national* memory and the struggle over the nature of history itself. According to Du Bois there were essentially five tragic flaws in American historiography: First, most American historians, consciously or unconsciously, conspired in an avoidance of conflict, especially on the issue of race; second, American historians spurned moral judgment or responsibility for the wrongs of the past; third, slavery, both as an institution and as a cause of the Civil War, had never forthrightly been confronted; fourth, the active role of blacks, as well as abolitionism broadly defined, in the achievement of freedom had been ignored or suppressed; and fifth, the highly developed "hideous mistake" thesis about Reconstruction was rooted in false assumptions, mass production, and popular racism. This wall of historiography could not easily be pierced. Its flaws were not sins, wrote Du Bois, of "mere omission and . . . emphasis."[33] They had to be engaged with counter-arguments and, indeed, counter-"propaganda." Du Bois' devastating critique of American historiography provides one of the most acute examples we have of the interdependence of history and society, of how deeply rooted collective historical memories are in social structure, popular beliefs, and professional academic interests. Du Bois' *Black Reconstruction* challenged much more than historiography; it challenged the racism and the social theory through which most Americans gained any level of historical consciousness.

American historiography concerning race has come so far since the 1930s that the avoidance of conflict no longer seems as pressing a problem as it once did. Likewise, since the turbulent 1960s and 1970s the notion of history as moral discourse may seem to have returned to its proper place on the periphery of historians' concerns. But almost all debates over "new" histories and "old" histories, over events versus social process, or over the various ways to return to "narrative" have hinged in great part not only on the proper subject matter of history but on these two issues: conflict/continuity, scholarly dispassion/moral judgment, and the inclusion of those still perceived as outsiders. Indeed, the current challenge of multicultural studies in the academy might benefit from the perspective of looking back at some prior models. The ship of "diversity" is not sailing in completely uncharted waters. Du Bois did not advocate a personal needs-based history; he resisted the kind of ahistorical chauvinism that the Reagan-Bush era has brought us from both ends of the ideological spectrum; and he saw pluralism as the source of a new American historical narrative, not its obstacle.

The two ideas with which Du Bois began his arraignment of American historiography in 1935—the avoidance of conflict and moral responsibility—still ebb and flow from our historical agenda about race. How much of Reconstruction was truly a political, social, and racial "revolution" and how much was left "unfinished"?[34] Are the legacies of slavery still a matter of national and social responsibility in America? Do we even discuss slavery in those terms anymore? How much did the victories of the modern civil rights movement accomplish for political democracy but leave undone for economic democracy? How much should blacks shape their current agenda by looking to the symbolic memory of Martin Luther King or Malcolm X? How are those memories being contructed? Is the apparent success or failure of recent history, and its widespread dissemination in print and film, distorting or inspiring the development of the long-term historical memory among blacks and among all Americans about race? Has Martin Luther King Day lent itself to historical consciousness or historical amnesia? It all depends, of course, on who is shaping the memory, how it is conveyed, and to what end. In contemplating this crucial element of America's collective memory, we would do well to remember Nathan Huggins' insistence that the greatest challenge in writing African-American history lay not in continuing to uncover "black history," important as that process will remain, but in subverting and redefining the master narrative itself, in understanding "that there can be no white history or black history, nor can there be an integrated history that does not begin to comprehend that slavery and freedom, white and black, are joined at the hip."[35]

Du Bois' comments on the meaning of conflict and moral responsibility in American history have had many interesting echoes in the more than half a century since he wrote them. Looking especially to the Civil War era, he warned against using history merely "for our pleasure and amusement, for inflating our national ego." A meaningful black history might so controvert white supremacy that it was deemed "neither wise nor patriotic to speak of all the causes of strife and the terrible results to which sectional differences in the United States had led." There had to be a place for slavery, massive civil war, and postwar racial violence in the doctrine of American progress. Avoidance might be the only effective remedy, then, to sustain a historical memory rooted in the contradiction of white supremacy and progress. Du Bois chastized "reticent" historians who blinked or bowed in the face of an issue such as slavery. "Our histories tend to discuss American slavery so impartially," he wrote, "that in the end nobody seems to have done wrong and everybody was right. Slavery appears to have been thrust upon unwilling helpless America, while the South was blameless in becoming its center. The difference of development, North and South, is explained as a sort of working out of cosmic social and economic law." In this passage Du Bois captured the spirit and substance of much that had been written, inside and out of the academy, about the meaning of slavery and the Civil War in the seventy years since Appomattox. He was trying to advance a new set of *facts* into the historical equation at the same time he insisted that history was inherently a moral discourse. "War and especially civil strife leave terrible wounds," he contended. "It is the duty of humanity to heal them."[36]

One of the facts with which Du Bois was most concerned in his critique of American historiography was the role of slavery in causing the Civil War. This question was, and still is, pivotal in the broad development of American historical memory. Du Bois was incredulous toward interpretations of Civil War causation that ignored the slavery question. He considered it simply self-evident that the Confederacy existed and fought for the perpetuation of slavery. No amount of stress on Unionism, states' rights, or "differences in civilization" could, in his view, ever diminish the centrality of slavery as the moral and political cause of the war. He identified the stakes involved between contending memories when he pointed to a monument in North Carolina that had, in his view, achieved "the impossible by recording of Confederate soldiers: 'they died fighting for liberty!' "[37]

These sentiments toward the Confederate dead and toward the whole conception of the Civil War as a struggle between white men over southern independence or national union are strikingly similar to those Frederick Douglass expressed a generation earlier. Douglass had deeply resented monuments to Confederate leaders and soldiers, and he especially resisted the way sectional reconciliation had been forged through the mutual respect of white southern and northern veterans. Du Bois restated these resentments and demonstrated how the values of honor and valor and the concept of the good fight on both sides had helped usher the idea of black emancipation into the background of America's memory of the Civil War. To forget about slavery as a cause of the war was one of the surest ways to forget about the challenges of black freedom and equality during the age of Jim Crow. One could "search current American histories almost in vain," wrote Du Bois, "to find even a faint recognition of" the thousands of black soldiers who fought in the Civil War, and of the fact that the freedmen were not "inert recipients of freedom at the hands of philanthropists."[38]

Du Bois observed that the greatest obstacle to any development of a new American historical memory regarding race was the "chorus of agreement" about Reconstruction. In the academy, in popular culture, and in the schools, when Americans reflected upon their past during the early twentieth century they tended to look to the "tragedy" of Reconstruction for lessons and meaning. The South had been "grievously . . . wounded," blacks had been "set back" by mistaken radical policies, and the nation as a whole was shamed and retarded in its growth to greatness. "There is scarce a child in the street," wrote Du Bois, "that cannot tell you that the whole effort was a hideous mistake." Du Bois explained why this historiography, both popular and academic, was so "overwhelming."[39] It had been initiated and sustained by two successful popularizers, James Ford Rhodes and Claude Bowers. Rhodes, an Ohio businessman, combined the techniques of mass production, an overriding thesis of Negro inferiority, and a conservative's contempt for democracy to "manufacture" (as Du Bois put it) his famous seven-volume *History of the United States from the Compromise of 1850* (the first volume published in 1903 and the remaining ones in 1906). Rhodes' wide popularity and influence over school textbooks and curricula were matched in the 1920s by the journalist Bowers' best-selling book *The Tragic Era* (1929), a work that took the tragic legend of Reconstruction to its highest development and largest audience yet. Du Bois' characterization of Bowers' work as a "classic example of historical propaganda of the cheaper sort" demonstrates both his disgust and his awareness that the popularization of historical amnesia is, in part, a struggle over power and social domination.[40]

Within the academy, according to Du Bois, the "frontal attack on Reconstruction" was most formidable of all. He surveyed the wide range of Reconstruction historiography produced in the first third of the twentieth century, but centered his critique on John W. Burgess and William A. Dunning. Burgess, a southerner by birth but a former Union soldier who became a professor of political science at Columbia University, used unabashed theories of white supremacy and Anglo-Saxonism, along with an overt defense of authority, to condemn Reconstruction as an attempt to overthrow the natural order. Readers of Burgess' work would not only witness the political mistakes of Reconstruction as well as the efforts to push history beyond its evolutionary limits; they also encountered a bold faced, academic argument that black people had simply not risen above "barbarism" and had never "created any civilization of any kind." At the turn of the century Burgess, of course, voiced the prevailing racial ideology of the age; his perspective was not unique and his work appeared to be scholarly by all existing conventions. History, rooted in such sentiments, had convinced Du Bois that all struggles over historical memory would, therefore, have to be fought on both sides with some degree of "propaganda." Du Bois respected the more careful and scholarly Dunning (also of Columbia) as a "less dogmatic" historian.[41] But in many ways, the "Dunning school" of Reconstruction historiography, with its enormous influence on two generations of scholars, its dozen or more state-by-state monographs, and even with its few exceptions that did acknowledge blacks as part of the story, provided the greatest obstacle of all to an alternative memory. Most of the work by the Dunning school, however scholarly or scientific, had been written in the service of a widely accepted thesis and a very popular theory: the tragic mistake of radical Reconstruction and white supremacy.

What Du Bois illuminates in the final chapter of *Black Reconstruction* is the social organization of remembering and forgetting. Versions of historical memory—their sources and meanings—can be suppressed in the interest of social cohesion or dominance. Following the lead of Carter Woodson and a handful of less visible black and white historians, Du Bois helped to launch the long attempt to rescue black history in America from what many scholars have called a "structural amnesia." In the United States during the early twentieth century no official state censor governed scholarship and ideas; no single authority could be said to have had the power of creation or erasure of official memories, as in totalitarian societies (with the possible exception of the World War I years).[42] But the authority structure of white supremacy in America had been almost as well served by the historiography on Reconstruction as it had been by Jim Crow laws, official acquiesence in lynching, or "coon songs" and blackface minstrel shows. Such was the aim, said Du Bois, of those Reconstruction historians who ridiculed "the Negro" as the "impossible joke in the whole development." Du Bois sadly described the results of this pervasive control of historical memory. "We have in fifty years," he wrote, "by libel, innuendo, and silence, so completely misstated and obliterated the history of the Negro in America . . . that today it is almost unknown." History had been effectively used, he maintained, to teach Americans to "embrace and worship the color bar as social salvation."[43]

Du Bois' critique of Reconstruction historiography led him, finally, to a meditation on the epistemology of history and on the proper role of the historian. By training and temperament he was exceedingly interested in how historians create and convey knowledge. Du Bois never stopped referring to history as a "science," and he always remained committed to the ideal of finding historical, if not objective, "truth." By the 1930s he certainly was no longer a hard-boiled empiricist, but he could not easily relinquish the belief in history "either as a science or as an art using the results of science." But Du Bois fully appreciated and exploited the subjectivity of the historian's craft. In a 1937 memorandum about his proposed *Encyclopedia of the Negro,* Du Bois demonstrated that, though he was never indifferent about the pursuit of truth, he knew its limitations. "No scientific work done by living, feeling men and dealing with humanity," wrote Du Bois, "can be wholly impartial. Man must sympathize with misfortune, deplore evil, hope for good, recognize human fellowship. All that social science can do is so to limit natural human feeling by ascertained facts as to approach a fair statement of truth."[44] Du Bois was a relativist, like most, with an evolving, sometimes clear, sometimes ambiguous, but often aggressive conception of right and wrong interpretations.

The restraint apparent in 1937 had seemed under great duress a few years earlier when Du Bois wrote the final chapter of *Black Reconstruction.* Because he wrote in a "field devastated by passion and belief," and because racism so infested the historiography of Reconstruction, Du Bois argued that of "sheer necessity" he had written an "arraignment of American historians and an indictment of their ideals." Although he vowed to "let no searing of the memory by intolerable insult" distract him from a search for facts, he acknowledged that the "one fact" driving his analysis was that most recent historians of Reconstruction "cannot conceive Negroes as men." Reconstruction historiography was understandable, Du Bois contended, as the result of intersectional attraction to a lost cause and a romanticized South. But it rested on a bedrock of "propaganda against the Negro since emancipation . . . one of the most stupendous efforts the world ever saw to discredit human beings, an effort involving universities, history, science, social life and religion.[45] Such propaganda demanded counter-propaganda, and hence the irony in the title of Du Bois' final chapter. Such an overwhelmingly powerful effort to forge a historical memory required all the weapons of art, persuasion, and scholarship to counter it.

The idealist in Du Bois prompted him to argue that Reconstruction historiography had "spoiled and misconceived the position of the historian." If history were to be the proper guide for a better future, historians had to distinguish between "fact and desire." In almost the same breath Du Bois made an objectivist demand for the "things that actually happened" and a relativist appeal for the "philosopher and prophet . . . to interpret these facts." These "two functions" of the historian, as Du Bois described them, are precisely the same two he reserved for himself. Confronting a racist historical memory in America, Du Bois had learned and demonstrated, could not be accomplished by a mere separation of fact and desire. It demanded contextualism and relativism, the careful chronicler and the moral prophet. Du Bois tried to do both but, in the end, chose primarily the latter role.[46]

In the final pages of *Black Reconstruction,* Du Bois turns aggressively to art to convey the stakes of contending historical memories. He portrayed the whole of black history from the slave trade through emancipation as a "magnificent drama" and a "tragedy that beggared the Greek." He likened this American epic to the upheavals of the Protestant Reformation and the French Revolution. Black people, he said, had "descended into Hell; and in the third century they arose from the dead, in the finest effort to achieve democracy for the working millions which this world had ever seen." This was more than a typical Du Boisian flight into hyperhole; the resurrection imagery frames his angry disavowal of those American historians who had constructed the dominant memory of Reconstruction. So much had been missed; so much had been suppressed. The Civil War, black freedom, and the Reconstruction of the South, Du Bois seemed to be saying, ought to have been the epic of American democracy. "Yet we are blind," he declared, "and led by the blind." Du Bois would have agreed (albeit for different reasons) with Walt Whitman's famous caveat that "the real war will never get into the books." The art of memory, Du Bois understood, was not a benign process; it thrived on great contention and a social need for consensus, "with aspiration and art deliberately and elaborately distorted."[47]

The despairing tone of Du Bois' ending in *Black Reconstruction* probably reflects an honest sense of the obstacles this book, and any future revision of Reconstruction history, would face. It also represents Du Bois's felt need to confront and provoke his fellow historians. He was not writing in 1935 as a typical professor inside the academy; he could not simply take his work to the American Historical Association's annual meetings, which were ironically raging at that time with debates over relativism and objectivity. Du Bois had to contend for American historical memory—for a new vision of the meaning of race and Reconstruction—with the weapons of language. He felt "so futile," he said, in confronting this task. Du Bois viewed the "truer deeper facts of Reconstruction with a deep despair." To him, it seemed an era of great lost opportunity in its own context, and great misapprehension in the works of historians.[48] Du Bois waxed nostalgic for the heyday of radical Reconstruction: "those seven mystic years between Johnson's [President Andrew] 'swing around the circle' and the panic of 1873" when Americans allowed themselves to believe in and experiment with racial equality (a yearning, for better or worse, shared by later revisionists during the modern civil rights movement). Such a season of hope he then juxtaposes with the "crash of hell" that followed in the late nineteenth century, a period of racial repression and organized forgetting. Du Bois ends the book with the image of a college teacher in an academic hall somewhere at the turn of the century. The teacher "looks into the upturned face of youth and in him youth sees the gowned shape of wisdom and hears the voice of God." "Cynically," the professor "sneers at 'chinks' and 'niggers.' " Then Du Bois places the words of the historian John Burgess in the mouth of the teacher. The nation, announces the lecturer, "has changed its views in regard to the political relation of races and has at last virtually accepted the ideas of the South on this subject. The white men of the South need now have no further fear that the Republican party . . . will ever again give themselves over to the vain imagination of the political equality of man."[49]

In this metaphoric classroom, with the actual words of a leading Reconstruction historian, Du Bois demonstrated that the real tragedy of Reconstruction was not in the history but in the histories. In this classroom, as in textbooks, in popular culture, and in historiography itself, white supremacy in the present remained secure as long as historical memories were controlled or suppressed. The hope embedded in Du Bois' tragic ending of *Black Reconstruction* is that when the marketplace for the construction of social memories becomes as free and open as possible, while still firmly guided by the rules of scholarship, then the politics of remembering and forgetting might be, here and there, overcome. Whether that is a vain hope or an occasionally realized ideal remains the principal challenge of all those seriously interested in American historical consciousness.

Notes

For their helpful readings and criticisms of this paper I would like to thank all participants in the History and Memory Working Group, Harvard University; the Five-College Social History Seminar, Smith College; and Herbert Aptheker, Karin Beckett, Thomas Bender, Rhonda Cobham-Sander, David Du Bois, Robert Gooding-Williams, Hugh Hawkins, Michael Kammen, Alan Levy, David L. Lewis, Wilson Moses, Alfred Moss, Barbara Tischler, and David Wills.

1. Martin Luther King, Jr., "Honoring Dr. Du Bois," speech delivered at celebration of Du Bois' one hundredth birthday, February 23, 1968, Carnegie Hall, New York City, sponsored by *Freedom Ways Magazine,* reprinted in Philip S. Foner, ed., *W. E. B. Du Bois Speaks: Speeches and Addresses, 1890–1919* (New York, 1970), 12–13, 15, 17. Emphasis added.

2. Frances A. Yates, *The Art of Memory* (Chicago, 1966); King, "Honoring Dr. Du Bois," in Foner, ed., *W. E. B. Du Bois Speaks,* 12; W. E. B. Du Bois, *Black Reconstruction in America: An Essay Toward a History of the Part Which Black Folk Played in the Attempt to Reconstruct Democracy in America, 1860–1880* (New York, 1935), 725. Examples abound of Du Bois' contentiousness about American history. For instance, in 1908 Charles Francis Adams had written an article on the "Negro Problem" and the "Solid South" for *Century Magazine.* Du Bois took such exception to the piece that he wrote to Adams: "One of the most unfortunate things about the Negro Problem is that persons who do not for a moment profess to be informed on the subject insist on informing others. This, for a person who apparently boasts of advanced scientific knowledge is most deplorable and I trust that before publishing further matter on the race problem, *you will study it. To this end I am sending you some literature.*" (italics mine). See Du Bois to Charles Francis Adams, Nov. 23, 1908, and Dec. 15, 1908; and C. F. Adams to Du Bois, Nov. 28, 1908, in W. E. B. Du Bois Papers (University of Massachusetts, Amherst), reel 1.

3. Arnold Rampersad, "W. E. B. Du Bois as a Man of Literature," in William A. Andrews, ed., *Critical Essays on W. E. B. Du Bois* (Boston, 1985), 49–66; Arnold Rampersad, *The Art and Imagination of W. E. B. Du Bois* (Cambridge, Mass., 1976). Also see Arnold Rampersad, "Slavery and the Literary Imagination: Du Bois' *The Souls of Black Folk,* " in Deborah E. McDowell and Arnold Rampersad, eds., *Slavery and the Literary Imagination,* Selected Papers from the English Institute (Baltimore, Md., 1989), 104–24. On Du Bois' broader literary impact, see Herbert Aptheker, *The Literary Legacy of W. E. B. Du Bois* (White Plains, N.Y., 1989). Students of Du Bois are indebted to Aptheker for his compilations, bibliographies, and republications of Du Bois' work. See especially *The Annotated Bibliography of the Published Writings of W. E. B. Du Bois* (Millwood, N.Y., 1973).

4. *The Autobiography of W. E. B. Du Bois: A Soliloquy on Viewing My Life from the Last Decade of Its First Century* (New York, 1968), 148; W. E. B. Du Bois, "My Evolving Program for Negro Freedom," in Rayford Logan, ed., *What the Negro Wants* (Chapel Hill, N.C., 1944), 43. Emphasis added.

5. See Rampersad, "Du Bois as a Man of Literature," 62.

6. W. E. B. Du Bois, "Jefferson Davis as a Representative of Civilization," Commencement Address, Harvard University, 1890, in *W. E. B. Du Bois: Writings,* The Library of America Series (New York, 1986), 811–14. On Du Bois' race theory,

and its rootedness in nineteenth-century philosophy, see Anthony Appiah. "The Uncompleted Argument: Du Bois and the Illusion of Race," *Critical Inquiry* 12 (Autumn 1985), 21–37; Robert Gooding-Williams, "Philosophy of History and Social Critique in the Souls of Black Folk," *Social Science Information* 26 (1987), 99–114; and Joel Williamson, *Crucible of Race: Black-White Relations in the American South Since Emancipation* (New York, 1984), 399–413. I would like to acknowledge the advice and inspiration of Nathan I. Huggins on the topic of Du Bois' Jefferson Davis speech. The speech and its meanings first came to my attention in a seminar discussion on the topic at the Du Bois Institute, Harvard, led by Huggins. It is also worth noting that, given his later stance about black participation in World War I, Du Bois himself also came to "love a soldier." Conversations with Wilson Moses were very helpful on this point.

7. See Manning Marable, *W. E. B. Du Bois: Black Radical Democrat* (Boston 1986), 22–23; and Aptheker, *Literary Legacy,* 11–13.

8. W. E. B. Du Bois, *The Suppression of the African Slave Trade to the United States of America, 1638–1870* (1896), in *Du Bois: Writings,* 193. See James Ford Rhodes, *History of the United States from the Compromise of 1850* 7 vols. (New York, 1893–1906). On reconciliation and the rise of the Lost Cause mythology as well as resistance to it, see Paul S. Buck, *The Road to Reunion, 1865–1900* (New York, 1937); Gaines M. Foster, *Ghosts of the Confederacy: Defeat, the Lost Cause, and the Emergence of the New South* (New York, 1987); Charles Reagan Wilson, *Baptized in Blood: The Religion of the Lost Cause, 1865–1920* (Athens, Ga., 1980); and David W. Blight, "For Something Beyond the Battlefield: Frederick Douglass and the Struggle for the Memory of the Civil War," *Journal of American History* 75, no. 4 (March 1989), 1156–78.

9. Du Bois, *Suppression,* in *Du Bois: Writings,* 194. See Rampersad, *Art and Imagination,* 68–90.

10. Nathan Irvin Huggins, "The Deforming Mirror of Truth," new introduction to *Black Odyssey: The African American Ordeal in Slavery* (New York, 1990), reissued edition, xiii. Du Bois, *Suppression,* in *Du Bois: Writings,* 196–97.

11. W. E. B. Du Bois, *The Souls of Black Folk,* (1903; rpt., New York, 1969), 45. On Du Bois and blacks as historical "outsiders," see Clarence E. Walker, "The American Negro as Historical Outsider, 1836–1935," *The Canadian Review of American Studies* (Summer 1986), 140–61

12. John Edgar Wideman, "Introduction," *The Souls of Black Folk,* Vintage–Library of America edition (New York, 1990), xi, xv–xvi. Du Bois to William James, June 12, 1906. W. E. B. Du Bois Papers (Univ. of Mass.), reel 2. On the reception and reviews of *Souls* across a wide racial and political spectrum, both in the United States and internationally, see Aptheker, *Literary Legacy,* 51–69. For blacks, the penetrating psychological insights of *Souls* at the time of its publication are represented in a telling letter by Jessie Fauset to Du Bois. "I am glad, glad you wrote it," wrote Fauset. "[W]e have needed someone to voice the intricacies of the blind maze of thought and action along which the modern, educated colored man or woman struggles." Jessie R. Fauset to Du Bois, Ithaca, N.Y., December 26, 1903, in Herbert Aptheker, ed., *The Correspondence of W. E. B. Du Bois, Selections, 1877–1934,* vol. 1 (Amherst, Mass., 1973), 66.

13. W. E. B. Du Bois, *The Gift of Black Folk: Negroes in the Making of America* (Boston, 1924), 135–36; Countee Cullen, "Yet Do I Marvel," in Langston Hughes and Arna Bontemps, eds., *The Poetry of the Negro, 1796–1970* (New York, 1949), 233; Du Bois, *Souls,* 45, 139.

14. Michel Foucault, *Language, Counter-Memory, Practice: Selected Essays and Interviews,* ed. Donald F. Bouchard, (Ithaca, N.Y.: 1977), 163, 144. I do not intend my

use of Foucault here to be a reification of language alone, nor do I in any way subscribe to a Foucauldian denial of specific content or subjects in history. Foucault's denial of even the intent of objectivity in research is far too cynical. I simply find his discussion of power in historical analysis useful in opening ways to understand how social memories rise and fall from dominance. An important cautionary treatment of Foucault's overall historical theory is Bryan D. Palmer, *Descent into Discourse: The Reification of Language and the Writing of Social History* (Philadelphia, 1990), esp. 24–29. Du Bois, *Black Reconstruction,* 714.

15. Foucault, *Language, Counter-Memory, Practice,* 148, 150–51; Du Bois *Black Reconstruction,* 726.

16. Peter Burke, "History as Social Memory," in Thomas Butler, ed., *Memory: History, Culture, and the Mind* (Oxford, 1989), 107. On memory in totalitarian societies, see Geoffrey A. Hosking, "Memory in a Totalitarian Society: The Case of the Soviet Union," in Butler, ed., *Memory,* 115–30. On the importance of words in relation to power, see Vaclav Havel, "Words on Words," *New York Review of Books,* Jan. 18, 1990, 5–8. On the significance of liberation through language in black writing from the slave narratives to the present, see Henry Louis Gates, Jr., *Figures in Black: Words, Signs, and the Racial "Self"* (New York, 1987), 14–24; Houston A. Baker, Jr., *The Journey Back: Issues in Black Literature and Criticism* (Chicago, 1980), 33–46; and Robert B. Stepto, *From Behind the Veil: A Study of Afro-American Narrative* (Urbana, Ill., 1979), 16–26. The stakes in debates over social memories are, therefore, quite real; material resources, political power, and life chances may all be at stake. Language is not life, but it is one major component in how we contend for the meanings of and control over historical memories.

17. Maurice Halbwachs, *The Collective Memory,* trans. Francis J. Ditter, Jr., and Vida Yazdi Ditter (1950; rprint. New York, 1980), 22–49. Also see David Thelen, "Memory and American History," *Journal of American History* (March 1989), 1122; David Lowenthal, *The Past Is a Foreign Country* (Cambridge, 1985), 196–97; and Paul Connerton, *How Societies Remember* (Cambridge, 1989). On the constructive and reconstructive nature of collective memory, see Frederick C. Bartlett, *Remembering: A Study in Experimental and Social Psychology* (1932; rpt., Cambridge, 1961), 205, 209; and Edmund Blair Bolles, *Remembering and Forgetting: An Inquiry into the Nature of Memory* (New York, 1988), 17.

18. Paul Ricoeur, *Time and Narrative* (Chicago: University of Chicago Press, 1985). Steven Knapp, "Collective Memory and the Actual Past," *Representations* 26 [special issue on memory and counter-memory] (spring 1989), 140; Frederick Douglass. "The Races," speech reprinted in *Douglass Monthly* (Aug. 1859).

19. W. E. B. Du Bois, *The World and Africa: An Inquiry into the Part Which Africa Has Played in World History* (New York, 1947), 1–2; Du Bois, *Suppression,* in *Du Bois: Writings,* 196–97; W. E. B. Du Bois, *The Negro* (New York, 1915); and Rampersad, *Art and Imagination,* 235.

20. Du Bois, *Souls,* xi.

21. Yates, *Art of Memory,* 2–26, 31–36, 129–59, 199–230; *The New Science of Giambattista Vico,* 3rd ed. (1744). tr. and ed. Thomas G. Bergin and Max H. Frisch (Ithaca, N.Y., 1970), 374–83; Patrick H. Hutton, "The Art of Memory Reconceived: From Rhetoric to Psychoanalysis," *Journal of the History of Ideas* 148, no. 3 (July–Sept. 1987), 376–92. On the idea of memory palaces or theaters, see Jonathan D. Spence, *The Memory Palace of Matteo Ricci* (New York, 1983), 1–22.

22. Rampersad, *Art and Imagination,* 34, 37. On Du Bois' writing style generally, see ibid., 33–41.

23. Rampersad, "Du Bois as a Man of Literature," in Andrews, ed., *Critical Essays,* 62; W. E. B. Du Bois, "The Spiritual Strivings of the Negro People," *Atlantic Monthly* Aug. 1987, 194–98; Du Bois, *Souls,* 250, 258.

24. Pierre Nora, "Between Memory and History: *Les Lieux de Mémoire," Representations,* 26 (Spring 1989), 7–25; Du Bois, *Souls,* 96, 102–3.

25. Du Bois, *Souls,* 140, 146, 152, 156; emphasis added. Ulrich Bonnell Phillips, *American Negro Slavery* (New York, 1906). On the idea of neoslavery, see Rampersad, "Slavery and the Literary Imagination," 113–14, 121–23.

26. Du Bois, *Souls,* 59.

27. Ibid., 68–69. Du Bois' use of the phrase "no man clasped the hands of these passing figures" is especially interesting because during the 1872 presidential campaign and for a long time thereafter, the slogan "clasping hands across the bloody chasm" (referring to Union and Confederate veterans) became quite popular. So far as I can tell, it was first popularized by Horace Greeley and the Liberal Republicans in the election of 1872. See William Gillette, *Retreat from Reconstruction, 1869–79* (Baton Rouge, La., 1979), 56–72.

28. Du Bois, "The Damnation of Women," orig. pub. in Du Bois, *Darkwater* (New York, 1920), in *Du Bois: Writings,* 958.

29. Du Bois, *Black Reconstruction,* "To the Reader," 3. In 1930, in response to a correspondent eager to know how to interpret the Reconstruction era, Du Bois asserted that "the story of Reconstruction from the point of view of the Negro is yet to be written. When it is written, one may read its tragedy and get its truth." In an attempt to obtain some last-minute funds from the Carnegie Corporation to complete his manuscript for *Black Reconstruction* Du Bois wrote an apt description of the long-term value of his own book before it was published. "I think I have a book of unusual importance," he said. "Of course, it will not sell widely; it will not pay, but in the long run, it can never be ignored." See Edgar H. Webster to Du Bois, Nov. 3, 1930; Du Bois to Webster, Nov. 10, 1930; Du Bois to F. P. Keppel, Carnegie Corp., Nov. 17, 1934, W. E. B. Du Bois Papers (Univ. of Mass.), reels 34, 41. On Du Bois as historian, I am indebted to Clarence E. Walker, "Black Reconstruction in America: W. E. B. Du Bois' Challenge to the Dark and Bloody Ground of Reconstruction Historiography," a copy in manuscript provided by the author. On the origins, publishing history, and long-term significance of *Black Reconstruction,* see Aptheker, *Literary Legacy,* 211–56. Also see Jessie P. Guzman, "W. E. B. Du Bois—The Historian," *Journal of Negro Education* 30 (Fall 1961), 27–46; Ferrucio Gambino, "W. E. B. Du Bois and the Proletariat in Black Reconstruction," in Dirk Hoerder, ed., *American Labor and Immigration History, 1877–1920s* (Urbana, Ill. 1983), 43–60; Paul Richards, "W. E. B. Du Bois and American Social History: The Evolution of a Marxist," *Radical History* 1 (1970), 37–65; and Charles H. Wesley. "W. E. B. Du Bois, Historian," *Freedomways* 5, no. 1 (Winter 1965), 59–72. For a discussion of Du Bois as historian that stresses his scholarly "isolation," see August Meier and Elliott Rudwick, *Black History and the Historical Profession, 1915–1980* (Urbana, Ill. 1986), 5–6, 70–71, 279–80.

30. Du Bois, *Black Reconstruction,* 9–11; Booker T. Washington, *Up From Slavery* (rpt. New York, 1965), 24. See Stanley Elkins, *Slavery: A Problem in American Intellectual and Institutional Life* (New York, 1959).

31. Frederick Douglass, as quoted in Du Bois, *Black Reconstruction,* 14–15.

32. Du Bois, *Black Reconstruction,* 13, 715, 14. Emphasis added.

33. Ibid., 717, 713

34. See Eric Foner, *Reconstruction: America's Unfinished Revolution* (New York, 1988). For one of the most interesting recent go-arounds about the issue of new and

old histories, see "AHR Forum: The Old History and the New," *American Historical Review* 94, no. 3 (June 1989), 654–98. The five essays include, Theodore S. Hamerow, "The Bureaucratization of History"; Gertrude Himmelfarb, "Some Reflections on the New History"; Lawrence W. Levine, "The Unpredictable Past: Reflections on Recent American Historiography"; Joan Wallach Scott, "History in Crisis? The Others' Side of the Story"; and John E. Toews, "Perspectives on 'The Old and the New History': A Comment." In the 1930s and even earlier, Du Bois, though not necessarily promoting new methodologies, was certainly suggesting "new" questions, subjects, and assumptions for American historiography. A reading of especially the last chapter of *Black Reconstruction* would give many historians a valuable perspective on where some of the "new" histories came from and the struggles and obstacles they have faced. A very useful discussion of how pluralism challenges American historiography to strive for a balance of "wholes" and "parts" is Thomas Bender, "Whole and Parts: The Need for Synthesis in American History," *Journal of American History* 73 (June 1986), 120–36.

35. Huggins, "Deforming Mirror of Truth," in *Black Odyssey,* xliv.

36. Du Bois, *Black Reconstruction,* 713–14.

37. Ibid., 715–16. Here Du Bois' historical polemicism is apparent. Indeed, it would be difficult for a black historian of his time to acknowledge the Confederate soldier's claim to be fighting for "liberty." But in their 1860s perspective, many Southerners, of course, saw no contradiction between fighting to preserve a slave economy and for the principles of Southern independence or self-determination. Memory is thus demonstrated to be a tricky and deeply political phenomenon.

38. Ibid., 716–17.

39. Ibid., 717

40. Ibid. See Rhodes, *The History of the United States;* and Claude G. Bowers, *The Tragic Era* (Cambridge, Mass., 1929).

41. Du Bois, *Black Reconstruction,* 721, 718–19. See John W. Burgess, *Reconstruction and the Constitution, 1866–1876* (New York, 1902); and William A. Dunning, *Reconstruction: Political and Economic, 1865–1877* (New York, 1907).

42. Burke, "History as Social Memory," in Butler, ed., *Memory,* 106–8; Hosking, "Memory in a Totalitarian Society," in Butler, ed., *Memory,* 118–19.

43. Du Bois, *Black Reconstruction,* 723.

44. W. E. B. Du Bois, "Confidential Memorandum Regarding the Significance of the Proposed Encyclopedia of the Negro" (1937), in Herbert Aptheker, ed., *Against Racism: Unpublished Essays, Papers, Addresses, 1887–1961, by W. E. B. Du Bois,* (Amherst, Mass., 1985), 161.

45. Du Bois, *Black Reconstruction,* 727.

46. Ibid., 722. On Du Bois as moral prophet, see Rampersad, *Art and Imagination,* 91–115; and Marable, *W. E. B. Du Bois,* 190–217. On historians' relativism, see Peter Novick, *That Noble Dream: The Objectivity Question and the American Historical Profession* (Cambridge, 1988), 164–67, 264–68, 282–91, 387–92; John Higham, with Leonard Krieger and Felix Gilbert, *History: The Development of Historical Studies in the United States* (Englewood Cliffs, N.J., 1965), 117–131; and Michael Kammen, *Selvages and Biases: The Fabric of History in American Culture* (Ithaca, N.Y., 1987), 3–62.

47. Du Bois, *Black Reconstruction,* 727; Walt Whitman, "Specimen Days," in Floyd Stovall, ed., *Prose Works* (1892; rpt., New York, 1963), *The Collected Writings of Walt Whitman,* 1:117.

48. The great irony of Du Bois' despair is that by the 1960s (the "Second Reconstruction" in America) the historiography of Reconstruction would come full circle to

essentially Du Bois' vision. Inspired in great part by Du Bois' monumental work, the "revisionists" produced an enormous outpouring of "new" history about the Reconstruction era. Led by Kenneth Stampp, Willie Lee Rose, John Hope Franklin, Richard Current, and others, the revisionists reversed virtually every tenet of the traditional, "hideous mistake" thesis. They tended to view the radicals as a complex lot who championed human rights but did not brutalize the South. The revisionists persuasively rehabilitated the carpetbaggers, demonstrated the growth of independent black institutions (family, schools, and churches), illuminated the remarkable growth of black politics, and argued that Reconstruction as a whole was by no means a complete failure; and if it was, they were fond of quoting Du Bois' claim that it had been a "splendid failure" (*Black Reconstruction,* 708). Indeed, no field of American historiography became so active and explosive, and no traditional interpretation was so fundamentally overturned as that of Reconstruction. A half century after the publication of Du Bois's *Black Reconstruction,* Eric Foner has portrayed the aftermath of the Civil War as a "massive experiment in interracial democracy without precedent in the history of this or any other country that abolished slavery in the nineteenth century." Foner's recent monumental effort at a coherent synthesis of this complex era is boldly organized around the theme of "the centrality of the black experience." See Eric Foner, *Reconstruction: America's Unfinished Revolution* (New York, 1988), xxiv–xxv. For the most complete collection of revisionist writings, see Kenneth M. Stampp and Leon Litwack, eds., *Reconstruction: An Anthology of Revisionist Writings* (Baton Rouge, La., 1969), a book dedicated in part to Du Bois. For two of the best among many historiographic essays on Reconstruction, see Bernard A. Weisberger, "The Dark and Bloody Ground of Reconstruction Historiography," *Journal of Southern History* 25 (Nov. 1959), 427–47; and Eric Foner, "Reconstruction Revisited," *Reviews in American History,* 10, no. 4 (Dec. 1982), 82–88.

49. Du Bois, *Black Reconstruction,* 726–28. The passage Du Bois quotes directly is from John W. Burgess, *Reconstruction and the Constitution, 1866–1876* (New York, 1902), 298.

5

African-American Commemorative Celebrations in the Nineteenth Century

GENEVIÈVE FABRE

The celebrative spirit has always been strong among African Americans. Slaves and free blacks punctuated their lives with many feasts and commemorative events. Even though these festive occasions followed a calendar set by whites—religious and political feasts, holidays, and seasonal events like the famous corn shucking—they were often radically transformed and reinvented in their ritual and forms as well as in their function and meaning. Finding ways to alter the time–space framework prescribed or suggested by whites, African Americans created their own cycle of celebrations away from white supervision and extended it into a territory which became their exclusive property.[1]

Leaving out the rituals of daily life—Christmas and New Year, Easter, Sundays, but also baptisms, weddings, and burials—this essay will deal mainly with the calendar of public celebrations observed in the North, in the postrevolutionary era, and through the antebellum years. Emerging at a time when blacks in the New Republic were experiencing both high hopes and disenchantment, these celebrations were informed by two movements: a will to remember and the determination to construct an African-American memory—one which often ran counter to the national memory—and a desire to accomplish a "dream deferred" and an unfinished revolution. The sense of betrayal and the enduring precariousness of their situation induced in African Americans a greater concern for the future. The commemorative spirit which permeated a wealth of celebrations was therefore oriented both toward the past and toward the future. Its mood was *subjunctive,* the *ought* and *should* prevailed over the *was*: with a feeling of urgency, of great impatience at the renewed delay, African Americans invented a future no one dared consider and forced its image upon black and white minds and spirits.

Looking at the calendar of celebrations created from the beginning of the nineteenth century till the outbreak of the Civil War, I shall argue that, in contrast to most observances which are devised to fix history, African-American feasts partook of the flux of history, commented upon its direction, and indicated, in subtle ways, paths to follow. Whereas commemorations are often seen as oriented toward the past and as a means of preserving tradition, black feasts were primarily concerned with forcing change and inventing a more viable future. If their purpose was to invent tradition, it was, one must emphasize, a tradition of struggle, jeremiad, and claim-staking. As such, these commemorations should be analyzed as a *political gestus* which contributed to the development of the collective memory—not just memory of past events but the *memory of the future,* in anticipation of action to come—and of the historical consciousness of a people who are often perceived as victims rather than as historical agents.

The future which was at stake was not only the future that slaves and free blacks were preparing for themselves; it was also the destiny of the republic and of American democracy. Even the feasts which seemed to involve mostly black people were in fact sending a message to white America. Each celebration charted the various steps toward gradual, then general emancipation, thus expressing its concern for black freedom and its commitment to liberty as a fundamental human right. This interpretation of festive events runs counter to commonly held assumptions on the presence and the role of African Americans in American history, as well as on the role of feasts in African-American culture. I shall attempt to show how freedom was constantly celebrated, not as a mere allegorical figure but as a fully developed idea; how these "freedom celebrations" belong to African-American intellectual, political, and cultural history and should not be seen as marginal—as the mere manifestation of a folklore which was allowed to come to life only in limited allotted time and place.[2]

Many religious and political leaders seized upon these occasions to address the world in sermons, speeches, and orations. They tried to evaluate the contribution of black people in the building of the nation, to assess the progress of the race and its capacity for self-government, and to develop race pride as well as race memory. Most significantly, the speakers were setting themselves in the place of the Founding Fathers, as those who could take the dream of liberty one step further and perhaps bring it to completion.

Celebrations gave rise to an impressive production of speeches which belong to an oral tradition of harangues and rhetoric. Delivered in a culture where the *spoken word* prevailed, they reached out beyond their immediate contemporary audiences and eventually found their way into written forms. They testify to the skills of "negro orators" and to the importance of the *word* among a people who were thought to express their feelings more easily through music and body motions. The ability to put ideas into words was also very much a part of their culture.[3] The power of ideas was related not only to the gestures and the quality of the voice but also to the ritualized and performative style which accompanied these celebrations, and it became an essential element in the commemorative spirit. Freedom celebrations were freedom *performed* with "much ado" and with a "will to adorn."[4] Images and symbols were created, displayed, interconnected in an unusual assemblage—in words, in gesture and movement, and in visual forms. Here again the concept of performance or ritual should not be understood in a limited sense

This steel engraving from the French Publication *Le Monde Illustré* (1863) depicts the first celebration of black freedom as proclaimed by the Emancipation Proclamation of January 1, 1863. (From the collection of Randall K. Burkett)

(in the perspective of strictly folkloric studies which sometimes draw too much attention to form at the expense of meaning). Feasts were crucibles in which a culture was constantly in process. African Americans were not simply performing culture, they were performing crucial social and political acts. They were using the power of the imagination to invent, visualize, and represent themselves in roles they had always been denied; and their symbolic acts held significances that transcended mere play, game, role-playing, or improvisation. Feasts were also "rites of passage," transitions from invisibility to visibility, which included collective responses to social and political injustice and wrongs; they marked the passage from various forms of subordination and enslavement to a "season" of change which could ultimately bring complete emancipation and liberation. "Performance" must here receive its full meaning: While performing during their celebrations, African Americans were training themselves and shaping their anticipated roles as full-fledged citizens, capable of participating in public affairs. Feasts were not only a "big time" to enjoy; they held out a promise to refashion a better world and wield new power.

Stages in the Quest for a National Black Commemoration

The Spirit of 1776: Independence Day

It seemed appropriate that blacks who had participated in the fight for independence should want to celebrate the spirit of 1776; yet observances of the Fourth of July became a hotly debated issue among African Americans.[5] This commemoration was promoted by those who gave priority to their American identity and were struggling to ensure their integration in the new nation; they put their trust in a new government which, even though it had failed to abolish slavery, was still animated with noble principles of equality and liberty that might one day prevail for all persons, regardless of "birth or color." Black orators, who spoke at the early Fourth of July celebrations, did not indict the nation for having left out of the republic part of its population; instead, they encouraged blacks to seek moral improvement in order to become worthy citizens. The best example of this plea is perhaps Jupiter Hammon's speech warning his brothers against certain vices (such as idleness for free blacks) and urging them not to "become servants of sin and slaves of Satan" but "to seek earnest living" by their "labour and industry."[6]

As the abolitionist movement grew, Independence Day became a keynote in the building up of the antislavery argument.[7] It was the occasion to remind the nation of the principles which had presided at its birth—and the Declaration of Independence, the Bill of Rights or the amendments were often read; speeches pointed at the obliviousness of those who could plan a new egalitarian society and forget the black population. The inequities which still persisted were more blatantly evident in the maintenance of slavery. If Liberty, "the great first motive passion which in all times . . . had impelled and agitated the world," in the words of Caleb Cushing's oration before the Massachusetts Colonization Society in Boston, on July 4, 1833, and had been the predominant idea and "the masterpiece" of the American Revolution, "liberty of thought . . . of speech . . . of action, liberty in government and in person," many black speakers asked, why not grant it to all, regardless of color of skin? The meaning of 1776 could not be the same for whites and for the members of "a long abused race."[8] Caleb Cushing, who was one of the white interpreters of Independence Day, expressed in another oration the traditional significance of the date: "Nothing is more surely fitted to invigorate the spirit of patriotism in our breasts than the return of an anniversary festival which like the present may freshen our recollections of the *persecution* to which our forefathers were subjected in their native land . . . and of the generous enthusiasm in the cause of religious virtue and freedom which animated all the exertions and accomplished the final *emancipation.*"[9] We shall not speculate here on the way patriotism could be invigorated in black minds by the solemnities of the day. Certain words, however, encapsulating key ideas ("recollections of the persecution" or "final emancipation"), kindled the spirits of black orators and audiences to formulate their own distinctive interpretations. Certainly, the Fourth of July could offer an opportunity to proclaim that persecution was not over and that emancipation was still far from reach.

As Fourth of July speakers, blacks persistently tried to demonstrate the scope of the injustice they were still enduring and elaborated on the ideas of liberty. Frederick Douglass's famous address of 1852—"What, to the American Slave, is your Fourth of July?"—best exemplifies black ambivalence and dissatisfaction: "Your prayers and hymns, your sermons and thanksgivings with all your religious parade and solemnity, are to him mere bombast, fraud, deception, impiety, and hypocrisy—a thin veil to cover up crimes which would disgrace a nation of savages."[10] This document is one of the most compelling antebellum expressions of discontent and outrage. Delivered seventy-seven years after the Revolution, it gives vent not so much to emotions inspired by that double consciousness so often referred to as to that spirit of jeremiad and anger which prompted many black petitions and informed the struggle for liberation. White Americans came to fear Fourth of July festivities. Either they encouraged separate celebrations—and ironically they did so when blacks were trying to hold integrated observances—or they simply prohibited or outlawed black participation. To black Americans, the Fourth of July could be a most menacing and perilous day, a day when they were more likely to be exposed to white violence, resulting in arson or total destruction of a meeting place (as in New York City in 1834 or in Canaan, New Hampshire, a year later), or in riots and murder.[11] Independence Day, this most controversial and often bleakest commemoration, became a key symbol around which all other slave celebrations converged not to emulate white festivities but rather to offset them and create a separate ritual. The *black* Fourth of July, however, in anticipation of black independence, was to be observed not on that day but through another calendar of feasts, deemed more relevant to African-American history and memory.[12]

History, during these antebellum years, suggested other more appropriate commemorative celebrations, other sites and more significant landmarks around which to weave communal aspirations and construct an alternative memory. This slow and deliberate elaboration of an African-American memory is to be seen in its dialectical relation to history—both complementary and oppositional—and in its diachronic movement from one site to the next. The recognition of a new site was often brought by the dissatisfaction with a former one or heralded by the demise of an earlier celebration. This fluctuation from one date to another, far from being the expression of inconsistency or lack of purpose, offers evidence of the determination with which blacks pursued their quest for a national commemoration in order to draw guidelines for taking action. It invites us to probe more deeply into the meaning of the concept "black history" seen here not so much in opposition to "white history" as the image and representation black people had of American history, and the history they managed to make for themselves against all odds. That African Americans should hold their destiny in their own hands was a firm belief shared by many leaders (Douglass, Walker, Garnet). Their collective memory selected certain events, moments, heroes, and figures more appropriate to convey this black perspective and to inspire their historical imagination to invent and create their future. Each new site suggests new interpretations, and the analysis of each site—in which a constellation of signs and messages can be read—is a precious tool for those who wish to study black history and culture.

The Abolition of the Foreign Trade: January 1, 1808

The abolition of the slave trade—a long-awaited event seen as a major step toward the abolition of slavery—was at the beginning of the nineteenth century the first site chosen for a national black celebration. In contrast to the Fourth of July, it was situated at the other end of the calendar. The New Year had always been a dreaded moment in slave life: It brought an end to Christmas festivities and heralded another long year of toil and humiliation. After 1808, however, it received a new meaning and became a harbinger of hope. It was observed in the spirit of gratitude and of rejoicing induced by most celebrations—as a day of public thanksgiving and as a day to remember for the hopes it brought of a brighter future. This new New Year's Day also developed a character of its own and set the pattern for commemorations to come. If one is to judge from the descriptions one finds in the speeches given on that day or in the black press, rejoicing was tempered by mourning, and thanksgiving by ardent protest. In 1809, Joseph Sidney noted the celebration's festive mood but insisted that the participants did not forget those still held in bondage.[13] January 1 also reminded Blacks of the historical impact of the slave trade, of the greed of "fleshmongers," and of the importance of gain and power in Anglo-Saxon history. It brought at the same time a heightened consciousness of Africa as a *lieu de mémoire*—the point from which the Black Odyssey had started—and the fear that the end of the trade might entail another dramatic break from the mother country. On the one hand, slaves and free blacks recalled their common origins, the communality of their fate as chattel property brought into the New World, and the importance of the African component of their identity. As in the other celebrations—the elections of Governors and Kings in New England, for instance—they could take pride in their African origin and bemoan the hardships of their bondage.

On the other hand, for the first time perhaps since their arrival on American soil, the continuity of the link they had managed to preserve with Africa was threatened. Viciously destructive as it was, slavery did mean that the constant arrival of new slaves had kept their memories of the homeland alive and had been instrumental in renewing and reviving their culture. The commemoration—celebrating as it did the end of a much dreaded trade and the opening of a more hopeful era—was fraught with mixed feelings. It was important that it should keep *American* blacks from forgetting their African origin, that it should also help them foresee their destiny in the United States. When the colonization movement started, the relation between these two poles—Africa, where some free blacks were encouraged to return, and America, where many thought they were either forced to stay (the slaves) or committed to remain (free blacks who felt bound to their enslaved brothers and sisters)—became more and more complex. January 1 observances provided the site of many debates between those who, like Delany, pleaded for a return to Africa; those who, like Douglass, opposed colonization; and those who, like Garnet, had more ambivalent feelings. It is therefore interesting to look at January 1 for the changes it brought to the memory of Africa. First the end of the foreign trade and then the beginning of the colonization movement, tended to divide and confuse blacks. January commemorations assumed a new function: to reorganize memory and to redefine the new components of the African-American identity. Bringing a great number of blacks together, these January firsts were also given the task of bridging the gap that threatened to endanger the unity of the community. This gap, as we shall see, was increased by the movement toward emancipation which spread across the Northern states and redistributed the free blacks/slaves division along starker geographic lines, opposing Northern liberty to Southern bondage. By reiterating commonalities of origin and values rather than conflicts and tensions, these black celebrations strove to correct certain inconsistencies of history. Memory became not only more selective but also prescriptive; it chose to ignore certain realities which could impair its work; or rather it attempted to change the course of history by cementing a unity which was constantly jeopardized. Since freedom was the main object of celebration, slavery had to remain the central issue, and abolition, through general emancipation, the ultimate aim.

The ritual followed for the New Year ceremonies, with the alternance of song/prayer/sermon/address/parade, was distinctly African American. It might have been partly inspired by Independence Day (it would be interesting, for example, to see to what extent black oratory developed as a nineteenth-century American tradition and to what extent it was a rather unique black creation); but the place chosen, the mood, and the styles of performance were definitely African American. Celebrations were organized, presided over, attended by blacks; the services were held in an "African" church; the opening address was given by a black minister, the anthem sung by a black choir; and, if the official document that was read was the Congressional Act of Abolition, the formal address was given by a black leader (Peter Williams in 1808, Henry Sipkins and William Hamilton in 1809 and 1815), and the congregation sang the hymns and prayers. The atmosphere was predominantly religious, more so than in later celebrations which became increasingly secular; but the orations, the reading, and the address transformed the event into one that was decidedly political.

In a lengthy account of the New York ceremonies, James McCune Smith shows how much the rituals of January the First were close to those of the governors' elections and to the Pinkster Festival (although the comparison is ours, not his). The styles of marching, of music, and of dancing were common to all these celebrations; the grand marshal of New York's New Year, Hardenburgh, with his attendants and "his aids on horseback dashing up and down the line," bore much resemblance to Pinkster King or to the Kings and Governors of New England.[14] The procession counted a great number of first-generation Africans, who marched not in separate clusters but all together. African languages were heard in speech and in song; but, in spite of the diversity, the feeling was one of unity, the procession bringing together *a* people of different backgrounds. The New York African Society for Mutual Relief, whose founding was celebrated in the 1808 feast, led the "grand procession." The name "African" was on many banners, at a time when many organizations still used that word as a sort of title and legitimate designation.[15] On the banners were also inscribed freedom mottos ("Am I not a man and a brother?"), and people "carried themselves with a free air, which showed that they thought themselves free." They paraded in large numbers "easily thrashing aside by their own force the small impediments [whites] which blocked their way." All the details we find in this description show the importance of visual effects (in banners, but also in costumes and trappings), of mood and demeanor as signs of freedom. All rituals and performances seemed to converge to celebrate major aspects of black life: African identity, freedom, leadership, solidarity between free blacks and bondsmen, between African-born and American-born blacks.

New Year celebrations were held mostly in New York and Philadelphia, the cities which had the greatest number of blacks. Black Bostonians apparently never observed January 1; instead they celebrated July 14, anniversary of the abolition of slavery in the Commonwealth of Massachusetts. This event was sponsored by the African Society of Boston, and occasionally involved white guest speakers. These celebrations often met with strong white disapproval and were often derided: in Boston, numerous broadsides, between 1815 and 1825, made fun of black pomposity and of the pretentiousness of "The Grand and Splendid Babolition of Slavery." Under these circumstances, friends of the Negro in Boston were unable to offer sufficient protection against those repeated attacks.

The January celebration, in spite of its popularity (it was observed also in England and in Denmark) was kept only eight years in New York and survived only until the early 1830s in Philadelphia. It never became a national day for all blacks until the Emancipation Proclamation of 1863 gave this date a newer significance. In the 1820s and 1830s, disillusionment over the impact that the abolition of the slave trade could have on the course of history caused many blacks to abandon this site on which they had set so much hope: The legislation had not been respected, it had not paved the way for the abolition of slavery; indeed, it was responsible for the development of the even more dreaded domestic trade. By 1830, too, the "peculiar institution" had been strengthened and supported by a diversified proslavery ideology and by a body of codes and acts which were to culminate in the 1850 Fugitive Slave Law.

State Emancipations and July 5 Commemorations: 1827

Following the example of Boston, some black Americans, in search of new anniversaries, chose to celebrate the abolition of slavery in their states. Thus, from 1827 on (the date when the 1799 and 1817 gradual emancipation laws became effective) New York forsook January 1 and held its annual celebration in July. But since the legislation took effect on Independence Day, the old debate about July 4 was resumed. The *Freedom Journal* stressed the necessity of creating a separate black ceremony. The fifth of July was chosen to set it apart from the American holiday. Five other states also commemorated the end of slavery, and records reveal eighteen different celebrations in eight years in eight different cities. Nathaniel Paul's emancipation day address in New York stressed the importance of the appearance of blacks in the streets of the city, and eloquently defined the themes of the day to be humiliation and exaltation. "We find much," he said, "which requires our deep humiliation and our most exalted praises. The power of the tyrant is subdued, the heart of the oppressed is cheered, liberty is proclaimed to the captive."[16] While he exposed the perniciousness of slavery, he praised the peaceful, bloodless revolution through which "so glorious an event" had been accomplished. His address thus offers a classic example of fifth of July speeches: an indictment of the evil of slavery (vilified for its "pure, unmixed, unsophisticated wickedness," for being "a hateful monster, the very demon of avarice and oppression, the scourge of heaven and the curse of the earth," and for the affliction and suffering it brought); the ardor with which it calls for vengeance and a just retribution ("Are there no forebodings of a future day of punishment, and of meeting the merited avenger?"); the way it points at the "medley of contradictions" and the "palpable inconsistencies . . . which stain the national character"; and finally its anticipation of the role the British Parliament, which had first permitted such an infamy, might play in "arresting its progress and effecting its expulsion."

The ritual was held partly in the private spaces of black churches and partly in spaces much more public. Parades were included more frequently, as a challenge to white power and authority. They were also a challenge to the American parades of the preceding day, the Fourth of July: a demonstration of orderliness and respectability on the part of those who claimed their right to be considered as fully responsible citizens. These outdoor performances were strongly opposed by some organizations, like the National Negro Convention, or by such leaders as Samuel Cornish or John Russwurm, editors of the *Freedom Journal.*

Yet the stage was set and the time was ripe for the entry of blacks into the public space.[17] The transition from the more secret, sacred space of the black church to the streets of major cities created a dramatic change and accounts for the transformation of celebrations. They became more of a community affair and were no longer placed exclusively under the control of the church; they sought more deliberately to attract the attention of white people. Forms also changed. Community dinners were organized with formal toasts. Military bands replaced religious choirs. These ceremonies now usually opened with the firing of guns in salute and the displaying of new emblems and other striking visual effects; they offered many black groups and associations the opportunity to appear publicly. These forms were not altogether new, for they had been present in feasts like Election Day, local festivals, and in some New Year ceremonies. Yet, coming right after the Fourth of July, they became more daring and more legitimate.

July 5 celebrations offered the opportunity to challenge more openly the national mood and to develop publicly a counterceremony. The occasion to resume the old debate on Independence Day was seized upon with much vigor and eloquence. Throughout these antebellum years, the fifth of July orations give the measure of the intensity of the confrontation with white America, and show clearly the development of the antislavery argument. They also allowed black abolitionists to offset the speeches of other American orators, to vent their disagreement with their white counterparts, and to take a strong stand against some of their assumptions and postures.

It is around this reflection on the Fourth of July—that cornerstone of American history—that African-American thought and political culture grew more elaborate and sophisticated. It is to that period that one is indebted for the wealth of black speeches addressed not only to blacks but to the nation at large. It is then also that speakers like Douglass refined their oratorical skills and their reflections; then that the stronger statements and the boldest indictments were made. It would be interesting to analyze the impact July 5 had on the abolitionist movement when it was in full swing, to see what support it received from the white abolitionists, and, most importantly, what inspiration it gave them. One is tempted to say that some white friends of the Negro were eager to follow a movement which arose without their initiative, while others were irritated or threatened by this arrogant display of black political independence.

Emancipation celebrations, consistently observed from 1827 to 1834 (and even up to 1859, when W. J. Watkins gave a well-known oration), just like celebrations for the end of the slave trade, became less memorable as years went by and as blacks realized the limits of the freedom granted. Emancipation brought little improvement to free blacks, who ironically saw their status decline as the increasing number of new "free" states voted new constitutions that imposed restrictions on the black vote—requiring, for example, property qualifications—or segregated the educational system. Negrophobia was widespread in the North, where the presence of free blacks was considered less and less desirable—even (or, should we say unsurprisingly?) in Philadelphia, where the free black community was large and influential. Efforts by advocates of Negro rights, reformers, or abolitionists to alleviate racial tensions and violence failed. Once again, dreams of freedom were deferred.

British Emancipation in the West Indies: August 1, 1834

In these times of shattered hopes, an act of the British Parliament ending slavery in the West Indies encouraged black Americans to think of their fate more in terms of a diaspora than in the limited frame of state or U.S. events. The August 1 celebration, which started in 1834, immediately assumed a much larger scale than all other observances. The act, which emancipated approximately 670,000 slaves, brought back on the scene the immense hope of general emancipation. A powerful country was setting an example which one day might be followed by the United States. (France, which had successively abolished and reestablished slavery in 1801 would emancipate its slaves only in 1848; after this date, praise of France was often included in orations). General emancipation offered a brighter prospect than gradual state emancipations. Discriminatory segregative practices and the upsurge of racism which had followed upon Northern emancipation left many free blacks powerless and vulnerable. Slavery was outlawed, but legislation brought new restrictions. General emancipation, by the sheer impact of numbers and liberating all slaves among a fast-growing population, would give blacks a greater power, restore their unity, and check the impending cleavage between free and enslaved, and between North and South. Free blacks, who were the initiators and the celebrants of August 1, also knew that only nationwide abolition of slavery could bring them the freedom they failed to receive from their emancipation; in other words, that as long as slavery existed, it would continue to affect the status of the entire black population.

One understands, therefore, why August 1 celebrations became such an important site of memory for the black community and for the abolitionist movement in its pre–Civil War years. They were occasions to reaffirm the solidarity of free and enslaved. Other ties were also emphasized: ties to a loyalist past and to Canadian brothers and sisters, who had organized their own celebrations in Canada West as early as 1835.[18]

August 1, 1834, thus significantly expanded the black collective memory by introducing two important symbols: England and Canada. England, at the time of the revolutionary war, had promised black loyalists freedom, whereas by contrast the American republic often betrayed black patriots; in the 1830s England also provided more official support to the abolitionist movement, offering it a broader international forum and an audience as well as institutional and financial help. England, which only a few decades earlier had been, in many patriotic speeches, presented as the perfidious despotic tyrant/enslaver of America, was now held up as a moral example "of humility and honest repentance" for the United States. A country that "still clung to the doctrine of the Divine Rights of Kings" was nevertheless ahead of the American republic.

Canada was likewise held up as a major symbol: a potential land of the free, a country where fugitive slaves could find refuge (especially after 1850, when it offered protection from slave catchers) and start a new life; the termination point of the Underground Railroad and of the slave's hazardous life and suffering; the incarnation of the North Star; the mythic Canaan Land—Canada.

Yet both England and Canada left blacks with ambivalent feelings. Black loyalists exiled on British territory often voiced their complaints to Parliament at the unjust treatment they received from British authorities and citizens. In Toronto, blacks proclaimed their loyalty to the British government and praised its humanitarianism. But speakers also raised the issue of white prejudice and racism, and drew a distinction between the tolerance of abolitionists in England and the harshness of colonial governments. The common fate of free blacks in the United States and Canada tightened their solidarity. For both communities, August 1 celebrations were again animated with two moods: hope and despair, praise and denunciation.

To American blacks, August 1 offered an opportunity for a drastic reconsideration of the significance of American history for their people. It spurred a resurgence of the movement against the Fourth of July, and a new and radically changed reflection on the American Revolution. August 1 became another countercelebration. Again, black orators (like Douglass in his speech delivered in Canandiagua on August 4, 1857) often took addresses delivered by whites on the Fourth of July as their main rhetorical targets.[19] Beyond the criticism, indeed the excoriations, of the American government, one is struck by the sharpness of their analysis of the pre–Civil War climate; by their intuition that Union interests would prevail over the antislavery cause; and by their conviction that the abolitionist movement would be perceived more and more as a threat to the Union. One finds in Douglass's writings, for example, an interesting point on one of the effects of slavery on the historical imagination: having noted that the Declaration of Independence and the Constitution make no reference to the slave and that these facts have been systematically obscured, he writes: "Slavery has taught us to read history backwards, sitting at the feet of [J. C.] Calhoun and [R. B.] Taney."[20] August 1 celebrations were thus meant to shape and orient the historical mind. With a sharp focus on past events, they could correct errors and presumptions. They could help set history straight.

As black leaders were revising history, they made insistent calls for future action and commitment, and for appropriate methods to achieve these aims. Orations abounded with exhortations: to support fugitive slaves and to demonstrate black ability to manage freedom; to become self-reliant and to distrust white philanthropy. Blacks were also urged to seek self-improvement, respectability, dignity, and exemplary conduct. Encouragement was also given to unite in the fight against pervasive racism, both in Canada and in the United States, and emancipated and fugitive slaves were called upon to bear witness to the prejudices and suffering they had endured. In addition, they were expected to describe their achievements as free men and women. In these testimonies, the individual memories of lived experience, rich and complex, contrasted with the simplified constructed collective memory. Both the fugitive slave whose "voice" had to be heard and the West Indian blacks were set as examples. They became central symbols. Jamaica often came into the picture (especially in Garnet's speeches after he had spent three years there), and the white press was often blamed for demeaning black accomplishment among newly freed West Indians.[21]

One must remember that August 1 celebrations took place at a time when proslavery forces were gaining ground, when efforts were being made to check the abolitionist movement, and when legislation was passed to limit the liberty of free blacks. It was most important then that blacks show some concern for the image they were presenting. Ceremonial events had to be well organized and orderly (on occasion, they even served as a model for white observances). Again, the Fourth of July, conducted with shame and confusion if we are to believe some retrospective depictions, became the foil. Douglass repeatedly attacked "Fourth of Julyism," not only for its lack of political relevance to blacks but also for the excess that presided over its ritual, for its "tall drinking, tall talking, tall swearing, tall speech-making."[22] Likewise, other more "carnivalesque" and popular festivals were also decried for being disreputable and impairing black dignity.

August 1 stands apart from other feasts precisely because of its orderliness, for the way it tried to impress whites not only with ideas—on the meaning and the course of history—but with images. And whites did react favorably. Not only did they participate more widely (and blacks did not try to check this white presence as long as black control was retained); they also expressed their approbation and admiration. If some newspapers like the *New York Herald* remained consistently hostile, most of the white press gave frequent reports and made laudatory comments on the spirit and proper behavior which prevailed.

The celebration ritual grew more complex over the years, perhaps as a result of the growing significance it held. Indeed, one should not neglect the role that ritual played in the creation and maintenance of commemorative spirit. Celebrations themselves became history, became important and memorable events—a memory to hand down to generations to come. Their number was impressive. August 1 was observed in thirteen states, in fifty-seven different places in the United States, and also in Liberia in 1859.[23] In London it became one of the most significant antislavery affairs. In 1851, at the Hall of

Commerce, West Indian Emancipation Day combined with a special meeting to welcome George Thompson home. The event was chaired by the black abolitionist William Wells Brown, and by leading British antislavery figures. Alexander Duval from Baltimore (who fled slavery in 1849 and settled in New Bedford) read the "Appeal of the People of Britain to the World," and Brown gave the formal address. In 1859, another famous August 1 meeting was held in London at Store Street Music Hall. Lord Brougham presided, and gave a speech reviewing the history of British agitation against slavery. It is probably in Britain that the most solemn ceremonies took place, with the attendance in 1859 of members of Parliament and of famous black abolitionists like Sarah P. Remond and Ellen Craft.[24]

In the United States, certain places and certain years also became famous for their ceremonies. This celebrity was due to the presence of a renowned speaker or to the importance of the gathering: Rochester, Canadaigna, 1847, 1848—because of Douglass; Poughkeepsie, 1857—because of Garnet and also for the (in)famous Dred Scott decision. In Canada, Chatham, Hamilton, Amherstburg, and (after 1854) Toronto became key sites.

An intense network of interaction and exchange was woven between these various sites, places, and times. Former celebrations were often referred to and established as examples to be followed or improved upon. Thus from one observance to the next a solid chain was created, each feast connected with some important event and with a particular spirit: the Fugitive Slave Law (1850) induced anger and a sense of outrage, whereas the general emancipation created a festive mood and exhilaration. Delegations, sent from other cities, often traveled hundreds of miles to the major sites. Celebrants traveled for days to Rochester, or from Canada West to New York, or from New York and Albany to Poughkeepsie, from Detroit and Windsor to Amherstburg. Boats occasionally were chartered. Although all of these celebrations occurred in the North, they related themselves to the slaves in the South. Participants were exhorted not to forget the enslaved. Memory of enduring servitude by fugitives was always present.

The celebrations were planned months in advance. Preparations involved churches and many African-American associations and societies. The events were well advertised, with local black militia plus horn and brass bands with high-sounding names brought forward to attract huge crowds.

These ritual occasions included fairs, parades, picnics, banquets, and dances; and thus blended the traditional religious elements with the secular and the military. Dance and drink alternated with prayer and speech. Many symbolic acts and gestures were performed: the ringing of bells, burning of powder, display of banners, all "offered on the altar of freedom." In spite of the organizers' determination to conduct the August 1 ceremonies with exemplary genteel restraint, the festivities became occasions for popular rejoicings and conviviality. Abundance and plenty replaced the prescribed sobriety. In 1846, an emancipation ball was introduced in spite of the objection of serious-minded observants. The celebration, over its thirty years of existence, grew in scope and, in the process, sometimes lost its original frame and meaning. It was the orators' duty to remind participants of the seriousness of the occasion, and they often did so with authority and eloquence. Nevertheless, the celebrations eventually got out of hand, and their popularity ironically caused them to lose their political and civic character.

Some leaders began to question the political meaning of August 1. Like their predecessors who opposed celebrating the Fourth of July or January 1, they argued that it commemorated acts of white people. James McCune Smith objected to celebrating "the deeds of a race by which we are so despised."[25]

An Alternative Calendar

As the initial thrust for commemorating August 1 declined, alternative celebrations were suggested or even observed: events deemed more worthy of remembrance or more centered on black history, anniversaries of death or prominent deeds of black leaders. While Baltimore preferred to commemorate Toussaint L'Ouverture and the Haitian revolution,[26] Cleveland recommended the downfall of slavery in Haiti or Nat Turner's birthday.[27] McCune Smith suggested Turner's rebellion of 1831 or Vesey's death in South Carolina in 1822. In the late 1850s, Massachusetts began to honor Crispus Attucks on March 15, in protest against the Dred Scott decision. The Commemoration Festival, held in Faneuil Hall in Boston, celebrated, together with Attucks, Peter Salem, Prince Whipple, the "Colored Patriots," the Sons of Freedom, and black soldiers who had fought in the American wars (the revolutionary war and the War of 1812), and famous places like Lexington, Bunker Hill, or King Street.[28]

In Syracuse, New York, another significant celebration, begun in 1851, was directly connected with immediate history: Jerry Rescue Day, in memory of the rescue of a fugitive slave and in protest against the 1850 law. Jermain W. Loguen, preacher and superintendent of the Underground Railroad, created this site of memory by appealing to the people of Syracuse's love of liberty. In one of the most powerful addresses of the times, he urged his fellow citizens to unite and fight, and to denounce the obnoxious statute, thus "sending" from Syracuse "an earthquake voice through the land. . . . I tell you the people of Syracuse and of the whole North must either meet this tyranny and crush it by force or be crushed by it." The speech he delivered three days after the Fugitive Slave Law went into effect is a compelling statement on the stand taken by former slaves. "They have taken their stand—they would not be taken back to slavery. . . . They will have their liberties or die in their defence." The call to defiance ("The time has come to change the tone of submission into tones of defiance") and to resistance against a government which has "transgressed constitutional and natural limits" is reminiscent of Walker's *Appeal.* The violence and the daring of Loguen, going to the rescue of his people, set the mood for celebration of black resistance, courage, and audacity: "I don't recognize this law—I don't fear it—I won't obey it! It outlaws me, and I outlaw it." Speaking in the name of all African Americans at a time when fear was stifling so many voices, he also set the fugitive slave as the central symbol in the struggle for liberation and the love of liberty as the core of all action. With Jerry Rescue Day, freedom celebration received its most uncompromising meaning.[29]

Thus there existed, besides the more official calendar of the three main celebrations—January 1, July 5, August 1—an alternative calendar which favored commemorations of black resistance (crushed or successful) of black heroic deeds and black resilience. The three main sites, supplemented by those of the alternative calendar, should not be interpreted, as Smith did, as simply honoring white deeds. As Douglass rightly pointed out, these legal acts by whites who were the only people entitled to pass any legislation were often forced upon them through the sustained struggle of black people, who through nonviolent or violent action (petitions, protest, escape, riots, and insurrections) consistently pursued their fight for freedom and managed to impose upon white minds their own idea of a free republic. Even if the acts celebrated were taken thanks to the support or the sympathies of whites, they were ultimately the doing of black people, who, obstinately and with determination, accomplished this long revolutionary process and broke open the institutional doors of their white rulers.

The fact that emancipation celebrations became such a firmly established institution in the life of antebellum Northern blacks reveals that their conception of freedom was linked with the end of slavery—a conception which was to be questioned after the Civil War. General emancipation then proved to be a necessary but insufficient step toward the recognition of civil liberties and rights and the erasure of racism.

In the pre–Civil War years, the antislavery cause was the most legitimate and crucial issue; and it was this character—the *legitimacy* of the claim—that was emphasized in "freedom celebrations." But with the strengthening of the proslavery movement in the 1850s, black leaders were less inclined to turn celebrations into thanksgiving ceremonies that honored white sympathizers or a republic which had repeatedly betrayed them. Instead, they shifted their celebration "sites" towards new symbols—black warriors here, rebels or fugitives there—demonstrating the force and courage of a people who had striven to bring to completion an imperfect revolution not as victims but as alert and diligent historical actors. The trend that was already present in some early celebrations—asserting the right to autonomy and *sovereignty* through legal or illegal and even violent action—became more manifest in the 1850s and accounts for the emergence of an alternative calendar.

Nineteenth-century celebrations created a tradition—of ritualization of civic life—which was to culminate in the Emancipation Jubilees of 1862 and 1863, and in Juneteenth. But such forms of remembrance also continued well into the twentieth century, still in anticipation of a freedom which general emancipation had failed to accomplish. The numerous organizations founded after the war resorted to ceremonial rites and commemorative events to continue reinforcing the idea of freedom. These groups patterned their meetings and conventions on the earlier celebrations. Later, freedom celebrations served as models for the organization of great demonstrations like those of the Garvey Movement or of the civil rights era. The persistence of the tradition attests not only to the unending struggle for liberty and justice but also to the significance of these ritual performances in the dynamics of black cultural, institutional, and political life.

Commemorative celebrations may also have another decisive meaning, in resolving some of the contradictions created by the distance between history and memory—history as it is lived and history as it is conceived, history as it is remembered and history as it is commemorated. These celebrations highlight the tension between the *is* and the *ought,* between the course of things and principles stated; but they also oscillate between presence and absence, making the presence more perceptible and proclaiming the absence (and there is clearly a greater sense of absence in African-American commemorative ceremonies). Moreover, they stage the dialectics of forgetting and not forgetting. On the one hand, they stress the necessity of forgetfulness (and not forgiveness) of certain aspects of the past which would be too inhibitive to construct the future; on the other hand, they correct the lapses and oblivions of memory and insist that some events be recollected. Standing as they do between history and memory, arbitrary in their selection, commemorations do not always do justice to complexities and uncertainties. They do violence by imposing simplification, exaggeration, stylization, or dramatization. Yet they lend to history and memory an organizing principle; they question their habitual workings by calling attention to unnoticed but nonetheless meaningful historical realities. On the eve of the Civil War, commemoration celebrations helped African-American people not only to grapple with their lives and destiny, but also to forge a collective memory which could challenge the national American memory and perhaps even change the course of a history otherwise violently oblivious of the fate of its black populations, enslaved and free.

Notes

1. A number of studies deal indirectly with African-American festivities and celebrations. Among them are John Blassingame, *The Slave Community* (New York: Oxford University Press, 1972); Eugene D. Genovese, *Roll, Jordan, Roll* (New York: Pantheon, 1974); Albert J. Raboteau, *Slave Religion* (New York: Oxford University Press, 1978); Eileen Southern, *The Music of Black Americans* (New York: Norton, 1971); Lawrence W. Levine, *Black Culture and Black Consciousness* (New York: Oxford University Press, 1978); Sterling Stuckey, *Slave Culture* (New York: Oxford University Press, 1987); Roger D. Abrahams and John Szwed, eds., *Discovering Afro-America* (Leiden: E.J. Brill, 1975); and Roger D. Abrahams, *Singing the Master* (New York: Pantheon, 1992).

2. For a study of these celebrations, see William Wiggins, " 'Lift Every Voice': A Study of Afro-American Emancipation Celebrations," in *Discovering Afro-America,* ed. Roger D. Abrahams and John Szwed (Leiden: E. J. Brill, 1975), pp. 45–46; William S. Gravely, "The Dialectics of Double Consciousness in Black American Freedom Celebrations," *Journal of Negro History* 6, no. 2 (Winter 1982), 302–16;

Leonard E. Sweet, "The Fourth of July and Black Americans," *Journal of Negro History* 61, no. 3 (1976), 266–75; John R. McKivigan and Joseph H. Silverman, "Monarchial Liberty and Republican Slavery: West Indies Emancipation Celebrations in Upstate New York and Canada West," *Afro-Americans in New York Life and History* 10 (January 1986), 7–18.

3. The most complete collection of sermons, addresses, and orations is in Dorothy Porter, ed., *Negro Protest Pamphlets* (New York: Arno Press, 1969); idem, *Early Negro Writing* (Boston: Beacon, 1971).

4. These expressions are borrowed, respectively, from Herbert Blau's *Eye of Prey* and from Zora Neale Hurston. On ritual performance, one may consult the works of Victor Turner, Richard Schechner, and Barbara Babcock.

5. Leonard I. Sweet, "The Fourth of July and Black Americans in the Nineteenth Century" *Journal of Negro History,* 61, no. 3 (1976), 256–75. July Fourth was a "major holiday"; observed more systematically after the 1812 War, it was then institutionalized as a sacred national holiday. It was celebrated by blacks in the North as well as in the South; yet this day of festivity was fraught with irony for the Southern slaves and for free blacks, who seized the occasion to voice their anger and protest. Insurrectionists like Nat Turner planned their rebellion on this symbolic date, while Northern orators delivered their most violent speeches on that day of "national vanity," as European observers sometimes viewed it. Every Fourth of July, blacks were confronted with this "singular anomaly" and "living paradox"—in the words of William J. Walkins (see Porter, ed., *Negro Protest Pamphlets,* pp. 7–8)—and devised diverse strategies to deal with the dilemma. The lie of freedom was also a bitter experience for many slaves: for Sojourner Truth, who did not receive her "independence" on July 4, 1826—the day her master had pledged to give her liberty—and, ironically, for Jefferson's slaves, who had to wait until that same year (1826) for the death of their master in order to receive their freedom.

6. Jupiter Hammon, quoted in Porter, ed., *Negro Protest Pamphlets,* p. 000.

7. The American Colonization Society, founded in 1816, and the abolitionist movement played very different roles in the interpretation and transformation of this celebration. The former turned it into rites in praise of colonization, the latter into a day of protest and accusation.

8. In this respect, one could compare the orations delivered by white speakers (Richard Furman at Charleston in 1802; William H. Sweard at Auburn, New York, 1825; and George W. Lindsly at Peru, Illinois, 1839; earlier orations of 1801 and 1803 have been collected in Caleb Bingham's *The Columbian Orator* [Troy, N.Y.; O. Penniman, 1803]) with black speeches (Peter Williams at Wilberforce, Canada, 1830; and G. F. Buncem, New York, 1830 in Porter, *Early Negro Writings,* p. 295; or Nathanial Paul in Albany, 1827, in Porter, *Negro Protest Pamphlets,* pp. 1–23; or again Frederick Douglass in Rochester in 1852).

July Fourth was occasionally another source of inspiration for Blacks, who not only wrote orations but songs and odes. A Buffalo barber wrote such an ode. See James M. Whitfield, *America and Other Poems* [Buffalo, N.Y. 1853]; see also *Freedom's Gift or the Sentiments of the Free* (Hartford, Conn.: S.S. Cowles, 1840), pp. 76–77, 97.

9. Oration delivered at Newburyport on the forty-fifth anniversary of American Independence, July 4, 1821.

10. In Philip Foner, ed., *The Life and Writing of Frederick Douglass* (New York: International Publishers, 1950) vol. 2, p. 443. Douglass further condemns the conduct of the nation as "hideous and revolting," adding that "America is false to the past, false to the present, and solemnly binds itself to be false to the future." (*Douglass'*

Paper, July 6, 1855; also in Foner, *Life and Writings,* p. 192). No one has expressed more slashingly the opposition between the *we* and *they,* ours and theirs, between the white and the black commemoration: "This Fourth of July is *yours* not *mine;* you may rejoice, I must mourn. . . . I am not included within the pale of this glorious anniversary! Your high independence only reveals the immeasurable distance between us" (ibid., p. 189). On July 4, 1862, Douglass delivered another speech—at Himords Corner, Yates County, New York—in which he provides not only an insightful analysis of the state of the nation at the outbreak of the war but also indicates how to reconstruct white and black memory on that "sacred day": "The claims of our fathers upon our memory . . . are found on the fact that they wisely . . . met the crisis of their day. . . . [T]he thought of to-day and the work of to-day are alike linked and interlinked with the thought and the work of the past. . . . We are all continuing the tremendous struggle which your fathers and my fathers began eighty years ago" (ibid., pp. 242–59).

11. For instances of these "July riots," see Sweet, "Fourth of July," pp. 258, 262, 264.

12. For reports on July Fourth celebrations, the best sources are travel accounts and autobiographies. For a reassessment of the role of blacks in American history, see "The American Negro from 1776–1876," an oration delivered by Reverend George W. Williams on July 4, 1871, at Avondale, Ohio (Cincinnati: R. Clarke, 1876). Curiously, July Fourth was observed in Haiti and in Liberia (which in 1847 framed its independence with the date of the American Declaration). In the States, celebrations resumed after 1864 and were related to tributes to Lincoln—who, almost a century after Jefferson, became another very controversial figure among blacks—in 1876 for the centennial.

13. Among the most striking orations delivered on the first of January, one should mention Absolom Jones, *Thanksgiving Sermon* in the African Episcopal Church, Philadelphia (Fry and Kammerer Press, 1808); orations by Peter Williams in the African Church, New York, (Samual Wood, 1808), Joseph Sidney before the Wilberforce Philanthropic Association, New York (J. Seymour, 1809), George Lawrence in the African Methodist Episcopal Church, New York (Hardcastle and Van Pelt, 1813), and William Hamilton in the Episcopal Ashbury Church, New York (C. W. Bunce, 1815); all are collected in Porter, ed., *Early Negro Writings.*

14. In Joseph Wilson, *An Introduction to A Memorial Discourse,* Philadelphia, 1865, pp. 17–19.

15. On the controversy over names and over African versus American identity, see Stuckey, *Slave Culture,* pp. 193–244. On representations of Africa, see Alexander Crummell, *Africa and America: Addresses and Discourses* (Springfield, Mass.: Wiley, 1891).

16. An address delivered on the celebration of the abolition of slavery in the state of New York, July 4, 1827, at the first African Baptist Society (Albany, N.Y.: J. B. Van Steenbergh, 1827), in Porter, ed., *Negro Protest Pamphlets,* pp. 1–23.

17. The 1827 parade has been studied by Alessandra Lorini in an unpublished essay. See also Mary Ryan, "The American Parade: Representation of Self in Nineteenth-Century Social Order," in *The New Cultural History,* ed. Lynn Hunt (Berkeley, CA: University of California Press, 1989), pp. 131–53.

18. In Robin W. Winks, *Blacks in Canada's History* (New Haven, Ct., Yale University Press, 1971), pp. 142–215, 248–52. See Jason H. Silverman, *Unwelcome Guests; Canada West's Response to American Fugitive Slaves, 1800–1860* (Millwood, N.Y., 1985).

19. In Foner, ed., *Life and Writings of Frederick Douglass* 2:426–39.

20. Douglass papers, August 12, 1858.

21. On Garnet, see Stuckey, *Slave Culture,* chap. 3.

22. *Douglass Monthly* 2 (1859), 113.

23. With Delany; see *The Anglo-African,* October 15, 1859.

24. John Ripley, ed., *The Abolitionist Papers,* p. 284, n. 3. See *Ladies Society to Aid Fugitives from Slavery* (London, 1855); R. J. M. Blackett, *Building an Anti-Slavery Wall; Black Americans in the Atlantic Abolitionist Movement, 1830–1860* (Baton Rouge: Louisiana State University Press, 1983); Howard R. Temperly, "The British and Foreign Anti-Slavery Society in 1858" (Ph.D. diss., Yale University, 1960).

25. Douglass papers, August 10, 1858.

26. One may wonder why the commemoration of the Haitian revolution, which created the second independent nation in the New World, never became an institutionalized celebration in the black calendar. On this issue, see Eric Foner, *Nothing But Freedom* (Baton Rouge: Louisiana State University Press, 1983), p. 11.

27. Nat Turner was praised for his "resistance to tyrants" by Garrison in his July 4, 1838, address. See Borman, ed., *Forerunners of Black Power,* p. 100.

28. One must see the reorganization of the calendar in relation to the publication of William C. Nell, *Colored Patriots of the American Revolution* (Boston, 1855).

29. J. W. Loguen, *The Rev. J. W. Loguen as a Slave and as a Freeman: A Narrative of Real Life* (1859; rpt. Washington, D.C.: Howard University Press, 1941), p. 394.

6

National Identity and Ethnic Diversity: "Of Plymouth Rock and Jamestown and Ellis Island"; or, Ethnic Literature and Some Redefinitions of "America"

WERNER SOLLORS

> "Yes, the Statue of Liberty still stands, and we still open our arms under our law to people that are politically oppressed," [President] Bush said. But he added: "I will not, because I've sworn to uphold the Constitution, open the doors to economic refugees all over the world. We can't do that." The crowd applauded.
>
> —*New York Times,* May 22, 1992

Ethnic and national identities are interrelated in ways that are important for an analysis of "minority" as well as "majority" cultures. For this reason the historical nature of categories such as "American" deserves close scrutiny in investigations of immigrant, ethnic, racial, and other cultural issues. This relationship could be looked at from many vantage points. I have here chosen to focus on the ways in which "America" and its national symbols have been defined, debated, and redefined in their relationship to ethnic diversity.

It is well known that modern geographers named the New World "America," honoring the Italian explorer Amerigo Vespucci. Initially the term "American" referred to the original inhabitants, or Indians; in Puritan New England, however, it was increasingly adopted to refer to the British colonists, as when Nathaniel Ward, in 1647, spoke of an "American Creed"—and meant the religious beliefs of the English settlers in North America. In the American Revolution the term was used to emphasize less the British origin than the new makeup of the settler population of the United States. In Crèvecoeur's famous answer to the question "What is an American?" in the third of his *Letters from an American Farmer* (1782) he singled out "that strange mixture of blood, which you will find in no other country" (Crèvecoeur 1957, 39). For Crèvecoeur the term "American" referred to the ethnic diversity of at least the white colonists in the New World.

Yet anchoring national identity in mixing goes back at least to Daniel Defoe's English model, which he advanced in *The True-Born Englishman* of 1701: "I would examine all Nations of Europe and prove, that those Nations which are most mix'd, are the best, and have least of Barbarism and Brutality among them" (Richards 1989). The hyphenated Anglo-Saxons thus provided a prototype for Crèvecoeur's supposedly uniquely mixed Americans and for the melting-pot metaphor.

Initially applied to the Indians, then taken on by the British and applied generally to white settlers, by 1900 the term "American" had become problematic. In 1907 Henry James asked:

> Who and what is an alien . . . in a country peopled from the first under the jealous eye of history?—peopled, that is, by migrations at once extremely recent, perfectly traceable and urgently required. . . . Which is the American . . . —which is *not the alien, over a large part of the country at least, and where does one put a finger on the dividing line. . . ?* (James *1968, 124)*

"American" could mean all sorts of things: the ethnic fault line could be drawn on linguistic or religious grounds, making the English language and a certain form of Protestantism touchstones of America. Even the Americanness of the first group of people who were called "Americans" could now become questionable. Thus the sociologist Robert Park mentioned the story of an old lady who visited the Indian village at the World's Fair and—"moved to speak a friendly word to one of these aborigines"—actually asked: "How do you like *our* country?" (Park 1934, quoted in Johnson 1979, xxi).

At the center of the debates about the nature and future of America was the problem of ethnic heterogeneity: how inclusive and how exclusive could America be? An extreme example was provided by the political journalist David Goodman Croly, who had coined the word *miscegenation* in 1863 and was also the father of the *New Republic*'s founder, Herbert Croly. In 1888 David Croly published *Glimpses of the Future, Suggestions as to the Drift of Things*. Croly's mouthpiece, "Sir Oracle," makes the following prophecy:

> We can absorb the Dominion . . . for the Canadians are of our own race . . . but Mexico, Central America, the Sandwich Islands, and the West India Islands will involve governments which cannot be democratic. We will never confer the right of suffrage upon the blacks, the mongrels of Mexico or Central America, or the Hawaiians. . . . The white race is dominant and will keep their position, no matter how numerous the negroes may become. (Croly 1888, 22–24; see Kaplan 1949)

According to Croly's view, "American" meant "white"—hence non-white and mixed races were not considered "absorbable" or eligible for full citizenship rights. Not even Central America counted as "American." Croly himself was an Irish immigrant but did not wish to extend the melting-pot metaphor to non-whites. Of all the fault lines, "race" or, more precisely, the decision whether a person was "white," and thereby a potential American, or "non-white," hence "nonabsorbable," has been the deepest dividing line.

On the other side were reformers such as the newspaper editor Hamilton Holt, who early in the century ran a series of first-person-singular accounts by people of many backgrounds in the *Independent.* When he published some of those "lifelets" in book form in 1906, he chose the programmatic title *The Life Stories of Undistinguished Americans: As Told by Themselves* (reprinted in 1990), stressing the compatibility of the elastic term "American" with a very broad spectrum of the populace: Rocco Corresca, and Italian bootblack; Sadie Frowne, a Jewish sweatshop worker from Poland; Amelia des Moulins, a French dressmaker; Ann, an Irish maid; Agnes M., a German nurse girl; Axel Jarlson, a Swedish farmer; a Syrian journalist; Antanas Kaztauskis, a Lithuanian butcher; an anonymous Negro peon, a Japanese manservant, a Greek peddler, a midwestern farmer's wife, and a handicapped Southern Methodist minister; a Chinese laundryman and businessman, Lee Chew; Fomoaley Ponci, a foreign nonimmigrant Igorot chief from the recently conquered Philippines who was on display at Coney Island; and an Indian, Ah-nen-la-de-ni. Holt includes everyone: black, white, Indian, Asian, native-born, immigrant, refugee, temporary migrant, sojourner—men and women from all walks of life. Their voices cover a broad ethnic spectrum, making the book one of the most inclusive "American" texts early in the century, as the collection virtually transformed the inhabitants of the whole world into potential Americans.

The contrast between Croly's exclusive and Holt's inclusive "America" was dramatic. On such a contested terrain, attempts at symbolizing the country had to yield contradictory and problematic results.

"AMERICANS ALL!" was the title of a poster designed by Howard Chandler Christy in 1917, used to promote Victory Liberty Loans and other war efforts. It depicts a scantily clad young blond woman in front of an American flag, holding a laurel wreath under which an "honor roll" of ethnic names appears: Du Bois, Smith, O'Brien, Cejka, Haucke, Pappandrikopolous, Andrassi, Villotto, Levy, Turovich, Kowalski, Chriczanevicz, Knutson, and Gonzales—they were all to be Americans at a time when World War I made undivided loyalties mandatory. At first glance this may have seemed to constitute an invitation to foreigners who were thus honored to become eligible as Americans—in the vein of Holt's *Undistinguished Americans.* Yet the allegorical figure who was meant to signal the incorporation of various ethnic groups into "America" is not a mulatto Madonna with an Indian headdress but "the American girl," an English-looking white woman, not sturdy like the Statue of Liberty—for which the Alsatian sculptor Frédéric-Auguste Bartholdi's mother had posed (Gilder 1943, 17; Trachtenberg 1977, 60)—but with a glitzy Christy-style look. The poster did not simply honor ethnic diversity: Christy's image contains a double message as ethnics are asked to assimilate to an Anglo-Saxon norm (its origins in mixing forgotten) that is constituted precisely in *opposition*

Americans All! (Howard Chandler Christy, 1917)

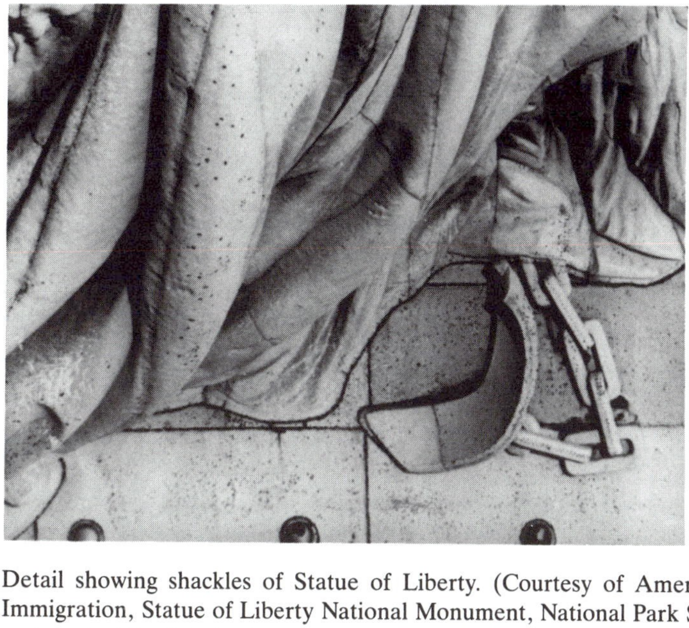

Detail showing shackles of Statue of Liberty. (Courtesy of American Museum of Immigration, Statue of Liberty National Monument, National Park Service, U.S. Department of the Interior.)

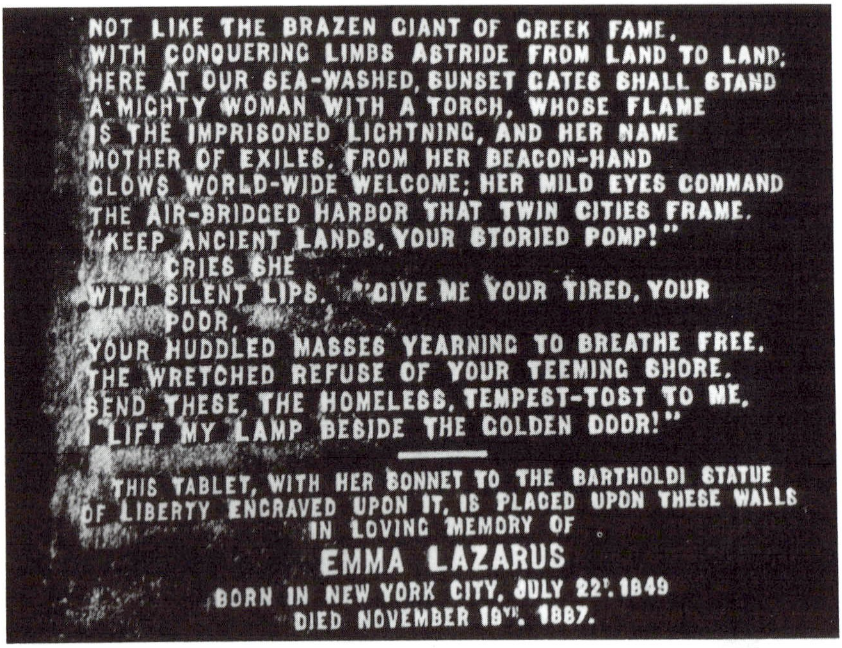

NOT LIKE THE BRAZEN GIANT OF GREEK FAME,
WITH CONQUERING LIMBS ASTRIDE FROM LAND TO LAND;
HERE AT OUR SEA-WASHED, SUNSET GATES SHALL STAND
A MIGHTY WOMAN WITH A TORCH, WHOSE FLAME
IS THE IMPRISONED LIGHTNING, AND HER NAME
MOTHER OF EXILES. FROM HER BEACON-HAND
GLOWS WORLD-WIDE WELCOME; HER MILD EYES COMMAND
THE AIR-BRIDGED HARBOR THAT TWIN CITIES FRAME.
"KEEP ANCIENT LANDS, YOUR STORIED POMP!"
CRIES SHE
WITH SILENT LIPS. "GIVE ME YOUR TIRED, YOUR
POOR,
YOUR HUDDLED MASSES YEARNING TO BREATHE FREE,
THE WRETCHED REFUSE OF YOUR TEEMING SHORE.
SEND THESE, THE HOMELESS, TEMPEST-TOST TO ME,
I LIFT MY LAMP BESIDE THE GOLDEN DOOR!"
THIS TABLET, WITH HER SONNET TO THE BARTHOLDI STATUE
OF LIBERTY ENGRAVED UPON IT, IS PLACED UPON THESE WALLS
IN LOVING MEMORY OF
EMMA LAZARUS
BORN IN NEW YORK CITY, JULY 22ND. 1849
DIED NOVEMBER 19TH. 1887.

Emma Lazarus plaque on Statue of Liberty.

Augustus Francis Sherman (1865–1925), *Women from Guadeloupe on Ellis Island* (1911) (William Williams Collection, New York Public Library)

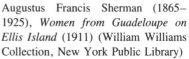

Slave ship

Meta Vaux Warrick Fuller, First arrival of Africans in Jamestown.

to them. They are told to be "Mr. American" by conforming to something that not even many of the European immigrants might ever become physically. The representative American body of 1917 does not include their features, and their names sound like those of many Hollywood actors and actresses *before* they changed them into more palatable ones:

Betty Joan Perske	=	Lauren Bacall
Anna Maria Italiano	=	Ann Bancroft
Anthony Benedetto	=	Tony Bennett
Dino Crocetti	=	Dean Martin
Margarita Cansino	=	Rita Hayworth
Bernard Schwartz	=	Tony Curtis
Doris von Kappelhoff	=	Doris Day

Incidentally, if Hollywood once exported an Anglo-American image, it now also propagates an openly ethnic look. Most performers and producers have stopped camouflaging their ethnic names behind Anglicized stage names: Whoopi Goldberg, Al Pacino, and Sissy Spacek stand for the new generation; and an Anglicized name may now be an ironic comment on the old status quo—as when a transvestite appears under the name "Holly Woodlawn."

Christy's World War I poster could be read both inclusively (as in Holt's *Life Stories*) and exclusively (as in Croly's *Glimpses*); and it is interesting to consider how important the manipulation of such symbols can be for the establishment of a national identity as well as for various ethnic identities.

A very famous example is the Statue of Liberty. The dedication of the statue in 1886 inspired the poet John Greenleaf Whittier—whose career had climaxed before the Civil War with his widely cited antislavery verse—to compose the poem "The Bartholdi Statue" (1886). Whittier stresses Franco-American liberty as an enlightening force, singing: "O France, the beautiful!" and concluding with the lines:

> Shine far, shine free, a guiding light
> To Reason's ways and Virtue's aim,
> A lightning-flash the wretch to smite
> Who shield his license with thy name!

Whittier thus presents the official "Franco-American" interpretation of the statue as advanced during the dedication ceremony, which included hardly any references to immigrants; yet the poet also celebrates the absence of slavery as the proof of American liberty:

> Unlike the shapes of Egypt's sands
> Uplifted by the toil-worn slave,
> On Freedom's soil with freemen's hands
> We rear the symbol free hands gave.
> (Whittier 1904, 295–96)

Whittier's national and "official" reading thus also contained his own cause, the memory of the abolition of slavery. This element was not to remain in the foreground of later interpretations of the statue, despite the inviting presence of broken shackles on the monument.

The poet Emma Lazarus saw a different statue in her sonnet "The New Colossus"; her poem—written in aid of the Pedestal Fund—constituted a recasting of the statue's officially intended meaning. Lazarus's Statue, a "Mother of Exiles," speaks:

> "Keep, ancient lands, your storied pomp!" cries she
> With silent lips. "Give me your tired, your poor,
> Your huddled masses yearning to breathe free,
> The wretched refuse of your teeming shore.
> Send these, the homeless, tempest-tost to me,
> I lift my lamp beside the golden door!" (Lazarus 1888, 202–3)

Whittier's apostrophe "shine far" contrasts markedly with Lazarus's well-known motto "send these to me." The New England poet James Russell Lowell seems to have been among the first to recognize the cultural significance of Lazarus's poem; when he was the United States ambassador to England, he wrote her: "Your sonnet gives its subject a *raison d'être* which it wanted before quite as much as it wanted a pedestal" (Handlin 1971, 61, 63; Jacob 1949, 179). A plaque with Lazarus's sonnet was affixed to the Statue of Liberty in 1903; and though this was noted in the Baedeker of 1909, and in some immigrant writing, it remained, according to John Higham's book, significantly entitled *Send These to Me,* relatively unnoticed until the mid-1920s, when the immigration restrictions were legislated (Higham 1975, 82–83). While the message of Lazarus's poem seemed to be an invitation to immigrants ("From her beacon-hand / Glows world-wide welcome"), the reference to the newcomers as "wretched refuse" also permitted a reading that an immigration historian convincingly paraphrased as "welcome, garbage!" (Shenton; see also Higham 1975, 85–86); and at least one nativist, James H. Patten, applied Lazarus's phrase "Wretched refuse!" in 1906 to "the beaten people of beaten races" who come to America in order ". . . to desecrate / Thy Sabbath and despoil thy rich heritage / Purchased with so much Anglo-Saxon blood and treasure" (Patten 1906, 16; Solomon 1972, 126). Even though the imagery of Lazarus's proimmigrant stance was multivalent, ethnic writers often adopted her reinterpretation of the Statue of Liberty as the symbolic space where "foreign" and "American" identities meet. In this fashion the Swedish-American journal *Valkyrian,* published from 1897 to 1909, had as its permanent cover illustration the image of a big Valkyrie, whereas a small Statue of Liberty in New York harbor was recognizable in the background (Thander 1991), thus connecting a Norse and an American goddess.

A curiously ironic testimony to the power of the statue as the dominant symbol of immigrant arrivals is given by the anarchist Emma Goldman, who remembered in her autobiography *Living My Life* (1931) how, when she first came to America, she was "enraptured by the sight of the harbour and the Statue of Liberty, suddenly emerging from the mist": "Ah, there she was, the symbol of hope, of freedom, of opportunity! She held her torch high to light the way to the free country, the asylum for the oppressed of all lands. . . . Our spirits were high, our eyes filled with tears" (Goldman 1970, 11; Giesen 1991, 513). Yet, as immigration historians have noticed, Emma Goldman *could not have seen* the statue, since she arrived in New York on December 29, 1885, months before the pedestal was completed and over half a year before the statue was assembled! (Giesen 1991, 515). In retrospect, even a radical anarchist like Goldman subjugated her own specific memory to the meaning of the statue that the other Emma had helped to propagate.

Lazarus's voice opposed not only the sentiments that Whittier was to express but also opinions like those of Croly that were later put into poetry by the New Englander Thomas Bailey Aldrich in his once-famous "Unguarded Gates" (1892). One may look at his poem as another interpretation of "Liberty":

> Wide open and unguarded stand our gates,
> And through them presses a wild motley throng—
> Men from the Volga and the Tartar steppes,
> Featureless figures of the Hoang-Ho,
> Malayan, Scythian, Teuton, Kelt, and Slav,
> Flying the Old World's poverty and scorn;
> These bringing with them unknown gods and rites,
> Those, tiger passions, here to stretch their claws.
> In street and alley what strange tongues are these,
> Accents of menace alien to our air,
> Voices that once that Tower of Babel knew!
> O Liberty, white Goddess! is it well
> To leave the gates unguarded?
>
> (Aldrich 1892; cf. Zangwill 1910, 199–200)

Aldrich's liberty is imagined not as a "Mothers of Exiles" but, in exactly opposite terms, as a "white Goddess" who should guard freedom *against* the menace of the beastly invaders. It is clear that Aldrich did not believe in the message "send these to me," but he also had little faith in liberty's ability to "shine" very "far." It is characteristic that Aldrich thought the closing of the Boston Public Library on St. Patrick's Day in 1892 showed that "Columbus didn't discover America; it was St. Patrick" and that he polemicized against immigration by arguing that America's true emblem was no longer the eagle but "some sort of unnaturalized mongrel" (Solomon 1972, 88).

It is a measure of the transformation of public memory that Lazarus's voice clearly won out over Whittier's and Aldrich's by the time of the statue's centennial celebration in 1986.

At the peak of the new immigration, some "old-stock" American intellectuals perceived themselves to be outnumbered by the "invasion" of "strangers" in the country their ancestors, real or adopted, had founded. I say "real or adopted" even in thinking of the group that was dubbed "the Brahmin Caste of New England" in the first chapter of Oliver Wendell Holmes's novel *Elsie Venner* (1861) in order to describe a "race of scholars" among students that was different from common country boys (Holmes 1891, 1–5). In fact, many of the intellectuals who adopted the term *Brahmin* were not old-stock descendants but upwardly mobile young men, several of whom had married into old families (Taylor 1979, 43–44).

Such intellectuals adopted and increasingly stressed the symbols of the *Mayflower* and Plymouth Rock as mythic points of origin. Their invention of Plymouth as an exclusivist ethnic symbol replaced earlier ideological readings in revolutionary, religious, or abolitionist contexts.

The Pilgrims had landed in 1620 at the Pamet Sound near Truro (Cape Cod), and leaving the *Mayflower* at Provincetown they sailed on to Plymouth a month later. The rock that commemorates this second landing is of dubious authenticity (Bradford 1952, 72n.; McPhee 1990, 112) and, geologically considered, seems to be of African origin (McPhee 1990, 114, 117). In 1741, Elder Faunce, then ninety-five years old, had identified a boulder as the "place where the forefathers landed," a phrasing that was probably misunderstood as referring to the "first landing" (Bradford 1952, 72n.; see also McPhee 1990, 115); this led to the increasing sacralization of the rock—as well as of fragments that were chipped off from it—in the nineteenth and twentieth centuries. Like relics, exhibits, or souvenirs, pieces of the rock have been taken to Immingham, Lincolnshire (the point of the Pilgrims' departure for Holland), and to the Plymouth Congregational Church in Brooklyn; other pieces were sold in the 1920s as paperweights by the Antiquarian Society of Plymouth; one fragment was sent to President Eisenhower by a citizen (McPhee 1990, 113). In a footnote to *Democracy in America,* Tocqueville observed:

> This rock has become an object of veneration in the United States. I have seen bits of it carefully preserved in several towns of the Union. Does not this sufficiently show how all human power and greatness are entirely in the soul? Here is a stone with the feet of a few poor fugitives pressed for an instant, and this stone becomes famous; it is treasured by a great nation, a fragment is prized as a relic. But what has become of the doorsteps of a thousand palaces? Who troubles himself about them? (Tocqueville 1951, 34 n. 8; see Sears 1985, 16)

In 1852 Lydia Huntley Sigourney viewed Plymouth Rock as a sacred stone, similar to the Muslim Kaaba:

> And give him praise, whose Hand
> Sustained them with His grace,
> Making this Rock, whereon ye stand,
> The Mecca of their race.
>
> (Sigourney 1852)

James Kirke Paulding wrote an "Ode to Jamestown" before the Civil War, in which he celebrated John Smith and Pocahontas; he also cast America as the peaceful synthesis of Plymouth and Jamestown, North and South:

> Jamestown, and Plymouth's hallowed rock
> To me shall ever sacred be,—
> I care not who my themes may mock,
> Or sneer at them and me.

And in the next stanza he wrote:

> He is a bastard if he dare to mock
> Old Jamestown's shrine or Plymouth's famous rock.
> (Stevenson 1922, 46–47)

This was apparently the special interest of a Northerner with strong sympathies for the South and for slavery who wanted to reconcile Puritans and Cavaliers and defy abolitionist readings of the rock in the wake of Daniel Webster's address of 1820.

In the world of widely shared national public memorialization Plymouth Rock still seems to have played only a minor role until after the Civil War (see, e.g., Lossing 1873, 36). The Society of *Mayflower* Descendants was founded in 1894 (Baltzell 1966, 115). The 1920 tercentenary inspired the National Society of the Colonial Dames (a women's association constituted in 1891 and dedicated to preserve shrines of Anglo-American history under the motto "Not Ancestry but Heredity") to erect the present memorial by architects McKim, Mead, and White, completed in 1921 (Lamar 1934, 19–44, 132–43).

Turn-of-the-century legends of Plymouth Rock pondered the question of who first touched shore. The first claimant to this honor was John Alden, the second the maiden Mary Chilton. One such version of 1906 concludes as follows:

> A youth in the full vigor of manhood, whose posterity should inherit the virgin land, sets his nervous foot upon the cornerstone of a nation, and makes it an historic spot. A young girl in the first bloom of womanhood, the type of a coming maternity, boldly crosses the threshold of a wilderness which her children's children shall possess and inhabit, and transforms it into an Eden. Surely John Alden should have married Mary Chilton on the spot. (Drake 1906, 380)

The story makes the supposed "cornerstone of a nation" nicely vivid in the dream of a founding couple, here imagined of purely English origin.

It seems likely that the new immigrants and their reinterpretation of the Statue of Liberty helped to strengthen the Brahmins' countervailing consciousness of Plymouth: thus the toga-clad allegorical figure representing "Faith," sculpted in granite, that crowns the National Monument to the Forefathers in Plymouth, was dedicated in 1889, three years *after* the Statue of Liberty, and does resemble her much larger sister in New York harbor: Faith's left "foot rests upon Forefather's Rock (supposedly another actual piece of Plymouth Rock); in her left hand she holds a Bible, not the Declaration of Independence; and with the right uplifted she points to heaven," rather than clasping a torch (Burbank 1916, 8).

Horace Kallen argued in 1915 that it was the new presence of vast non-English populations, the feared "barbarian hordes," in the United States that had the effect of throwing back "the Brito-American upon his ancestry and ancestral ideals," a development that manifested itself in a heightened public emphasis upon "the unity of the 'Anglo-Saxon' nations" and in the founding of societies such as the Sons and Daughters of the American Revolution "that have arisen with the great migrations" (Kallen 1924, 98–99).

The more heterogeneous the country was perceived to be, the more Plymouth origins came to be stressed as a mark of distinction. This tension erupted in the controversy about the Russian Jewish immigrant Mary Antin, the author of the autobiography *The Promised Land* (1912). Antin suggested the compatibility of Jewish and American identity, viewing her transatlantic crossing as a new exodous (as the Puritans had done); and she expanded Lazarus's interpretation of the Statue of Liberty as a symbol of immigrants:

> Let it . . . be repeated that the Liberty at our gates is the handiwork of a Frenchman; . . . that the verses graven on a tablet within the base are the inspiration of a poetess descended from Portuguese Jews; . . . that the love of liberty unites all races and all classes of men into one close brotherhood, and that we Americans, therefore, who have the utmost of liberty that has yet been attained, owe the alien a brother's share. (Antin 1914, 25–26)

Though the word was not yet in use, this was, indeed, a "multicultural" reading.

What Antin did for the Statue of Liberty, she boldly extended to the core symbols of Brahmin descent: "The ghost of the Mayflower pilots every immigrant ship, and Ellis Island is another name for Plymouth Rock" (Antin 1914, 98). Antin courageously equated the Pilgrim Fathers' increasingly enshrined American beginnings with the modern clearing center in which approximately 12 million immigrants were processed from 1892 to 1924 alone—and about three thousand committed suicide (Bolino 1985; Perec 1980, 16). Thereby Antin attempted to subvert the point of view from which a Plymouth Rock and *Mayflower* ancestry gave a speaker the right to reject an Ellis Island immigrant as a potential citizen. For Antin *any* arrival in America after a transatlantic voyage was thus comparable; and her view of Ellis Island as a synonym for Plymouth Rock, as well as her self-inclusion as "American," were to become centerpieces of the expansion of the term "American." In developing her elaborate analogy between Puritans and immigrants, she invokes the Brahmin James Russell Lowell and (probably without knowing about his endorsement of Lazarus) finds that he is a writer who chips "away the crust of historic sentiment and show[s] us our forefathers in the flesh. Lowell would agree with me that the Pilgrims were a picked troop in the sense that there was an immense preponderance of virtue among them. And that is exactly what we must say of our modern immigrants . . ." (Antin 1914, 69). Antin's position illustrates the complications of national integration in a polyethnic country: nations often need founding myths and stories of origins, beginnings in the past that authenticate the present. Those who do not share such pasts, or at least their myths, can then be excluded from the concept of the nation: if they mean "foreigners" when they say "our forefathers" they may define themselves as aliens (e.g., "Our Forefathers' Day" celebrations desired by Swedish Americans in 1890); if they mean the Puritan and revolutionary heroes, as Antin did, they "forget who they are." By contrast, a myth of origin in a mésalliance may stimulate polyethnic integration as ever newly combining mixed marriages (not just ethnically endogamous unions à la Mary Chilton and John Alden) can then be regarded as the fulfillment of a prophecy in the national past, and not as a novel and threatening penetration by foreigners; the children of such unions may combine memories of different, even antithetical pasts. By such myths of origins, immigrants and ethnic minorities can become directly related and affiliated with a shared national past.

In 1918 the New York trial of the Russian Jewish anarchist immigrant Jacob Abrams, who had arrived at Ellis Island in 1908, brought to the surface the same problem. At the point in the trial when Abrams was about to defend himself for having distributed English and Yiddish leaflets against Wilson's war policies by invoking American revolutionary beginnings, saying, "When our forefathers of the American Revolution—" the federal judge Henry DeLamar Clayton, Jr., from Alabama, interrupted, "Your what?" When Abrams repeated, "My forefathers," the judge asked in disbelief, "Do you mean to refer to the fathers of this nation as your forefathers?" In the course of the trial Abrams was asked twice, "Why don't you go back to Russia?" Later the judge recalled responding to Abrams's phrase "our forefathers": "What? You were born in Russia and came here four or five years ago and not a citizen, an anarchist, who can never become a citizen. Our forefathers . . . why, just look at it." Abrams received a twenty-year sentence (Polenberg 1985, 397, 407; Fuchs 1990, 68; see also Goldman 1970, 666–67). As Everett V. Stonequist generalized, "individuals of subordinate groups" are sometimes "made to feel that they do not really belong," adding that "in the United States members of such groups may be quite fully Americanized and yet be referred to as 'Jews,' 'Negroes,' 'Chinese,' etc. The native American unconsciously excludes them when he speaks of 'Americans' " (Stonequist 1937, 185). Some Americans were resentful of the erosion of the very word *American*. Alternative terms emerged such as "native Americans," "100% Americans"—or "real Americans," as a white neighbor stylizes himself in order to distinguish himself from Chinese immigrants in Sui Sin Far's short story "Mrs. Spring Fragrance," although the Chinese-American characters so much accept the identification of "American" and "white" that Mrs. Spring Fragrance quotes "a beautiful American poem written by a noble American named Tennyson" (Siu 1912, 12, 3). Both Nicholas Roosevelt and Brander Matthews called themselves "American-Americans" when they reviewed Horace Kallen's *Culture and Democracy* in 1924 (Mann 1979, 141–142).

Like the Abrams case, Antin's literary reception shows how difficult the process of becoming "American," of adopting another country's past, could be. The New Englander Barrett Wendell, for example, who was among the first professors of English to teach American literature at Harvard University, wrote in a letter of 1917 that Antin "has developed an irritating habit of describing herself and her people as Americans, in distinction from such folks as Edith [Wendell's wife] and me, who have been here for three hundred years" (Howe 1924, 282). Wendell's genealogical consciousness rests on the male line of descent. He says little about his mother's ancestors, and her middle name, Bertodi, is mentioned but not explained in a detailed genealogical account (Howe 1924, 6–11). His wife Edith Greenough Wendell served, incidentally, as president of the Colonial Dames' Plymouth Executive Committee in 1920.

Wendell conceded that the Antin's grandchildren "may perhaps come to be American in the sense in which I feel myself so—for better or worse, belonging only here."

In 1916 the conservative *Atlantic Monthly* journalist Agnes Repplier was also troubled by Mary Antin's presumptuousness in calling the Pilgrim fathers "our forefathers," as well as by her critical attitude. "[W]hy should the recipient of so much attention be the one . . . to reproach us for . . . our failure to observe the precepts and fulfill the intentions of those pioneers whom she kindly, but confusedly, calls "*our* forefathers" (Repplier 1916, 226–27). Repplier failed to see any parallels between Plymouth Rock and Ellis Island:

> Had the Pilgrim Fathers been met on Plymouth Rock by immigration officials; had their children been placed immediately in good free schools, and given the care of doctors, dentists, and nurses; had they found themselves in infinitely better circumstances than they had ever enjoyed in England, indulging in undreamed-of luxuries, and taught by kind-hearted philanthropists,—what pioneer virtues would they have developed . . . ? (Repplier 1916, 219–20)

Reviewing some evidence of the new ethnic heterogeneity, Repplier concluded with the question that gives away her restrictive sense of a national identity: "It is all very lively and interesting, but where does the American come in?" (Repplier 1916, 205). Repplier (incidentally, not of Brahmin New English but of Franco-German background) resented Antin's use of Lowell as a misquoting of the dead (Repplier 1916, 197–201; Lowell 1892, 220–54) and, in turn, invoked the antiassimilationist Horace Kallen in order to support her dislike of "Mrs. Amadeus Grabau (Mary Antin)," alluding publicly to the fact that Antin had married a non-Jewish German-American professor. Kallen had criticized Antin earlier when he considered her "intermarried, 'assimilated' even in religion, and more excessively, self-consciously flatteringly American than the Americans" (Kallen 1924, 86); yet Kallen had also partly adopted Antin's argument and, for example, compared Polish immigrants with the Pilgrims when he wrote: "The urge that carries [the Poles] in such numbers to America is not so unlike that which carried the pilgrim fathers" (Kallen 1924, 106).

Repplier recognized the danger with Antin's position: assimilation, full American identity, even if adopted unilaterally by declaration of will rather than by birth or acceptance from old-stock Americans, and the notion of equal merit of Plymouth Rock and Ellis Island origins entitled Antin to criticize her adopted "promised land" quite openly.

Young intellectuals among old-stock Americans also found ethnicity useful for their purposes and invoked the promise of a future multiethnic intelligentsia in their melodramatic battle against the "Anglo-Saxon" genteel tradition, which they could thereby reject as the result of a British colonial mentality (Higham 1989, 23–26). The most outstanding of them was the culture critic Randolph Bourne, who was acutely aware of the political implications of the New Englanders' reaction to Mary Antin. "We have had to watch," Bourne wrote in his famous essay of 1916, programmatically entitled "Trans-National America," "hard-hearted old Brahmins virtuously indignant at the spectacle of the immigrant refusing to be melted, while they jeer at patriots like Mary Antin who write about 'our forefathers' " (Bourne 1977, 249). Ellery Sedgwick, then the editor of the *Atlantic Monthly* (in which both Antin's autobiography and Repplier's critique had appeared) and a long-standing admirer of Bourne, wrote him: "I profoundly disagree with your paper." Sedgwick sounded the voice of an older gentility when he insisted that the United States was "created by English instinct and dedicated to the Anglo-Saxon ideal"—exactly the tenets Bourne sought to undermine. Sedgwick criticized Bourne by saying: "you speak . . . as though the last immigrant should have as great an effect upon the determination of our history as the first band of Englishmen" (Bender 1987, 246–49). Like Repplier, Sedgwick simply could not accept the analogy of Plymouth Rock and Ellis Island—though he thought that Antin had written an important autobiography. For Sedgwick, Bourne's essay was "radical and 'unpatriotic' "—though he did publish it in the *Atlantic Monthly* (Bender 1987, 246–49).

In the course of Bourne's essay, the "American" core definitions and their symbolizations were again revised: "Mary Antin is right when she looks upon our foreign-born as the people who missed the Mayflower and came over on the first boat they could find. But she forgets that when they did come it was not upon other Mayflowers, but upon a 'Maiblume,' a 'Fleur du mai,' a 'Fior di Maggio,' a 'Majblomst' " (Bourne 1977, 249). While implying in this example that various ethnic histories could be understood as "translations" of an original *Mayflower* voyage, Bourne did perceive the tremendous cultural opportunity for a nation in which each citizen could also remain connected with another culture (Matthews 1970). Bourne laid the foundation of the concept of a cosmopolitan intelligentsia that attempted to struggle free from a English orientation in American culture and from the requirement that newcomers shed their cultural, religious, or linguistic pasts upon becoming Americans (Hollinger 1985, 56–73). He also did not think that immigrants could remain fixed to their pasts. Instead Bourne advocated the new ideal of "dual citizenship," both for immigrants who came to the United States and for the increasing number of internationally oriented individuals who, like American expatriates in France, were born in one country but lived in another. In Bourne's hands the contemplation of Americanness in the face of diversity led to a reconsideration of the nationalist premises of citizenship; and Bourne's American nationalism is, in fact, anchored in diversity: "Only the American—and in this category I include the migratory alien who has lived with us and caught the pioneer spirit and a sense of new social vistas—has the chance to become that citizen of the world" (Bourne 1977, 262).

In order to strengthen his argument Bourne also recapitulated the substance of Antin's plea to regard the new immigrants as latter-day Puritans, and with a touch of Henry James's perception of the difficulty of drawing a line between the "alien" and the "American": "We are all foreign-born or the descendants of foreign-born, and if distinctions are to be made between us they should rightly be on some other grounds than indigenousness" (Bourne 1977, 249). It is this proposal, clearly a minority voice in 1916, that became the semiofficial core of a redefinition of "America" during World War II and, finally, the official line for celebrations from the Bicentennial in 1976 to the dedication of Ellis Island in 1990. Immigrants had slowly become accepted as prototypical Americans after being considered among the problematic exceptions (Gleason 1980, 248–54).

However, those redefiners of "America" who wanted to make it more "ethnic" and "pluralistic," such as Kallen, Antin, and even Bourne, paid little or no attention to non-white Americans in their attempts at broadening American cultural categories. As Higham writes, their theses were "from the outset . . . encapsulated in white ethnocentrism" (Higham 1975, 208). As Higham also stresses, however, the victory of pluralism may have been bought at a terrible price: the battle (Higham calls it a *Kulturkampf*) pushed the conservatives toward racism, anti-Semitism, nativism, and anti-intellectualism, and it alienated radical young intellectuals from "the rank and file of the American working people—that is, from all the people except the culturally distinctive minorities" (Higham 1989, 25–29). It helped to create an atmosphere in American intellectual life in which many participants value various ethnic backgrounds more than the ideas that emanate from them, a trend that may have persisted to this moment. Nowhere is Bourne's blind spot more apparent than in his venomous disdain for the marginal man who does not answer Bourne's Procrustean definition of ethnic identity: "It is not the Jew who sticks proudly to the faith of his fathers and boasts of that venerable culture of his who is dangerous to America, but the Jew who has lost the Jewish fire and become a mere elementary, grasping animal." (Bourne 1977, 254). It is telling that Bourne, too, used the sinister animal image as well as the nativist term *hordes*—in order to deplore the assimilated "men and women without a spiritual country, cultural outlaws, without taste, without standards but those of the mob" (Bourne 1977, 254). Bourne surrendered to a strikingly paradoxical argument for ethnic purity in the service of cosmopolitan diversity. In order to construct a dynamic and pluralistic national identity Bourne needed monistic stable ethnic identities based on fixed origins (that he questioned elsewhere); there was no room for "dangerous" marginal men and women and little sympathy for intermarriage (which threatens the neat system of the enclosed subcultures). This is the dilemma of many pluralistic models of American culture, and it may be an inherent problem in "multiculturalism" too. Kallen's "Democracy vs. the Melting-Pot" may also mark the multicultural position: resistance to true and messy syncretism is what models of America as Plymouth Rock or as Ellis Island could share.

After the battles of the 1910s and 1920s (which resulted in the enactment of immigration restrictions), the change from monoethnic to polyethnic thinking gained ground in the period from the late 1930s to the 1950s. In the late 1930s and early 1940s the Slovenian immigrant Louis Adamic helped to further superimpose the American origins at Plymouth Rock and those at Ellis Island, in the section "Ellis Island and Plymouth Rock" in his book entitled, in the Antin tradition, *My America* (1938), and in lectures to hundreds of audiences, with references to Emma Lazarus (Adamic 1938, 195; Adamic 1940, 292; see Higham 1975, 85, and Gleason 1980, 244). Adamic wanted to

> work toward an intellectual-emotional synthesis of old and new America; of the Mayflower and the steerage; of the New England wilderness and the social-economic jungle of the city slums and the factory system; of the Liberty Bell and the Statue of Liberty. The old American Dream needs to be interlaced with the immigrants' emotions as they saw the Statue of Liberty. The two must be made into one story. (Adamic 1940, 299)

Adamic reiterated the parallels between "old" and "new" American symbols, exclaimed "Americans All!" (now with more varieties of body features), and invoked Walt Whitman's revived poetic formulation from the preface to *Leaves of Grass* (1855): "Here is not merely a nation but a teeming nation of nations" (Whitman 1982, 5; see also Adamic 1945), presenting a line that John F. Kennedy would ultimately help to make the official one. One must remember, however, that as late as 1956—two years after the Immigration and Naturalization Service had abandoned Ellis Island—the U.S. government tried unsuccessfully to sell the island and its buildings (Smith 1992, 84), which suggests that its symbolic role had not yet been officially accepted.

Comparisons between Plymouth Rock and Ellis Island became more and more widespread up to the present moment at which the two alternatively conceived symbols seem to have merged. No satirists seem to comment on the strange fact that America's former first lady, Barbara Bush, paid one hundred dollars to commemorate her Puritan ancestor Thomas Thayer (who emigrated from England in 1630) by having his name put on a copper plaque on the Wall of Honor now surrounding the Ellis Island immigrant museum (Stanley 1990), a wall that displays nearly two hundred thousand other names, among them Myles Standish and John Alden, though not Mary Chilton. It is also perfectly fitting that Pamela Berger's 1989 film *The Imported Bridegroom,* based on a story by Abraham Cahan, represents the Old World Jewish shtetl by what looks very much like the living-history museum of Plymouth Colony. Plymouth Rock and Ellis Island seem to have become interchangeable in contemporary American culture. And this is where accounts of an American success story sometimes end.

Yet the "old-stock" / "new immigrant" distinction on which much of the thinking about "America" and "ethnicity" rested did not, of course, apply to all ethnic groups. Unless forced into the somewhat misleading notion that they constituted "America's first immigrants," American Indians may have an equally problematic relationship to Plymouth Rock and Ellis Island, though attempts have been made to connect them with both symbols. At Plymouth they are celebrated as the coinventors of Thanksgiving; and when during the restoration work of Ellis Island Indian skeletal fragments were found there, they were blessed in a public ceremony performed by Willy Snake of the Delaware Indians ("Indian" 1987), a ritual that seemed intended to connect American Indians with the new national core symbol of Ellis Island. When Native Americans occupied Alcatraz they may have wished thereby to create an alternative symbol.

Those Mexican Americans whose ancestors became Americans by annexation and conquest are also likely to have a somewhat ironic relationship to the "nation of immigrants" and its symbols of arrival as well as to the narrowing of the meaning of "America" to stand for the United States rather than for the whole continent.

Among immigrant groups proper, American citizens of Japanese descent who lived in the western part of the United States were, exactly at the time that Adamic popularized the reinterpretation of the immigrants as new Puritans, stripped of their rights as citizens and property owners and interned in detention camps—as a *race* (unlike German or Italian enemy aliens, who were generally detained only on the grounds of individual affiliations or political acts).

And other trans-Pacific immigrants? Maxine Hong Kingston ends a long story about her father's possible arrival in the United States as he is being smuggled into New York harbor—where he notices a "gray and green giantess" and is told that she is not a goddess but "the symbol of an idea"—only to continue: "Of course, my father could not have come that way," followed by a long scene on Angel Island that contrasts sharply with his imagined happy observation that "Americans saw the idea of Liberty so real that they made a statue of it" (Kingston 1980, 52–53; one might regard this also as an answer to Goldman). The 17,500 Chinese immigrants who, from 1910 to 1940, were processed through the detention center at Angel Island in San Francisco Bay may have gone through a clearing house modeled on Ellis Island; yet Angel Island, called "Devil's Pass" by the Chinese migrants, undoubtedly treated immigrants worse than its model. Several of the (fairly recently published) Chinese poems that were written on the walls of Angel Island comment explicitly on the immigration procedure. For example:

> Alas, yellow souls suffer under the brute force of the white race!
> Like a homeless dog being cursed, we are forced into jail.
> Like a pig chased into a basket, we are sternly locked in.
> Our souls languish in a snowy vault; we are really not even the equal of cattle and horses.
> Our tears shower the icy day; we are not even equal to bird or fowl.
> (Lai, et al., 1991, 141)

One also wonders what significance any of the old arrival points or doorstep and threshold symbols can have for the new immigrants who have come to the United States since the 1960s: borderlands? Kennedy Airport? or the "Green Card"? How can such diverse ethnic histories be reconciled with a generalizable American identity?

I shall, in conclusion, concentrate on the problematic situation of black Americans, one of the "oldest" and most "indigenous" yet most persistently excluded groups that consists mostly of descendants of people who did cross the Atlantic, though involuntarily and as slaves. Is Ellis Island a more appropriate myth than Plymouth Rock for African Americans? How would the American story have to change in order to accommodate black history? In his last writings the late historian Nathan Huggins raised such questions, taking American historians to task for dealing with African-American history only too rarely, and then usually as an "exception" and "anomaly," in their generalizations about America (Huggins 1990, xliv–xlvi); I would like to continue his questioning with literary texts.

Identifying himself in the *Atlantic Monthly* merely as "a peaceable man," an astute observer wrote during the Civil War that there was a special affinity between Puritans and southern blacks:

> There is an historical circumstance, known to few, that connects the children of the Puritans with these Africans of Virginia, in a very singular way. They are our brethren, as being lineal descendants from the Mayflower, the fated womb of which, in her first voyage, sent forth a brood of Pilgrims upon Plymouth Rock, and, in a subsequent one, spawned slaves upon the Southern soil,—a monstrous birth, but with which we have an instinctive sense of kindred, and so are stirred by an irresistible impulse to attempt their rescue, even at the cost of blood and ruin. The character of our sacred ship, I fear, may suffer a little by this revelation; but we must let her white progeny offset her dark one,—and two such portents never sprang from an identical source before. (Hawthorne 1862, 50)

The observer was Nathaniel Hawthorne and his appears to have been a lonely voice. The relationship between Plymouth Rock and American slavery more typically has been drawn as a contrast rather than as an affinity. *The Autobiography of Malcolm X,* for example, formulated the relationship of a critically conceived black history with the "old" American story most vividly: "We didn't land on Plymouth Rock, my brothers and sisters—Plymouth Rock landed on *us!*" (Malcolm X 1966, 201). This may be a statement with a "separatist" thrust; yet Malcolm X may also have been thinking of Cole

Porter's song "Anything Goes" (1934), which opens with the claim that if the Puritans were to arrive today, they might not drop onto Plymouth Rock, the old Rock might just drop onto *them.*

In "Plymouth Rock and the Pilgrims," an address given at the First Annual Dinner, N.E. Society, Philadelphia on, December 22, 1881, Mark Twain said that "those Pilgrims were a hard lot. They took good care of themselves, but they abolished everybody else's ancestors" (Twain 1977, 64). Then he offered his own putative genealogy:

> My first American ancestor, gentlemen, was an Indian—an early Indian. Your ancestors skinned him alive, and I am an orphan. . . . The first slave brought into New England out of Africa by your progenitors was an ancestor of mine—for I am of a mixed breed, an infinitely shaded and exquisite Mongrel. I'm not one of your sham meerschaums that you can color in a week. No, my complexion is the patient art of eight generations. . . . (Twain 1977, 65–66)

This led Mark Twain to a full-fledged attack on the genealogical associations:

> O my friends, hear me and reform! . . . Oh, stop, stop, while you are still temperate in your appreciation of your ancestors! Hear me, I beseech you; get up an auction and sell Plymouth Rock! . . . Disband these New England societies, renounce these soul-blistering saturnalia, cease from varnishing the rusty reputations of your long-vanished ancestors—the super-high-moral old iron-clads of Cape Cod, the pious buccaneers of Plymouth Rock—go home, and try to learn to behave! (Twain 1977, 67)

Just to continue with an excerpt from a great canonical American author who resisted placid American myths of ancestry from another angle, consider William Faulkner's observation in his novel *Flags in the Dust* (1973):

> In the nineteenth century anywhere chortling over genealogy is poppycock, but it is particularly so in America, where we all have a common ancestry and the only house from which we can claim descent with any assurance is the Old Bailey. Yet the man who professes to care nothing about his forefathers is only a little less vain than he who bases all his actions on blood precedent. (Blotner 1974, 6)

And in *Absalom, Absalom!* (1936) he specifically connected the reminder of the immigrant as ex-convict to such high-toned views of Jamestown as those articulated by Paulding: Faulkner's narrator describes the American arrival of the Sutpen family with the phrasing "when the ship from the Old Bailey reached Jamestown probably" (Faulkner 1987, 278).

African-American writers have, for a long time, taken on the special responsibility of questioning American national symbols by confronting them with the history of slavery and segregation. In the first novel published by an American Negro, William Wells Brown's *Clotel, or the President's Daughter* (1853), the author dedicated a whole page to the contrast between the two American beginnings of the "May-flower" and of Jamestown, of freedom and of slavery

(Brown 1970, 147). At the end of the novel, the titular heroine and slave woman dies, pursued by slave catchers, in the Potomac, "within plain sight of the President's house and the capitol of the Union" (Brown 1970, 177). Her father, Jefferson, was the "author" not only of the Declaration of Independence but also of unacknowledged slave children—whether or not this was literally the case is not important since it is, as Nathan Huggins argued, "*symbolically* true" (Huggins 1990, xlvii).

In his famous work *The Souls of Black Folk* (1903), W. E. B. Du Bois developed the well-known formula "an American, a Negro," and specifically mentioned the slave ship that "first saw the square tower of Jamestown" as an American beginning point (Du Bois 1986, 424; see also Griggs 1969, 197). Near the end of the book, he asks: "Your country? How came it yours? Before the Pilgrims landed we were there" (Du Bois 1986, 545). Richard Wright, in *Twelve Million Black Voices* (1941), came close to Hawthorne's critique when he wrote: "The *Mayflower*'s nameless sister ship, presumably a Dutch vessel, which stole into the harbor of Jamestown in 1619 and unloaded her human cargo of 20 of us, was but the first ship to touch the shores of this New World, and her arrival signalized what was to be our trial for centuries to come" (Wright 1941, 14). For black writers "Jamestown" memorializes *not* 1607 and John Smith with or without Pocahontas but 1619, the first arrival of Africans in the English colonies that were to become the United States. This is, incidentally, an event not remembered much even in Jamestown itself. It has hardly played a part in the various anniversaries of the founding of Jamestown (Hatch 1957, 23–24; *Anniversary* 1958, 78; *Jamestown* 1958; True 1983), though Meta Vaux Warrick (Fuller) contributed sculptures on the "advancement of the Negro since he landed" to the tercentennial of 1907, and Duke Ellington publicly claimed Jamestown descent (Washington 1909, 293–94; Adamic 1945, 195).

A poetic example is James Edwin Campbell's poem "The Pariah," which makes an explicit case for the merger of Plymouth Rock and Jamestown through the union of the black–white couple that follows the formula: "She the Brahmin, I the Pariah." Speaking about the woman's father, the poem explicates:

> Traced he back his proud ancestry
> To the Rock on Plymouth's shore,
> Traced I mine to Dutch ship landing
> At Jamestown, one year before.
> (Campbell 1895, 82)

Whereas Paulding wanted to see a northern–southern merger of Puritans and Cavaliers, and immigrant enthusiasts such as Antin and Adamic thought that the whole American synthesis was embodied in the fusion of Ellis Island and Plymouth Rock (leaving out the legacy of slavery that way), the black poet Campbell viewed the merger of the Pariah and the Brahmin (as in Paulding's "Ode to Jamestown," with echoes of the Pocahontas story and with a focus on an intermarriage) as the hope for a casteless country of Jamestown *and* Plymouth Rock (ignoring the arrival point of immigrants). Both the "Jamestown" of African Americans and the "Ellis Island" of European immigrant were, in different fashions, symbolic alternatives to the narrow interpretation of America as *Mayflower*-descended, yet alternatives that—even though they were both "thresholds"—could also exclude each other.

In 1942 the black modernist poet Melvin B. Tolson contributed to *Common Ground* the poem "Rendezvous with America," in which he seems to have desired to represent America as the merger of all points of arrival. The poem opens with the lines:

> Time unhinged the gates
> Of Plymouth Rock and Jamestown and Ellis Island,
> And worlds of men with hungers of body and soul
> Hazarded the wilderness of waters,
> Cadenced their destinies
> With the potters'-wheeling miracles
> Of mountain and valley, prairie and river.
>
> (Tolson 1942, 3)

Tolson's critique of American symbols is directed against their exclusiveness, which he tries to break (unhinging Aldrich's "gates") by the addition of many points of entry. The Whitmanian conflation of old and new national symbols reaches a higher pitch when Tolson explicitly makes a special place for those groups (such as Indians) not automatically included by the "Plymouth Rock and Ellis Island" formula, when blind bigots are rebuked for their prejudices, or when the question "America?" is answered in the following way:

> America is the Black Man's country,
> The Red Man's, the Yellow Man's,
> The Brown Man's, the White Man's.
> America?
> And international river with a thousand tributaries!
> A magnificent cosmorama with myriad patterns and colors!
> A giant forest with loin-roots in a hundred lands!
> A mighty orchestra with a thousand instruments playing
> *America!*
>
> (Tolson 1942, 4–5)

Tolson worries about inadequacies in the image of the Statue of Liberty; yet his poem, written upon the occasion of Pearl Harbor, sees this inadequacy in a tranquilized Uncle Sam's lack of watchfulness: he "Pillows his head on the Statue of Liberty" (Tolson 1942, 7). In his harmonic vision of a polyethnic America the shadow of one enemy—Japan—remains. Perhaps this enemy image may even have helped with the project of integrating red, black, and white (though Tolson does mention "Patriots from Yokosuka and Stralsund" in one of his melting-pot catalogs [3]).

The incorporating mood of the war years affected even politically radical writers such as Richard Wright. He not only published American paeans such as "Transcontinental" (Salzman 1978, 314–20), but he also let his character

Boris Max defend the black murderer Bigger Thomas in the model *Native Son* with the plea: "In him and men like him is what was in our forefathers when they first came to these strange shores hundreds of years ago." (Wright 1940, 332). When Wright was invited to go to France shortly after World War II and repeatedly was denied a passport, he sounded a different note. His friends, among them the painter Marc Chagall, appealed to the French cultural attaché Claude Lévi-Strauss, and Wright received an official invitation by the French government and, finally, after more maneuvering, a U.S. passport too. In an allusion to the classic scene in the manner of Adolph Treidler's World War I poster "Remember your first thrill at the Statue of Liberty" and of Louis Adamic, Wright described his emotions in the essay "I Choose Exile": "I felt relieved when my ship sailed past the Statue of Liberty!" (Wright 1948). The feeling is familiar, except that Wright was *leaving* the United States for France!

Exclusion of any group from national symbolism may generate not only the insistent argument for the group's compatibility with those symbols ("our forefathers") but also a rejection of such symbols. This rejection may be undertaken with the intention of facilitating an ultimate integration on equal footing. Wright's ironic reversal of interpreting the Statue of Liberty was not a unique occurrence. Thus, Du Bois described in his *Autobiography* how, upon returning from Europe in 1894 on an immigrant ship, he saw the Statue of Liberty: "I know not what multitude of emotions surged in the others, but I had to recall [a] mischievous little French girl whose eyes twinkled as she said: 'Oh yes the Statue of Liberty! With its back toward America, and its face toward France!' " (Du Bois 1968, 182). This strategy is, of course, a politically radical as much as an ethnic device. Thus Emma Goldman may have misremembered her happy arrival in America *with* the Statue of Liberty precisely in order to build up a more dramatic contrast between what "the generous heart of America" (Goldman 1970, 11) meant to her when she arrived and her political imprisonment—she highlights a Fourth of July in prison (Goldman 1970, 663)—before she was ultimately deported from Ellis Island in 1919; when she has embarked the *Buford* in order to go back to Russia, she writes:

> On the deck above us I could hear the men tramping up and down in the wintry blast. I felt dizzy, visioning a transport of politicals doomed to Siberia, the *étape* of former Russian days. Russia of the past rose before me and I saw the revolutionary martyrs being driven into exile. But no, it was New York, it was America, the land of liberty! Through the port-hole I could see the great city receding into the distance, its sky-line of buildings traceable by their rearing heads. It was my beloved city, the metropolis of the New World. It was America, indeeed, American repeating the terrible scenes of tsarist Russia! I glanced up—the Statue of Liberty!" (Goldman 1970, 717).

While both Du Bois and Wright titled the interpretation of the statue from the immigrant toward the Franco-American reading—which they, however, inverted—neither of them drew here on Whittier's connection between the Statue of Liberty and slavery.

Yet in our days the symbol of Ellis Island is used explicitly to incorporate African Americans too. Thus the black former congresswoman Barbara Jordan, together with Frank Sinatra, was awarded the Ellis Island Medal of Honor by the Statue of Liberty–Ellis Island Foundation ("Chronicle" 1990); more recently, Alex Haley was honored posthumously with the same medal, along with Natalie Cole, Norman Schwarzkopf, Connie Chung, Elie Wiesel, Strom Thurmond, and Arnold Schwarzenegger ("Chronicle" 1990).

It was during World War II and in the Supreme Court decisions and civil rights bills of the 1950s and 1960s that the term "American" actually became intertwined with ethnicity and flexible enough to include—in widely accepted public usage—such groups as immigrants, African Americans, and American Indians. Minorities have moved into the center of the cultural industry, and the metaphor of the "invading hordes" seems to have fallen into disfavor. The growth of a more flexible term for an American national identity thus *seems* to be a success story. Yet it is not only that, and the hymnic synthesis invoked by some poets has hardly become an American reality. After all, the successful expansion of the term "America" came about only in the heated debates about national loyalty generated by two world wars, and after immigration had been severely limited along racial categories. The broad notion of "America" has never really included everybody, all the redefinitions notwithstanding, and the inclusive use of "American" remains ambiguous even today. Xenophilic cosmopolitanism may have helped to alienate some liberal intellectuals from people other than those in distinctive ethnic groups and encouraged some conservatives to embrace racism and anti-intellectualism with little restraint. The educational system confronts tough debates over *which* American culture should be taught to children and adolescents. The battle for "America" continues, and there are today more contradictory notions and definitions of what is, or ought to be, "American" than there are views of the Statue of Liberty.

References

Adamic, Louis. 1938. *My America, 1928–1938.* New York and London: Harper and Brothers.

———. 1940. *From Many Lands.* New York and London: Harper and Brothers.

———. 1942. *What's Your Name.* New York and London: Harper and Brothers.

———. 1945. *A Nation of Nations.* New York and London: Harper and Brothers.

Aldrich, Thomas Bailey. 1892. "Unguarded Gates." *Atlantic Monthly* 70:57.

Anderson, Benedict. 1985. *Imagined Communities: Reflections on the Origins and Spread of Nationalism* (1983). Rpt. London: Verso.

Anderson, Philip. 1990. "The Risberg School in Chicago: American Aid and Swedish Immigrant Ministerial Education." Lecture at Emigrant Institute, Växjö, Sweden, June 2.

Anniversary. 1958. *The 350th Anniversary of Jamestown, 1607–1957: Final Report.* Washington, D.C.: National Park Service.

Antin, Mary. 1912. *The Promised Land.* Boston and New York: Houghton Mifflin.

———. 1914. *They Who Knock at Our Gates: A Complete Gospel of Immigration.* Boston and New York: Houghton Mifflin.

———. 1969. *The Promised Land.* Ed. Oscar Handlin. Boston: Houghton, Mifflin. (Sentry edition.)

Baedeker, Karl. 1909. *The United States, with Excursions to Mexico, Cuba, Porto Rico, and Alaska.* Leipzig: Baedeker.

Baltzell, E. Digby. 1966. *The Protestant Establishment: Aristocracy and Caste in America* (1964). Rpt. New York: Vintage.

Banta, Martha. 1988. *Imaging American Women: Idea and Ideals in Cultural History.* New York: Columbia University Press.

Barber, J. W. 1839. *Historical Collections Relating to the History and Antiquities of Every Town in Massachusetts.* Worcester [Mass.]: Dorr, Howland.

Barringer, Fred. 1991. "U.S. Minorities' Share of Melting Pot Soars." *International Herald Tribune,* March 12, 1–2.

Barth, Fredrik, ed. 1969. *Ethnic Groups and Boundaries: The Social Organization of Culture Difference.* Boston: Little, Brown.

Bender, Thomas. 1987. *New York Intellect: A History of Intellectual Life in New York City, from 1750 to the Beginnings of Our Own Time.* Baltimore: John Hopkins University Press.

Bennett, Hal. 1967. *A Wilderness of Vines.* New York: Pyramid Books.

Blanck, Dag. 1990. "An Invented Tradition: The Creation of a Swedish-American Ethnic Consciousness at Augustana College." In: *Scandinavia Overseas: Patterns of Cultural Transformation in North America and Australia,* 2nd ed, ed. Harald Runblom and Dag Blanck. Uppsala: Center for Multiethnic Research.

Blotner, Joseph. 1974. *Faulkner, a Biography.* New York: Random House.

Bolino, August C. 1985. *The Ellis Island Source Book.* Washington, D.C.: Kensington Historical Press.

Bourne, Randolph S. 1977. *The Radical Will: Selected Writings, 1911–1918,* ed. and introd. Olaf Hansen. New York: Urizen Press.

Bradford, William. 1952. *Of Plymouth Plantation 1620–1647.* Ed. and introd. Samuel Eliot Morison. New York: Modern Library.

Briggs, Rose T. 1988. *Plymouth Rock: History and Significance.* (1968). Rpt. Plymouth: Pilgrim Society.

Brown, Sterling A., et al. ed. 1969. *The Negro Caravan* (1941). Introd. Julius Lester. New York: Arno Press.

Brown, William Wells. 1970. *Clotel; or, The President's Daughter* (1853). Rpt. New York: Collier Books.

Browning, Elizabeth Barrett. 1974. *The Poetical Works of Elizabeth Barrett Browning,* Cambridge ed.. Introd. Ruth M. Adams. Boston: Houghton Mifflin.

Brownstone, David M., et al. 1979. *Island of Hope, Island of Tears.* New York: Rawson, Wade.

Burbank, A. S. 1916. *Guide to Historic Plymouth: Localities and Objects of Interest.* Plymouth: A. S. Burbank.

Cagidemetrio, Alide. 1989. "A Plea for Fictional Histories and Old-Time 'Jewesses.' " In: *The Invention of Ethnicity,* ed. Werner Sollors. New York and Oxford: Oxford University Press, 14–43.

Campbell, James Edwin. 1895. *Echoes . . . from the Cabin and Elsewhere.* Chicago: Donohue and Henneberry.

Chametzky, Jules. 1977. *From the Ghetto: The Fiction of Abraham Cahan.* Amherst: University of Massachusetts Press.

Chesnutt, Charles. 1968. *The Wife of His Youth and Other Stories of the Color Line* (1899). Ann Arbor: University of Michigan Press.

Christopher, Robert C. 1989. *Crashing the Gates: The De-WASPing of America's Power Elite.* New York: Simon and Schuster.

"Chronicle." 1990. *New York Times,* December 8.

Crèvecoeur, J. Hector. 1957. *Letters from an American Farmer* (1782). Rpt. New York: Dutton.

Croly, David. 1888. *Glimpses of the Future: Suggestions as to the Drift of Things.* New York and London: Putnam's.

Devereux, George[s], et al. 1943. "Antagonistic Acculturation." *American Sociological Review* 7:133–47.

Drake, Samuel Adams. 1989. *A Book of New England Legends and Folk Lore in Prose and Poetry* (originally published 1884, rev. ed. 1906) Rutland, Vt.: Tuttle.

Du Bois, W. E. B. 1968. *Autobiography.* New York: International Publishers.

———. 1986. *Writings.* New York: Library of America.

Duyckinck, Evert A. and George L. eds. 1866. *Cyclopedia of American Literature* (1855). Rpt. New York: Charles S. Scribner and Co.

Elliott, Emory ed. 1988. *Columbia Literary History of the United States.* New York: Columbia University Press.

Fairchild, Henry Pratt. 1926. *The Melting-Pot Mistake.* Boston: Little, Brown.

Faulkner, William. 1987. *Absalom, Absalom!* New York: Vintage.

Fuchs, Lawrence H. 1990. *The American Kaleidoscope: Race, Ethnicity, and the Civic Culture.* Middletown, Ct.: Wesleyan University Press, 1990.

Giesen, Bernhard ed. 1991. *Nationale und kulturelle Identität: Studies zur Entwicklung des kollektiven Bewusstseins in der Neuzeit.* Frankfurt: Suhrkamp.

Gilder, Rodman. 1943. *Statue of Liberty Enlightening the World.* New York: New York Trust Company.

Gleason, Philip. 1980. "Americans All: Ethnicity, Ideology, and American Identity in the Era of World War II." In *The American Identity: Fusion and Fragmentation,* ed. Rob Kroes. European Contributions to American Studies 3. Amsterdam: Amerika-Instituut, 235–64.

Goldman, Emma. 1970. *Living My Life* (1931). Rpt. New York: Da Capo Press.

Gomes, Peter J. 1971. *The Pilgrim Society, 1820–1970.* Plymouth, Mass.: Pilgrim Society.

Griggs, Sutton. 1969. *The Hindered Hand: or, The Reign of the Repressionist* (1905). Miami: Mnemosyne Publishing Co.

Handlin, Oscar. 1971. *Statue of Liberty.* New York: Newsweek Book Division.

Hane, Misiko. 1990. "Wartime Internment." *Journal of American History* 77:569–75.

Harlan, Louis, et al., eds. 1977. *Booker T. Washington Papers,* vol. 6 Urbana: University of Illinois Press.

Hatch, Charles E. 1957. *Jamestown, Virginia: The Townsite and Its Story* (1949). Washington, D.C.: National Park Service.

[Hawthorne, Nathaniel]. 1862. "Chiefly About War-Matters. By a Peaceable Man." *Atlantic Monthly* 10:43–61.

Higham, John. 1975. *Send These to Me: Jews and Other Immigrants in Urban America.* New York: Atheneum.

———. 1989. "The Redefinition of America, 1910–1930," ms.

———. 1990. "Indian Princess and Roman Goddess: The First Female Symbols of America." *Proceedings of the American Antiquarian Society* 100.1:45–79.

Hönnighausen, Lothar. 1990. "Washington D.C. and the National Myth." *Rivista di studi anglo-americani* 6.8:225–43.

Hollinger, David A. 1985. *In the American Province: Studies in the History and Historiography of Ideas.* Bloomington: Indiana University Press.

Holmes, Oliver Wendel. 1891. *Elsie Venner: A Romance of Destiny* (1861). Rpt. Cambridge, Mass.: Riverside Press.

Holt, Hamilton. 1990. *The Life Stories of Undistinguished Americans: As Told by Themselves* (1906). New York and London: Routledge.

Howe, M. A. DeWolfe. 1924. *Barrett Wendell and His Letters.* Boston: Atlantic Monthly Press.

Howells, William Dean. 1891. *An Imperative Duty.* New York: Harper and Brothers.

Huggins, Nathan Irvin. 1990. "Introduction: The Deforming Mirror of Truth." In *Black Odyssey: The African American Ordeal in Slavery.* New York: Pantheon.

Hurwitz, Samuel J. 1975. "Lazarus, Emma." In *Notable American Women* (1971), vol. 2, ed. Edward T. James et al. Rpt. Cambridge, Mass.,: Harvard University Press.

Hutson, Charles Woodward, ed. 1926. *Editorials by Lafcadio Hearn.* Boston and New York. Houghton Mifflin.

Inauguration. 1887. *Inauguration of the Statue of Liberty Enlightening the World by the President of the United States. Issued Under the Authority of the Committee.* New York: D. Appleton.

"Indian." 1987. "Indian Ceremony on Ellis Island." *New York Times,* June 29, B3.

Jacob, Heinrich Eduard. 1949. *The World of Emma Lazarus.* New York: Schocken Books.

James, Henry. 1968. *The American Scene* (1907). Rpt. Bloomington: Indiana University Press.

Jamestown. 1958. *Significant Addresses of the Jamestown Festival, 1957.* Ed. Ulrich Troubetzkoy. Richmond (Virginia) (with addresses by Queen Elizabeth, President Eisenhower, Richard Nixon, and others).

Johnson, Charles S. 1979. *Shadows of the Plantation* (1934). Rpt. Chicago and London: University of Chicago Press.

Kallen, Horace M. 1924. *Culture and Democracy in the United States: Studies in the Group Psychology of the American Peoples.* New York: Boni and Liveright.

Kaplan, Sidney. 1949. "The Miscegenation Issue in the Election of 1864." *Journal of Negro History* 34.3:274–343.

Kingston, Maxine Hong. 1980. *China Men.* New York: Knopf.

———. 1989. *Tripmaster Monkey: His Fake Book.* New York: Knopf.

Kivisto, Peter, et al. eds. 1990. *American Immigrants and Their Generations: Studies and Commentaries on the Hansen Thesis After Fifty Years.* Urbana and Chicago: University of Illinois Press.

Lai, Him Mark, et al., eds. 1980. *Island: Poetry and History of Chinese Immigrants on Angel Island 1910–1940.* San Francisco: HOC DOI (History of Chinese Detained on Island), Chinese Cultural Foundation.

Lamar, Mrs. Joseph Rucker. 1934. *A History of the National Society of the Colonial Dames of America from 1891 to 1933.* Atlanta: Walter W. Brown.

Lazarus, Emma. 1888. *Poems of Emma Lazarus,* vol. 1. Boston and New York: Houghton Mifflin.

Lejeune, Philippe. 1989. *On Autobiography.* Ed. John Paul Eakin, trans. Katherine Leary. Minneapolis: University of Minnesota Press.

Levine, Benjamin et al. 1957. *Statue of Liberty: National Monument, Liberty Island, New York.* Washington, D.C.: National Park Service Historical Handbook Series no. 11.

Lossing, Benson J. 1873. *A Common-School History of the United States; From the Earliest Period to the Present Time.* New York: Sheldon and Co.
Lowell, James Russell. 1892. *Literary Essays,* vol. 3. Boston and New York: Houghton Mifflin.
———. 1897. *The Poetical Works.* Boston and New York: Houghton Mifflin.
McPhee, John. 1990. "Travels of the Rock." *New Yorker,* February 26, 108–17.
Malcolm X. 1966. *The Autobiography of Malcolm X* (1965). Rpt. with the assistance of Alex Haley. New York: Grove Press.
Mangione, Jerre. 1978. *An Ethnic at Large: A Memoir of America in the Thirties and Forties.* New York: Putnam's.
———. 1982. *Mount Allegro: A Memoir of Italian American Life* (1942). Rpt. New York: Columbia University Press.
Mann, Arthur. 1979. *The One and the Many: Reflections on the American Identity.* Chicago: The University of Chicago Press.
Marsden, R. G. 1904. "The 'Mayflower.' " *English Historical Review* 19:669–80.
Massachusetts. 1937. *Massachusetts: A Guide to Its Places and People* (Federal Writers' Project). Boston: Houghton Mifflin.
Matthews, F[red] H. 1970. "The Revolt Against Americanism: Cultural Pluralism and Cultural Relativism as an Ideology of Liberation." *Canadian Review of American Studies* 1.1:4–31.
Morris, Edmund. 1990. "Short and Simple Annals." *New Yorker,* June 11, 100–103.
Morse, Samuel F. B. 1835. *Imminent Dangers to the Free Institutions of the United States Through Foreign Immigration.* New York: J. P. Trow.
Old Colony. 1990. *Old Colony Memorial: Plymouth Rock. Old Colony Sentinel,* vol. 68, n. 31. Plymouth: August 3, 1889.
Ovington, Mary White. 1927. *Portraits in Color.* New York: Viking Press.
Patten, James H. 1906. *The Immigration Problem and the South.* Raleigh, N.C.:
Perec, Georges. 1980. *Récits d'Ellis Island: Histoires d'errance et d'espoir.* Paris: Editions du Sorbier.
Pierpont, John ed. 1835. *The American First Class Book; or, Exercises in Reading and Recitation.* Boston: Carter, Hendee.
Pilgrim. 1823. *The Constitutional Articles of the Pilgrim Society, Incorporated February 24, 1820.* Plymouth, Mass.: Allen Danforth.
Pitkin, Thomas M. 1975. *Keepers of the Gate: A History of Ellis Island.* New York: New York University Press.
Polenberg, Richard. 1985. "Progressivism and Anarchism: Judge Henry D. Clayton and the Abrams Trial." *Law and History Review* 3.2:397–408.
Programme. 1886. *The Official Programme. The Statue of Liberty: Its Conception. Its Construction. Its Inauguration.* New York: B. W. Dinsmore.
Repplier, Agnes. 1916. *Counter-Currents.* Boston and New York: Houghton Mifflin.
Richards, Earl Jeffrey. 1989. "European Literature and the Labyrinth of National Images: Literary Nationalism and the Limits of Enlightenment." Diss., University of Aachen.
Ripley, William Z. 1908. "Races in the United States." *Atlantic Monthly* 102:742–59
Rizk, Salom. 1943. *Syrian Yankee.* Garden City, N.Y.: Doubleday, Doran.
Rodriguez, Richard. 1982. *Hunger of Memory: The Education of Richard Rodriguez.* Boston: Godine.
Roosevelt, Theodore. 1924. "The Settlement of Jamestown" (1907). In *The Works of Theodore Roosevelt* (memorial edition), vol. 12. New York: Charles Scribner's, 585–96.

Rose, Peter I. ed. 1969. *The Ghetto and Beyond.* New York: Random House.
Ross, Edward Alsworth. 1914. *The Old World in the New: The Significance of Past and Present Immigration to the American People.* New York: Century.
Russell, William S. 1846. *Guide to Plymouth and Recollections of the Pilgrims* (with an appendix "Airs of the Pilgrims"). Boston: George Coolidge.
Salzman, Jack et al. ed. 1978. *Social Poetry of the 1930s: A Selection.* New York: Burt Franklin.
Samuels, Charles E. 1965. *Thomas Bailey Aldrich.* New York: Twayne.
Scudder, Horace Elisha. 1901. *James Russell Lowell: A Biography.* Boston and New York: Houghton Mifflin.
Sears, Charlotte. 1985. *The Peregrinations of Plymouth Rock.* Plymouth, Mass.: Antiquarian Society.
Sigourney, L. H. 1852. *National Era,* n. 281 (May 20).
Solomon, Barbara Miller. 1972. *Ancestors and Immigrants: A Changing New England Tradition* (1956). Rpt. Chicago: University of Chicago Press.
Stanley, Alessandra. 1990. "Ellis Island Will Reopen in a Subdued Mood." *New York Times,* September 3, 1, 32.
Stevenson, Burton Egbert, ed. 1922. *Poems of American History* (1908). Rpt. Boston and New York: Houghton Mifflin.
Stewart, Randall, ed. 1962. *The English Notebooks by Nathaniel Hawthorne* (1941). Rpt. New York: Russell and Russell.
Stonequist, Everett V. 1937. *The Marginal Man: A Study in Personality and Culture Conflict.* New York: Scribner's, 1937.
Stowe, Harriet Beecher. 1982. *Uncle Tom's Cabin; or, Life Among the Lowly* (1852). In *Three Novels.* Rpt. New York: Library of America.
Sui, Sin Far. 1912. *Mrs. Spring Fragrance.* Chicago: A. C. McClurg.
Taylor, William. 1979. *Cavalier and Yankee: The Old South and American National Character* (1957). Rpt. Cambridge, Mass.: Harvard University Press.
Thacher, James. 1835. *History of the Town of Plymouth.* Boston: Marsh, Capen and Lyon.
Thander, Gunnar. 1991. "*Valkyrian,* a Mediator Between Cultures." Lecture at Emigrant Institute Växjö, Sweden, June 2.
Thernstrom, Stephan, et al., eds. 1980. *Harvard Encyclopedia of American Ethnic Groups.* Cambridge, Mass., and London: Harvard University Press.
Thernstrom, Stephan. 1990. "The Minority Majority Will Never Come." *Wall Street Journal,* July 26, A16.
Tolson, Melvin B. 1942. "Rendezvous with America." *Common Ground* 2:4.
Tocqueville, Alexis de. 1951. *Democracy in America.* (1835). Henry Reeve text, ed. Phillips Bradley. Vol. 1. Rpt. New York: Knopf.
Trachtenberg, Marvin. 1977. *The Statue of Liberty* (1976). Harmondsworth and New York: Penguin.
True, Ransom B. 1983. *Jamestown: A Guide to the Old Town.* Richmond: Association for the Preservation of Virginia Antiquities.
Twain, Mark. 1977. *The Comic Mark Twain Reader: The Most Humorous Selections from His Stories, Sketches, Novels, Travel Books, and Speeches.* Ed. Charles Neider. Garden City, N.Y.: Doubleday.
Ware, Caroline F., ed. 1940. *The Cultural Approach to History.* New York: Columbia University Press.
Washington, Booker T. 1909. *The Story of the Negro: The Rise of the Race from Slavery,* vol. 2. London: T. Fisher Unwin.

———. 1986. *Up from Slavery* (1901). Rpt. New York: Penguin.

Wendell, Barrett. 1907. Letter to Horace M. Kallen, November 3 (manuscript, American Jewish Archives, Cincinnati).

Whitman, Walt. 1982. *Complete Poems and Collected Prose.* New York: Library of America.

Whittier, John Greenleaf. 1904. *Complete Poetical Works.* Boston and New York: Houghton Mifflin.

Wright, Richard. 1940. *Native Son.* New York: Harper and Brothers.

———. 1945. Publicity statement for *Black Boy* (manuscript, James Weldon Collection, Beinecke Library, Yale University).

———. 1948. "I Choose Exile" (manuscript, James Weldon Collection, Beinecke Library, Yale University).

———. *Twelve Million Black Voices: A Folk History of the Negro in the United States* (New York: Viking, 1941).

———. 1964. *White Man, Listen!* (1957). Garden City, N.Y.: Doubleday.

Yamamoto, Hisaye. 1988. *Seventeen Syllables and Other Stories.* Latham, N.Y.: Kitchen Table: Women of Color Press.

Yin, Xiaohuang. 1991. "Gold Mountain Dreams: Chinese American Literature and Its Socio-Historical Context, 1850–1963." Diss., Harvard University.

Zangwill, Israel. 1910. *The Melting-Pot* (1909). Rpt. New York: Macmillan.

———. 1925. *The Melting-Pot* (with an appendix). New York: Macmillan.

7

International Beacons of African-American Memory: Alexandre Dumas père, Henry O. Tanner, and Josephine Baker as Examples of Recognition

MICHEL FABRE

Abroad as well as in the United States, African Americans have created different *lieux de mémoire* according to their divergent interests. The most well-known example of the black American presence in France remains that of the "Hell Fighters of 1918." As members of the American Expeditionary Force, these soldiers marked the official French recognition of black heroism—in spite of America's Jim Crow regulations—and came to symbolize black American enjoyment of the warm welcome extended by the average French citizen.

During the nineteenth century the African-American literary and artistic elite created their own *lieux de mémoire* in France. In this essay on the lives of Alexandre Dumas Père, Henry O. Tanner, and Josephine Baker, I will examine the ways in which the black artist becomes a cultural beacon. Their professional and personal successes illustrate that prominent blacks, whether American or not, become African-American *lieux de mémoire* for reasons quite different from the generalities which explain their appeal to the whites, and the recognition granted by them. For black Americans it takes not only talent and economic success to become a *lieu de mémoire*—it also requires official recognition or international popularity. Not only have Dumas, Tanner, and Baker served as role models for other African-American artists, but their very names evoke a feeling of racial pride and "togetherness" on a worldwide scale. The moral and ideological implications are that other nations, in providing an atmosphere or personal and artistic freedom, recognize black achievement to a greater extent than does their own country.

Black Americans, having had little international recognition before emancipation—Phillis Wheatley was a rare example—paid close attention to foreign "luminaries of the race." These included ancient or contemporary military leaders such as Antar, the chevalier de Saint-Georges or Toussaint

L'Ouverture, and also novelists such as Pushkin and Alexandre Dumas Père. There seem to be several reasons why Dumas became, and for so long remained, a cultural beacon in the eyes of African Americans. One may be that his father was a general in Napoleon's armies: Although Napoleon restored slavery after it had been abolished in 1790, eliminating Toussaint L'Ouverture by unfair means, he ranked surprisingly high in black American esteem. Because Napoleon had promoted the son of a black woman to the position of general, Marcus Garvey honored and admired Napoleon. (Rogers).

There is no way to overestimate the appeal of the elder Dumas on blacks worldwide before Emancipation. The grandson of the Marquis de la Pailletterie, a Santo Domingo planter, and of dark-skinned Marie Césette, he was a dazzling example of French recognition of black literary merit. Although his contemporaries knew him to be a mulatto, few French people spoke of his "color"; but to American blacks he was most assuredly a Negro. Understandably, Dumas was first claimed as a black literary lion and emulated by a handful of French-speaking free men of color from New Orleans, artists who chose to live in France in the nineteenth century. Dramatist Victor Séjour, poet Pierre Dalcour, and musician Eugene Macarthy—all cultivated his acquaintance.

One of the few antebellum African-American visitors to France, William Wells Brown testified to the reverence in which Dumas was held during those years. In Paris as a delegate to the 1849 peace conference, Brown was received only as a fugitive slave and militant abolitionist. By 1853, however, he would be known as the first black American to write both a full-length play and a novel. Holding Dumas in high esteem and eager to meet him, Brown had been given a letter of introduction to his friend, the novelist Eugène Sue, by revolutionary Louis Blanc. To no avail. Although Brown suspected that Dumas might not condescend to give an audience to a slave, while attending a performance of *Norma* at the Opéra he delighted in noticing:

> a light-complexioned mulatto, apparently about fifty years of age,—curly hair, full face, dressed in a black coat, white vest, white kids,—who seemed to be the centre of attraction not only in his own circle but in others. Those in the pit looked up, those in the gallery looked down, while curtains were drawn aside at other boxes and stalls to get a sight at the colored man. So recently from America where caste was injurious to my race, I began to think that it was the woolly head that attracted attention when I was informed that the mulatto before me was no less a person than Alexandre Dumas. Every move, look and gesture of the celebrated romancer were watched in the closest manner by the audience. (Brown, 129)

Brown remarked that no writer filled a more important place in the literature of his country than this son of a Negro general. He considered Dumas's success as a tribute paid to the race, and proof that France rewarded artistic merit regardless of color.

For black Americans, Dumas's achievements testified to the capacity of his race to "rise," and contribute to the culture of mankind. In the black press, his name would appear as frequently as that of Pushkin or even Toussaint L'Ouverture, and his portrait graced the first issue of *The Anglo-African Magazine* in 1859. In tribute, several African-American visitors to France made a point of visiting his grave in Villers-Cotterets.

The spirited black recognition granted Alexandre Dumas is reflected as late as 1892 in *Iola Leroy,* the novel by Frances Ellen Harper. The protagonist is an octoroon upon whom her white husband cannot impose his acquaintances. He decides to settle in France, knowing that their children can only be properly educated "abroad where merit and ability will give them entrance into the best circles of art, literature and science" (85). And the African-American character cites the examples of Ira Aldridge and Alexandre Dumas, who "was not forced to conceal his origin to succeed as a novelist" (84).

The tragedian Ira Aldridge performed in Paris in 1866, opening at Versailles in a performance of *Othello* which the French press generally described as memorable. Many a Parisian celebrity attended, including Guizot of the French Academy and the elder Dumas, who, upon this rare occasion, insisted upon hugging Aldridge on his breast and proudly proclaiming, "My dear brother, I too am a Negro!" (Marshall and Stock, 324).

Still, Frederick Douglass's race consciousness prevented him from admiring Dumas wholeheartedly, for Dumas generally did not define himself as a Negro. Douglass saw the statue of Dumas by Gustave Doré as an acknowledgment of the literary genius of a colored man but refused to honor the character of a man to whom, as a Negro, he felt he had no grounds to be thankful. He was more enthusiastic about white abolitionists like Victor Hugo and Victor Schoelcher. However, the day after his arrival in Marseilles Douglass took his wife for a boat trip to the Château d'If, the old rock from which Edmond Dantès had been reportedly hurled in *The Count of Monte Cristo.* Douglass made this special trip, he says, "because the genius of the Negro writer had woven around it such a network of enchantment" (568).

Thirty years later another black American, Mary McLeod Bethune, would hail Marseilles for the same reasons as Douglass: the presence of many Africans in the harbor and the fictional memory of Dumas, the "black writer" feted by France for his talent (Bethune).

Dumas's star continued to shine over black America during the Harlem Renaissance. When John F. Matheus, a contributor to *The New Negro* anthology, visited Paris in 1927, he likewise noted that Marseilles, with its large African population, was a "discovery," and went to the Château d'If as a tribute to Alexandre Dumas. Matheus remained an untiring propagandist for French culture among black Americans, and in 1936 he prepared an edition of the only work signed by Alexandre Dumas that has a Negro protagonist, *Georges.*

When young Langston Hughes told his father of his ambition to become a writer, he could only think of Alexandre Dumas as an example of a colored writer who had made money. And his father countered: "Yes, but he was in Paris where they don't care about color" (Hughes, 62).

In 1925 young Gwendolyn Bennett made it to Paris as an art student but was also inspired to write poetry. Her "Lines Written on the Grave of Alexandre Dumas" sound unexpectedly solemn:

> Thou, great spirit, wouldst shiver in thy granite shroud
> Should idle mirth or empty talk
> Disturb thy tranquil sleeping.
> A cemetery is a place for shattered loves
> And broken hearts.
>
> (Cullen, 159)

It is noteworthy that, in the minds of black Americans, Alexandre Dumas was rarely associated geographically with his abode and grave at Villers-Cotteret (or that of his son at the Montmartre cemetery) but mostly with the place that affected Douglass and Bethune: the Château d'If. Their favorite reference to his fiction was not to the better-known *Three Musketeers,* and the deeds of d'Artagnan, but to *The Count of Monte Cristo,* possibly because, in this novel, the victory of Edmond Dantés over injustice could function as a parable for black endurance and eventual freedom. As late as November 1944, Communist Hugh Mulzac, author of *A Star to Steer By,* was able to see Marseilles again in a troop transport ship. He remembered that before the war, boatmen used to beg the visitor to ride out to the Château d'If, the legendary site of *The Count of Monte Cristo.*

In the 1920s Alexandre Dumas's role as a literary beacon had been partially superseded by the contemporary French West Indian René Maran. While serving as a colonial administrator in Oubangui in 1921, Maran was awarded the prestigious Goncourt prize for his "authentic Negro novel," *Batouala,* set in central Africa. The *New York World* of January 9, 1921, referred to French General Mangin in the headline: NEGRO REAL EQUAL OF PALE BROTHER, SAYS GEN. MANGIN. Mangin was quoted as stressing the meaning of the award: "It is a witness to the fraternal sentiment of our country for all of her sons without distinction of shade or origins, when those sons honor the country by their words and deeds." The article went on to recall the rougher treatment reserved for blacks in the United States. Langston Hughes, Alain Locke, Gwendolyn Bennett, Countee Cullen, Walter White, and many others met René Maran. In the September 1924 issue of his newspaper *Les Continents,* Maran published an article by Locke on the "New African-American Poetry," which was the first mention of the New Negro movement to appear in France. Countee Cullen, inspired by his reading of *Batouala,* wrote a poem entitled "The Dance of Love."

Maran played a major role as a bridge between the Harlem Renaissance writers and the *négritude* poets; and one is led to wonder why a man whose talent was crowned by the Goncourt prize, who was far more race conscious than Dumas, and who actually helped publicize the New Negro movement never became an important cultural beacon for black Americans. One reason may have been his modest, retiring personality; another, the lesser dimension of his success, compared with that of Dumas. Mostly, however, Maran's career was hampered by World War II. He suffered because he refused to collaborate with the Nazis; also, the war meant disruption of cultural relations between the French and the Americans, with the result that Maran's mild criticism of the abuses of French colonialism now seemed somewhat outdated when contacts were reestablished in 1945.

When he visited Paris at the turn of the century, Booker T. Washington was received as an important American, an international figure. He attended several receptions given by American officials, met Justices Fuller and Harlan of the Supreme Court, and was asked to speak from the pulpit of the American Chapel. Convinced that southern blacks did not suffer from comparison with Europeans "in all that marks a lady or a gentleman," he strongly advised them against coming to France with the hope of finding employment unless they had prior contacts and wealth. Booker T. Washington never mentioned any personal interest in Alexandre Dumas, but wished to visit the grave of Toussaint L'Ouverture and could not because it was in the north of France and without a monument. For Washington, Henry O. Tanner was a personal *lieu de mémoire* in Paris.

To the editor of the *Colored American* Washington wrote at length of his visit to Tanner's studio on boulevard Saint-Jacques, noting the painter's perseverance, his talent, and his success at being one of the few American artists exhibited at the Luxembourg museum: "Mr. Tanner is determined that he shall not be known as merely a successful Negro artist but that his work shall stand upon its merit alone," Washington said. "Here in France no one judges a man by his color. The color of the face neither helps nor hinders" (Harlan, 142).

Like Dumas, Henry Ossawa Tanner was a role model but also an embodiment of black American artistic merit recognized by France after having been spurned in the United States. After becoming convinced that his color would always prevent his work from being recognized in America, Tanner had gone into self-exile in France in 1891. In Booker T. Washington's eyes, the recognition granted Tanner in Paris was not especially an indication of a French lack of racial prejudice but, as he stated in *Up From Slavery*—in guarded words, not to displease American whites—a reinforcement of his belief that "any man, regardless of colour, will be recognized and rewarded just in proportion as he learns to do something well" (280). True to his gospel of self-help, he stressed excellence in any field, however humble, without remarking on the specificity of artistic achievement.

When it became known that Tanner's painting *The Raising of Lazarus* had been bought by the French government and was hanging in the Luxembourg gallery, the event and its implications became the object of a racial/cultural pilgrimage. In 1904 Mary Church Terrell went to Paris with the expressed wish of seeing Tanner's *Raising of Lazarus* in the Luxembourg, but she was told by the curator that the painting had already been taken to the Louvre. After one of the guards was sent to the Louvre with her to show her the painting, she commented: "Thus it was that I had the rare privilege and the great pleasure of feasting my eyes upon the masterpiece of a colored man" (Terrell, 211). This experience gave her yet another reason for liking Paris and the French!

In 1929, when Countee and Yolande Cullen honeymooned in Paris, he rented an apartment for them close to Tanner's place on the boulevard Saint-Jacques because he wanted to be able to visit him easily. In similar fashion, although the pages of *Fifty Years After* recounting John Paynter's few weeks in Paris in 1936 read like a guide to the architectural treasures of the city, Paynter was race conscious to the point of knowing that Tanner's studio stood at 51, rue Saint-Jacques.

Entertainer and dancer Josephine Baker soon attracted more attention than Henry O. Tanner, not only from mass audiences but also from the "colored elite." Having come to France as a member of "La Revue nègre," Josephine Baker soon outshone Maude de Forest. Baker's "clowning" and her shapely body were an acceptable shade of blackness; she could present herself as animallike enough to titillate, but she also could be polished and Parisienne. And she was an astute businesswoman: after winning over Paris through her grotesquerie in "La Revue nègre," she changed her style and became almost feline, satisfying the expectations of audiences—and producers. A couple of years later, after touring Europe, she was earning $250 a night at the Folies Bergères. In 1929 drama critic Lincoln Kirstein was stopped in Paris by an English-speaking lady who asked him, "Where is la rue Baker?" meaning "la rue du Bac," to which he could answer: "It doesn't exist yet, but there will be one."

Most of Baker's dark-skinned compatriots felt that seeing her performance in Paris was a must. Many an artist, entertainer, or writer visited her with a reverence comparable to that shown toward Henry Tanner. Mary McLeod Bethune, Gordon Taylor, John Paynter, Countee Cullen, and Alain Locke all commented on seeing her perform. John Matheus, when he saw the city of Dumas, also made a point of sampling the cabarets. At the Folies Bergères, the dark-skinned Algerian who played the devil in the show told him about the Frenchman's own brand of prejudice, even though Paris had welcomed Josephine ecstatically. However, American tourists behaved much worse, and Matheus saw a couple of his white compatriots leave the room in outrage when his new acquaintance, the devil, appeared on stage among the white female cast! John Paynter gives a more precise account of the same performance:

> Part of the crowd poured into the Folies and, as we drove up, from the flaming billboard, a gorgeously gay presentment of the star, Josephine Baker, greeted us in that characteristic fly-away pose which seems to have captivated the whole Parisian world. In the crush of the lobby, M. Achille found his friend, M. Feral Benglia, a colored gentleman who, himself, has been a star in many of the Bergères performances. The cast of some forty beautiful girls was almost naked, and the highlight of the performance was a jungle scene, a tribute to black beauty:
>
>> [T]he gently rolling turf of a wooded dell had been abandoned to the lone occupancy of a recumbent exotic Venus. Suddenly, there appeared, descending cautiously from the hills, a brown-skinned native of giant stature, who espied the slumbering nymph on coming into the

> clearing. . . . And then intently gazing for a second or two, [he] turned abruptly, his long arms cleaving the air—and fled back into the hills. A typical French moment of suspense was the climax. (82)

By the early 1930s, Josephine Baker had become a "must." On December 24, 1932, Paul Robeson's wife, Eslanda wrote Harold Jackman that she would be flying to Paris the following day to interview Josephine Baker to complete an article about the Negroes in Paris: "I thought that the white folks would be interested to read all about what our folks are doing all over the world, but when I started in Paris I found that I was more interested myself than any white folks would ever be. Our people, if you will excuse the term, sure made progress." When Langston Hughes traveled to Paris in 1937, he went to the Folies Bergères to meet Josephine after her show.

Clearly, Dumas, Tanner, and Baker were instances of such black "firsts" as can still be found in *Ebony* magazine. The choice of a foreigner like Dumas may seem surprising since, in the literary field, African Americans had produced several notable writers from their own ranks—Phillis Wheatley and Jupiter Hammon, for example. What made the projection of the elder Dumas as a desirable *lieu de mémoire* was the extraordinary range of his international popularity during the antebellum period. With the passing of time and increasing recognition of their achievement in art and literature, blacks in the United States needed to depend less on blacks from other parts of the world as "race heroes." However, because of the prestige and money involved, visual art as an area of achievement had long been reserved for whites, and Henry Ossawa Tanner was certainly justified in seeking recognition in Europe at the end of the nineteenth century. Spoken reports about him abounded in black artistic circles, and incited painters like Hale Woodruff in the 1930s or Lois Mailou Jones in the 1950s to try their chance in Paris.

It may seem more surprising that Josephine Baker should have been selected as a cultural beacon, given the widespread acceptance and stereotyping of blacks as entertainers. What made Baker's success exceptional was, on the one hand the magnitude of its economic rewards (of which blacks had traditionally been deprived); and, on the other hand, the legitimization of her dancing as a highbrow aesthetic contribution (not only entertainment) in Europe—very much in the way that jazz was considered there. Also, isn't it significant that in spite of the way black American women were seen by white Americans, this girl from St. Louis was viewed as one of the most attractive women on earth? Later, too, her activism, her services during the war, and her adoption of children of many ethnic backgrounds won her universal esteem. On April 15, 1975, when the funeral procession for Josephine Baker arrived at La Madeleine, Jo Bouillon wrote:

> The Rue Royale was literally banked with Josephine's enormous public. They had come as they were, impressive in their dignity and silence. . . .
>
> In the huge church, packed to capacity . . . the service was also that of Lieutenant Josephine Baker. The coffin, followed by a bearer carrying Josephine's decorations, was saluted by twenty-four flags representing various

> branches of the military. Many public authorities, ministers, generals and ambassadors were in attendance. The funeral was of almost national scope, decorous yet crowded with spectators. Still it was a deeply personal occasion. Next to the President of the Republic's wreath lay roses "from Papa and the children," a heart made of flowers from Brialy and Levasseur, and a Star of David fashioned out of roses from an anonymous friend, honoring Josephine's personal attachments and fight against racism." (Baker and Bouillon, 292–93)

As such, Baker's triumph can be seen as embodying the legitimization of African-American cultural offerings. Alexandre Dumas, Henry Ossawa Tanner, and Josephine Baker symbolically signaled a recognition of racial equality by European cultural institutions, and thus they heralded the desirability and/or imminence of comparable moves in the United States.

References

Baker, Josephine, and Jo Bouillon. *Josephine.* New York: Harper & Row, 1977.

Bethune, Mary McLeod. Unpublished travel diary. Amistad Research Center, New Orleans, La.

Bennett, Gwendolyn. "Lines Written on the Grave of Alexandre Dumas." *Opportunity* 4 (June 1926), 136–37.

Brown, William Wells. *The Black Man: His Antecedents, His Genius, His Achievements.* New York: Thomas Hamilton, 1863; New York: Johnson Company, 1968.

Cullen, Countee, ed. *Caroling Dusk.* New York: Harper, 1937.

Douglass, Frederick. *Life and Times of Frederick Douglass* (1892). New York: Macmillan, 1962.

Harlan, Louis, ed. *Booker T. Washington Papers,* vol. 5. Urbana: University of Illinois Press, 1976.

Harper, Frances Ellen. *Iola Leroy or Shadows Uplifted* (1892). New York: McGrath, 1969.

Hughes, Langston. *The Big Sea* (1940). New York: Hill & Wang, 1963.

Marshall, Herbert, and Mildred Stock. *Ira Aldridge, the Negro Tragedian.* London: Rockcliff, 1958.

Paynter, John. *Fifty Years After.* New York: Margent Press, 1940.

Rogers, J. W. "Alexander the Greatest: The Story of France's Renowned Black General." *Norfolk Journal and Guide,* February 16, 1929, sec. 3, p. 1.

Terrell, Mary Church. *A Colored Woman in a White World.* Washington, D.C.: Ransdell, 1940.

Washington, Booker T. *Up From Slavery* (1900). New York: Doubleday, Page, 1925.

8

On the Wrong Side of the Fence: Racial Segregation in American Cemeteries

ANGELIKA KRÜGER-KAHLOULA

> For the first time in the history of the management of Cave Hill Cemetery, the colored people were yesterday admitted to the beautiful city of the dead and they accepted the opportunity and enjoyed the delightful scenery with evident satisfaction.[1]

Residential segregation in the United States has been widely studied and commented upon. The black ghetto is usually understood to have been generated by oppression and maintained by discrimination and poverty.[2] The categories of caste and class that affect the residential patterns of the living also touch the homes of the dead. In the cemetery, *lieu de mémoire par excellence,* geography meets history and sociology. The sacred and the profane converge at the grave. Burial patterns reveal religious beliefs and social distinctions; they reflect intra- and intergroup as well as interpersonal relationships and project them into eternity. Racism pervades the metropoles and the necropoles, biography and memory.

Integrating the Graveyard

The history of the civil rights movement against discrimination and segregation has a chapter on the integration of cemeteries, even though in this case the moves toward desegregation did not usually make it to the front pages of the national newspapers. The Korean and the Vietnam wars brought home, with the bodies of soldiers killed in action, the realization that people good enough to die for their country were not even good enough to be buried in a place of their choice.

The Schomburg Center for Research in Black Culture keeps a vertical file on "Cemeteries" in its microfiche archive. The clippings conserved there document the fight for admission to previously all-white burial grounds in the years from 1951 to 1963. Copies of the following nine articles are to be found in the above-mentioned file.

On January 19, 1952, *America* reported that the body of Pfc. Thomas C. Reed, nineteen, killed in Korea, lay unburied in the Phoenix, Arizona, mortuary from November 28 to early January. Greenwood Memorial Park, the only non-Catholic cemetery in Phoenix to allow the burial of blacks on its premises, requested letters of petition from three veterans' organizations before accepting the body. Such a procedure was not followed in the case of white veterans. In order to put an end to this discriminatory pattern, the local American Legion, the Veterans of Foreign Wars, and the Disabled American Veterans did not supply the requested letters. On January 8, 1952, the cemetery trustees voted to admit black veterans on the same terms as whites in future.

On March 22, 1959, the *Worker* related that several black families living in Flint, Michigan, buried their kin in Saginaw because only one undertaker and one burial ground in their hometown accepted black customers. The same newspaper reported on August 10 the successful attempt of a black district engineer's widow in Michigan to have her husband buried in a "white" cemetery even though she received hate calls after pushing for his funeral. A number of whites trying to disrupt the ceremony with violence were arrested.

In August 1960 the *New York Times* featured three articles that documented a Winnebago family's problems of laying George Nash, a World War I veteran, to rest after he was taken out of the grave at the burial in Detroit, Michigan. The newspaper headlines followed the body's odyssey: "Indian Denied Burial" (August 12); "Indian's Burial Set: Family of George Nash Finds Plot in Pontiac, Mich." (August 13); "Indian Given Burial" (August 14).

On August 12, 1960, the *New York Post* ran an article on the racial exclusion policy of a graveyard aptly named White Chapel Memorial Cemetery: "For the Dead, 74% Won't Do." In order to be admitted, corpses had to be 75% Caucasian. On July 16, 1963, the *Post* revealed "Bias in an Oklahoma Graveyard." A black man was finally buried across the border from his home state, in Coffeyville, Kansas, where an integrated cemetery was available. The *Times* comment on the same issue ran: "U.S. Negro Colonel Bars a Bitter View over Burial Dispute."[3]

In the year after the March on Washington, on April 4, 1964, the *New York Times* announced: "Episcopalians in Capital Clash on Negro Burial in Church Plot" (L12). The article was fittingly set between one on libel proceedings in the aftermath of 1962 racial rioting in Mississippi and another one on Little Rock authorities bowing to federal law on school issues.

The few blacks ever to be buried in Rock Creek Cemetery in Washington, D.C., owned by Episcopal St. Paul's Rock Creek Church since 1719, were the slaves of wealthy church members. In 1962 the church approved a policy of nondiscrimination in the sale of lots, but for parishioners of St. Paul's only. Two other cemeteries owned by the church were to remain segregated. A seventy-nine-year-old black woman who had died on March 13 was denied interment at Rock Creek Cemetery even when another Episcopal church, St. Stephen and the Incarnation, applied for a plot for her. On Easter Monday, the congregation voted 38 to 22 to reaffirm its segregation policy with regard to outsiders. On April 15 the *Times* correspondent reported that the vestry had voted to "bury the dead in the churchyard cemetery without regard to race, religion or national origin."[4]

In 1966 Flint, Michigan, was in the news again: "Court Backs Negro on Bias in Burial."[5] Black mortician J. Merril Spencer had bought a plot in Memorial Park, an all-white cemetery, but was not allowed to have his mother buried there in 1964. The Michigan Court of Appeals upheld his case and stated that the cemetery had violated a civil rights law. When, on December 7, 1966, the *Times* announced "Cemetery Owners Ending Racial Bias in Flint, Michigan," all the cemeteries in the county were dropping their bans against nonwhites (L38).

On July 26, 1969, the *Times* readers learned that the wife of Pvt. William Henry Terry, Jr., was suing Elmwood Cemetery in Birmingham, Alabama, for refusing to bury her husband. The suit, believed by the journalist to be the first of its kind, was supported by the NAACP Legal Defense and Educational Fund. The article referred to the case of another black man killed in Vietnam whose family tried in vain to have him buried in a public cemetery in Wetumpka, Alabama. Their request was refused on the ground that all available space had been sold. No court action was filed.[6] Five months later, on December 24, 1969, Terry was permitted burial in Elmwood,[7] and on January 4, 1970, his reinterment with military honors and twelve hundred mourners present was reported: "Black Soldier Burial Among Whites." A photograph showed the funeral procession framed by two police motorcycles.

On August 23, 1970, the *New York Times* ran an article entitled "Mother of Black G.I. Slain in War Vows Burial in White Cemetery" (L3). Hillcrest Memorial Gardens in Ft. Pierce, Florida, had advertised free plots for servicemen but refused to admit black veterans. Mrs. Williams, the mother of Army Specialist 4 Pondexteur E. Williams, was quoted as saying: "I feel that he being black and can't be buried in Hillcrest, then he didn't have any business going to the war. He died for nothing." A white acquaintance of the family had donated a gravesite, next to that of her infant grandson, but was forbidden to let the Williamses use it.

On August 23 Williams was given military and religious honors at an armory and then carried to a mortuary awaiting interment. The eulogy characterized him as "a man without a country."[8] On the following day, the U.S. government joined the suit filed by the veteran's family and friends against the cemetery. The same petition brought suit on behalf of another black G.I. who had also applied for one of the Hillcrest plots for honorably discharged Vietnam veterans.[9]

On August 27 the Federal District Court ordered Hillcrest to accept Williams' body. The court ruling came after a close pretrial conference, with a U.S. attorney on instructions from the Justice Department participating.[10] On

August 30, 1970, the *Times* readers learned: "Black G.I. Buried in White Cemetery."

In the same issue of the *Times* Fred P. Graham gave an account of the Fort Pierce affair, putting it in the context of other civil rights legislation. He reminded the readers that as late as in 1955 California Courts had conceded that cemeteries were not places of public accommodation and therefore they were entitled to excluding blacks. Cemetery desegregation was only to be achieved via the Supreme Court's 1968 *Jones v. Mayer* decision, which actually referred back to an 1866 civil rights law. The original provision guaranteed blacks equal rights in making and enforcing contracts and purchasing personal property.[11]

Jones v. Mayer made the erection and maintenance of invisible walls and fences illegal, although it did not tear down the visible ones that had separated black and white burials for generations. Who had decided to build them in the first place?

Old Barriers in a New World: Fencing In and Walling Out

The history of racially segregated burial places for Africans and Europeans is older than their joint settlement of the New World. In fifteenth-century Spain, for instance, one of the objectives pursued by Afro-Spanish brotherhoods was to purchase graveyards for their members who were barred from those of white Spaniards.[12] In the North American colonies, segregated burial facilities appear to have been the rule. They took the form of internal segregation of plantation burial grounds or of larger premises, with separate sections for whites and blacks, or of external segregation, with different graveyards serving the black or the white community. The areas reserved for blacks might be evocatively referred to as an "African reservation," as in Shawshine Cemetery, in Bedford, Massachusetts, or simply as "Burial Ground for Negroes," "For Negro People," or "Colored."[13]

Writing about colonial Connecticut, Bernard Steiner observed in 1893: "Each large village had its negro corner in the Meeting House gallery and in the graveyard."[14] Winthrop D. Jordan points out that the segregation of blacks in colonial churches and graveyards reflects a social worldview that is based on distinctions. It categorizes "the orders of men," white and black. Such models of the social order place African Americans at the lowest rung of the ladder.[15] Or up the stairs, if the most remote corner happens to be above ground level: in Rocky Hill church, Connecticut, blacks were banished from the body of the building and the galleries; they had to go to a stall "high up behind the singer's gallery, and at the farthest possible remove from the pulpit."[16] In such seating arrangements social distance was literally carried to extremes.

Following the hierarchical worldview, the graves of blacks in biracial cemeteries were "carefully relegated to the obscure corners of the ground, along with those of paupers and criminals."[17] Projected onto the flat surface of the burial ground, this model of society assigned people of inferior social standing and outsiders the margins of the cemetery, as they had occupied the margins of the community. In Boston, grave diggers petitioned the town in 1744 to provide a place for burying "stranger and negroes."[18] In Worcester, Massachusetts, blacks were buried in the far left corner of the Burial Ground on Mechanic Street, behind the strangers' section.[19]

The gravesites of the few eighteenth- and nineteenth-century black New Englanders whose gravestones are still extant indicate their marginality. The markers for John Jack in Concord, Massachusetts, for Boston Trowtrow in Norwich, Connecticut, and for Jack York in Pittsfield, Vermont, are on the periphery of their respective cemeteries, or on what used to be the edge when they were buried. Interestingly enough, in the Old Wethersfield, Connecticut, burying ground, the gravestones of Tenor Abro, François, and Quash Gomer were set off the rest of the graves in the early nineteenth century, but due to cemetery crowding the space once left between the different ethnic populations has been filled in the meantime. Population growth, not rapprochement between the races, caused this forced integration to happen. The three markers are situated at the foot of a hill, still close to the border, a fence separating the cemetery from a playground.

To be sure, blacks were not the only group to be discriminated against in early American cemeteries. Indian graves were also relegated to isolated corners. In the burial ground next to the Wapping Community Church in South Windsor, Connecticut, the racial segregation that was practiced in the last century is still clearly visible. New grounds were made available before the old graveyard was completely full, so the latter has remained in its historical state and presents the contemporary visitor with a glimpse of the order of Windsor society in the early decades of the nineteenth century. The graves are arranged in a field of neat rows next to the church. At the edge of the elevation on which church and cemetery are set, four sandstone markers are clearly segregated from the larger population. The one that is best preserved reads:

In memory of
Molley Mohalk
who Dieb Desember
AD 1766. In the
28 Year of Her
Age. A Squaw.

Molley Mohalk's identity is defined for eternity by her gender and her ethnicity, or at least for as long as her stone withstands the onslaught of natural erosion and of pollution. The physical separation of her gravestone and those of her neighbors, Augustus M (. . .), (. . .) Cesar, and two children, conveys a sense of their social isolation when alive.

New York City was equally discriminating in respect to mortal remains. The "Old Negroes' Burying-ground" was located in Lower Manhattan in the vicinity of the poorhouse, the workhouse, and the debtor's prison in 1755. In

1794 a new "burying-ground for the Black people" was established by the city at the present 195 Chrystie Street on the Lower East Side.[20]

Social distinctions were sometimes made between different classes of blacks. The city of Richmond, Virginia, for example, established two black cemeteries in 1815, one for slaves and one for free blacks.[21] Oakland Cemetery in Atlanta, Georgia, also had separate sections for slaves and free blacks.[22]

The West proved to be more democratic, anarchic even, in its treatment of the dead. A report on Yerba Buena Cemetery in San Francisco dated 1855 describes with disgust the chaos of posthumous racial togetherness.

> American and European, Asiatic and African are now the same filthy substance. In life, the white man prided himself that his veins held not the blood of yellow, red or black races; the man of 'progress,' that he was not like the slothful, ignorant, slavish native of warm climates: now in Yerba Buena Cemetery there is none better, none worse in all human respects.[23]

Equality of the races beneath the dust: in the western cemetery, the promise of the melting pot is finally fulfilled.

The topography of American cemeteries reflects race, class, age, gender, and religious distinctions. Hierarchy and marginality are very often displayed in a literal sense. In 1805 the Episcopal Christ Church of New Orleans was given a rear section of St. Louis Cemetery No. 1 for the burial of non-Catholics. A graveyard for blacks was situated behind the Protestant section, that is, in the rear of the rear.[24] Pushed into the lowest levels of socioeconomic status, African Americans had to accept the least attractive locations for their final resting places.

In the mid-nineteenth century, Frederick Law Olmsted visited one black cemetery in Richmond, Virginia, located beyond the city's principal cemetery, and called it "a desolate place."[25] William Cullen Bryant described the black cemetery of Savannah, Georgia:

> At a little distance, near a forest, lies the burial-place of the black population. A few trees, trailing with long moss, rise above hundreds of nameless graves, overgrown with weeds; but here and there are scattered memorials of the dead, some of a very humble kind, with a few of marble, and half a dozen spacious brick tombs like those in the cemetery of the whites.[26]

The humbler appearance of the black graveyard compared to that serving the white population can be observed in both the South and in the North, in both the past and in the present.[27]

God's Acre, Forbidden Ground: Different Persuasions

Most churches allowed racial segregation of the dead, but sometimes condemned the indiscriminate burial of Christians. The Catholic church tolerated segregation, but not the casual burial of Catholics in nonsanctified grounds.

The *Code Noir* required baptized slaves to be buried in cemeteries, with church ceremonies. In Louisiana, Loquet de Lapommeray was fined 30 livres in 1738 for having a slave girl interred outside the graveyard. The girl's body was to be exhumed and reinterred in proper grounds.[28]

Differential treatment was practiced by the Quakers, whose cemeteries appear to be so highly egalitarian. Yet, Colonial Philadelphia had a black cemetery outside the city. Other communities either had separate burying grounds for blacks or they fenced off areas in interracial grounds. Some provided graves in masters' orchards or on the edge of woods.[29] Others, in a more enlightened spirit, broke fresh ground. The charter of Allegheny Cemetery in Pittsburg, Pennsylvania, stated in 1844 that everybody had a right to a dignified burial, regardless of "race, color, or creed."[30]

Perhaps most dramatic are the individual acts of protest against discriminatory policies. Joseph Carpenter, a Quaker from New Rochelle, New York, donated the ground for an integrated cemetery when he learned that blacks were excluded from the town's cemeteries. He was buried there, on his own instruction, to express his disapproval of racism.[31] An eloquent condemnation of differential segregation in death is made in the epitaph of Thaddeus Stevens, the majority leader in the House of Representatives during the Civil War, who initiated and championed the passing of the Fourteenth Amendment.

I repose in this quiet and secluded spot,
Not from any natural preference for solitude
But finding other cemeteries limited as to race
By charter rules,
I have chosen this that I might illustrate
In my death
The principles which I advocated
Through a long life
Equality of Man before his Creator.

Before his death in 1868, Stevens had arranged for his interment in Shreiner's Cemetery in Lancaster, Pennsylvania, because it did not practice segregation. His burial provided the occasion for an ultimate symbolic act of integration.

Evidently, the major Christian churches of the United States did not pursue a firm and clear-cut policy in their treatment of black bodies to be buried. Sometimes they reinforced patterns of segregation, sometimes they mitigated the effects of discrimination. Similarly, Jewish communities signaled contradictory messages to blacks. Whereas African Americans who belonged to or worked for Jews seem to have been encouraged to follow Jewish religious practices, they were apparently discouraged from seeking interment in Jewish burial grounds. Necrogeographic mapping was taken quite seriously in Jewish graveyards.[32] Legend has it that one black woman, Lucy Marks, made it into the Jewish Mikveh Israel Cemetery in Philadelphia. She worked as a cook for a Jewish family and observed their rites and holidays. When her employers were refused permittance to bury her in Mikveh Israel, they (according to lore) interred her there secretly, at night.[33]

In Conspicuous Company: A Mixed Blessing

While looking at the provisions white Americans made to avoid physical contact with blacks before and even after death, we should keep in mind that contact between the races nonetheless took place within a social framework that, rigid as it may have been, did not meet the requirements of a caste system. There was spatial separation and a well-practiced choreography followed by members of the different races, but there was no strict ritualistic avoidance.[34] The spheres of action of masters and slaves interlocked, black and white people extended into each other's territory. Similarly, their resting places adjoined and occasionally overlapped.

In some family burial grounds, favorite servants were allotted space in the white section, as an act of final grace on the part of the master. "Family" as a socially constructed entity can be based on ancestry, matrimony, and household membership. By including the latter category in their definition of "family," slaveholders were able to manipulate group membership. Certain slaves, who were part of the racial out-group, were drawn into the circle of the primarily biologically defined in-group of the white "family," usually irrespective of their own matrimonial and lineage ties.

For self-assured slaveholders, race boundaries were so clearly defined that they were less apprehensive about mingling their dust with that of blacks than other white Americans. Emotional attachment as well as an acknowledgment of loyal service prompted masters to have certain slaves buried close to themselves. Andrew Jackson's body servant Alf, for instance, was buried close to his master in the Hermitage grounds.[36]

Whereas burial within the same area may reflect equal status, the actual disposition of graves may also suggest domination and subjugation. Assembling family and servants around the master's grave projects the latter's patriarchal image into the beyond. Those arranging for a burial in a particular lot were no doubt aware of the symbolic significance of a grave's location.

The Blackwell family burying ground is located in Cobb County, Georgia. After the Civil War, friends of the family, Mr. and Mrs. Oliver, were buried outside the fence of the burying ground, close to yet separate from the biologically related in-group. A former slave of the Olivers is buried with his masters: at their feet.[36]

Chase C. Mooney reports the following rare example from Tennessee:

> Colonel James Tubb of DeKalb County requested that Caleb, his body servant, be buried next to him. After the war and Tubb's death, Caleb cared for Mrs. Tubb and the youngest child until they died. . . . James, Jr., carried out his father's wish and buried Caleb at the head of the family section.[37]

"At the head of the family section" is the appropriate place for a patriarch. It is an unusual position to be accorded to a black man in a white family lot.

Longfellow's poem "In the Churchyard at Cambridge" (1858) captures the ambiguity involved in interring masters and slaves in close proximity.

In the village churchyard she lies,
Dust is in her beautiful eyes,
    No more she breathes, nor feels, nor stirs;
At her feet and at her head
Lies to a slave to attend the dead,
    But their dust is white as hers.

Was she, a lady of high degree,
So much in love with the vanity
    And foolish pomp of this world of ours?
Or was it Christian charity,
And lowliness and humility,
    The richest and rarest of all dowers?

The question is not answered: "Who shall tell us? No one speaks; / . . . At the rude questions we have asked; / Nor will the mystery be unmasked / By those who are sleeping at her side."[38]

We do not usually know what the beneficiaries of such favors thought of the arrangement.[39] One slave biography, however, provides an explanation of why a slave might not want to be close to his master or mistress in perpetuity. In 1846 Lewis and Milton Clarke pointed out that slaves preferred to be buried at a distance from their master because they did not want to be terrorized by his presence even after death. In a humorous anecdote told by the Clarkes a slave refuses the "honor" of being interred in his master's vault by explaining that when the devil comes to get the master, he might carry him, the slave, away by mistake.[40]

Grounds for Exclusion

Fear of spiritual contamination is not the only cause behind the choice of separate burial places by African Americans. When black communities were able to exercise authority over their graveyards they did not practice indiscriminate burial. The spatial structure of black cemeteries in the United States reflects ordering principles such as biological descent, cultural community, and social hierarchy. The dead are assembled according to family ties and/or membership in the community, church, fraternal society, et cetera. The social distinction of the deceased may be expressed in the decoration and in the location of the grave. In the local cemetery, the in-group (in the true sense of the word) may be kept separate from outsiders or relative newcomers to the area. A black resident of Sunbury, Georgia, affirmed in the late 1930s: "Ebrybody wannuh be buried in deah own town. An we nebuh bury strainjuhs wid our own folks. Ef a strainjug die yuh, we bury em in duh strainjuh's lot."[41]

The categories of in- and outsiders appear to be accepted by both parties concerned in the rather closed communities of the Sea Islands, where recent arrivals tend to meet with coldness if not open hostility.[42] After living on St. Simon's Island most of her life, Bessie Jones consciously assumed the role of the stranger and explained in 1983 that she would not be buried with the local folk:

> I know I'm a stranger. Let me die and you'll see where I go. I ain't going to King's cemetery, no sir. I'm going to Strangers' Cemetery, or out there at Rose Hill, wherever my children put me—but not in the others. We have a lot in Strangers' Cemetery. And a number of people who we thought weren't strangers, when they died they went down there. They sure did. . . . St. Simons is a spot. You stay here long enough, you'll find what you are.[43]

The statement "We have a lot in Strangers' Cemetery" indicates that close kin ties are maintained before and after death, and that geographic attachment, lineage, and local roots can be traced for generations.

> In some Sea Island communities, ancestry outweighs matrimony. The belief is strong among the Negroes that your body must lie with those of your ancestors. Sometimes this meant that a husband and wife were buried in different cemeteries, the woman being buried by her parents in one burying ground while the husband was laid with his family in another. Even today when Negroes die elsewhere their bodies are brought back from great distances that they may rest with their own people.[44]

For people who take home burial very seriously the idea of posthumous relocation for the sake of so-called "development" purposes is an abomination. Thus an eighty-six-year-old Sea Island resident expresses her discontent: "I buried two husbands on Fuskie, and now those folks talking about removing the cemetery. If the construction companies bother my husbands' graves, that is the day I'll put *them* in one."[45] It should be noted that she used to be the best shot on the island, who could shoot alligators between the eyes from a distance.

Consciously discriminatory burial patterns and customs as found in the Sea Islands appear in geographic areas where demographic and political factors have allowed for a certain measure of black cultural autonomy. Members of black minorities living in predominantly white settlements, on the other hand, had a severely limited choice in where they buried their dead. John Jack in Concord and Boston Trowtrow in Norwich probably did not ask for solitary places in the overwhelmingly white cemeteries; they were assigned their lonesome spots in accordance with their standing in the community. The posthumous isolation of black individuals, as well as the ghettoization of small groups within larger biracial cemeteries, illustrates their subordinate status. Forced segregation in cemeteries also furthered the development of distinctive traditions relating to death. For better or worse, physical separation has played a part in keeping African-American folk customs alive. The laying out, marking, and decorating of graves has been done according to local and ethnic traditions. Adaptation to the mainstream model, with streamlined gravestones and leveling lawn, has come with political equality and socioeconomic advance. Gentrification, that is, "cleaning up" the graveyard, usually entails removal of folk decorations and plants that might obstruct the run of the electric lawn mower.[46]

The following section looks at a historic New England cemetery that has not entirely succumbed to the power of the lawn mower. While it has never encouraged the use of folk grave decoration, its upright markers are held in esteem and good repair and provide tangible links to the past.

Margin and Center in New Haven

The present Grove Street Cemetery in New Haven, Connecticut, offers an interesting illustration of the hazards of necrogeographic mapping. It was by accident rather than intention that the marginalized populations of this burial ground were moved to the center in the nineteenth century.

On September 9, 1796, thirty-two citizens of New Haven decided to purchase a field of six acres situated at the northern limit of the city in order to establish a cemetery. They eventually bought ten acres and founded the "New Burying Ground in New Haven." It was the first in the country to be owned and managed by a corporation and to be divided into family lots. Lots were drawn for the tiers assigned to the ecclesiastical societies of the city (United, Episcopal, and First) and for the president and fellows of Yale College. For the remaining fifth section the following was laid down:

> Noted: That Lot No. 1 in the fifth Tier be appropriated for the burial of Strangers who may die in this City.
>
> That Lots No. 3–5 5–&7 of the fifth Tier be appropriated to the burial of the deceased poor of this Town who have not title to any other Lots.
>
> That Lot No. 1 of the 6th Tier be appropriated for the burial of people of colour.[47]

A meeting of the proprietors on September 8, 1800, recorded another zoning division: "Noted that Lot No. 3 in the 5th Tier be appropriated for the Burial of Negroes who are not otherwise provided for."[48]

The orderly layout in the new cemetery contrasted sharply with the haphazard dispersal of interments on the crowded New Haven City Burial Ground on the Green as described by a later historian:

> We only know that within a space of three or four acres the bones of six generations lie indistinguishably intermingled. Magistrates and criminals, preachers, soldiers, merchants, lawyers, doctors, colonial dames, paupers and negro slaves are all consorting together in promiscuous companionship.[49]

To avoid such indiscriminate mingling, the reform-minded proprietors of the New Burying Ground established the rectangular grid pattern of domestic units in a mirror image of the social groups existing in town.

The fifth tier was situated in the southwestern border of the burial ground, on the corners of Grove Street and Plainfield Road, diagonally opposite "Jethro's Corner" on Grove and York Streets.[50] A city map of 1748 identifies the property as that of "Jethro a blackman / Farmer."[51]

For black New Haveners, the abodes of the living and the dead were both on the periphery. At the end of the eighteenth century most blacks who had homes of their own lived in the State, Union, Fleet, and Water Street areas.[52] Even as late as 1845, however, almost one-quarter of New Haven's black population lived with their employers.[53] In 1800 there were about eighty slaves resident in New Haven, out of a slave population of almost one thousand in all of Connecticut. The first, partial Emancipation Act of the state was passed in 1784, and it specified that no black person born after March 1 of that year would be a slave after reaching the age of twenty-five. In 1797 the age was reduced to twenty-one. The holding of slaves was finally forbidden in 1848.[54] Not many New Haven blacks appear to have been included in their employer's or master family's last abode.[55]

In 1814 the corporation bought another tract of land to enlarge the cemetery. Eight acres were added to the original ground on the west side.[56] Owing to the cluttered condition of the City Burial Ground on the Green, burials there had been discontinued after 1812. In 1819 the city of New Haven acquired a lot in the New Burying Ground and divided it into six squares for the general population, adding one each for Yale College, for strangers, and for "people of color."[57]

Again, the black section was relegated to the periphery: it was situated in the northwesterly corner of the grounds. With the availability of a new potter's field, owned by the city, the old one in tier five was sold off to individuals. As the stigma of former black occupancy was attached to this neighborhood, the "invasion—succession" cycle took its course. Lots in that vicinity were acquired by black individuals for their families: for example, by Alexander Dubois (W. E. B. Du Bois' grandfather), the Reverend Jacob Oson, and Ebenezer D. Bassett (later U.S. minister and consul general to Haiti).

Then, in 1828, a solitary act of desegregation was performed. On August 25, Jehudi Ashmun, the first agent of the African Colonization Society at Monrovia, Liberia, and a white man, died of hepatitis in New Haven, shortly after his return from Africa. I have not found any information on the choice of his burial site, but as Ashmun appears to have been quite in control of the circumstances surrounding his dying, I assume that he himself decided to be buried in the "African" section of the New Burying Ground. Contemporaries noted that there was "moral sublimity in his death," and his later biographer wrote in a letter to a friend: "As he has taught us how to live, he is now teaching us how to die."[58]

Before his death, Ashmun meticulously put his affairs in order, donating most of his possessions to the African Missions.[59] His interment in the lot reserved for "people of color" was a final statement, a visual reminder of the role he had assumed in leading African Americans to what was considered their place. His humble act was to be understood as a token of solidarity, of identification with their situation. He relinquished his privilege to be buried in one of the more attractive sections of the graveyard. "Burying down" may be more acceptable to supremacists than mixing freely and on equal terms with the living members of the other race. We are left to wonder what the families of the black individuals in tier five thought of the new neighbor.

The monument on Ashmun's grave was erected by the American Colonization Society in 1829. It is a sarcophagus on a pedestal, made of red sandstone, very similar to the Eli Whitney monument which is in the same cemetery. Ironically, Ashmun, who wanted to take black Americans back to Africa, is buried in the vicinity of the inventor of the cotton gin, which caused the demand for slave labor in the American South to rise.

In another ironic twist, the inconspicuous corner was moved to the center of public attention. At the time of Ashmun's death, the New Burying Ground had two gates: one between tiers two and three, another between tiers eight and nine. When, in 1846, the cemetery was provided with a wrought iron fence and an arched sandstone gate in the Egyptian revival style, the new entrance was located opposite tier five. Visitors walking in would first see Ashmun's sarcophagus and the lots acquired by black New Haveners. The margin had become center.

When portions of the new potter's field were sold for private lots in 1836, the proprietors confirmed that the sections for ancient monuments, for college members, for strangers, and for blacks would be kept available for the groups intended.[60] Toward the end of the century, however, the proprietors noted that there had not been any interments in the place set apart for blacks and ordered the human remains from that section to be removed to another former potter's field and to specified vacant locations. The vacated lots of the pauper section were put up for sale.[61] Black New Haveners had preferred to bury their dead in less distinguished ground for several decades.

Jim Crow Dying: Discrimination in Other Areas of the Mortuary Complex

Separation and degradation occur in more ways than by the location of graves in allocated, unattractive burial grounds. In slavery, certain masters even had to be reminded to bury their dead slaves. The convenient disposal of slave corpses by throwing them into the river was interdicted by a cabildo ordinance passed in Vera Cruz, Mexico, in 1547. As a burial method, the procedure had proved to be hygienically doubtful but attractive to sharks.[62] Disparagement was also expressed in the prohibition against the use of caskets by people of color in colonial Latin America. Only Spaniards were permitted to use them.[63]

Restriction might take the form of controlling funeral rites. African Americans were policed into their very graves. In the South and in the North, constraints were imposed, ostensibly out of fear of black conspiracies.[64] In New York, for instance, night burials of Indian and black slaves were prohibited in 1722. The interdiction was repeated in 1731, 1748, and 1763. Slave funerals were to be attended by not more than twelve slaves and deprived of such trappings as palls, gloves, and favors.[65]

There were even segregated railway compartments for the deceased. In 1835 a railroad was planned for the transport of corpses and mourners from St. Claude Street to the cemetery at Bayou St. John in New Orleans. The city council stipulated that the contractor had to provide separate cars for white, free colored, and slave corpses, with fees ranging from fifty cents for slaves to three dollars for whites.[66]

One (arguably) positive consequence of differential segregation and white America's disregard of black mortuary and memorial needs was the establishment of black-owned business to supply the African-American community with goods and services. When the Gupton-Jones School of Embalming opened in Nashville, Tennessee, in 1920, embalming course in May and November catered to white pupils, courses in July and February to blacks. In 1921, 135 of the 597 embalmers registered in Georgia were black. Black funeral directors had their own state organizations, some founded as early as 1897 (Virginia) and 1916 (Tennessee).[67]

The present National Funeral Directors and Morticians Association started out as the Independent National Negro Funeral Directors Association in 1925. The name underwent a series of changes, from the Progressive Funeral Directors Association a few years after its founding, to the National Negro Funeral Directors Association in 1938, and to National Negro Funeral Directors and Morticians Association in 1957, before the racial tag was dropped.[68]

With desegregation and/or demographic changes, African-American professionals have attempted to broaden their customer base, sometimes neglecting or surrendering some black cultural values while adopting mainstream standards. In order to expand his business in a predominantly white area, black funeral director Lincoln Ragsdale had to reach out for white customers. Conscious of the political aspects involved, he changed the name and the ethnic image of his funeral home: "When I was losing money, I made a business decision. I took down my pictures of Martin Luther King Jr. and Booker T. Washington and put up some white folk. I hired white personnel and my business increased over 300 percent."[69] Giving up part of his cultural identity and redefining the ethnic makeup of his firm paid off for him.

More fundamental than segregated facilities in institutions pertaining to death and dying is, in the eyes of posterity, the denial of basic elements of commemoration and thus of historical record for blacks. First of all, during slavery, the vital statistics of African Americans were much more likely to appear in wills and inventories and plantation diaries than in the vital records kept by political or church authorities. Blacks were often listed among items of livestock, crops, and household furniture. The dreadful consequences of the legal status of chattel slaves for their life, health, and death need not be reiterated here.

The lack of recognition for blacks was shown in manifold ways. On a monument dedicated to the revolutionary soldiers who fell at the storming of Fort Griswold, the names of the two blacks who were killed, Lambo Latham and Jordan Freeman, were not only entered last but with a blank space left between them and their white fellow soldiers.[70]

How strict the categories of separate and differential commemoration were defined becomes apparent in the following case of mistaken identity. A man who had been passing for white drowned in a river in the Deep South. The newspapers gave the story the appropriate attention, with headlines on the front page and continuous coverage during the search for the body. The race of the drowned man was not mentioned, which signified classification with the white population. When his true racial identity was revealed, however, the newspaper coverage was shortened and committed to an inside page, and the man was referred to as a Negro. In spite of his mother's efforts to have him buried in the white cemetery, he was interred in the black one.[71]

In the antebellum North, categories were similarly established and maintained. In the decades preceding the Civil War, New Haven vital records were classified according to church affiliation and community status, corresponding to the tiers reserved for each group in the New Burying Ground: First Congregational Society, United Society Second Congregational, Episcopal Society, Methodist Society, Baptist Society, Yale College, Colored Persons, and Deaths at the Almshouse.[72] Until 1865, New Haven directories identified blacks by adding "col'd" to their names.

Even the legislation against vandalism in cemeteries made different provisions for white and black offenders. A city ordinance of 1857 that applied to Oakland Cemetery in Atlanta prescribed fines of up to fifty dollars and imprisonment of up to thirty days for white violators. Free blacks were fined a maximum of thirty dollars, but if they failed to pay they were given thirty-nine lashes and hired out at public outcry. The maximum penalty for slaves was seventy-five lashes.

In 1878, when the grounds were crowded in Oakland Cemetery, the city council had the human remains removed from the so-called slave square "to be reinterred in colored pauper grounds without any distinction of graves, except those who may have headboards." The former slave square grounds were to be leveled and divided to be sold at fifty dollars or more per lot.[73] Dispossessed of individual rights in life, slaves were also deprived of lasting records of their existence in history. Profit margins outweighed considerations of piety and respect for the dead. Not even the repeated relocation of burials, however, destroyed underlying patterns of racial segregation in cemeteries. Segregation had to be perceived as an economic and cultural anachronism to be attacked.

Mending Fences?

When civil rights legislation had cleared the grounds for cemetery integration, white supremacist resentment made use of its traditional repertoire of intimidation to maintain de facto segregation in the graveyard. In September 1971, one year after the Federal District Court's decision against Hillcrest Memorial Gardens, a white couple in Dade City, Florida, had the body of a black man, the husband of their domestic employee, removed from their plot in a hitherto all-white cemetery after receiving threatening telephone calls.[74] A few days after their decision was disclosed, the widow, accompanied by an NAACP representative, bought a single plot in another part of the same cemetery. The UPI reporter noted that "there were no objections to the purchase."[75]

Another possible reaction to cemetery integration is white flight. In 1979 black funeral director Alfonso Dawson of Atlanta became the sole owner of the almost all-white Resthaven Gardens of Memory, a twenty-seven-acre property in Decatur, Georgia. White families began to remove the remains of their relatives at an average of twenty-five per year. In 1985 the cemetery population was still 90 percent white, but the rate of disinterment seemed to be growing. *Jet* magazine published this case of necropolitan migration on May 6, 1985.[76] About a year after the publication of the article, the "flight" seemed to have run its course, with disinterments trickling down to approximately one every four months.[77]

Even if we disregard such exceptional cases of discrimination and resistance to change, the persistence of ethnic (self-) segregation in American cemeteries is hard to overlook. Voluntary segregation is not necessarily based on white supremacist or black nationalist thinking. Nor is customary separation inextricably linked with economic necessity. Families may want to bury their dead with relatives, with members of the church or lodge the deceased were part of. Communities thus formed in the cemetery span the lifetimes of several generations. The inclusion of trips to the cemetery in African-American homecoming rites underlines the function of family graves in traditions that foster a strong sense of community identity. The graveyard, *locus mémoriae* in the literal sense, provides the members, of a given community with geographic and historical roots. It is a place to return to, in life or in death.

The connections between the choice of burial site and socioeconomic advancement, between migration patterns, residential mobility, and necrogeography have yet to be explored. A close look at biracial cemeteries may reveal whether inclusion has led to egalitarian confusion or whether distinctions are being upheld through the position of burial plots and the exclusiveness of grave markers. As we know from the inner cities, the marginalized are sometimes found in the center.

NOTES

1. Newspaper clipping quoted in Samuel W. Thomas, *Cave Hill Cemetery: A Pictorial Guide and Its History* (Louisville, Ky., 1985) and in review article by Robert A. Wright, *AGS Newsletter* 11, no. 4 (1987), 3. North American whites-only policy was rarely carried as far as in Cave Hill, where blacks were denied access to the cemetery grounds as late as 1870.

2. For a more sophisticated analysis of the factors that may account for ongoing residential segregation, see W. A. V. Clark, "Residential Segregation in American

Cities: A Review and Interpretation," *Population Research and Policy Review* 5 (1986): 95–127.

3. July 17, 1963. This is the last entry in the Schomburg Vertical File.

4. "Church to Broaden Burial Integration," *New York Times* April 15, 1964, L42.

5. *New York Times,* September 14, 1966, L23.

6. "Negro G.I.'s Wife Sues Cemetery," L3.

7. "White Cemetery Burial Cleared for Negro G.I.," L23.

8. "Black Soldier's Burial Is Held Up in Florida," August 24, 1970, L38.

9. "U.S. Backs Suit to Drop Racial Bar at Cemetery," August 25, 1970, L5.

10. On August 28, 1970, the *New York Times* had the news: "Court Tells Florida Cemetery to Bury Black G.I.," (L1, L10). Fort Pierce is an interesting landmark in the African-American political and cultural map. In addition to the case of enforced desegregation related here, Fort Pierce has the burial place of Zora Neale Hurston in the Garden of the Heavenly Rest. The story of her almost forgotten grave and Alice Walker's pilgrimage to find and mark it is described in Walker's essay "Looking for Zora" in her collection *In Search of Our Mothers' Gardens* (San Diego, 1983; the original version, entitled "In Search of Zora Neale Hurston," was published in *Ms.* magazine in March 1975).

11. "Blacks Get Equal Rights Even in Death," August 30, 1970, E 14.

12. *Creative Survival: The Providence Black Community in the 19th Century* (Providence, The Rhode Island Black Heritage Society, n.d.), 23.

13. Abraham English Brown, *History of the Town of Bedford, Middlesex County, Massachusetts* (Bedford, 1891), 32, 34; Richard Wade, *Slavery in the Cities* (New York, 1964), 270–71.

14. Bernard Steiner, "History of Slavery in Connecticut" (1893), *Slavery in the States: Selected Essays* (New York, 1969), 20.

15. Winthrop D. Jordan, *White over Black: American Attitudes Toward the Negro, 1550–1812* (New York, 1977), 132.

16. Sherman W. Adams and Henry R. Stiles, *The History of Ancient Wethersfield,* vol. 1 (1904; rpt., Wethersfield, Ct.: Wethersfield Historical Society, 1974), 945.

17. George Tolman, *John Jack, the Slave, and Daniel Bliss, the Tory* (Concord, Mass., c. 1902), 4.

18. Lorenzo Johnston Greene, *The Negro in Colonial New England, 1620–1776* (New York, 1942), 284.

19. *Inscriptions from the Burial Grounds in Worcester, Massachusetts, from 1727 to 1859* (Worcester, 1878), map of 1798.

20. Margaret F. O'Connell, "Potter's Field Has Found a Resting Place at Last," *New York Times,* August 31, 1975, R4.

21. Mary H. Mitchell, *Hollywood Cemetery: The History of a Southern Shrine* (Richmond, Va., 1985), 9.

22. "Oakland in Atlanta," *American Funeral Director* (October 1978), 44.

23. Helen Marcia Bruner, *California's Old Burying Grounds* (San Francisco, 1945), 22.

24. Samuel Wilson and Leonard V. Huber, *The St. Louis Cemeteries of New Orleans* (New Orleans, La., 1963), 11.

25. Frederick Law Olmstead, *A Journey in the Seaboard Slave States* (New York, 1856), 24.

26. William Cullen Bryant, *Letters of a Traveller* (London, 1850), 94.

27. Fiction captures the subtle mechanisms of social difference in this excerpt from David Bradley's novel *The Chaneysville Incident* (New York, 1982, 77): "In my home

town, white people and black people aren't buried together. It isn't anything official, like down South. It's just the way things are done. I expect that if somebody black wanted to be put away in a white cemetery, nobody would say a thing. But the practice is we have our place and they have their places. And our place is a little shabby." In spite of legal equality, customary segregation defines de facto interracial codes and territories.

Of another community on the black American literary map, *Linden Hills,* Gloria Naylor writes, "Unlike the South, the North didn't care if blacks and whites were buried together so long as they didn't live together," only to undercut even that claim to partial equality: "Appalled by the reports of the evils that lay below the Mason-Dixon and the cry that 'the only good nigger is a dead nigger,' Wayne County let it be known that any of their sable brothers who were good and dead were welcome to a Christian burial right next to a white person—Tuesdays, Thursdays, and Saturdays, the days assigned for colored funerals." (1985; New York, 1986, 3) The truth underlying Naylor's caustic irony is no less strange than fiction.

28. *Vicar General v. Treasurer General,* June 14–July 5, 1738; Helen T. Catterall, *Judicial Cases Concerning American Slavery and the Negro,* vol. 3 (Washington, 1932), 412.

29. Timothy E. Drake, *Quakers and Slavery in America* (New Haven, Ct., 1950), 16; Henry J. Cadbury, "Negro Membership in the Society of Friends," *Journal of Negro History* 21 (1936), 161, 160.

30. Alan B. Govenar, "Allegheny Cemetery," *Stone in America* (June 1979), 38.

31. Cadbury, "Negro Membership," 161.

32. In nineteenth-century New Orleans non-Jewish wives could be interred in the southwest corner of the Jewish cemetery "in the walls of the burial ground." As gentiles allied with Jews they were granted proximity to the in-group while being kept separate (Graenum Berger, *Black Jews in America* [New York, 1978], 21). In the Glasgow Necropolis, Jews who married gentiles were buried just outside the walls of the Jewish enclosure (James J. Berry, *The Glasgow Necropolis* [Glasgow, 1985], item 35).

33. Berger, *Black Jews,* 14–15; John Francis Marion, *Famous and Curious Cemeteries* (New York, 1977), 148.

34. Cf. Orlando Patterson, *Slavery and Social Death: A Comparative Study* (Cambridge, Mass., 1982), 50.

35. Chase C. Mooney, *Slavery in Tennessee* (Bloomington Ind., 1957), 91.

36. Sarah B. G. Temple, *The First Hundred Years: A Short History of Cobb County, in Georgia* (Atlanta, 1935), 809.

37. Mooney, *Slavery in Tennessee,* 90.

38. Henry Wadsworth Longfellow, "In the Churchyard at Cambridge," in Gay Wilson Allen, Walter B. Rideout, James K. Robinson, eds., *American Poetry* (New York, 1965), 159–60). The poem is believed to have been inspired by the grave of Madame Vassall, the original owner of Longfellow's house in Cambridge (Edward Wagenknecht, *Henry Wadsworth Longfellow: His Poetry and Prose* [New York, 1986], 132).

39. Testimonies from biased white observers cannot be taken at face value. One such questionable source describes the burial of "Uncle Jim" in Kentucky: "They buried him in his own soil, next to the wall near the Fort Myer gate. Likely they did not know the old man wanted to sleep near the iron railing that guards the graves of his first white people ("Orland Kay Armstrong, *Old Massa's People: The Old Slaves Tell Their Story* [Indianapolis, 1931], 355).

40. Lewis Clarke and Milton Clarke, *Narratives of the Sufferings of Lewis and Milton Clarke* (Boston, 1846), 119. The same story was told in Connecticut (William D. Piersen, *Black Yankees* [Amherst, Mass., 1988], 109).

41. Georgia Writers' Project, Works Progress Administration, *Drums and Shadows: Survival Studies Among the Georgia Coastal Negroes* (Athens, Ga., 1940), 113. The informant is Elizabeth Roberts.

42. Patricia Jones-Jackson, *When Roots Die: Endangered Traditions on the Sea Islands* (Athens, Ga., 1987), 23.

43. Bessie Jones, *For the Ancestors: Autobiographical Memories,* ed. John Stewart (Urbana, Ill., 1983), 147.

44. Margaret Davis Cate and Orrin Sage Wightman, *Early Days of Coastal Georgia* (New York, 1955), 213. Cf. Jones-Jackson, *When Roots Die,* 25.

45. Charles L. Blockson and Karen Kasmauski, "Sea Change in the Sea Islands: 'Nowhere to Lay Down Weary Head,' " *National Geographic* 172, no. 6 (December 1987), 756.

46. For detailed discussions of African elements in black American grave marking and decoration, see Robert Farris Thompson, *Flash of the Spirit: African and Afro-American Art and Philosophy* (1983; New York, 1984), 132–42; John Michael Vlach, *The Afro-American Tradition in Decorative Arts* (Cleveland, Ohio, 1978), 139–47; Lil Fenn, *Honoring the Ancestors* (videocassette: North State Public Video, 1986); Elaine Nichols, ed., *The Last Miles of the Way: African-American Homegoing Traditions, 1890–Present* (Columbia, S.C., 1989).

47. At a meeting of the proprietors, October 30, 1797, *Records of the Proprietors of the "New Burying Ground in New Haven" 1796–1859; thence, "New Haven City Burial Ground"* (Manuscript no. 74, New Haven Colony Historical Society), 13.

48. *Records of the Proprietors,* 18.

49. Henry T. Blake, *Chronicles of New Haven Green. From 1638 to 1862* (New Haven, Ct., 1898), 276.

50. "Doolittle Map of 1812", Map G 3784.N4 D667, 1812, at the New Haven Colony Historical Society map collection.

51. Engraving done in 1806, exhibited at the New Haven Colony Historical Society, after James Wadsworth's map of New Haven in 1748.

52. Afro-American Collection, Manuscript no. 119, Box I, Folder F New Haven Colony Historical Society.

53. Robert Austin Warner, *New Haven Negroes: A Social History* (New Haven, Ct., 1940), 23.

54. Mary H. Mitchell, "Slavery in Connecticut and Especially in New Haven," *Papers of the New Haven Colony Historical Society* 10 (1951), 286–312; Steiner, "History of Slavery in Connecticut."

55. I know of only three black employees buried at their employer's charge in nonsegregated parts of the cemetery. All of them were pointed out to me by Superintendant William M. Cameron, Jr.

56. Henry H. Townshend, "The Grove Street Cemetery," paper printed for the New Haven Colony Historical Society, 1948, 14.

57. *Report of the Committee, Appointed to Inquire into the Condition of the New Haven Burying Ground, and to propose a plan for its Improvement* (New Haven, Ct., 1839), 10.

58. Leonard Bacon, *Discourse Preached in the Center Church, in New Haven, August 27, 1828, At the Funeral of Jehudi Ashmun, Esq. Colonial Agent of the American Colony of Liberia* (New Haven, Ct., 1828), 23. R. R. Gurly, August 25, 1828, quoted in Charles Woodbury McLellan, *Some Notes on Jehudi Ashmun* (Champlain, N.Y., 1959), 9.

59. Ralph Randolph Gurly, *Life of Jehudi Ashmun, Late Colonial Agent in Liberia* (Washington, D.C., 1835), 392. A poetical rendering of his funeral is given by

Lydia Sigourney in "Burial of Ashmun, at New-Haven, Aug. 1828," *Zinzendorff, and Other Poems* (New York, 1836), 288–89.

60. *Report of the Committee,* 11.

61. Entries for January 20, 1897; November 1, 1900; November 25, 1901, in the *Records of the Proprietors.* By this time the cemetery was called New Haven City Burial Ground.

62. Colin A. Palmer, *Slaves of the White God: Blacks in Mexico, 1570–1650* (Cambridge, Mass., 1976), 42.

63. Rolando Mellafe, *Negro Slavery in Latin America* (Berkeley, Calif. 1975), 114.

64. David R. Roediger, "And Die in Dixie: Funerals, Death, and Heaven in the Slave Community 1700–1865," *Massachusetts Review* 22 (Spring 1981), 164–65.

65. Edith Vernon Morgan, "Slavery in New York," reprinted in *Slavery in the United States: Selected Essays* (New York, 1969), 22. In colonial Spanish America, an ordinance issued in April 1612 restricted the number of black participants in the funeral of a mulatto or black person to four (W. H. Dusenberry, "Discriminatory Aspects of Legislation in Colonial Mexico," *Journal of Negro History* 33 [1948], 292).

66. Wilson and Huber, *The St. Louis Cemeteries of New Orleans,* 29.

67. Charles R. Wilson, "The Southern Funeral Director: Managing Death in the New South," *Georgia Historical Quarterly* 67, no. 1 (1983), 67, 58.

68. Robert W. Habenstein and William M. Lamers, *The History of American Funeral Directing,* rev. ed., (Milwaukee, Wisc., 1968), 541, 611.

69. "The Business Side of Bereavement," *Black Enterprise* 8 (November 1977), 57.

70. William C. Nell, *The Colored Patriots of the American Revolution* (Boston, 1855), 136. Even a few decades ago a Georgia parochial historian happily perpetuated the custom of benign neglect of recording black lives when dressing an inventory of gravestones of Cobb County. She explained: "Records have been taken only from the cemeteries in which white citizens are buried. In the Citizens Cemetery in Marietta there are a number of Negro citizens buried, and in this case the records of the entire cemetery are given" (Temple, *The First Hundred Years,* 586).

71. Allison Davis, Burleigh B. Gardner, and Mary R. Gardner, *Deep South: A Social Anthropological Study of Caste and Class* (Chicago, 1941), 43–44.

72. *Vital Records of New Haven: 1649–1850,* 2 vols. (Hartford, Ct., 1924).

73. "Oakland in Atlanta,": 24, 27.

74. "Threatened Couple to Remove Negro in White Cemetery," *New York Times,* September 23, 1971, L49.

75. "Negro Buys a Plot in White Cemetery," *New York Times,* September 26, 1971, L58.

The screenplay for "Resting Place" (Writer: Walter Halsey, Director: John Korty, Producer: CFT Marian Rees Associates) takes several elements from the Williams case. Set in imaginary Rockville, Georgia, in February 1972, it involves a black Vietnam hero's parents, a white officer sent by the army to investigate, and a white woman, benevolent and condescending, who is a friend of the black family. The burial in an all-white cemetery takes place only when the killed soldier's fellow soldiers and subordinates provide an escort for the casket.

76. Harmon Perry, "Whites Remove Dead from Cemetery Now Owned by Black Man," *Jet,* May 6, 1985, 38–40.

77. Personal communication, Alfonso Dawson, March 11, 1986.

9

What One Cannot Remember Mistakenly

KAREN FIELDS

I chose this title deliberately to provoke. Nothing is more fully agreed than the certainty that memory fails. Memory fails, leaving blanks, and memory fails by filling blanks mistakenly. In filling blanks mistakenly, memory collaborates with forces separate from actual past events, forces such as an individual's wishes, a group's suggestions, a moment's connotations, an environment's clues, an emotion's demands, a self's evolution, a mind's manufacture of order, and, yes, even a researcher's objectives. In these collaborations, and in others I have not thought of, memory acquires well-noted imperfections. We seek to understand these imperfections systematically if we are scholars of memory in itself, and we seek to correct for them if we are scholars who use memory as a source. As researchers, we bind ourselves to skepticism about memory and to a definite methodological mistrust of rememberers who are our informants. We are fully attentive to the fact that memory fails.

But memory also succeeds. It succeeds enormously and profoundly; for it is fundamental to human life, not to say synonymous with it. A large capacity for memory is an integral component of the complex brain that sets Homo sapiens apart. And, without it, the social life that is characteristic of our species would be inconceivable. Thus Nietzsche[1] spoke of memory in terms of our human ability to make, deliver, and collect upon enduring agreements, an ability from which much if not all else is constructed. So although nothing is more certain than that memory fails, equally, nothing is more certain that that memory succeeds. Systematic thought about how it succeeds, and at what, is thus as much in order as the reverse. Otherwise, we who turn to it as a resource fall into paradox.

My work with my grandmother, Mamie Garvin Fields, on her memoir, *Lemon Swamp and Other Places,* offers me a starting point for reflection about what memory succeeds in doing and about the ways in which it does its work. For it is important to refine continually our methods of observing and thinking about memory as a matter of scholarly or scientific enterprise. However, I will also reflect a bit upon this sort of enterprise itself; for it is equally important to refine continually our awareness of certain oddities and particularities that shape this enterprise, and that therefore shape our inner attitude as we go about our work. As researchers we systematically doubt what we systematically count upon as ordinary human beings in the routine of daily life.

One of the particularities of the enterprise is the paradox we flirt with when we turn, with methodological mistrust, to memory as a source. This danger was present from the beginning of my work on *Lemon Swamp.* I turned to my grandmother as a source about the past, aspects of which I had few or no other ways of knowing. The book deals with public and private events (from submarine infiltration during World War II to her marriage just before World War I), attributes and assumptions current in her milieu (from race consciousness to notions of proper dress), aspirations (from racial "uplift" to middle-class consumption), judgments both collective and personal (Who is an Uncle Tom? To whom is a moral person accountable?), habits about the body (from details of housekeeping to color consciousness), natural and man-made objects in Charleston and elsewhere (from Calhoun's statue on the Citadel Green to Lemon Swamp itself), and much else.

At the time of working on this rich material, I liberated myself from the constraints of scholarship or science by refusing to call it sociology, history or even *oral* history. (The constraints tightened no less if I added to "history" the modifier "oral.") Grandmother's term for what we were about was "stories" (and I will say something about stories later on); in the end, we settled for the term "memoir," *Lemon Swamp and Other Places: A Carolina Memoir.* I made this liberation clear in the Introduction to the book by saing "It is a subjective, personal account of life and work in South Carolina from 1888 to now." Nonetheless, the two of us then, no less than the reading audience we imagined, thought of it as a source about the past. And since I was trained as a sociologist and had done historical research, this liberation remained incomplete. It was not possible for me to run methodological red lights unself-consciously—although I most certainly ran them. The running of them occasioned reflection about what some of the green lights permit.

Consider, for example, the predicament that arises when we treat informants with the methodological mistrust that social science conventionally requires. A special existential condition arises between two human beings communicating face to face. Contrary to the face value methodology of everyday human encounters, ours requires skepticism, suspicion, a certain condescension, and above all a constantly open second channel in which to place those bits of testimony that are destined to float out of the interaction, back toward some source of corroboration. This is alien to normal human communication. (The closest everyday-life kin to it involves the interrogations of police and special agents.) Equally alien to everyday life is the patronizing of an interlocutor with silent knowingness when other information establishes that he or she is wrong, or even lying. Suppressing the social commonplaces of contradiction, correction, or dismissal belongs to that special existential condition I am talking about, the one our methodological green lights permit. Now, if the condition of gaining knowledge is first to create a surrogate of human interaction, thereafter deliberately to diminish it, this proceeding demands its own scrutiny—quite apart from the scrutiny the testimony itself gets. This scrutiny amounts to examining our tools, in order to see clearly what they are accomplishing above and beyond our intended purpose. When a surgeon sterilizes the knife with which he cuts through flesh in order to repair the heart, he or she nevertheless still has to attend to the knife's secondary work.

I ran the red light that blocks arguing with an informant. Liberated from the constraints of scholarship, I said to Gram one day that I intended to corroborate her testimony about the high regard certain white folks downtown had had over many years for the residents of her street, Short Court. I made my announcement after the departure of an elderly employee of the gas company. (Gram had commented that he must have been coming to her home for sixty some odd years.) Gram was outraged: one, that I would consider going around behind her to check on stories; two, that I even had the idea of talking about her to somebody who operates gas meters. She was furious at this multilayered violation of our confidence in one another. At one level, I think she thought I thought she would lie. I argued back that scholarly historical work had to go by cross-checking of this kind. She didn't care about history, then. We fought that afternoon over what would and would not be part of my method. In more usual circumstances of doing research, penetration to this level of what is latent in the routine of interviewing most likely would not have come up.

In the end, I could not establish as "fact" that white folks downtown considered Short Court residents to be "aristocratic," in Gram's terms, although I certainly know from other contexts that white Charleston, for some intents and purposes, distinguished "respectable" black people from others. What our argument did establish is that Gram believed in, and perhaps was invested in, the special distinction, to white eyes, of the stratum to which she belonged. Was Gram remembering an aspiration or a fact? Later on that afternoon, her longtime friend Mrs. DaCosta dropped by to sit a spell on the porch, and Gram by skillful direction obtained corroboration from this dignified lady. (Not only that, we got quite a lot about special distinctions of her own family. I should come over one day and learn more . . .)

Fighting with my informant is a red light I ran on many afternoons. One of these fights was about what is or is not a relevant set of facts in an account of a public event—in Charleston—for presentation to a public much larger than Charleston's—the future readers of *Lemon Swamp and Other Places*. In this case, Gram did the cross-checking of memory, and it was I who rejected the process. The issue was what can be called the "wedding list" or the "church program" sort of memory.

This sort of memory has quite particular features: the utter necessity of getting it right; the methodological assumption of ordinary folks that any mistake is meaningful; a corresponding anxiety about forgetting on the part of the rememberer; the consequential nature of the result; and, last but not least, a god-awful exhaustiveness that can overwhelm all it touches. Everyone knows the gnawing fear that accompanies this kind of remembering. And I dare say as well, no one has not at one time or another upheld it—by drawing conclusions about omissions deemed incapable of being inadvertent, or, from the other side, by clenching jaws and making omissions with cold-blooded intent. The enforcement of flawless memory of this sort is in the nature of many kinds of sociability. It embodies what not only cannot but must not be remembered mistakenly. But when we shift to our historical mode in regard to memory, even memory aimed at answering historical questions that are clearly embedded in sociability, the wedding list/church program sort of memory is out of place, an encumbrance, and trivial. Such was the scene for a particularly passionate argument with Gram. Standards imposed by sociability battled with others. Decisions about the inclusion or exclusion of details were subject to different rules for the two of us.

Gram was a leader in establishing integrated public day care in Charleston. I put the story in the book's epilogue. The typescript I gave to Gram said that Charlestonians got together to care for the children of working mothers.

> Grandmother Fields will tell you, reeling off the names of the Charlestonian places from which people came to help—"Holy Communion Episcopal, Zion Olivet Presbyterian, Plymouth Congregational, to name those in the neighborhood, then St. Phillip's and St. Michael's, which are South of Broad, over toward the Battery, and, of course, Centenary, Old Bethel, and Wesley Methodist." Her list goes on. "And you know what?" she will go on, reeling off the name of pastors who came forward.

When Gram saw this, she got down to historical business. She checked with others in a position to know, and added, added, added. My epilogue absolutely would not do. It needed to mention Mrs. So and So, of Such and Such Street. It could not possibly be published without remembering Pastor This and That. "Why these are the people I have worked with for decades. They deserve the credit. These are the people who have been waiting to see my book, who put their names down to buy the first copies off the press." My rejoinder, that no one outside Charleston would care, did not count: The important audience was in Charleston. If the details got tedious to outsiders, well we couldn't help that. Gram's purpose assigned those details to what cannot, nay, must not be remembered mistakenly. My purpose consigned them to just as obligatory forgetting.[2]

These details are of a category familiar to scholars who try to reconstruct Africa's history using oral tradition. Gram's church-program memory (or anyone's) is an instance of ideologically tainted memory summoned in a view of present political purposes. Like that observed among African groups, it has the function of legitimizing and stabilizing a claim to some distinction. And part of its purpose is to perpetuate, by rendering it creditable to those concerned, a respectable consciousness of we-feeling. In that case memory "tainted" by interest is a dead-serious party to the creation of something true. The "mistakes" it may embody represent an imperfection only in light of the particular purposes scholarship has. Our scholarly effort to get the "real" past, not the true past required by a particular present, does not authorize us to disdain as simply mistaken this enormously consequential, creative, and everywhere visible operation of memory. It may be the case that human memory has it as a large-sized portion of its nature to be, in the psychologist Craig Barclay's splendid phrase, "true but not veridical."[3] Considerations of this sort carry us back to Nietzsche's identifying memory as a building block of sociability.

Returning again to our onions, however, we can take such considerations as a way of reminding ourselves of the biases scholarship requires us to adopt in our vocation to correct for bias in our data, and to select what is "significant" in terms of a given research program. In our dealings with informants, we constantly look beyond the encounter toward a scientific horizon where what matters is literal facticity, veracity, representativeness, general applicability, relationship to a set of questions generated by theory, and, above all, relevance in terms of a scheme that designates what we need—and what we do not need—to know, what needs to be remembered and what is legitimately forgotten.

Although I did try to compromise, I did not make all my grandmother's amendments, which she crammed into the margins, and which still spilled over onto extra pages—publishable remembering required their deliberate forgetting. On the other hand, I have kept them for our archive, well imagining some future historiographic predicament from which these names and places may provide a scholarly exit. Nonetheless, this action did not provide Gram an exit from her social predicament. It has troubled me ever since to reflect that preparing *Lemon Swamp* for publication required for me a certain condescension toward Gram and her compatriots.

This certain condescension was essentially no different from the systematic condescension toward the not-great with which we routinely tax documentary sources. I ask myself, now, how the church-list episode with Gram was different from what happened to my grandmother's great-great Uncle Thomas, who she said accompanied his owner's sons as their valet, when they were sent to Oxford to have the rough edges knocked off their "aristocratic" South Carolina slaveholders' upbringing. Having been taught by those boys during slavery, Thomas educated his own and others' children, in a clandestine school—English, Latin, Greek, and Hebrew, according to Gram. In consequence, Thomas' children were among those well-educated freedmen whom the missionary churches recruited to be leaders. Face to face with a remarkable set of facts, and trained to mistrust such claims, I deputized a friend, off to Oxford for studies, to find out what he could about slaves resident in the colleges in the 1830s or thereabouts. The answer: records of who lived where 150 years ago were scarce; names of servants residents with them were nonexistent—because irrelevant. What would have been the conceivable purpose of remembering one "Tom," who laundered the shirts of Masters So-and-So and Such-and-Such Middleton? Those details held no more interest then than somebody else's church-program list does for us now—or that Gram's list of Charleston luminaries in the day care movement has. Only a then unimaginable future historiography could make the names of slave servants resident at Oxford worth remembering. So while the contents of my grandmother's communication about her great-great Uncle Tom are rich and suggestive about a number of issues, Gram's communication could not be transformed into information.

I did, however, take one more stab at transforming Gram's story about Thomas Middleton into information about Charleston's past. The source for most of the stories about dead Middleton kin had been Anna Eliza Izzard, whom everyone called Cousin Lala. Lala had graduated from Avery Institute, a private high school for freedmen established by the American Missionary Association, and then from Claflin University, established by the Methodist Church. (One of Thomas' sons, J. B. Middleton, was among those recruited to Claflin's first Board of Trustees.) After earning her B.A., Lala established a private school at her parents' home in Short Court. There she taught "black history," part of which was family history, including the saga of Thomas. Now, sometime in the 1920s a black doctoral student named T. Horace Fitchett had come to Charleston to collect oral testimony from local black people. Gram told me he collected a great deal from Lala. Thereafter he had taught for many years at Howard University. Reasoning that his notes and papers might yield corroboration, I contacted Howard's Moorland Collection, and through it, his widow, Mrs. Fitchett, told me his papers would eventually be turned over, but that tragic circumstances at present made my consulting them impossible. Thus ended for purposes of the book my attempt either to make of Gram's story a bit of information or to discredit it as that. The historical fact that neither could be done appears in the next as the naming of Gram's sources—mainly Lala and a less distinct figure called "Aunt Jane." Therewith I abandoned a would-be "fact" on the less respectable territory, so far as scholarship is concerned, of mere communication.

But then, not long ago, I happened to read an essay that made me think further about this respectable territory of verifiable fact: "The Storyteller," by Walter Benjamin.[4] In it he observes that the main form communication takes in the modern world is that of information, a form which, in his words, "lays claim to prompt verifiability." He goes on to characterize this development, not as an advance, but as an impoverishment. Storytelling dies, he says, as this new form of communication arises. Storytelling's successor, information, represents an impoverishment because, and to the degree that, the producer of information accomplishes precisely what we scholars strive to do: namely, to induce some body of material to deliver up explanation of its own accord, without our adding anything to it. "But the finest stories," according to Benjamin, "are characterized by the lack of explanation." Because the hearer or reader is left to interpret according to his own understanding, "the narrative achieves an amplitude that information lacks." If it involves our own participation, achieving this "amplitude that information lacks" is precisely what we as researchers strive not to do. Therefore while we seek narrative from our informants, we are specifically precluded from handling it in such a way that it remains what it was at birth.

According to Benjamin, it is the nature of every real story to contain "openly or covertly, something useful." And the utilities of stories include "counsel." "Counsel," he goes on, "is less an answer to a question, than a proposal concerning the continuation of a story that is just unfolding. To seek this counsel one would first have to be able to tell the story. . . . Counsel woven into the fabric of real life is wisdom. The art of storytelling is reaching its end because the epic side of truth, wisdom, is dying out." Anyone who said in a conference on oral historical method that the researcher sought "wisdom" or "counsel" from his informants would, I believe, be met with stunned silence. We are usually free not to attend to these possible features of what we hear. But, when we exercise this freedom to disregard an inborn feature of what we encounter, what does this do to memory contained in it? What have we done, and what have we foregone, by carrying out surgery so as to put "fact" in a specimen bottle while throwing the unexamined rest of the body into the disposal unit?

My own freedom from the constraints of scholarship went along with unfreedom in this regard. Since the project of doing *Lemon Swamp* did not change the relationship of grandmother and granddaughter, the elements of "wisdom" and "counsel" were not ignorable and hidden, but explicit and obligatory. She was, after all, addressing the child of her child. Gram was didactic. My attempt to transform another of her communications into information, into something that laid claim to prompt verifiability, engendered another fight. In this case, the offending deed was to take a photograph of the Calhoun statue for inclusion in the book, offering readers thereby a kind of "proof" for an observation of Gram's, thus replicating the trip I made to see the object she referred to. Key points of the story were not verifiable, as I will now show. Let me start by quoting her on the subject of the statue of Senator John C. Calhoun, the indefatigable defender of slavery and states' rights.

> We hated all that Calhoun stood for. Our white city fathers wanted to keep what he stood for alive. So they named after him a street parallel to Broad—which, however, everybody kept on calling Boundary Street for a long time. And when I was a girl, they went further: they put up a life-size figure of John C. Calhoun preaching and stood it up on the Citadel Green, where it looked at you like another person in the park. Blacks took that statue personally. As you passed by, here was Calhoun looking you in the face and telling you, "Nigger, you may not be a slave, but I am back to see you stay in your place." The "niggers" didn't like it. Even the "nigger" children didn't like it. We used to carry something with us, if we knew we would be passing that way, in order to deface that statue—scratch up the coat, break the watch chain, try to knock of the nose—because he looked like he was telling you there was a place for "nigger" and "niggers" must stay there. Children and adults beat up John C. Calhoun so badly that the whites had to come back and put him up high, so we couldn't get to him. That's where he stands today, on a tall pedestal. He is so far away now until you can hardly tell what he looks like.[5]

The point of that story, made repeatedly in many different ways, was that even during the ascendance of Jim Crow, even when it appeared from the outside that black people had capitulated to their defeat, they resisted, even the children resisted. The counsel was, You resist, too. Be a worthy descendant of Thomas and J.B. and Lala and the others. You do it, too. "You do it, too" is not something we researchers are prepared to take seriously from informants. Indeed, this aspect of the narratives we hear for our scholarly purposes raises a danger flag marking bias, ideological special pleading, and the like. The flag marks a familiar site of mis-remembering, where the "should-have-been" displaces the "was," where wishes fill the blanks where facts are to be placed by dint of our own industry.

I proceeded with industry. I made myself conspicuous in the reading room of the Charleston Historical Society, depository of many documents pertaining to the past of a very historically conscious city. Conspicuous: because I, like other black people of southern heritage, still do not enter such formerly segregated places unself-consciously or unnoticed. I spent two days searching for "information." I expected or hoped to learn that "rowdy" members of the "coloured race" had vandalized this public work of art. Instead I learned something that prevented the facts from speaking for themselves, that pushed into a dead end my search for mere information. What I found out was much more interesting. It opened out instead of pinning down Gram's story.

It turns out that in 1854, the year Calhoun died, the Ladies' Calhoun Memorial Association began planning the memorial. In 1879, they were finally able to commission A. E. Harnisch of Philadelphia to execute a bronze statue of Calhoun on a Carolina granite pedestal, surrounded by allegorical figures—Truth, Justice, the Constitution, and History—at a cost of forty thousand dollars. But Harnisch in the end built the memorial with only one of the female figures—and she in such a state of disrobement that some of the ladies are said to have fainted at the unveiling. When the white folks recovered themselves sufficiently for straight thinking, they found historical fault with the clothing besides the aesthetic fault with the nakedness: Harnisch had put Calhoun into a Prince Albert coat, an anachronism. Black Charlestonians figured in the citywide uproar in a curious way. The public work of art began to be called, in Gullah syntax, "Calhoun and his wife." A newspaper article says, "Because of the female figure's state of disattire, the nickname greatly distressed the ladies of Charleston and Mrs. Calhoun who was still alive."

Besides, the statue's construction was poor, the pose bad, and "his right index finger pointed in a different direction from the others, a habit peculiar to him in speeches, but in this instance exaggerated to the point of deformity." The various discomfitures continued until 1895, when the *Charleston Post* was able to report that "the old statue which has so long been a thorn in the flesh of the ladies of the Calhoun Monument Association . . . to say nothing of the general public, will be taken down and consigned to oblivion." Massey Rhind of New York won the commission to execute Mr. Calhoun No. 2, erected in June 1896. No. 1 found his resting place in the Confederate Home Yard. A finger (it is not said which) was placed in the Charleston Museum. There ends the story obtainable at the Charleston Historical Society.

There is no mention of the oddly tall pillar that stands on top of the grand, wide conventional pedestal with its luxuriating scrolls at the corners and its dignified plaques of speeches on each side. No explanation is offered for the remarkable disproportion of line that the pillar creates nor for the fact that if you want to study Calhoun's features with your eye, or with that of a camera, you are interfered with by the sun and sky. Nothing I could find mentions certain Charlestonians' notice of the statues beyond the raucous Negro laughter implied by the nickname "Calhoun and he wife."

Gram and I fought about the picture I took of the statue. Innocently, I had intended it to illustrate her story. Gram said she would never have a picture of "that man" in her book. She was still passionate about a personage dead by then for nearly a century and a half. She intended, with malice aforethought, to exclude him from the list of guests—just as surely as the ladies society intended to include him on their own.

I have already devoted more time to topics regarding the color line than my grandmother would have approved of. I need to pause to say something about this fact. Gram would be the first to say that *Lemon Swamp* is about her own life: it is not about the racist system that partly enclosed it. Matters of race and color are a permanent presence without being her principal subject. They are constituent to life, but they do not define life. For example, Gram fondly remembers the details of her very fancy wedding—a black affair, from beginning to end—but yet notices that curious white people from the neighborhood slipped into Wesley Church's gallery silently to behold the occasion's splendor. On the other hand, when she decided to go to Boston to get her trousseau, and took the Clyde Line Ship, she did not at first remember whether it was segregated. The point was the adventure. She did not pay attention to where white people were on the ship. And in her story of the time she collided with a car driven by a white man, the initial subject had been proper dress, the motto mothers and aunts of all colors tell their nieces and daughters, "Dress, you never know." It turned out that she had thrown a coat atop her nightgown on the day of that accident. Her Aunt Harriet, severe exponent of "Dress, you never know," was proved right (such women usually are!) as Grandmother made her way through downtown offices after the accident. But the fact that all the officials were white and all the aftermath unfolded downtown, among "downtown white folks" colors for her in a distinctive way a comeuppance anyone could have had. I would call these features "involuntary memory," if the term had not already been filched from Proust and assigned a technical meaning. I use the term "unintended memory" instead, and I sometimes think it is also unintendable.

Even so, such features are often not the main subject of the story, from Gram's point of view. This point needs emphasizing because, as I continue exploring matters of race and color here, I acknowledge that these did not command Gram's front-burner attention as they do mine. They are there in the way Mt. Kilimanjaro is there in Africa. For many intents and purposes, it is *merely* there, rising to its snow-capped peaks over the luxuriant tropicality of the town of Moshi: it is hardly to be missed yet hardly to be noticed, at once native and alien to the life around it. Tourists are the ones who preoccupy themselves with looking at it. I am saying this to give warning that, as Gram's interlocutor, I was a tourist to her life with a tourist's habit of gawking. Gram criticized me more than once for my preoccupation. She called me "angry." Once she even called me "ugly" on the subject and asked, "What must those people be doing to you up there?" ("Up there" was Massachusetts at the time.) So I invite you to exercise methodological mistrust in my case, to be suspicious of the selections I have made in my own exercising of remembering. It is a fact that I cannot help gazing at Kilimanjaro.

The Kilimanjaro I gaze at, not always uncovered by clouds and mist, often comes into view in the form of unintended or unintendable memory. The inner horizon of the South's racial order is not the aspect we generally tend to think of first. It is easier to think of the South's Jim Crow regime in its outward and visible signs—its laws, its segregated spaces, its economic arrangements, its intermittent physical atrocities, and its civic iconography, items such as Calhoun's statue. But one learns through the testimony of inhabitants that it can at the same time be mapped out as an inward and invisible topography. It has objects analogous to mountains, rivers, and the like, which must be climbed, crossed, circumambulated, avoided, or otherwise taken into account. At the same time that these are not visible to the naked eye, and not immediately obvious to aliens on the scene, to insiders, much of the time, they are not specifically noteworthy. They remain, in the phrase of Harold Garfinkle, "seen but unnoticed" features of social life.[6] As such, they enter human memory. They often emerge in oral testimony as unintended memory. In actual life they emerge above all as social order.

Whenever we start from a remove in time and space, these topographical features begin to seem less substantial than they are. We tend to think of them as movable by a mere movement of thought. Consider, for example, the seventeenth-century English revolutionaries whom Christopher Hill describes in *The World Turned Upside Down.* These people embark on militant political projects by shaking and quaking, talking in tongues, and listening for the voice of prophecy. To us, they seem to be making a bizarre detour around a God present on the ground of ordinary experience that we nevertheless cannot see. To us, it seems there are more practical straight ahead routes. It is as thought we watch from above as human beings walk, as we might walk, across a flat heath. But, unlike us, they then turn to walk around what seems to us a nonexistent obstacle. Of course the obstacle is really there, unavoidably and materially there; but the knowledge of what it is, where it is, and *that* it is, they carry in memory.

The memory I am talking about is not the individual's own. It is instead the fruit of a collaboration among the inhabitants of a common social locale. Having said this much, I think I can avoid the troubling yet expressive term "collective memory,"[7] although I mean something like it. Or, rather, I mean to say that fundamental features of human memory are not grasped at the level of the isolated individual. Upbringing—or, to use my discipline's term, socialization—provides the context in which the human brain's, and mind's, imperfect capacity for memory develops. It is also a process by which human beings acquire things that cannot be remembered mistakenly. I want to present one example of this that emerged as unintended memory.

Last spring while I visited my grandmother, a middle-aged woman dropped by. This woman and her brother had been Gram's pupils on James Island. They started to reminisce about those school days over forty years ago. After a time, Gram spoke about the brother. What a fine, bright pupil he had been over the years. And very cute as a little fellow: his mother had liked to dress him in outfits with Peter Pan collars. And, oh, he was smart, he had a grand future because of his mind. The conversation seemed to be humming along in trivial sociability (generous recollections about someone's family being very good form), but then I heard my grandmother saying, "What they did to him was such a tragedy. How they could take that fine young man and put him in jail for all those years! How it broke his mother down!" They both shook their heads in commiseration. My antennae went up. When I finally got my question in between the head-shaking, the sister turned to me. "Well, he didn't do it. The other boy did it, but he never would admit, *never would admit,* so all those years my brother was in jail for what he did. He walked all around among us big as day, year in, year out, may he rot . . ." and so forth in that vein, the anger at the other boy coming alive again, boiling, and engulfing the English syntax. Well, what happened? "What happened: He never did ask for no drink of water, they said he sassed that white girl, talking about how he want some water, my brother ain't do that, know better than that. Ain't stop to ask that girl nothing'. That other boy did, and *my* brother went to jail, never would own up that *he* ask for that drink of water. My brother went to jail in place of him." In a rush of renewed emotion, the woman had arrived at an invisible mountain and begun to walk around it.

I piped up that neither one of them should have gone to jail twenty years over asking for a drink of water, not your brother and not the other boy either. If I hadn't seen the mountain yet, the awful way she looked up at me, and then ignored me, let me see it. I let further comment die in my mouth. I then saw what she saw, a black teenager who let his friend be convicted in his place. She did not see what I suddenly saw, a southern tableau: the impressionable white girl and her oppressive male kin (or perhaps the oppressive girl and her impressionable kin) enforcing an unjust etiquette of domination. A black young man did not ask a white young woman to address any sort of personal or bodily need. Her outrage at the wrong injustice revealed the Jim Crow order with an immediacy that intentional testimony never could. For this kind of unintended memory, I submit that cross-checking is redundant.

For those of us who try to glean from personal testimony the movement of history, as well as history's congealment in an order, what is interesting in the end is the ferment. We went to glean from people's recollection what territory remained unsubdued, perhaps unsubduable, by the Jim Crow regime's obligatory remembering. We want to find out when and how they come to note, and wonder at, the positively audacious presence of Kilimanjaro. Not accidentally, it is the domain of education that we find continuous evidence of such ferment and continuous guerrilla war, for education is about what we agree that the young should carry in their minds: what schoolbook lessons and what non-schoolbook lessons they should receive, about where they stand in the world and what that world is made of. In the 1950s, when the issue was desegregation, the guerrilla battles to fill the mind differently made the transition to conventional warfare.

But in the 1920s and 1930s, Gram's heyday, this fight proceeded in the South on a personal or local scale, underground, and hit and run. But I would maintain that the larger fight that later entered national awareness is inconceivable without it. On Tuesday night of this week, PBS's "MacNeil/Lehrer NewsHour" ended with one of its learned essays about national life. Roger Rosenblatt invited us to contemplate how Dwight D. Eisenhower, the "sleepy, conservative" president, surprised those who had elected him, by "launching the civil rights era." His memory could not have been more mistaken. The launching was done by the people whose business it was.

This launching was done not only by those who put their hand on the plow, and their eyes on the prize, in the 1940s and 1950s, but also by others who began long before that. Gram loved to tell the story of old Mrs. Burden, who lived on the same James Island where black people in a thousand ways were inculcated with the unjust etiquette I described. No doubt in many of those ways Mrs. Burden was inculcated, too. But as a military widow, she was collecting a pension, which meant that she had to collect her check from the downtown white powers-that-be. When Gram began to teach her pupils' parents and grandparents, Mrs. Burden made it her business, old as she was, to learn to sign her name. People asked her why she bothered and asked Gram why she bothered with a pupil so old. But Mrs. Burden kept on coming and brought the teacher, Gram said, "more eggs than the law allows." She was determined to be able to walk into that office of downtown white folks one day and sign for her pension properly. Mrs. Burden was after a schoolbook lesson, she was after a non-schoolbook lesson. She was determined to stop having to put herself down as "X." Gram said, "The day Mrs. Burden could go into that office and write 'Mrs. Samuel Burden,' she almost didn't need her walking stick." In fights as small-scale and personal as this one—the fight to be known by one's own name—the guerrilla war went on in the worst of times, blasting away bit by bit the invisible mountains of the Jim Crow South.

Let me close by saying that, during my time of liberation from scholarly constraint, Gram assigned me a part in a continuing guerilla war in which memory is not only a source of information about the past but also a force in creating the future. But, in a development that gave me many hours of methodological bad conscience, coming to grasp history in this immediately human sense involved departing from rules that define its incomparably paler counterpart, a mode of scientifically disciplined study. In the process, I had to think again about what this scientific discipline is for, what a present-day scholar's pursuit of knowledge is and is not, and after thinking again, to see how called-for modesty is about what it can add to civilization. What does inquiry disciplined by the ideals of science accomplish—if it is neither here nor there in terms of the growth of the individual, if it must by its nature remain silent, as my mentor Max Weber says, on the question What shall we do, and how shall we live?, if it paradoxically says that one way we shall live, as researchers, is according to an ethics of research that pertains to research and aught else, if it cuts through the flesh of human communication to expose for viewing an internal organ but marvels not at the act of surgery, if it is passionately committed to a search for truth that is not, cannot, and must not be a quest for wisdom?

None of this is meant to disparage the scientific model of knowledge; but it is meant to take note of the possibility that the very prestige of this model in an Age of Information may obscure what is particular and odd about it and thus obscure what vital tasks this mode of pursuing knowledge leaves undone, unconceived, perhaps even unconceivable. With this conundrum about method, I leave off speaking for myself and let the Polish poet Ceslaw Milosz say what I think I have come to understand.

> "To see" means not only to have before one's eyes. It may also mean to preserve in memory. "To see and to describe" may also mean to reconstruct in imagination. A distance achieved thanks to the mystery of time must not change events, landscapes, human figures into a tangle of shadows growing paler and paler. On the contrary, it can show them in full light, so that every event, every date becomes expressive and persists as an eternal reminder of human depravity and human greatness. Those who are alive receive a mandate from those who are silent forever. They can fulfill their duties only by trying to reconstruct precisely things as they were, and by wresting the past from fictions and legends.[8]

It is by trying to reconstruct things as they were by *all* means—those that partake in scientific method, and those that display the method's limits—that we fulfill our historic duties and, at the same time, fulfil our quintessentially human desire to know with nourishment worthy of it.

Notes

We are grateful for permission to print this paper to Professor Tom Charlton, organizer of the important conference of psychologists of memory and oral history at Baylor University, Texas, February 25–26, 1988, at which this paper was presented. The conference proceedings were published in Jaclyn Jeffrey and Glenace Edwall, eds., *Memory and History* (University Press of America, 1993).

1. Frederick Nietzsche, "Second Essay. 'Guilt,' 'Bad Conscience,' and the Like," in *The Genealogy of Morals: A Polemic,* trans. Horace B. Samuel (London, 1910), pp. 68ff.

2. I note in this connection that it is very good form in church-program memory to thank people for effort they did not expend—yet.

3. "Truth and Accuracy in Autobiographical Memory," in *Practical Aspect of Memory: Current Research and Issues,* vol. I, ed. M. M. Gruneberg, R. N. Sykes, and P. E. Morris (London).

4. Walter Benjamin, *Illuminations,* edited and with an introduction by Hannah Arendt, trans. Harry Zohn (New York, 1969), pp. 83–109.

5. Mamie Garvin Fields, *Lemon Swamp and Other Places: A Carolina Memoir* (New York, 1983), p. 57

6. Harold Garfinkle, *Studies in Ethnomusicology* (Englewood Cliffs, N.J., 1967)

7. I find this notion to be fascinatingly explored, in all its riches and some of its troublesomeness, in Bogumil Jewsiewicki, "Collective Memory and the Stakes of Power: Reading of Popular Zairian Historical Discourses," *History in Africa* 13 (1986), 195–223.

8. Ceslaw Milosz, Nobel lecture, December 8, 1980, Oslo, the Nobel Foundation, 1981.

10

History-Telling and Time: An Example from Kentucky

ALESSANDRO PORTELLI

A Multivocal Art

"History-telling" is a form of verbal art generated by the cultural and personal encounter in the context of fieldwork. It differs from more traditional forms of storytelling in narrative range, and in kind and degree of audience involvement. The narrative range is wider: prompted by the interviewer, the history-teller weaves personal recollections into a broader historical background, and is encouraged to expand the tale toward a full-sized oral autobiography in which the self-contained narrative units of anecdotes or tales are included in a more complex framework. In terms of audience involvement, while all oral speech acts and verbal arts imply a degree of interaction, history-telling differs in several respects.

First, the interviewer is not usually a member of the speaker's immediate circle. Thus, mutual discovery is intrinsic to history-telling: the interviewer tries to learn the history of the interviewee, while the interviewee tries to figure out who the interviewer is, and how to deal with her, or him.

Second, the interviewer is an especially active listener. Not only has he/she created the history-telling situation, but he/she shapes it by asking questions which are much more directive than the antiphonal audience reactions of traditional storytelling. Often, in fact, the interviewer will pose unexpected questions, encouraging the history-teller to explore new areas of experience, or to verbalize explicitly what is taken for granted and remains unsaid when speaking to members of the immediate community. A good interviewer facilitates the history-teller's overall strategy, but a good history-teller subtly shapes the tale according to the presence and manner of the interviewer. To a degree much higher than other oral verbal arts, history-telling is a multi-authored, multivocal genre.

Third, storytelling is a direct tapping of existing, outcropping memory; history-telling, as a cooperative effort between several narrators or between them and the interviewer, is an attempt to *reconstruct* memory. Thus, in a history-telling situation, listeners will prompt the principal narrator's memory ("tell him about the time when you . . .") or take narrative turns themselves in order to achieve a more complete reconstruction of the group's memory (as is the case, for instance, in *Black Elk Speaks,* in which the protagonist's narrative is occasionally supplemented by those of his friends).[1] While storytelling is largely an end in itself, history-telling is finalized to the production of an artifact (a tape) and eventually a text. These differences result in a diversified use of space: rather than the single speaker facing a circle of listeners, history-telling is done in a face-to-face exchange between narrator and interviewer or, alternatively, a circle of narrators facing a usually lone listener/interviewer across a space mediated by the strategic placement of a microphone. Therefore, while memory is the stuff of both storytelling and history-telling, the latter is also specifically *about* memory. The spaces and times of history-telling sessions, therefore, are in themselves *lieux de mémoire.*

"You're free to tape jus' what you want"

In this essay I will use as my text one interview in which two narrators—a man and a woman—tell about life from the 1930s to the present in the coalfields of Harlan County, Kentucky. These Kentuckians tell their story with a wealth of detail and an extraordinary command of personal style and skill of language. Oral history is usually keen to frame individual stories in the collective discourse which is "history." But by concentrating on a single interview, I hope to show that an oral personal narrative can achieve levels of structural complexity comparable to those of literary texts, and can therefore stand the close individual analysis we usually devote to written literature.

I sought out Reverend Hugh Cowans and his wife, Julia Cowans, in Lexington, Kentucky, in October 1983, because friends at the Highlander Center for Social Research told me they were both very fine speakers, singers, and organizers for the union and the civil rights movement. Reverend Cowans had worked many years in the coal mines of Kentucky and Virginia, until he lost his sight from the consequences of an old war wound; a few years later, he received the call to preach. I went to see them on a Sunday afternoon. They lived in a nice house in a middle-class area (they were the only black family I saw on the block; they have since moved back downtown). At least three generations of children, grandchildren, and great-grandchildren kept coming and going through the living room. Also, my wife and another woman, a student/colleague from the University of Rome, were with me. The context was halfway between a formal interview and a social visit, culminating in a dinner of fried chicken.

This was my first interview in the Appalachian project, so I was there to listen rather than to assert a specific agenda of questions I wanted to ask. So it was Reverend Cowans who asked the first question: "You in the United Mine Workers?" After I explained that I was a union member back home, the history-telling could begin.

> Now, you all. Now you're free to tape jus' what you want. I mean. First of all, I mean, you know, I'll just let you know my name. My name is Reverend Hugh Cowans, Junior, and I reside at 3753 Marriot Drive. And, you have come for information and I'll readily give it to you. Now back in the 'thirties when I started in the coal mines. I was nothin' but a boy. I had't reached my, I had not reached my thirteenth birthday—fourteenth birthday, rather—you know, because, at that time, you could go in the mines, they'd take you at any age.[2]

Reverend Cowans went on for about forty-five minutes, without pauses or interruptions; the conversation then lasted all afternoon. The monologic form of the first section was shaped by several factors: Reverend Cowans's experience of public speaking as a preacher and organizer; his blindness, which made it easier for him to abstract himself from his listeners; and the fact that we, as interviewers, did not yet ask any interrupting questions. He delivered, then, what was largely a set piece, a public performance, which developed into a more personal dialogue only after his wife entered the conversation.

In his opening monologue, Reverend Cowans told the story of his life not, however, in linear fashion, but cyclically, shuttling twice back and forth from "back in the 'thirties" to the present, and breaking the second cycle into two very distinct sections—before and after he quit work in the mines. His speech may thus be divided in sections in which shifts in the handling of time and narrative form designate shifting layers of personal experience; his story moved from public history rendered in the third person to more personal biograpy rendered in the first person.

History-Telling and Narrative Modes

In earlier articles, I have described these *modes* of "history-telling," that is, three ways of organizing historical narrative in terms of point of view, social referents, and space referents:

1. *Institutional*
   - social referent: politics and ideology; government, parties, unions, elections, etc.
   - space referent: the nation, the state
   - point of view: third person, impersonal
2. *Collective*
   - social referent: the community, the neighborhood, the job; strikes, natural catastrophes, rituals; collective participation in the institutional level
   - space referent: the town, the neighborhood, the workplace
   - point of view: first-person plural
3. *Personal*
   - social referent: private and family life; the life cycle (births, marriages, jobs, children, deaths); personal involvement in the two other levels
   - space referent: the home
   - point of view: first-person singular.[3]

These modes are never totally and explicitly separate, or separable, in oral history narrative; in fact, history-telling is precisely the art of combining the modes into meaningful patterns. Also, their characteristics are more a matter of tendency than of norm: each history-telling event is unique and creates its own style and grammar. We may, however, use these categories as a map to orient ourselves in the analysis.

Each of the three sections of Reverend Cowans's opening narrative is controlled by a different mode: first the institutional, then the communal, and finally the personal, with frequent overlappings but with a recognizable overall pattern. As we listen to the first section, we can see that it is dominated by the impersonal pronouns and iterative verbal forms of the institutional mode:

> And you worked under all kinds of oppressive conditions. I mean, no organized labor and they had gun thugs. Now what we mean by that, they would go to the high sheriff of the county. He would deputize 'em, and then the company would pay their salary. That was in ordinance to keep United Mine Workers OUT.

The iterative form ("they would go") and the impersonal pronouns ("they," "you") designate a general and lasting condition. First-person pronouns and singulative verbs are introduced in anecdotes intended as examples of this broader situation; the narrator then quickly reverts to the impersonal iterative:

> And if you joined it, they would come in and beat your head and throw your family outdoors and throw you off the job and everything. I remember once on the job that they had my uncle to pull 'is britches down and they whipped 'im right before my face. And if you had to lay off, you had to lay off in the mines, they didn't allow you to lay off at home.

The social referent is the union as political institution, with emphasis on the leadership. Reverend Cowans begins by associating himself with the top leaders—"And we were glad when John L. Lewis came along and God sent the man along in, uh, '37–'38 because I was instrumental in the drive, I was one of the leaders of that organization"—and ends with a discussion of the current leadership crisis, in the union and in the country:

> I'm sorry that all o' this corruptness come about in the organization, but that happens everywhere, you can look at Washington right now. The chief of corruption is right there. And some of it sprung from the Oval Office . . . And I feel sorry for our president Rich Trumka . . . And I don't know what is going to happen 'cause when Reagan taken office, he went in bustin' union . . . I mean, all he cares about is the rich, ya' understand? And, we are at, roughly, a deep-end. It's just about to go over it. If God don't help us, I mean, we're sold out.

Having reached the present, Reverend Cowans goes back to the beginning and tells his story all over again in the very next sentence. But he now shifts to the first-person point of view: "I have gone in the mines now, I want you to hear this good." He uses the first person consistently from now on, and soon shifts also from iterative synthesis to linear narrative ("Going on forward, I have many things happen to me") and to singulative verbs: "I had left Harlan County where I was instrumental in organizing . . . Left Harlan in '40, and I went to Gary, West Virginia, June—oh, I don't exactly—June 1940. And I started driving mules in the mine."

This second section is an interesting combination of the communal and personal modes. In fact, while Reverend Cowans uses the first-person pronoun of the personal mode, the space and social referents are those of the communal mode: the union local, the workplace. While the first cycle was the story of how the union changed the coal mines, the second section is the story of a representative working life. By combining the two modes, Reverend Cowans manages to project his own image as a *representative* man. He is a representative worker who shares the experiences of others like him and knows his job: "I said I could do anything around [a coal mine]—and could. I could help on 'lectricity, I said I could lay track, I can timber, I said I can help on the motor, machine, anything you have to." And, as an organizer in the union, he is also an institutional representative of the collectivity of the miners. This section, in fact, includes a variant of the typical standing-up-to-the-boss story which recurs in stories or organizers and celebrated working men.[4] And again he brings it up to the present by comparing the ethnic composition of the work force in the mines of the thirties and the situation there today.

So far, the working life had dominated the narrative. We have seen that he begins the story of his life—as many working-class narrators do—not with the day he was born but with the day he started in the mines.[5] Symmetrically, the second section ends with "the last shift of work I performed was August 31, 1956." In the third section, although the narrative goes forward in chronological terms, the mode shifts dramatically. As he tells about losing his sight, leaving the mines, haggling with the Veterans Administration, being called to preach, Reverend Cowans no longer tells a story of political and union struggles, but one of intense personal struggle for identity and survival. Now the story is no longer about John L. Lewis, Ronald Reagan, or the mine management, but about his eyes and his God:

> And from then I kept moving and I had not accepted my callin' in the ministry. But eventually the Lord bear down so heavy. And I, just one day backed in—that was in '60—I just backed my automobile in the driveway. And the doctors always did predict I'd lose my sight. I just backed my automobile in the driveway and woke up the next morning blind as a bat. But the Lord has been good to me. He brought us thus far.

The space referents again shift toward the personal mode: the hospital, a very important space in personal narratives; and the home: "We lived in a house in Harlan. It was a rent house." Symmetrically, the stories of confrontation no longer deal with bosses, but with landladies.

"Now, I don't want you preachin' "

"And this is where we are today," Reverend Cowans concluded for the third time. And he passed on the floor to his wife: "Is that right, baby? That's right. And she know because she was raised up on the coal cabin. She may have something she might wanna add. Do you have something, baby, you might wanna add?"

This, in fact, is where I asked my first interruptive question—mentioning that I had heard that they had met for the first time when they were on opposite sides of a picket line. So Reverend Cowans resumed the floor to tell that story, and again asked, "Do you have, do you wanna say anything?" "Well, not really," Mrs. Cowans replied, but then she took over and spoke for almost thirty minutes.

> I mean, I, I was born and raised by there in Cardinal, Kentucky, down South, up in the mountains there, Bell County. That's the only life, you know, that I knew was coal mining. My father, grandfather, great-grandfather—they were all coal miners. And, as my husband said, when I was growing up, the coal mining was just very bad. You didn't really live, you just existed, just existed.

Mrs. Cowans's time and space referents are different from her husband's. Her life story does not begin with getting a job but with being born; and in her narrative there is no break comparable to the "last shift" of work. In her experience, life and working life are never totally distinct: she was never formally employed outside the home and, symmetrically, she is never unemployed, even in her old age, inside the home. Even in her old age, she is helping to raise more than one generation of grandchildren. Her only outside work was housework, a continuation of what she did inside:

> Fourteen years old, I had to come out o' school and take care of my mother, my four sisters and brothers. And you know I wasn't trained for anything, all domestic, you know. I knew how to keep house. And that's how I took care of my mother, my sisters and brothers—on my knees, scrubbing floors, climbing walls, just whatever I could do. And I worked all day long for one dollar. One dollar. I mean I worked all day long.

In this part of her narrative, however, the mode is communal rather than personal, and the space referent is the town rather than the home. She did not volunteer (and we did not feel confident enough to ask) much information about children and marriages: partly because we were strangers, but also because of her husband's presence. When interviewed alone, five years later, she was much more open about these topics. Also, she understood our approach to be social and political, rather than personal, and felt she was also giving us what she thought we wanted, as well as staying on safer ground. The coal camp had been absent from her husband's story: his community was the workplace, not the town. Thus the male–female symmetry of space referents in this interview followed the division of experiences in the mining community, where the men spent most of the time underground, while the women had to deal with the outside world. According to Mrs. Cowans,

> My mother would send me to the store, you know, the grocery and I never remember axing for but a dollar. One dollar. I've never gone to the window say two dollars, three, five dollars . . . Whatever you had to have, you go to that company store and buy it. You did not leave off of that company property, to go to the next town to buy anything and bring it back in there. No, you didn't do that. And that kept the persons more or less, especially if you had a family of any size, that kept you in debt, all the time, you know, you just stayed in debt. Work a lifetime and be in debt to the company, you know; and some of the old coral camps, they had fences. They had guards to let you in there and guards to let you out . . . Like a concentration camp or something . . . And we grew up under those conditions.

Her description of the coal camp, however, is also a way of explaining why she had been on the other side, throwing rocks at the union pickets, when they met. While her husband uses personal stories as examples of a general condition, she uses the communal background to make sense of her personal behavior: she threw rocks at the picket because the employers' power extended to the control of what their workers knew and believed.

> Whatever the company officials said, that was the law . . . And all we knew was they were comin' to stop the men from workin', you know. That's all we knew about it. And so I used to get a bunch of kids and we'd line up and get us a pile o' rocks and we'd see them comin' and we start throwin' rocks at 'em, you know.

When she recalled having to seek outside domestic work, she explained that "there were no human resources, no welfare, no nothing in Kentucky, that I know about, at that time." Her narration was, indeed, much closer to the form of history-telling that I was looking for: it was making politics and social conditions come alive through their impact on individual lives.

From this moment on, Mrs. Cowans was firmly in command of the conversation. She delegated to her husband—to whom she deferred openly and sincerely—all discourse in the institutional mode, either by giving him the floor or by telling stories in which he played the central role. On the other hand, she successfully resisted her husband's attempt to regain control of the general drift of discourse. She allowed him to interrupt her, and frequently invited him to speak, yet retained discursive control: it was she who prompted his memory, suggested topics and episodes, and managed the timing and form his contributions:

> REV. COWANS: Baby, let me say somethin'.
> MRS. COWANS: Now, I don't want you preachin'; lemme hear.
> REV. COWANS: I'm not gonna preach. I just wanna tell ya . . .

In this, she was also helped by the fact that we, as interviewers, were much more responsive to her approach and encouraged it by our occasional questions. The result is a much more multivocal, interactive discourse in which all participants take a creative and explicit role.

Place of Memory

In this multivocal discourse, the handling of time becomes more erratic than in the two monologues. Rather than the earlier combination of cyclical and linear structures, we find a free flow of achronological associations. This is, in fact, the more frequent form in oral history interviews, determined by the interplay of the structure of memory and the dialogue situation.

In memory, time becomes "space": all the recollected past exists simultaneously in the same "place." Speakers therefore may tend to arrange events along paradigmatic lines of similarity rather than along syntagmatic lines of chronological sequence. From the strike of 1939, Mrs. Cowans shifted to the Brookside strike of 1973, and Reverend Cowans associated the 1938 union drive to the national miners' strike of 1978.

A more complex form is the multivocal association generated by the interaction of different speakers in conversation. In a typical sequence, a story told by Reverend Cowans about a speech he made in Detroit prompted me to ask him a question about preaching, which in turn unleashed a reminiscence of childhood on an Alabama plantation: "And you see, to make a good minister, you got to bring things to people's remembrance. I remember that now and then that when we worked on the farm and [were] boys down there—you had to go to the plantation owner. . . ." The story thus begun evolved into a sermon fragment, which drifts into a speech on civil rights and then stories about his work in the movement. At this point Mrs. Cowans is reminded of other powerful speeches he made and takes us all the way back to the Detroit speech we had started out with.

In all this free association, however, an underlying structure remains unchanged: the vision of history as a contrast between a generalized "then" and a generalized "now." The watershed between these two epochs is the rise of the union in the coalfields: the past is "before they became organized." Stories about the rising of the union—the organizing drive of 1938, the dramatic strike of 1939—are, therefore, pivotal to the whole structure of the conversation, and both narrators keep going back to them. We might define these events as "sites of memory," and their significance as such is also revealed by the formal organization of the narrative. In the stories about these watershed events all modes—institutional, communal, personal—come together, as if all meanings converged there. The first-person point of view, the communal space referent of town and workplace, the institutional social referent of union and government—all intermingle in Reverend Cowans's story of the union drive: "They [the union] came and the first mass meeting we had was at Verda, Kentucky. That's where I worked." All three pronominal forms—"they," "we," "I"—are concentrated in this opening clause. He then goes on:

> It was a fellow called Chester Smith. He had a large pasture out there and he built a flat for 'em and we had many speeches. And we would go and try to get individuals to sign a check-off slip. That was in ordinance to set up a local. And you'd crawl, and I'd crawl up in men's places [in the mine] on my knees and beg them to sign the cut-off slip. And they would cuss me out. But eventually . . . we were victorious, after I guess you can recall—when Mr. John L. Lewis had gone into Washington, that time.

Mrs. Cowans also tells about those times, weaving the personal mode (mother and home) together with the communal (the miners, the town) and the institutional (the National Guard, the governor):

> You jus' certainly wouldn't believe it . . . but before they got organized . . . Harlan County blood ran like water. Many a man lost their lives . . . and, oh, they were slaughtered like hogs. I remember right there in Cardinal, baby, when governor Chandler, Happy Chandler, sent those tin horns [National Guard] in 'ere to guard those, what they call scabs, in the mine and out. My mother used to take in washings and ironing. And she did they laundry, you know . . . my mother used to do the laundry for these soldiers that were there. . . .

The pivotal function of this "site of memory" is shown by the fact that this is where the narrative becomes most movingly bivocal. Both narrators take the floor, swapping tales back and forth, reinforcing each other's testimony with converging points of view. "I faced the machine guns that morning," Reverend Cowans breaks in.

> You see, we had a women's local in Carney, Kentucky. And their sons was manning the machine guns. And we went for them. And they came down the road with clubs in their hands singing "Amazing Grace" and all o' these spiritual songs. And one woman looked up from singin' her songs and she said, "What you doing up there?" . . . And she got him off that machine gun. . . .

After he has told this story, he gives the floor back to his wife: "Sorry, I just wanted to—Go ahead." As she resumes, the story connects back to her early antiunion days and forward to the women's role in the Brookside strike of the seventies:

> And we had women picket lines. I gone on a picket line after, you know, growing and knowing what this was all about . . . And we takin' coffee and doughnuts to the men—you know about this Brookside episode, that Brookside deal. Well, we were just about three miles above this at that time.

"There's always gon' be a line"

In many oral history narratives, all modes converge not only on pivotal events but also on crucial themes. War, for instance, has such a total impact that it can be narrated in all modes: "Mussolini ruined the country" (institutional); "our town was destroyed" (communal); "I lost a son" (personal). In the Cowanses' interview, all modes converged on another pervasive theme: race.

In Reverend Cowans's opening monologue, each section contains a reference to racial discrimination. The first occurs when he is describing the impact of unionism: it is a personal anecdote, told in the framework of the political, institutional discourse.

> My father, he's passed and gone now, he told me, says, uh, "You're crazy to go on those picket lines. You'll get killed." He said, "It's not going to benefit anybody but the white man." I says, "Well, I know it will benefit him more than it benefits me, but I see some good in that for you and I see some in it for me. In you' old age I see, I see medical benefits, I see retirement, and everything, I says, although, I said I know that it is discriminatory practice in it but it's better than what we have working in those water holes and slave condition. And, sure enough, when he reached the age of retirement, he had medical benefits. He died drawing his pension. Now I've lived up to the age where I draw my pension. And there's nothin' better than United Mine Workers.

At the end of the second section, the reconstruction of his working life, Reverend Cowans takes time for another comparison between "then" and "now." This time, it has to do with the presence of blacks in the communal space of the workplace:

> Now if you were black, back—when I went in the mines and there was stevedore work, you got your job. All the man wanted to know [was]: if you were black, you get a job. If you were white you probably were layin' track or you were running a motor. Very few blacks operated the motors then. They, if you worked on a motor at all, you had to be a brakeman. And my father, he was a machine operator. And they would put whites with him to learn him how to operate the machines and after he learned them, then he was subject to be fired . . . And, when the mantrip[6] used to run, y'all believe it or not, the mantrip looked like a bunch o' blackbirds. But now when it run, it look like a flock of geese, white. You might see one black in there that looks like a fly.

Reverend Cowans concludes his speech with a final reference to racism, which stresses again the political approach, and an optimistic view in the "then" and "now" framework: "But now although there is prejudice within the ranks of the United Mine Workers, but here is the best thing for the working man in the mine because all of these issues can be straightened out and it is somewhat better now than it was a long time ago." Throughout his performance, Reverend Cowans never discusses the impact of racism on his own life and personal feelings. Only later, after his wife has shifted the mode, he tells a story with a personal space referent, about a white lady who refused to rent to them when she found out they were black.

When Mrs. Cowans begins to speak, she shifts the discourse on race from the institutional to the personal mode, from politics to feelings. At first, she also speaks in rather abstract terms, about the KKK, divisions in the civil rights movement and in the black community, the NAACP. Then, a sudden change of pace: "And we've been—I'll tell you another thing. We've been—'we' as a race—we been oppressed." The change is palpable also on the linguistic plane, in the shift from the standard English "we've been" to the black English "we been." As she goes on to describe the discrimination and exclusion of black people in Harlan County, and her struggle, with her husband, against these conditions, the communal forms and referents are animated by a deeply personal urgency of feelings, revealed by the gushing of words and the intensity of her tone:

> And I'll be da—— . . . And if I have to die for standing up for what I believe in, that's just the way it'll be. 'Cause fear if, if—see, that's what it's about anyhow, they rule you with fear, that's what they did to us—threats and fears . . . 'Cause I, I, I, I would rather be dead than to live under the oppressive condi——I don't want my children and grandchildren to come under what I did, what I had to come through.

Finally, as if making another conscious decision to escalate, she touches where it hurts most, at the very personal level of sexual politics, of lynching, miscegenation, the white fear of rape. "And I'll tell you anytime . . . anytime, that they wanted to have to have trouble, bring trouble with the minorities, they'd use a black man and a white woman." Referring to a nephew of hers who is involved with a white girl, she says:

> I told 'em at, a meeting, I said, now, I'll tell ya right now, if you think you prejudiced, I said, you just meetin' prejudiced. That's 'cause I don't want my daughter to marry your son any more than you want you son to marry my daughter . . . I said, that's just the way I'm raised. I'm, I'm black. God didn't make no mistake when he made me, I said. I didn't make myself. He made me what he wanted me to be . . . But now I'm telling you, I don't want my son to have your daughter any more than you want your daughter to have my son . . . I said, ain't nobody gonna drag my son or my daughter out, like they have done and, and, and hang them or whatever. I said, have been a time that this happened, didn't nobody die but black. I said, but, brother, you better believe that if they bury somebody black, they gonna bury somebody white. I said, you'd better believe that.

This rugged speech about a dramatic confrontation and the horror of lynching is a long way from the blandly optimistic view of evolving race relations in the union. This progression, from the institutional to the personal mode, is shaped to a large extent by another factor: the interpersonal authorship of history-telling. Race is not only a pervasive element in the black experience, but is also a very touchy subject when black history-tellers are interviewed by white historians. The formulaic "I'll tell you," which marks each new step in Mrs. Cowans's narrative, signals also a new step in the relationship—as if she had decided either that she could talk to us or that certain things needed to be told anyway. In the passage in which Mrs. Cowans confronted her deepest feelings toward white people, the historical discourse mingled with an implicit statement about the interview:

> My grandma they, they—she was a daughter of—s-s-slaves. Her parents were slaves. And they used to sit around and tell things, you know, that happened when they were children and what they parents said. And I'll tell

you what that will do for you: although you might not have done a thing in this world to me, but because you're white, of what my parents said . . . I don't trust you, you know. And so for being misused by a white person, I've never been. But I've seen conditions of others, you know—[of] blacks as a whole. So I was raised; my grandmother always told us I don't care what nobody say, I don't care how good they look, how good they talk, you gonna always be black. There's gonna always be a line.

"I don't trust you." She is ostensibly, and perhaps intentionally, speaking in general terms, using the impersonal "you." But I could not help feeling that this broad, political mode was indissolubly twined with a very personal, immediate mode. She was talking in general, but she was also talking to me.

Several passages later in the conversation, Mrs. Cowans endeavored to attenuate the impact of this statement by historicizing it. "So, that's what I had in mind all of my life. O.K., but as you live, time changes, see. . . ." "And so when God changed my heart toward a lot of things, then I could see better. And learn to just love people because you're you, not because you black." During my second visit five years later, she was hospitable, talkative, eloquent. But it was said, it remained said, and it was the most important lesson I learned that day.

One part of the lesson was political: why, indeed, should she trust me, just because I may have acted and spoken nicely and sympathetically? As a character in Toni Morrison's *Beloved* puts it, "Nothing in the world more dangerous than a white schoolteacher."[7] There's gonna always be a line, Mrs. Cowans said: it takes more than goodwill and good manners to overcome the historical barrier between blacks and whites—and I had learned from Richard Wright's Mary Dalton that it is not up to me to decide when I can be allowed to step across. Perhaps one reason for her relative openness may have been, indeed, that we showed no inclination to invade her territory.

Another part of the lesson was methodological. The concept of "line" is intimately related to writing, and thus evokes the fact that my own role in the multiauthored and multivocal enterprise begun with Reverend and Mrs. Cowans's narrative was to write it down, turning history-telling into "oral history" and literary text, which can be distanced from the original narrators and performers. On the one hand, the line is also a class line (between the coal miner's wife and the intellectual); on the other, it stands as the boundary between orality and writing: a written trace of the absence of the voice. Indeed, the polysemous word "line" connects the very concept of geographical and social boundaries in a primary reference to writing. For instance, in an essay on resistance to enclosures in South Africa, Isabel Hofmeyr demonstrates that "fencing . . . has a number of cultural functions that are not unrelated to the preconceptions of literacy":

Fences, for example, "write" certain forms of authority into the countryside, and by representing the thin, fixed line of the boundary in the earth, they imprint the textual world of maps, treaties, and surveying on the landscape. While oral or, more precisely, paraliterate societies obviously recognize and

> mark boundaries, these are always fluid and have none of the fixity of the pencil-thin boundary of the sheer, narrow fence. Since boundaries are never rigid and, in any event, have to be accommodated to the character of the landscape, they are always subject to some form of negotiation.[8]

Thus the interplay of line as metaphor and line as writing points to a complex question of representation: the braiding of "artificiality" and "reality." Ultimately, the line itself becomes a physical *lieu de mémoire.* On the map, the Kentucky–Tennessee "line" just southwest of Harlan County across Cumberland Gap looks just as if someone had penned a straight line across uncharted territory; but on the other side of the county, the Kentucky–Virginia border follows the winding "natural" outline of the mountain ridges. By now, the "written" Tennessee line is no less real than the physical Virginia line: history has its own way of making the artificial real. This also applies to Mrs. Cowans's "line": "You don't even be aware of this prejudice," she said, " 'till you become a certain age and the parents go to separatin', you know"; but because this line is artificial, there's no reason to pretend it isn't there. As W. E. B. Du Bois put it long ago, "The problem of the twentieth century is the problem of the color line," and it's still with us.

One of the clichés of fieldwork is that the interviewer must endeavor to win the confidence and trust of the interviewee, and to a certain extent, this happened also in our encounter with the Cowanses. But the plural authorship of history-telling requires a plurality of subjects, and therefore a degree of difference. Thus, much of the eloquence and drama of the interview was generated precisely by the awareness of the distance and difference which still stood between us. When Mrs. Cowans said "I don't trust you," in one breath she both drew and erased the line; as she declared her inability to overcome the line, by recognizing it openly she was already speaking across it.

Notes

A different, shorter version of this essay originally appeared in *The Oral History Review,* 20, nos. 1–2 (Spring–Fall 1992), 51–66.

1. *Black Elk Speaks* (1932), as told through John G. Neihardt (Lincoln: University of Nebraska Press, 1979); Arnold Krupat (*The Voice in the Margin* [Berkeley: University of California Press, 1989], 159–60) notes that this is a common practice in Native American oral narration.

2. The interview is quoted here as transcribed by Ms. Julia Hairston.

3. See "The Death of Luigi Trastulli: Memory and the Event," and " 'The Time of My Life': Functions of Time in Oral History," both in A. Portelli, *The Death of Luigi Trastulli and Other Stories: Form and Meaning in Oral History* (Albany: State University of New York Press, 1991); also relevant is "Form and Meaning of Historical Representation: The Battle of Evarts and the Battle of Crummies, Harlan County, Kentucky, 1931–1941," lecture presented at the European Oral History Conference, Essen, Germany, March 1990, to be published in the conference proceedings, forthcoming.

4. See "Life and Times of Valtéro Peppoloni, Worker," in *The Death of Luigi Trastulli,* for several stories of this kind told by Italian steelworkers.

5. For another Harlan County example, compare this excerpt from an interview with Mr. James Hall, a black miner from Lynch, Kentucky: "I went into the mines when I was sixteen years old." "What year were you born in?" "I was born in 1917. When I went in the mine. . . ."

6. The mantrip is a vehicle which carries miners into the mine.

7. Toni Morrison, *Beloved* (London: Picador, 1988), 266.

8. Isabel Hofmeyr, " ' 'Nterata'\'The Wire': Fences, Boundaries, Orality, Literacy," *International Journal of Oral History* 11 (1990), 69–91. An example of "fluid" boundaries in paraliterate societies is found in the case related by Harlan County lawyer Sidney Douglass of the land deeds in which the boundary between two properties is marked by "a snowbank," which obviously melts in the summer; interview with Sidney Douglass, Harlan County, Kentucky, July 13, 1987.

11

Memory and Mass Culture

SUSAN WILLIS

The relationship of history and memory to African-American life cannot be fully addressed today without confronting the influence of mass culture. In the United States, the nineties marked the burgeoning of an African-American presence throughout the media. Rap is everywhere. Cars pulse and throb through the suburbs to its rhythms, rendered all the more effective with the windows rolled up. Rap-inspired music dominates the pop charts, making it acceptable for white teenybopper consumption. Meanwhile, campus radicals debate the politics of Public Enemy, Ice-T, and the notorious 2-Live Crew. Rap monologues are even used in TV and radio commercials for everything from furniture to toothpaste.

Television programing as a whole has opened itself up to African-American actors, styles, and language. Where some fifteen or twenty years ago television shows occasionally featured a singular black character, such as Uhuru in "Star Trek," black actors today have become an all but mandatory feature in TV's weekly diet of cop thrillers, dramatic series, and family, slice-of-life sitcoms. Not surprisingly, the controversial series "In Living Color" recently presented its take on "Star Trek." The skit held Captain Kirk up to ridicule for his privileged indulgence in authority over a diverse crew whose multiethnicity was the basis for each member's subservient position.

As TV and radio have given way to an expanding black cultural presence, so too have the newsstands. Where *Ebony* was once an anomaly on the magazine rack of white fashion trends and life-styles, there are now many new black magazines, each corresponding to a particular marketing niche in the black community. One of these is the up-tempo magazine *Young Brothers and Sisters,* intended for the adolescent and young teen reader/consumer, whose horoscopes urge black youths to get part-time and after-school jobs in order to buy all the things advertised on the pages of the magazine.

The influx of African-American participation in the media and in mainstream American mass culture represents a striking change for a country that less than thirty years ago tried to maintain the separate but (un)equal status of black Americans. My intent here is not to undermine the significant gains that entry into the media mainstream includes. Nor do I want to lose sight of the consequences that ethnic diversity has for white Americans who may have been schooled to think that reality was the world of the primer that Toni Morrison deconstructs on the first page of *The Bluest Eye*. Nevertheless, I want to pose some difficult questions about the relationship of African-American culture to the mass-culture industry. None of what follows will be definitive, nor will there even be tentative answers. The field of cultural studies, which is my academic base, is itself in formation; it stands to gain from raising issues, exploring possibilities, and posing—rather than answering—questions. The intersection of cultural studies and African-American studies ought not be foreclosed by definitive statements, but allowed to give shape to the practice of interdisciplinary inquiry.

The central question is whether or not mass culture provides a site for the recovery of history and the expression of cultural memories. Put another way, does mass culture offer African Americans (or, for that matter, any disenfranchised group) a means for preserving cultural practices and the group's history over time as these were once preserved and conveyed in folk culture and oral traditions? I want to suggest some distinctions that I use as a way of conceptualizing the difference between folk culture, popular culture, and mass culture. Basically speaking, these are historical categories. Each articulates a different relationship to the mode of production. While history doesn't fall into neat periods and there is much interplay among these cultural forms, folk culture largely pertains to the precapitalist world, an agrarian or tribal mode of production, and all the traditional cultural objects and practices that enhanced people's spiritual and secular lives. By comparison, I see popular culture corresponding to the centuries-long transition, which is in no way complete, to a fully capitalized globe. I would define the slave cultures of the Americas as popular cultures representing the articulation of many different folk forms under an emerging capitalist economy. In determining the difference between popular culture and subsequent mass-cultural forms, I would make one crucial distinction. That is, popular culture defines a cultural community where the producers of culture are also its consumers. For instance, the workers in the Florida turpentine camps whose tales were recorded by Zora Neale Hurston were simultaneously the producers and the consumers of their tales. Hurston's book *Mules and Men* represents the transition of the popular form to a consuming audience whose only separation from a mass cultural audience is the literary nature of Hurston's book.

Popular-culture forms are extremely resilient and may erupt out of the homogeneity of mass society. The hootenanny is a recent countercultural example, for the way it called upon the audience/consumer to hoot and join in the production of the event. This community of production/consumption is canceled out by mass culture, which is synonymous with capitalist culture, and the commodity form, whose primary feature is the distinct separation between those who control and produce the cultural commodity and those who buy it. Mass culture limits participation to consumption.

I offer this model not as a device for categorizing all forms of cultural expression but rather as a means for recognizing cultural expressions that stretch the categories. Most minority cultural forms emerge as instances of popular culture and undergo transformation to mass culture. For instance, break dancing claimed the public space of urban street and sidewalk for the articulation of community. Harking back to traditional dance forms as old as the diaspora, break dancing featured a "calling out" format where dancers challenged one another to acrobatic combat. Being spectator and being participant were one. However, the reciprocity between production and consumption gave way when break dancing was picked up by the media for wider distribution and consumption. Movies like Harry Belafonte's *Beat Street* attempted to preserve the cultural integrity of break dancing while taming its dangerous relationship to urban street culture and gang rivalry. As a final development of the form, break dancing troupes began to provide entertainment at mass-market venues like suburban shopping malls, thus recreating a social dynamic as old as the plantation that distinguishes the black, exotic dancer from the dominant white spectator. At this point the dancer undergoes transformation and becomes a performer rather than a producer of culture. Production is now controlled by unseen organizers and owners of venues, while the spectator becomes a consumer, wholly removed from the possibility of ever being challenged or "called out" to join in the production of culture or to question the racially defined separation between performers and spectators.

These considerations have a bearing on the question of history and memory in mass culture. The example of break dancing suggests that distinctly recognizable African-American cultural forms including rhythms, dance patterns, and the phenomenon of "calling out" can be transmitted across geographic space and historical time to emerge in new communally produced cultural forms. However, it is not clear by this example whether cultural memories continue to inform cultural expressions once they attain mass form. If MTV is any indication of cultural trends, then the dominant culture seems to have an insatiable need for the ethnic and the new. Furthermore, expanding technologies facilitate the immediate assimilation of diverse culture expressions for mass-audience consumption. Break dancing existed for a number of years before it was channeled into the mass market. So, too, did the combination of floppy socks and high-top sneakers before Nike made them into the look of Michael Jordan in order to sell a basketball street style back to black youth at $100.00 a pair. What are the consequences for cultural memory if the day should arrive when there are only mass forms available? Recently, I observed an aerobics class at a suburban gym in a small southern city. The gym's membership, like the demographics of the town, is 40 percent black. The class was jumping and sweating to a loud and rapid beat, the participants densely packed with no room for a mistake. Curiously, all the black participants were dancing their way to fitness, while the white participants looked like (white) cheerleaders. Moreover, the body movements of the black participants—their use of shoulder, arm, thigh, and hip—included many of the same movements that specialists on African-American dance have recognized as African dance forms. Aerobics is clearly a mass-cultural form. Like the mass media, it was once a whites-only cultural practice which has broadened its constituency to include many working-class and ethnic populations. In my book on daily life in capitalist culture,[1] I define the workout as the commodification of labor and leisure. It puts the practitioner in an individualized and competitive environment and replicates the sort of fragmentation and specialization that characterize the division of labor in the workplace. In working out, the individual turns self into commodity: the perfectly honed workout body. Does, then, the performance of African-American dance patterns in the commodified setting of aerobics constitute historical memory? Has African-American culture taken over the commodified mass-cultural setting and turned it into the site for the enactment of cultural memories; or has the mass-cultural form simply absorbed the "other's" cultural discourse, hollowed it out, and made it a performance where the performer no longer has access to cultural memories?

One way to begin to think through these questions is defined in the extensive body of scholarship produced by the Center for Contemporary Cultural Studies, located in Birmingham, England. The emphasis of the center is on collective intellectual investigation. Culture is understood as practice, with particular interest in the resistant practices of subcultural groups. Dick Hebdige's book *Subcultures* is a landmark text for its analysis of the way different subcultural styles that have developed in post–World War II Britain, from the teddy boys to the punks, articulate the politics of emergent class factions.

Hebdige is concerned primarily with class as the motive force behind style, particularly as postindustrial capitalism erodes the cohesiveness of the working class, causing fragmentation and the sort of cross-class rivalries expressed in the antagonism between subcultural groups. Nevertheless, his work on reggae and crossover music in Britain[2] delves into the complicated relationship between West Indian immigrants and working-class skinheads. On this basis something of a case might be made for translating the notion of subculture into the North American context and using it as a basis for understanding the relationship of African-American cultural practices to the dominant culture. The biggest obstacle toward such a translation is the history of slavery which defines African Americans as an internal oppressed minority rather than an emergent class faction. Nevertheless, the theory of subcultures facilitates an analysis of rap music culture along the lines that Hebdige develops in interpreting punk. Punk music and dress represented a rejection of bourgeois culture and its emphasis on upward social mobility. It expressed resistance in a style concocted out of discards and the affirmation of everything the bourgeoisie sees as loathsome in working-class dress and behavior. In analogous but contrasting fashioning, African-American rap expresses a challenge to bourgeois cultural values by way of "fronting out." Significantly, the challenge is lodged primarily by and in the figure of the black male rapper, who, to the extent that he represents all black men, comes also to represent what the media have designated as an "endangered species." Interpreting rap as a form of "fronting out" would find support in Kobena Mercer's analysis of the conk hairstyle.[3] Contrary to popular opinion which saw the conk as a pitiful attempt made by black men to "whiten" their appearance, Mercer interprets the look as an audacious, red-hued challenge and resistance to white-defined style and identity.

In these examples resistance is related directly to the production of new meanings in style. This is the cornerstone of subculture theory which apprehends mass culture as a site where disenfranchised groups make new meanings out of the debris, the odd juxtapositions, and the glut of mass-produced commodities. Rather than seeing mass culture as imposing limits on the sorts of meanings that can be made, subculture theory promotes the empowering attitude that the degraded and alienated raw materials of life in capitalist culture can be appropriated and reworked to produce affirmation.

The emphasis on new meanings poses problems for the adoption of subculture theory as a means for fully addressing the relationship of African-American cultural expression to mass culture. There is nothing in the British account of subcultures that speaks to memory. Indeed, the very notion of subculture represents a refusal of history, just as its theoretical elaborations prioritize the new over any possible rootedness in previous forms of working-class resistance. One of the reasons I think this is so has to do with a critique of authenticity, which runs throughout poststructural theory but finds thorough elaboration in James Clifford's *Predicament of Culture,* a scrutiny of the political and historical function of anthropology and the position of the anthropologist. The question Clifford asks, which I would pose here as well, is whether it is possible for social minorities to enact the memory and recovery of history in culture without simply bowing to the dominant culture's requirement that all marginal groups be authentic. Clifford fleshes out the politics of authenticity in the conclusion of his book, where he documents the court proceedings of the Mashpee Indians' attempt to restore tribal title to Indian Town on Cape Cod, Massachusetts. Winning the right to the land demanded that the Native American plaintiffs prove they really were "Indians." In an area defined by three centuries of colonization and assimilation, they were put in the position of having to demonstrate an unbroken relationship to "Indianness." Clifford's descriptions of interaction in the courtroom suggest that the outcome for the plaintiffs hinged on whether or not they lived up to the court's (and jury's) expectations of authenticity. Plaintiffs who wore braids and headbands were felt to be more authentically Indian that those who showed up to testify in suits.

In a strikingly similar context of judgment, Toni Morrison exposes the power relations bound up in the notion of authenticity. In her novel *Song of Solomon,* she portrays Pilate's transformation from a courageous, resourceful, and independent woman into a submissive, stooped, black mammy in a head rag. In the stereotypically authentic guise of Hollywood's version of the plantation slave, Pilate wins the release of her nephew from police custody. Morrison's treatment shows that authenticity has no real attachment to people's histories and experiences but resides in the dominant culture's ideological stereotypes. Clifford's solution to authenticity is the notion of radical inauthenticity. His vision of multiethnic cultural borrowings on a global scale, in which Native Americans would employ objects from Africa, Eastern Europe, and Latin America in their practice of traditional religious ritual, corresponds with the subcultural practice of making meanings out of the world's range of mass-cultural possibilities. In contrast, Morrison's response to the burden of authenticity is to demystify its historical and social roots. The urban white cops who are fooled by the "black mammy" enact a desire for subservient black women that is as old as the plantation.

The dominant culture's desire for authenticity has been enhanced rather than eroded by the mass-market, mass-media-generated postmodern culture, whose fascination with diversity requires that the entirety of the world's "ethnic" populations represent themselves in authentic "native" music and costumery. Only as authentic can they be appropriated for use by the metropolitan-style machines and upscale decor factories. The only culture not required to be authentic, to replicate its past in its present, is the invisible, never stated, but all-powerful central void of the dominant culture. Can anyone imagine the white middle class put on trial and asked to prove its claim to property on the basis of cultural authenticity.

"Fronting out" states the individual in opposition to authenticity but not necessarily in opposition to historical memory. Currently many black men choose to wear gold-chain necklaces. The style cuts across the entertainment industry and the black working class. It is a less obvious example of "fronting out" than the conk, but it has occasioned a great deal of controversy with respect to violence committed over the theft of chains and the focus on wealth competitiveness that the chains represent. The widespread use of gold-chain necklaces among black men represents much more than a cosmetic improvement on the heavy iron chain that Mr. T wore on the popular TV series *The A-Team.* No matter what they mean in terms of competition over wealth and commodities, chains, whether they be gold or iron, make reference to slavery. As such they articulate the embeddedness of history in style and the contradictory meanings that style statements make precisely because they are defined simultaneously by history and by consumer society. Furthermore, the meanings associated with chains are already historically complex because the chains of slavery were worked upon and redefined in the African-American system of signification whereby the chains as a means of enforcing enslavement were also the basis for making connection to Africa and the idea of release. Shango, the African god who presided over lightning—thus fire, thus the forge, thus iron—was present in the chains, carried over the ocean as a hard-and-fast desire for freedom. Chains are the simultaneous and contradictory embodiment of slavery and liberation.

This complicated set of relationships gives shape to John Agard's visually lyrical and rhythmic poem "Man to Pan." Agard tells the story of the suppression of the steel drums in Guyana; and in so doing expands the metaphoric relationship between Shango and chains to include the steel drums whose music creates a rhythmic web. This image, which Agard reproduces on the printed page by ordering the words in the shape of a spider's web, summons up a different reference to Africa and liberation in the figure of Anansi, the spider known throughout the folklore for his subversive trickery. Agard's poem is a masterful piece of historical memory, meant to be read aloud to the beat of the drums for the collective fusion of history in cultural expression.

Agard's poem poses a different sort of question that has to do with conscious versus unconscious memory. As an artist and an intellectual, Agard is culturally literate. The beauty and power of his poem reside in his ability to articulate all the historical references that are implicit in the music of the drums, buried in the steel itself but not rendered immediately accessible in the music. By comparison, most black men who wear gold chains are conscious of making a style statement and are also conscious of a sort of resistance to white cultural norms in their choice to wear gold-chain necklaces. But how many have the cultural literacy to experience the whole range of historical meanings that their style includes but does not render accessible? The presence of these meanings may even be canceled out by the fact that they are absorbed in a commodified, memoryless form.

The acquisition of cultural literacy may offer a means for revealing and recovering the submerged historical references that the mass-cultural commodity requires for its production but denies by its fetishism just as it also denies reference to the work force that produced it. Mickey Mouse offers a good case in point because Mickey Mouse is black.[4] I doubt any of today's generation of cartoon consumers sees Mickey Mouse as a derivative of African-American culture even though it is common knowledge that mainstream white culture has continually "ripped off" black music and style. Notwithstanding his little black body, Mickey Mouse is thought to be as white as white bread. Nevertheless the black body that debuted in "Steamboat Willie" dancing a jig and singing and whistling to "Turkey in the Straw" makes direct reference to minstrelsy.

There are some who would argue that the minstrel shows are hardly worthy of being reclaimed by African Americans. The notion of cultural literacy responds to this objection by demonstrating that the struggle is not simply to reclaim cultural reference points but to work through the complicated relationship between white and black cultures as these have been articulated in mass form and structured by the politics of domination, exploitation, and at times, subversion. In any society defined by social inequality, culture is a terrain of struggle. No cultural form is so unilaterally defined as to preclude contradiction. The minstrel shows which presented themselves as plantation comedy include complex forms of representation that transcend stereotypes. These include black actors who blackened themselves so as to be "blackface" actors and white and black actors who played black female roles. The theatrics of crossing gender and race categories in the context of a form that was already satirical animates innumerable social contradictions, all of these contained and managed by the notion of entertainment. The fact that Mickey Mouse partakes of this tradition (as do many of the early cartoon characters whose antecedents can be traced through vaudeville to minstrelsy) suggests that mass culture is the site where highly contradictory social and historical forces come together for their eventual erasure. As a cartoon commodity, Mickey Mouse has no past; he is only Mickey Mouse. Seen from this perspective, cultural literacy supplies a tool for unlocking the commodity and revealing the suppressed traces of its counterhistories.

The acquisition of cultural literacy may not have been a problem for folk communities where historical memory is enunciated in oral tales and the lessons of forebears are embedded in the process of producing the artifacts of daily life. However, cultural literacy is not the same in a highly stratified society such as our own. In her short story "A Girl's Story,"[5] Toni Cade Bambara portrays a culture worker. Dada Bibi is a repository of traditional knowledge, and for confused and abused black teens she is the source of responsive feminist nurturing. Hired by public money and housed in a neighborhood community center, the culture worker defines a model for the community-based transmission of cultural literacy. Reaganomics and the relentless drive toward a wholly privatized economy put the question of cultural literacy squarely in terms of class. As public monies for community-based social services are withheld, cultural literacy is redefined as a privilege of those who can afford higher education. As the privatization of the economy eliminates culture workers, it replaces these with a professional class of experts, hired by the corporations and universities. Cultural literacy is bent to meet the needs of writing advertising copy or channeled into academic discourse. Cultural literacy in the era of privatization and professionalization does not inform (nor is it informed by) community.

Speculation on the possibility of using cultural literacy to deconstruct the commodity form or to build community in more socialized economic environments suggests ways of thinking about cultural literacy in positive terms. There is, however, an equally compelling negative argument that would cast cultural literacy as an exercise in futility. Such a reading would adhere more closely to Marx's theory of the commodity. From this perspective the commodity is apprehended as wholly fetishized and therefore incapable of rendering submerged social meanings no matter what the deconstructive lever. According to Marxian theory, the commodity cannot be looked to for the revelation of social meanings and relationships because its very existence is the alienation of the social. The can of peas on the supermarket shelf presents itself as if it had spontaneously emerged out of the shelf itself. The can of peas cannot be deconstructed so as to reveal the interlocking but fragmented and isolated work forces that produced the peas from seed to store, the can and its label, nor the corporate structures that control and abstract the process of production. These can only be grasped by coming to understand the economics of capitalism. Only the Marxian critique of capital can reveal the labor and productive relationships that fetishism denies. Without such a critique, the consumer has no way of reckoning her relationship to the numbers of people whose creativity and labor supply her needs. She only has a relationship to the can of peas and all the other commodities that fill a shopping basket.

While Toni Morrison's doesn't go so far as to suggest the need for a Marxian critique of capitalist economics, she does condemn commodity consumption as a dead-end street. *Song of Solomon* is an inquiry into the process of recovering African-American histories through cultural practice. Using the antithetical characters Milkman and Hagar, Morrison questions the influence of consumer society on the possibility of recovering historical meanings. Milkman, whose journey south maps a process of reclaiming his family's history and by extension the larger history of postemancipation blacks, learns to relinquish all the commodity trappings and egotistical practices that defined his bourgeois life as cloistered and ignorant. Contrariwise, Hagar is unable to reclaim her past even though her female forebears embody significant histories shaped by migration and urbanization. The only journey Hagar makes is her heartrending trek through the department store, from perfume and cosmetics, to shoes and fashion, and then to the beauty salon. Morrison's painstaking enumeration of Hagar's purchases highlights the contradicton between their promising brand names and the hollow fulfillment each has to offer as the whole shopping bag full eventually becomes sodden in the rain. As Hagar stands before her grandmother disheveled, feverish, and close to death, Morrison enunciates in dramatically human terms the dehumanization and destruction inherent in the concept of fetishism. Morrison's portrayal of Hagar facilitates a comparison between all mass-produced commodities and crack cocaine. Indeed, in Morrison's treatment the flood of readily available consumer goods is as addictive as it is destructive. Actually, the point is not to see consumer goods as a drug but to recognize to what extent crack, as a mass-produced and therefore cheap and accessible drug, is a commodity only slightly more lethal than a steady diet of fast food.

Morrison's critique of consumer society brings the discussion back to the work of the Birmingham cultural critics who posit the possibility of making and reckoning meanings through the articulation of style and the practice of consumption. Morrison's portrayal of Hagar is a bleak negation of any possible meaning making or historical recovery in consumption. Rather, she suggests that memories are social and can be accessed only by becoming aware of one's place in a complicated system of interlocking life stories.

In considering the relationship of African-American cultural memory to mass culture, I have implied as much about the field of cultural studies as I have about the object under question. Clearly, cultural studies is polarized between theories that see peoples' cultural practices as empowering for the resistant and creative meanings they produce and the more traditional Marxian interpretations that see all cultural practices as limited if not manipulated by the structures of capitalist social formations and the commodity form. There is a great need in cultural studies to question this polarization and to begin to articulate a theorization that would bridge this impasse. In my opinion, grappling with the specificity of a particular culture, rather than theory per se, asking the sort of questions that I have posed, and undertaking the extensive and painstaking research it would require to answer these questions offer a means to unblock the polarization in theory. I am reminded of an observation a student made recently in class. We were discussing the "new" trend toward world music. "Black music is world music," he said, "and it is very old as well as new." He went on to trace the "call and response" tradition through the history and geography of the diaspora to embrace the a cappella sounds of South Africa's Ladysmith, Black Mambazo, plantation work songs and gospel music from the South, even Motown and much of rap. When memory is conceptualized as form rather than content, it suggests a structure of meanings more fundamental than the sort commonly attached to theories of resistance that focus on the content of meaning making. Memory as form also provides access to a continuum of cultural forms—some older than capitalism—whose influence on social relationships may continue into the present, as an alternative to alienation and abstraction. The possibilities that my questions evoke can be met only by collective, interdisciplinary scholarship. Such endeavor would define the radical potential of claiming cultural literacy.

Notes

1. Susan Willis, *A Primer for Daily Life* (London: Routledge, 1991).
2. Dick Hebdige, *Cut 'n' Mix* (London: Routledge, 1987).
3. Kobena Mercer, "Black Hair/Style Politics," *New Formations* 3 (Winter 1987): 33–54.
4. Susan Willis, "I Want the Black One," *New Formations* 10 (Spring 1990): 77–98.
5. Toni Cade Bambara, "A Girl's Story," in *The Sea Birds Are Still Alive* (New York: Random House, 1982).

12

Performing the Memory of Difference in Afro-Caribbean Dance: Katherine Dunham's Choreography, 1938–87

VÉVÉ CLARK

Ironically, the development of *lieux de mémoire* as a concept among scholars of French revolutionary history presupposes emotional and intellectual distance from memory and history. In African diaspora cultures where peasant communities continue to survive—and their memories with them—the evolution toward *lieux de mémoire* has been far more simultaneous. Distinctions among memory, history, and *lieux de mémoire* in Africa and the Caribbean result primarily from class distinctions rather than the erosion of trust in telling one's history which currently defines the deconstructionist agenda in France. Pierre Nora's rereading of the French Revolution and his notion of *lieux de mémoire* can be applied universally to traditions of historiography and history, and to significant events celebrated worldwide.[1]

Milieux de mémoire, alluded to briefly in Nora's essay, are especially relevant to an understanding of *lieux de mémoire* in African-American dance, largely because certain obscured black environs or *milieux* retained the memory from which choreographers of the 1930s drew their artistic inspiration.[2] To name the more obvious cases, Asadata Dafora Horton, Katherine Dunham, and Pearl Primus represented on the concert stage dance cultures they had studied in either Africa or the Caribbean. When Dunham and Primus transferred these dances of the diaspora to performance spaces in North America, their choreography challenged the norms of male-centered African-American performance of the 1930s and 1940s confined significantly to nineteenth-century formulas, namely shuffling and tap—no matter the degree of improvisation (e.g., Baby Lawrence or Bill Robinson) or attempts at sophisticated representation (e.g., Coles/Atkinson or Astaire/Rogers). I shall focus here on the transition from research (*milieux*) to performance (*lieux*) as one significant tradition within African-American dance history. While many of these milieux exist to this day, it is clear that some of the dances had lost their cultural base of support even in the 1930s and could, with the passing of an older generation, depart from memory.[3]

Early in the twentieth century, ethnology replaced both colonial historiography and alleged scientific theories that prevailed in the colonies and in France during the nineteenth century. Ethnologists became present-day historiographers whose studies in West Africa, for example, reflected memories and a history forgotten deliberately by the keepers of Hexagonic records.[4] Certain Caribbean historians of the eighteenth century, like the Creole writer Moreau de St. Méry, early on had published chronicles attempting to blend memory and history.[5] In 1935–36, when Katherine Dunham sought out *milieux de mémoire* in various Caribbean countries and succeeded in documenting aspects of dance culture, she uncovered cultural artifacts revealed to only a small cadre of scholars during that era. Between 1937 and 1945, Dunham established a research-to-performance method to which her first dance company was exposed. She would use this method of scholarly inquiry as a means to recreate the memory of regional dances among her dancers and a variety of audiences in North America and abroad. For this essay, I shall focus on the *memory of difference* to examine Dunham's research methods, dance technique, and performance principles, and to evaluate critical response by reviewers.

Ethnology, the New History

An epistemological break with the narrative of European history and memory occurred during the Haitian revolution (1791–1804). No longer would black history be remembered solely as an appendage; a former colony was producing a memory of its own. Later in the nineteenth century—during the period when Nora claims that certain French historians were becoming more scientific in their analysis—French writers, such as Gobineau, were defending the notion of European racial superiority in response to Darwin's theories of evolution. To European arguments for racial hierarchy, several Haitian writers responded vehemently in opposition.[6] Their views were dismissed and did nothing at the time to influence or overturn the prevailing white colonial versions of memory and history. Having inherited a tradition of exclusion from Western narrative history, a number of Caribbean and African intellectuals of the 1920s turned to ethnology for support. Ethnology, or the history of the Other, established in the 1820s and 1830s by the nation-states of Europe (notably England, France, and Germany), created a branch of memory and history whose purpose was to record tribal practices in the regions dominated by European powers. The French historian Delafosse and others, writing at the turn of the century, revealed the integrity of African sociopolitical structures as well as a hitherto ignored memory of family/clan rule—Africa's forgotten history, as it were.[7]

In *Ainsi Parla L'Oncle* (1928), Haitian scholar Jean Price-Mars attempted to prove the continuity of memory and history in the New World colonies, particularly Haiti, despite colonialist narratives arguing the contrary. Ethnology soon became the new history, the preferred methodology which encouraged the inclusion of folk memory in historical narrative; more importantly, however, Price-Mars's study became an antidote to the warped historiographies that colonialists wrote based on their memory of exile in the colonies. Price-Mars was followed by Herskovits, Roumain, and Métraux.[8] In the 1930s, such ethnologists accumulated *a memory of difference* deriving from folk memory and ritual observance that ultimately challenged official histories written by European colonists.

Price-Mars and others uncovered what Nora would call *milieux de mémoire*—discrete, regional remembrances beyond the pale of official history—so insignificant as to be known only among practitioners, a living chronology revealed to members only. In the Caribbean, *milieux de mémoire* survived in Haitian Vodoun, Shango cults of Trinidad, and the urban dance halls of Martinique and Jamaica. Dunham was attracted to all of these milieux. In 1935–36, when she traveled to Jamaica, Haiti, Martinique, and Trinidad, she was following an ethnological tradition established a decade before by her mentors, Robert Redfield and Melville Herskovits. Ethnology in the 1930s did indeed privilege the study of peasant culture or the *milieux de mémoire* of rural, nonliterate communities, and Dunham followed the precedent into the field. She was interested especially in observing and documenting dance cultures that had been overlooked by others. The privilege Dunham gave to peasant culture persevered throughout her career but was accompanied by an equal devotion to urban and rural black dance research in the United States. Consequently, the Dunham shows became a repository of black dance of both North America and the Caribbean. Moreover, Dunham's research became the basis for character dances and ballets, all of which demonstrated her extensive knowledge of dance forms recreated from African diaspora memory. When the dance steps, music, and other cultural forms were transformed for stage representations, they become *lieux de mémoire,* reworkings and restatements of historical danced events whose memory Dunham had also preserved in writing or on film.[9] Dunham's *lieux de mémoire* became at once a celebration of Caribbean memory and history preserved in dance form and a reminder of cultural artifacts one should not forget.

In four of Dunham's works, one witnesses a creative dialogue between *milieux* and *lieux de mémoire.* The dialogues appear in the choreography she created for the film *Stormy Weather* (1943), with the full ballet *L'Ag'Ya,* set in Martinique (1938–44), and two overtly political works, *Tango* (1954) and *Southland* (1951), first performed in South America. My interpretations here are meant to encourage innovative critical approaches to black dance, particularly to the work of choreographers who, like Dunham, participated in a research-to-performance method. I urge dance historians to provide readings that go beyond pure description, beyond the choreographer's biography, beyond the definitions of black dance as "ethnic" dance or as "concert" dance, the genre ghetto to which much of black dance history has been banished.[10] In Dunham's case, one must set her research and performance style in historical context. Her writing on the dances of Haiti applied a form/function, structuralist analysis to the dances she observed, while her choreography belongs to the narrative, modernist tradition.[11] When we view the Alvin Ailey Dance Company's recent reconstructions of several Dunham pieces, we as audience members, critics, and scholars perceive them in poststructuralist/postmodern intellectual and artistic environments, whether or not we acknowledge the existence of this fundamental change in artistic form and audience expeditions. Given the current taste for nonnarrative, decentered, or abstract choreography, the postmodern perspective may, indeed, inhibit our abilities to appreciate the history and memory embedded in Dunham's Caribbean and African-American dances.

The challenge, then is to develop a critical literacy for dance analysis so that we may decipher and interpret choreography just as we read literary texts closely or "read" the language of cinema. Performance studies by such scholars as Richard Schechner, Victor Turner, Judith Lynne Hanna, and Robert Farris Thompson provide models for analysis of this kind.[12] When dance scholars participate more fully in current critical discourse, their work will, no doubt, encourage comparative studies across genres—with the novel, with theater, and the fine arts.

Developing a critical discourse that is appropriate for the Dunham oeuvre is a complicated affair, because unlike most choreographers, she was trained both in dance and in anthropology. Consequently, her sources and allusions are extensive, and refer to dance styles she learned in Chicago as well as to the dance vocabularies she observed in the Caribbean and South America between 1935 and the mid-1950s. The South American dance idioms appeared in her shows as individual numbers (*Congo Paillette* or *Choros*), while the Caribbean dances were incorporated into ballets, the likes of *L'Ag'ya,* (*Beguine, Creole Mazurka*). Dunham applied a similar method of recovery when she studied urban black dances of the 1920s (Charleston, black bottom, mooch) which reappeared in *Flaming Youth.* Long before Dunham sought out black dances of the diaspora, she was trained in modern and character dance by her Russian-born instructors Ludmilla Speranzeva and Vera Mirova; her exposure to black community theater and ballet came by way of Ruth Attaway, Mark Turbyfill, and Ruth Page. These eclectic influences would later define the dance training style known as the Dunham technique, a specific set of exercises and movements that she developed in the early 1940s, whose vocabulary evolved through the late 1960s to include Asian performance styles as well.

Inevitably, critics not as learned as Dunham have applied their own standards to evaluations of the company's performances. Many expected Dunham to represent Caribbean regional dances in documentary form. When she did not do so, she was chided for stylizing authentic dance forms.[13] Criticism of this kind is irrelevant, because it fails to understand that Caribbean dance has been stylized and transformed throughout its history. More important, stylization has been a tradition in American modern dance since its inception. Note, however, that other moderns were not criticized when they visualized *milieux de mémoire* that no longer existed (e.g., Martha Graham's *Primitive Mysteries*) or never possessed a danced tradition (e.g., Helen Tamiris's *Negro Spirituals*).

Research to Performance Inverted

My original method for studying Dunham's choreography was to trace her research and/or creation process to the ultimate performance of a particular piece. Useful as that approach was in the research stages begun in 1983, I decided to change direction when I overheard negative responses to the Dunham ballets during the 1987 Ailey reconstruction of her choreography in New York City. At that point, I realized that American audiences have not been trained to see black dance historically. Consequently, I reversed my process of analysis by following the performances backward to research and by setting my analysis in the postmodern climate that informs our contemporary perceptions of dance. That inversion has raised questions that my chronological approach had failed to notice. Before turning to the study of specific dances, however, I will describe the dance research environment a half century ago into which Dunham was drawn as dancer and scholar.

In the 1930s dance ethnology offered American scholars a new field within cultural anthropology where the potential for rediscovery seemed limitless. The discipline attracted the attention of social scientists, dancers, folklorists, and writers alike. Franziska Boas, daughter of the eminent Franz Boas, was among the neophytes who brought credibility to the burgeoning field, as were Geoffrey Gorer, Harold Courlander, and two African-American choreographers, Pearl Primus and Dunham—the former directed toward African dance, the latter focused primarily on Caribbean culture and dance.[14] With the support of a Rosenwald grant in June 1935, Dunham departed for the Caribbean with dance archaeology on her mind. The significance of her first eighteen-month stay in the Caribbean lies in the breadth of her exposure to sacred and popular culture and the example she later established as a black choreographer for herself and others who were, in the 1930s and 1940s, reinterpreting for staged presentations the secular and sacred dances indigenous to African diaspora communities in the Caribbean and North America.

Dunham was drawn to folk culture rather than elite society because of her interest in African art forms surviving (albeit transformed) in the Caribbean. Her orientation reflected the scholarly concerns of her mentors Redfield and Herskovits, who were respectively attempting to reveal the dimensions and integrity of Mexican and African diaspora culture. Dance had been neglected prior to 1935 primarily because anthropologists and sociologists had gravitated toward the "hard" specializations of their disciplines. Dance was not among them. Moreover, none of these scholars was a trained dancer who could understand the language of dance without the aid of an interpreter. Herskovits, whose field experiences in Dahomey and Haiti were well known, directed Dunham's work. He suggested approaches that influenced her way of seeing and her subsequent manner of documentation. Nonetheless, Dunham diverged radically from prevailing methodology by becoming a participant-observer in Haitian Vodoun during an era when only a minority of social scientists practiced this form of information gathering.

Herskovits cautioned against such engagement in a letter dated January 6, 1936:

> Once again, I am disturbed at the amount you are trying to do, his time principally because of your health. I hope you haven't contracted malaria, but whatever it is, you owe it to yourself not to try to do quite as much as you are. I am a little disturbed also at the prospect of your going through the *canzo* ceremony, and I am wondering if it would not be possible for you to attend merely as a witness. Of course, as you know, the trial by fire is an integral part of this initiation, but I wouldn't like to see you suffer burns as a result of going through it. However, you know best in such matters. I am not surprised that the natives are amazed at the way you pick up the dances, and that it induces them to believe that you probably have inherited *loa* (ancestral spirit) that makes this possible.[15]

Dunham did not follow her mentor's advice, nor had she done so previously in Jamaica, Martinique, and Trinidad, where she gained entry into *milieux de mémoire* whose practices were shrouded in secrecy and mystery as a means of protection against censure by adversarial religious orders—Catholic and Protestant—ultimately the keepers of the status quo in the Caribbean of the 1930s.

When the research-to-performance method is reversed, a viewer's attention is drawn first to Dunham's stagings—the *lieux de mémoire* that exist on film and in the recent Ailey reconstructions. Looking back from performance to research inspires a number of questions, and when one studies the archival footage Dunham shot in 1935—say, in Martinique—issues of reconstruction for the stage become apparent. In the case of the martial dance form *ag'ya,* an explicitly male *milieu,* one wonders how Dunham gained access. Given the potential for bodily harm during these bouts, I question whether *ag'ya* was repressed by the constabulary or, as one sequence suggests, these bouts may have been sanctioned by local authorities and their constituencies as well. In her filming of *ag'ya,* Dunham documented a memory of difference that has been forgotten by most Martinicans. The dance form does appear frequently in advertisements for tourism; however, representations of *ag'ya* in contemporary Martinique are equally as stylized as were Dunham's presentations in the 1930s and 1940s. To my knowledge, no historical record exists in Martinique to remind us of the distinctions which must be made between *ag'ya* as *milieux de mémoire* and the *lieu de mémoire* it has become in recent decades.

The relationship that exists between mimesis and figuration is a central issue in the research-to-performance method; the process is highly complex, particularly when the transfer of research is cross-cultural, as it was in Dunham's case. The notion of performing the memory of difference may suggest ways in which historians of black dance might assist contemporary audiences and those of the future in seeing and appreciating the dialogue, both cultural and performative, that Dunham's better-known choreography represents.

Performing the *Memory of Difference*

The *memory of difference* in dance provides a paradigm for examining the dialogues between research and performance; between research and the training of dancers; and between the established order of repertoire and the ways it changes over time as well as the portrayals of class and gender differences that have not always been acknowledged as significant elements in Dunham's choreography. As of this writing, I have isolated seven elements, all or some of which may affect our readings of dance when difference in diaspora culture is represented on stage. These elements come into play on several levels whether the problems refer to research, performance, criticism, or scholarship:

1. historiography of a researcher's individual memory of regional dances;
2. representations of African-American and Caribbean *milieux de mémoire* on stage;
3. style and mood conveyed to the audience through characteristic movements memorized, as it were, during the training and rehearsal process;
4. allusions in the text to which audiences respond differently as a company tours (e.g., *L'Ag'Ya* in Japan);
5. subtle differences in performance over the period of a company's history as principal dancers are replaced;
6. responses to cultural difference on the part of mainstream critics whose literacy of black dance varies;
6. class and gender differences that challenge an audience to recognize variations in black culture.

In *L'Ag'Ya,* for instance, we are confronted with the lives of peasants in a small fishing village in Martinique. Through mime, posture, and costume—all mimetic in character—the Dunham company brought us closer to peasant environments that, in the 1930s and 1940s, were viewed principally from the outside. Gender differences appear in pieces Dunham choreographed for the men in her company who, as she says, needed a display of their own. Thus *Nañigo*. Dunham's ballet *Women's Mysteries* from the 1950s was another attempt at developing gender-specific dance language and settings. *Stormy Weather,* although designed for a mixed group of performers, privileges the lead woman dancer. This convention dominated American dance throughout the 1930s and 1940s, when dance dramas created by women choreographers replaced male fantasies and prowess as they appeared, for example, in Nijinsky's *Afternoon of a Faun* (1912) and Asadata Dafora Horton's wonderful display of male athleticism, *Kykunkor* (1934).

In illustrating the various modes of rereading the process of performance to research, a number of approaches seem relevant, including stylistic/aesthetic (à la Robert Farris Thompson), agitprop (as in Dunham's *Southland* and *Tango*), cultural, and semantic. The latter two are representations of memory I shall discuss in *Stormy Weather* and *L'Ag'Ya.*

The Break in *Stormy Weather:* Envisioning Modernism in Black Dance

Stormy Weather (1943) is a *lieu de mémoire* which serves as a dictionary of black dance including nineteenth-century forms such as the cakewalk and shuffling as well as twentieth-century versions of cool tap performed by Bill Robinson. In addition, black performers parody the Astaire/Rogers elegant variety, and in one short sequence a young man performs modernized tap accompanied by interpretive moves that would later become the sign of Gene Kelly's cinema dance.

The section in which the Dunham company appears occurs during the break as Lena Horne performs Harold Arlen's urban white version of the blues, *Stormy Weather.* Her blues is uptown, sophisticated, and smooth, stylistically well removed from the Ma Rainey and Bessie Smith variety largely because technical advances like the microphone and boom had erased the need for singers to belt out their lines. Dunham's choreography literally replaces the section in a blues song during which musicians improvise on the theme; in this instance, black dance is improvising, and it is here that Dunham's visions of modernism in black dance are expressed forthrightly. The vision contrasts dramatically with the opening scene in which the performers (all but Dunham) lean forward on each other and in a casual but deliberate manner recapture the movements of 1920s black American get-down social dancing. Their style is meant to be mimetic, and John Pratt's wonderful costumes suggest a reality of the Chicago streets. The angular lines in the costumes reflect the reticulations of the elevated train tracks above, under which this disparate group has huddled. This same angularity will be restated in the following section. I would argue that both sections are *lieux de mémoire:* the first is mimetic, representing the tradition of black popular dance and its transmission from generation to generation; the second is figurative and visionary.

As the music becomes increasingly jazzy in the second section, the dancers' movements take on an off-center perspective. (I am speaking here of the leaning, falling, shoulder, and pelvic moves that Dunham chose to illustrate her vision of black modern dance to come.) Only recently had this modernist tradition been established publicly, in 1937, during a presentation by Edna Guy, Dunham, and others at the YMHA in New York.[16] Dunham's vision of a new dance is also ironic considering the background theme to which the dancers perform—namely stormy weather. As many black choreographers and dancers of the era and afterward would testify, their art was indeed caught in the "stormy weather" of unpredictable obstacles that would confront a black company performing the memory of difference in the United States.[17]

Paradox in *L'Ag'Ya*

This ballet was Dunham's first. It was performed for the WPA series of productions in 1938 and has always intrigued me. Even though I have written elsewhere on the structure of *L'Ag'Ya,* I have felt that my analysis was insufficient, that there was far more to learn from the narrative and from Dunham's use of various Caribbean dance idioms.[18] When I began to focus on the sequences, I realized how deeply this *lieu de mémoire* expresses the paradoxical nature of black culture in the "New World." History in *L'Ag'Ya* visualizes dramatic moments in the silenced working and recreational lives of peasants and working-class individuals. The setting is a village in rural, southern Martinique of the 1930s, known as Vauclin. Mundane fishing and marketing activities in which the dancers participate daily are offset by feast days when they transform themselves into "another." To dance the Creole mazurka, the *mazouk,* villagers dress in former colonial apparel imitating ruling-class behavior of a century ago. This type of transformation seems to be socially acceptable. When Julot, one of the featured characters, engages in sorcery as a way of seducing Loulouse (played by Dunham) away from her lover Alcide (Vanoye Aikens), his attempts to transform reality are considered antisocial and a transgression against the community. The ballet ends with a martial-arts duel, the *ag'ya* between Julot and Alcide. The latter is killed in the process and Julot is chased away from the scene and the community as a form of reprimand.

Memory in the ballet is cross-culturally presented through a sequence combining ballet, modern dance, and Caribbean dance. Of the Caribbean dances, the sequence includes the *habañera* (Cuba), *majumba* (Brazil), *mazouk, beguine,* and *ag'ya*—the latter three from Martinique. *L'Ag'Ya* is the quintessential ballet of memory because of its composite representation of dances from the wider Caribbean. Dunham's mélange of cultural references in the piece leads to a more profound portrayal of Martinican society of the 1930s. At the time, Caribbean culture was entering a second phase of creolization through emigration on the one hand and cross-cultural communication among intellectuals associated with the Harlem Renaissance, indigenism, *indigenísmo,* and *négritude* movements. Some of these intellectuals would share their coming to consciousness in the salons of Paris or meeting-halls of New York City.

The syntax of Dunham's choreography in *L'Ag'Ya* reflects the profound class and color antagonisms that existed in 1930s Martinique. *L'Ag'Ya* is a perfect example of oxymoron in dance; the narrative opposes work/feast days, seaside/jungle, love/fantasy, respectable, community-oriented behavior/questionable, ego-centered desire. The subtext of the ballet reinforces such a reading: consider the constant use of dance movements which by their style are opposed—modern/ballet; Old World/New World; colonial/postemancipation; ecstatic/martial. Dunham's choreography reflects social oppositions existing simultaneously and paradoxically in a society governed at a distance from France, and further controlled economically and socially in those days by former plantation families known as *békés* or their elite mulatto co-conspirators. In such an environment, dance of the majority black population demonstrates the contradictions of New World acculturation.

Having settled on paradox and oxymoron as the principal semantic devices operating in *L'Ag'Ya,* I looked back at one of Dunham's letters to Herskovits written in September 1935 when she reported on the barriers she was then facing:

> This is a very difficult country. It is small, and the people are much amalgamated. There is much more to be done here psychologically than artistically or anthropologically. The country is slowly decaying and the people with it. I have been not so well here physically, partly because my work has gone so poorly, I suppose. There is just nothing to see, but I hang on, hoping. I've seen several phases of the *Béguine,* the *Ag'Ya,* an acrobatic dance that much resembles the Dahomean thunder dance, and Sunday I go to see an (East) Indian ceremony which is climaxed in cutting the throat of a sheep. But I can't seem to get any pictures.[19]

Seventeen years later, the Martinican theorist Frantz Fanon would analyze some of the same behavior, using as documentation two literary works written by Antilleans rather than the opposing traditions of their danced history that Dunham had observed.[20] While the sequence in which *Mazouk* is followed by *Béquine* maintains an established custom during set dances in Martinique where the memory of Old/New World form persisted side by side, Dunham's juxtaposition of other dance traditions was unconventional. *L'Ag'Ya* was Dunham's "Ballet des Antilles," the title she gave to the work in an early summary.[21] It was her attempt to consolidate the various dance styles of her training and research efforts. In the company's repertoire, *L'Ag'Ya* represented Dunham's vision of diaspora culture, a concept that in the 1990s seems more real than imagined.

Agitprop Transforming *Lieux de Mémoire*

Agitprop is not a performance technique associated generally with dance. Normally, the practice has been confined to dramatic representations: workers' theater of the 1920s and 1930s in both Europe and America; subsidized versions during the Federal Theatre Project; experiments in the 1960s among, for example, the San Francisco Mime Troupe and El Teatro Campesino.[22] Throughout the 1930s, however, several choreographers associated briefly with the Workers Dance League, the likes of Anna Sokolow and Sophie Maslow or Helen Tamiris, participated in their versions of social protest in dance, and did so following the precepts of agitation–propaganda as a showcase for left-wing political objectives.[23] In the historiography of the Dunham company, agitprop is a term which does not apear—perhaps because it may seem abrasive in its suggestion that control has been lost, the very reverse of the company's aesthetic. The Dunham style was elegant, intense, and at times raunchy in the ballets and single pieces based on the reformation of American, Caribbean and South American dance idioms for world stages.

Yet two works, a dance piece and full ballet—*Tango* and *Southland*—both of which were first performed during the 1950s in South America, Dunham engaged in agitprop to respond to political situations as they were then unfolding. Unlike the choreography analyzed earlier which focuses on modernism and transcultural adaptations, the agitprop works in the Dunham corpus were deliberate recastings of regional dances designed to express anger and protest against certain sociopolitical practices. These two texts were part of the European tours seen first in South American and later in Paris but, in the case of *Southland,* never performed in the United States. As *lieux de mémoire,* the dances were evaluated as sites of comparison by critics who had enjoyed the company's performances earlier in the late 1940s and early 1950s. Although these works were newly created, they reworked familiar idioms, such as the tango, plantation dances, and the blues, in a performance climate playing clearly upon difference.

Reviews of *Southland* from Paris bristled with expectation not only because the ballet dealt with lynching but also because four years after the initial tour the program generally had become a *lieu de mémoire* critiqued by association with memories of earlier performances.[24] In part, the return of the company to South America or Europe, and later to the United States, was a typical lesson for reviewers and audiences in *reading choreography* as Susan Foster has defined the phenomenon which I am calling the *memory of difference:*

> Only the viewer who retains visual, aural and kinesthetic impressions of the dance as it unfolds in time can compare succeeding moments of the dance, noticing similarities, variations, and contrasts and comprehending larger patterns—phrases of movement and sections of the dance—and finally the dance as a whole.[25]

Tango (1954), presented for the first time in Argentina for audiences accustomed to the forms of their national dance, allowed "readers" of Dunham's choreography to appreciate the ways in which the tango might be used to express defiance.

Buenos Aires theaters were not new to the company in 1954. The dancers had performed there in the fall of 1950 a program including *America!, Son, Choros, Nañigo, Batucada, Shango, L'Ag'Ya, Flaming Youth, Barrelhouse,* and *Jazz Finale.* But no *Tango.* During that first tour, the company participated in a benefit performance for Eva Perón's *Ayuda Social.* Four years later, the political climate had changed so significantly for the worse that Dunham used the tango as an agitprop form of persuasion that would both distance her company from former support of the Perónist agenda and record the degree to which disappearance (*los desaparecidos*) was becoming a mainstay of Argentinian political life.[26] In advance of her arrival, she informed the composer of *Tango,* Osvaldo Pugliese, and the pianist/conductor, Bernardo Noriega—both Argentineans—that she intended to make a political statement with this particular number in which she was to appear with the black Argentinean Ricardo Avalos, a member of the company, and three others, Vanoye Aikens, Lenwood Morris, and Lucille Ellis.[27]

There is no filmed record of the dance, although it stayed in the repertoire well into the 1950s. Only a few photographs remain, but these are striking because they show Dunham in the lead role and angry in performance. These pictures, housed in the Dunham Archives in East St. Louis, prompted me to inquire about the tone of *Tango,* with what seemed a dramatic departure from Dunham's usual persona on stage. According to her recollections, *Tango* played upon the implied Argentinean audience's probable readings of sentimentality, sexuality, and brutality in her reconstructed work. Members of the audience knew that Dunham intended to use their national dance as a form of protest and were prepared that the usual confrontations between male and female would allude to a particularly disturbing occurrence within their midsts. Dunham's remembrances of *Tango* explain how she used the memory of difference as an agitprop technique among an audience which would implicitly comprehend her political statement about death and repression advancing under the Peróns:

> *Tango* is a street number. I used to go walking in a Buenos Aires district which is very much like Les Halles in Paris, and used to do so well past midnight after our shows had closed. There were a number of taverns and cafes nearby where tangos were played, and when the dance was not being performed socially, I thought of it as though it were occurring on a street in Afro-America. When the woman in *Tango* enters, she is going somewhere with great urgency, looks back over her shoulder as if she were being pursued. She meets one partner then two others and has a brief tango step with the first partner. She is suffering from high, nervous tension. When she performs with her central partner (Vanoye Aikens), she demonstrates several authentic tango steps, but also engages in confrontation with him. She executes a series of movements in which she very sharply opens her thigh due to his pressure; he hits her with his knee so that she opens hers, and there are two or three movements like that which imply sexual motivation, but also refer to the clashing of two people ideologically even though they are politically on the same side. In the process, however, she seems to fling away everything around her in an intent to express another political position. The piece ends on a harsh, sharp note of defiance. The defiance is directed toward the Argentine people, the Peróns and the situation. I was a different person then. That was my second trip back to Argentina and I had no illusions about the political situation by then.[28]

The political references in this danced text were so clear that audiences previously drawn to the Dunham company's performances in 1950 either gave a standing ovation after *Tango* was premiered or stayed away, possibly for fear of reprisals.

Why was Katherine Dunham so angry, in 1954, when she returned to Buenos Aires? The program notes, reworked as the company toured throughout the 1950s, suggest in understated form the political context surrounding her own emotions at the time: "In the Argentine, there have been many changes in recent years but the vast city of Buenos Aires still covers the underbeat of the tango. In the *cantinas* of the street people, Katherine Dunham felt the nostalgia of the tango and the restlessness of the times."[29] Other versions of these Notes contain equally personalized references to Dunham's experiences in the city and to the memory of Pepita Cano, a personal friend and one of the first women to become a radio announcer, who died in the interim between the 1950 and 1954 tours. She died under mysterious circumstances and might have been murdered by the tango player whose career she had launched—as either a *crime passionnel* or a political assassination connected with "disappearance" methods of dispensing with activists, or both. Moreover, *Tango* was reacting to similar harassments of the composer and conductor—the former jailed and the latter known for his anti-Perónist sentiments.[30] The memory of difference in *Tango* contains a quality of agitprop which some members of the audience feared to sanction and others applauded forthrightly. Such, indeed, is the contrastive climate within which this particular style of performance has been received since the 1920s in both theater and dance.

Southland became Dunham's Achilles' heel after its premiere in Santiago de Chile in January 1951. This full-length ballet depicting lynching was her undoing as a trusted representative of American culture abroad as far as the State Department was concerned.[31] By portraying overseas our country's dirtiest social laundry, Dunham betrayed a trust of silence. As in *Tango,* the work expresses anger, this time reporting about the trial of the Martinsville Seven and Willie McGee in a replay of the rape *topos* surrounding the Scottsboro trials of the 1930s. Having recently experienced institutional racism herself during her company's tour of Brazil in the summer of 1950,[32] Dunham was reminded of similar acts of discrimination against which she had fought legally during the 1940s within her own country. She believed in the 1950s that the practice was typically American, and moreover had been resolved. In Brazil, the pervasiveness of color prejudices surfaced once again when she was denied entry into one of the better hotels because she was black. From this personal experience and news about the recent lynchings back home, she created *Southland.*

The work is a dance drama in the Kamerny tradition and closer in aesthetic to tragic ballets presented by the Ballets Russes. As such it reflects Dunham's early training with Speranzeva, who had worked in Kamerny, and the choreographer's expressed desire in the 1930s to create her own Ballet Nègre. Before arriving in Chile for the premiere, Dunham composed dialogue for *Southland* in two acts which the dancers, to their dismay, had to memorize in preparation for actually performing these feelings in pantomime on stage. In production, however, dramatic action was sustained by a "Greek" chorus of singers who explicitly express and comment upon the dialogue which the dancers enact but do not express in words.[33] At intervals, the chorus engages in irony and allegory. In the opening scene they literally signify upon Southern plantation sentimental melodies, "Is it true what they say about Dixie?" by responding ironically with the Other truths about the plantation South known among black Americans. When the lynching occurs, the tone of the chorus shifts to allegory as Claudia McNeil sings the Billie Holiday version of "Strange Fruit," thereby setting in broader perspective the endurance of this pernicious social phenomenon in American social history.

The curtain opens to reveal a huge magnolia tree and the whitened pillars of an old, Southern mansion—a wonderfully understated set by John Pratt. Throughout *Southland* the time frame is condensed so as to associate the memory of plantation oppression with segregation and despair among the urban black populace. Briefly, the problem of this dance drama unfolds in the following manner: "Two young country folk (Lucille Ellis and John Lei or Ricardo Avalos) express affection for each other. The joyful ease of their relationship is reflected in the carefree performance of plantation square dances drawn from the company's *Americana* repertoire. Following this opening sequence, a young white woman (played by Julie Belafonte) is battered by her white companion (Lenwood Morris) and left unconscious just below the magnolia tree. The field hands returning to the scene come upon the woman's body, and one of them shows compassion while the others draw away, knowing instinctively that a black man should not try to console a white woman in such a state of disarray. The tragic consequences of such an effort were implied. When the woman awakens to a black man hovering over her, she calls him "Nigger," and through pantomime arouses an invisible mob to defend her pristine virtue and punish a "reckless black eyeballer" instead of the white companion who actually abused her. Although the young black man attempts to escape mob violence through every possible exit on stage, he does not succeed, and in the next sequence his body is seen hanging from the lofty branches of the magnolia tree. In the final act the performers are on Basin Street, dancing the blues. They are anesthetized equally by segregation and alcohol, as a New Orleans–style funeral cortege passes through the cafe bearing the lynched body. Most of the clients do not know how to react. At ballet's end, only the blind beggar recognizes the depths of the tragedy which has transpired.

In 1951 *Southland* was a daring dance drama indeed. Beyond the subject matter itself, the use of *lieux de mémoire* exemplifies agitprop in dance. All of the four dance idioms were familiar to company members, audiences, and critics alike, as the company toured Europe following the South American engagements. Basically, Dunham transformed the setting of these *lieux de mémoire* within the repertoire in order to make a political statement. The apache in the pseudorape scene had appeared in *Windy City* (1947); the habañera performed to incite the mob was used in the zombie scene of *L'Ag'Ya* (1938); the plantation dances and blues had been long-standing numbers within the company's repertoire since the 1930s and 1940s. But here they were performed with a difference. The apache and habañera signified anger and arousal on the part of a woman "victim"; the American dances provided comforting yet paradoxical brackets for the violence developing at the center of the drama. For those viewers aware of how these dances appeared earlier in Dunham shows, they were witnessing the memory of difference. References to a culture's authentic dances suggested that communities surrounded by familiar traditions—whether square dances or blues—might be disrupted periodically and perhaps predictably by racial hysteria with its own set of "performance" tactics learned, practiced, and ultimately leading to the death of an individual hanging without trial by the neck.

As one would expect, the State Department responded negatively to *Southland* during a period of congressional conflict prior to the McCarthy proceedings and the civil rights movement between 1952 and 1954. Criticism of the ballet was mixed, particularly in Paris, where the ballet was performed in 1952. As in the response to *Tango,* the reviews were partisan—from Communist Left to conservative, from enthusiastically supportive to bored.[34]

On a broader level, agitprop in these two works is not nearly as unconventional in the Dunham oeuvre as it might appear to be. In fact, *Tango* and *Southland* are examples of a persistent choreographic tendency, beginning with the early experiment *Tableaux of Spanish Earth* (1937), one of many pieces performed at the time in support of the Abraham Lincoln Brigade's efforts during the Spanish civil war, through the Federal Theatre Project in Chicago where *L'Ag'Ya* premiered (1938), followed by a show sponsored by the ILGWU, *Pins and Needles,* for which Dunham served in 1939 as dance director. These commitments to the representation of political issues prepared the way for *Tango* and *Southland,* as well as Dunham's work with poet Eugene Redmond on *Ode to Taylor Jones* (1968) in East St. Louis, Illinois. *Ode* was a dance drama dedicated to the memory of a black activist killed in an automobile accident the year before.[35] When this type of dedication to representing social issues radically in dance is recognized as part of the Dunham legacy, the move to East St. Louis and the work with gang members of the 1960s are not the startling and abrupt changes in life-style that they appear to be among many observers of her company's successes in America and worldwide throughout the 1940s and 1950s. The memory of difference in Dunham's choreography is complex and still misunderstood. This brief survey of several works provides glimpses of the ways in which her transformations of indigenous Caribbean, African-American, and South American dances challenged her dancers, audiences, and critics to develop their dance literacy as they appreciated the changing same.

Notes

A version of this essay was presented at the Dunham Symposium organized by Yvonne Daniel and Halifu Osumare of the Committee on Black Performing Arts, Stanford University, May 12, 1989.

1. Pierre Nora, "Entre mémoire et histoire: La problématique des lieux," in *Les lieux de mémoire,* ed. Pierre Nora (Paris: Gallimard, 1984), xvii–xlii.

2. Nora, "Entre mémoire et histoire," xvii.

3. Katherine Dunham, *Journey to Accompong* (New York: Henry Holt, 1946).

4. Fred W. Voget, *A History of Ethnology* (New York: Holt, Rinehart and Winston, 1975).

5. Elie Moreau de St. Méry, *Description topographique, physique, civile, politique et historique de Saint-Domingue.* (Philadelphia: Imprimeur Libraire, 1797); and *Dance,* trans. Lily and Baird Hastings (New York: Dance Horizons, (1796), 1975).

6. The major writings are by Arthur de Gobineau, *Essai sur l'inégalité des races humaines* (1853–55) (Paris: Belfond 1967), and Clémence Royer, "Du groupement des peuples et de L'Hégémonie universelle," *Journal des économistes* 6, no. 5 (1877).

Gobineau has been translated into English by Michael D. Biddiss, *Gobineau's Selected Political Writings* (New York: Harper & Row, 1970), and his works studied by Biddiss in *Father of Racist Ideology: The Social and Political Thought of Count Gobineau* (New York: Weybright and Talley, 1970). The Haitian response appears in Louis Janvier's *L'Egalité des races* (1884), Anténor Firmin's *De l'égalité des races humaines* (1885), and Hannibal Price's *De la réhabilitation de la race noire* (1900).

7. Maurice Delafosse, *Haut-Sénégal-Niger* (Paris: Payot 1911), *Les Noirs de L'Afrique* (Paris: Payot, 1922), and *Les Civilisations négro-africaines* (Paris: Librairie Stock, 1925).

8. Jean Price-Mars, *So Spoke the Uncle,* trans. Magdaline Shannon (Washington, D.C.: Three Continents Press, 1983); Melville Herskovits, *Life in a Haitian Valley* (1937), (New York: Doubleday, 1971; Alfred Métraux, *Voodoo in Haiti* (1959) (New York: Schocken, 1972; Jacques Roumain's writings on Haitian culture are summarized in Carolyn Fowler's biography *A Knot in the Thread: The Life and Works of Jacques Roumain* (Washington, D.C.: Howard University Press, 1980), 213–23.

9. Kaye Dunn (pseudonym), "La Boule blanche," *Esquire* 12, no. 3 (September 1939): 92–93, 158, "L'Ag'Ya of Martinique," *Esquire* 12, no. 5 (November 1939): 84–85, 126. Katherine Dunham, *Dances of Haiti* (1947), (Los Angeles: Center for Afro-American Studies, 1983). The film footage shot in 1935–36 is in the archives of the Dunham Fund, East St. Louis, Illinois.

10. Joyce Aschenbrenner has reviewed the early critical response to Dunham Company performances in *Katherine Dunham, Reflections on the Social and Political Contexts of Afro-American Dance* (New York: Congress on Research in Dance, 1981); for a comprehensive history of African-American dance, see Lynne Fauley Emery, *Black Dance in the United States from 1619 to 1970* (Palo Alto, Calif.: National Press Books, 1972).

11. Katherine Dunham, "Form and Function in Primitive Dance," *Educational Dance* 4, no. 10 (October 1941): 2–4.

12. Richard Schechner, *Ritual, Play and Performance* (New York: Seabury, 1976); Victor Turner, *Dramas, Fields and Metaphors* (Ithaca, N.Y.: Cornell University Press, 1974); Judith Lynne Hanna, *To Dance is Human* (Chicago: University of Chicago Press, 1979); idem, *Dance, Sex and Gender* (Chicago: University of Chicago Press, 1988); Robert Farris Thompson, *Flash of the Spirit* (New York: Vintage, 1983).

13. See Aschenbrenner, *Katherine Dunham,* 41–59.

14. Franziska Boas, ed., *The Function of Dance in Human Society* (New York: Dance Horizons, 1972). Includes papers from 1942 by Gorer and Courlander delivered during a seminar organized by the editor.

15. The correspondence between Melville Herskovits and Dunham (1932–39) is in the Herskovits archives at the Africana Library of Northwestern University.

16. The "Negro Dance Evening" occurred on March 7, 1937, and included Edna Guy's Dance Spirituals, and Asadata Dafora Horton's and Dunham's choreography performed by members of their respective companies. See Emery, *Black Dance,* 251–52.

17. Racial discrimination in hotels and southern concert halls presented the major barriers as the Dunham company toured North America. VèVè Clark and Margaret Wilkerson, eds., *Kaiso! Katherine Dunham: An Anthology of Writings* (Berkeley, Calif.: Institute for the Study of Social Change, 1978), 37–38, 85–88.

18. VèVè Clark, "Katherine Dunham's *Tropical Revue,*" *Black American Literature Forum* 16, no. 4 (Winter 1982): 147–52.

19. Letter to Melville Herskovits, September 10, 1935.

20. Frantz Fanon, *Black Skin, White Masks* (1952), (New York: Grove Press, 1967).

21. The document is in the Katherine Dunham papers, Morris Library, Special Collections, Southern Illinois University, Carbondale, Illinois.

22. Douglas McDermott's article "The Workers' Laboratory Theatre: Archetype and Example" provides an excellent performance history of agitprop from its inceptions in both Europe and America. See Bruce McConachie and Daniel Friedman, eds., *Theatre for Working Class Audiences in the United States, 1830–1980* (Westport, Ct.: Greenwood Press, 1985), 121–42.

23. McDermott, "The Workers' Laboratory Theatre," 123–24.

24. The reviews of the opening in Paris at the Palais de Chaillot on January 9, 1952, and subsequent critiques are from the scrapbook of Julie Belafonte. Those to which I am referring are from *Humanité,* a French Communist party newspaper, and other periodicals, none of which are dated.

25. Susan Leigh Foster, *Reading Dancing: Bodies and Subjects in Contemporary American Dance* (Berkeley: University of California Press, 1986), 58.

26. On the disappearances of some eleven thousand Argentineans during the 1970s, see Argentina Comisión Nacional Sobre la Desaparición de Personas. *Nunca Màs: The Report of the Argentine Commission on the Disappeared (New York: Farrar, Straus & Giroux, 1986).* Robert Cox has argued in "The Second Death of Perón?" (*The New York Review of Books,* December 8, 1983) that the police state of Juan Perón prepared the way in the 1950s for these horrors to occur and be repressed.

27. Interview with Katherine Dunham, July 22, 1983.

28. Ibid.

29. Program notes in the Dunham Collection at Southern Illinois University.

30. Interview with Katherine Dunham, July 22, 1983.

31. The company's unofficial status as artistic/cultural representatives and issues of censorship during the 1950s is related in Ruth Beckford's biography, *Katherine Dunham* (New York: Marcel Dekker, 1979), 59–60. Proof of the latter assertion will not emerge until Dunham's FBI file, if it exists, is released through the Freedom of Information Act.

32. See the column by Mason Roberson in the *Daily People's World,* March 23, 1951, 5.

33. The working notes for *Southland* are in the Dunham collection at Southern Illinois University; the lengthy program notes were reproduced in Clark and Wilkerson, eds., *Kaiso! Katherine Dunham, An Anthology of Writings.* The action summary here is drawn from these two sources and from interviews with Katherine Dunham, July 23, 1983.

34. See n. 24.

35. See Eugene Redmond, "Cultural Fusion & Spiritual Unity: Katherine Dunham's Approach to Developing Educational Community Theatre," in *Kaiso! Katherine Dunham: An Anthology of Writings,* ed. VéVé Clark and Margaret Wilkerson (Berkeley, Calif.: Institute for the Study of Social Change, 1978), 265–69.

13

"With a Whip in His Hand": Rape, Memory, and African-American Women

CATHERINE CLINTON

> A hill of black people, falling. And above them all, rising from his place with a whip in his hand, the man without skin, looking. He is looking at her.
>
> —Toni Morrison, *Beloved*

In the time it takes you to read this sentence, in the time it will take me to open my paragraph, someone will be raped. Somewhere a person is being violated. One person is forcing himself on another and leaving a mark—a bruise, a scar from a cigarette burn, some torn tissue mixed with blood, some semen, perhaps none of these. In every case of rape, whether the mark is invisible or permanent, life or death, a mark remains: the memory of a violation—force without consent.

The mark may only be an ineradicable memory. The actual act of rape may not be defined legally as a criminal act, so much sexual violence remains outside the law. Could a slave claim rape by his or her master? Could a prisoner accuse a jailer? Until recently, could a wife charge her husband with rape? If a rape remains unreported, as do the majority of incidents, the rapist remains free to rape again. If a rape is reported, the burden of proof rests with the accuser, and many court systems allow the victims of sexual assault to be put on trial through publicity.[1] In all cases memory will replay the circumstances, allowing the rapists to prey again and again on the psyches of their victims.

Whether or not rape is a political act, it remains a politicized topic. And when race and rape intersect as they have throughout our history, the topic becomes explosive. Sensationalist headlines plunge us into emotionally charged intellectual debates over these questions. To the scholar, the terms of the debate seem depressingly familiar. The voices of individual black men and women, as well as the opinions of feminists of all colors, are drowned out by the screech of tabloid journalism.

Despite editorializing on rape, we need some sensible data to put much of this into perspective: recent surveys tell us that less than 20 percent of the rapes in this country are committed by unknown assailants, and that in one out of three reported rapes the victim had multiple assailants. Despite increasing consciousness about sexual matters and sexual politics, we live in a culture saturated in rape: a 1985 survey of six thousand college students found that one in six women report having been raped or having fought off an attack. In addition, one in fifteen men surveyed report committing rape or attempting rape.

Despite the incontrovertible evidence that only a small fraction of rapes are interracial, race continues to inflame the issue and to obscure the fact that African-American women are represented in rape statistics in dangerously disproportionate numbers. *In America today, a black woman is six times more likely to be raped than a white woman.* Not only this shocking contemporary data but also the actual texts and textures of the African-American past have led me to explore the roots of violence against black women—slavery's legacy and racism's rawest nerve within our culture.

In 1982 I wrote, "American slavery bred many strong and sturdy monsters. Racism, class oppression and sexual exploitation remain indestructible among us; they have outgrown their parent and prowl with little restraint; . . . We flatter ourselves that we have slain the dragons, conquered the devils, defeated the deadly relics of our past. Yet we are haunted by the rattling of the chains."[2] Over a decade later, little has changed.

Within academic literature, the taboo subject of the sexual exploitation of slaves and its consequences has been broached in the work of Calvin Hernton, Angela Davis, bell hooks, Dorothy Sterling, Paula Giddings, Deborah Gray White, Jacqueline Jones, Melton McLaurin, and Darlene Clark Hine, among others.[3] Feminist scholarship on rape—what little there is—provides scant remedy. Susan Brownmiller's pioneering work *Against Our Will: Men, Women and Rape* (1975) was riddled with insensitivity to race and class dynamics. And equally problematic was her proposition that rape can be defined as an act by which "all men keep all women in a state of fear." This is a partial truth at best. Men and women have long been convenient categories for discussions of rape, but this is imprecise and incomplete. Although all rapists arguably might be masculine and all violated are feminized—not all victims of rape are women and not all violations are performed by men.

Class, ethnic, and racial factors are central to our appreciation of the power dynamics of rape. Rape has been employed as a collective as well as an individual means of social control—for the perpetrators and the victims. Slavery systematically fostered patterns of sexual violence, with consequences which have clear impact today. The challenge is enormous, but evidence provides a tremendous stumbling block to our full appreciation of the scope of the problem. I have argued elsewhere that antebellum white slave owners tried to erase the records of rape of slave women, and indeed for all women of color within their culture.[4]

Within the Old South, a slave woman was denied the power of consent by legal definition: she could not be raped. This was not neglectful, but deliberate avoidance. If a rapist was suspected of the sexual assault of a slave woman, he was charged with "assault and battery" and, in the case of conviction, damages were paid to her owner, as would be the case in any other "property damage." The law very specifically withheld from a slave woman the rights of personhood and concomitant protection of the state. Sexual abuse could break a slave woman's will and spirit. She was denied her right of consent and, under the law, her own body.

Despite the absence of formal legal charges, we do have evidence of these crimes against slave women. Upon occasion, the rape of a slave woman is revealed in the courtroom. Most powerful, a Missouri court case formed the basis for Melton McLaurin's *Celia: A Slave* (1991). In another example, as part of the legal defense of a slave accused of murder, a lawyer introduced the evidence that the slain man had raped his killer's wife.[5] Evidence from the slave narratives, both the published nineteenth-century texts as well as the Works Progress Administration (WPA) interviews, affords significant insight. Interestingly, in those WPA interviews conducted by black women, 18 percent of the ex-slaves described sexual coercion by whites, directed either at them or at others on their plantations. Family historians and oral interviews provide further testimony.

In her family history *Proud Shoes* (1978), Pauli Murray gives us a vivid account of her grandmother, Cornelia, who was the product of a relationship betwen a slave woman and her master's son. Unlike most autobiographies and testimonies which tend not to give full accounts of forced sex, Murray's work reveals that Cornelia was born after her mother suffered a series of violent rapes. Murray's level of detail is rare, although African-American family lore often includes references to both interracial and nonconsensual unions.[6] In some cases children of these liaisons are unclear as to their parental lineage, and their father's motives, as Pricilla Butler confided to an interviewer: "I don't know if it was rape or money or lust or affection or what that caused the mingling up. I never talked to no one about it in those terms. In my mother's case, I don't know. I've spent a lot of my life trying to know, but I don't."[7] Despite the ambiguity some sources present, scholarly interpretation and analysis have been either absent or conspicuously racist and sexist.[8]

Scholars in African-American women's literature and critics celebrating "women's voices" have provided historians with new and important insights. Hazel Carby's compelling study of the African-American women novelist reminds us that in almost all black women's accounts of rape—including the narratives of slave women—resistance is as thematically central as is victimage.[9]

Many scholars of slavery refuse to recognize the pervasiveness and significance of sexual abuse of slave women. Some deny that rapes took place or claim that, if they did, they were either rare or isolated instances. Some historians concede relationships between white men and slave women were coercive. A handful wrap themselves in a cloak of concern for these black women: "Should we inflict more damage to black women's images by dwelling on slave women as victims?" "Must we paint them as powerless?" Angela

Davis, bell hooks, Darlene Clark Hine, Nell Painter, Mary Francis Berry, and others suggest that we must see these women as subject to institutionalized sexual abuse—that rape was an integral part of slavery, not an aberration or dysfunction.[10] I am willing to move beyond images of slave women as rape victims, but while rape remains unacknowledged and crimes go unrecorded—while these liaisons are characterized by leading scholars as white men winning over pliant colored concubines—these violations of African-American women must be placed squarely within the historical foreground.

We need to integrate sexual abuse as a by-product of slavery, not aberrant behavior or "abuse" of the system. Establishing the fact of these relations in no way implies women's complicity. Can we measure collaboration or gauge "complicity" within such a coercive society?

Within the Old South, I argue, the refinement of patriarchy resulted in a system of "penarchy"—a system whereby the males of the elite use sexual terrorism to control women of all classes and races, as well as men within the subordinate classes. Women of their own class are judged by the dominant males by one system of standards and those of the subordinate group by another. Within the slave-owning South, white women were placed on the pedestal while black women were put on the auction block.

Penarchy emphasizes that male and female categories are necessary but not sufficient means to determine power relationships within society. Whereas patriarchy defines sexual categories as reflections of biological functions (mother/father) and power relationships are modeled on family roles (father/son or mother/daughter), penarchy emphasizes sexual categories which reflect power relationships and their sexual manifestations.

Unlike patriarchy, penarchy is not a system which merely divides people into the categories of men and women. Within patriarchal frameworks, it is assumed that all sons can become fathers, and that all daughters can become mothers, although all children are subject to parental will within the family matrix. Within penarchy, status is sexualized and inextricably linked to power relationships within society. Sexual identity cannot be encoded without a specific cultural context of power and status. Within penarchy, social/class/race/ethnic identity is incorporated into gender systems at the outset. Status, of course, may change over time, as one conquering nation may become a conquered nation, and so on and so on. But the sex act must be informed by context, and sexual identity is meaningless without it. Penarchy incorporates class and race considerations without privileging gender.

Like patriarchy, penarchy reflects the reigning power of masculinity. Men of subordinate groups can be subject to masculine trappings of power. On Southern plantations, power rituals were sexualized and directly reflected masculine values. Men and women were subject to physical restraints that had explicitly sexual overtones: collars, cuffs, ropes, and other icons of submission. Slaves frequently were subjected to public nudity. One of the first laws of racial differentiation in the Virginia colony was that white indentured servants might not be stripped for punishment. Finally, whipping itself can be a symbol of male will and lashing a form of sexual sublimation.

The sexually charged undertone of this ritual was underscored in Elizabeth Keckley's account of an incident she suffered as a young female slave. One evening a "Mr. Bingham," a local schoolmaster and member of Keckley's master's church, announced his intention to whip her. Keckley was shocked by the unprovoked threat—by a man not even her master. Bingham declined to state his reasons for the punishment, and Keckley resisted his attack. In her memoir she commented: "Recollect I was eighteen years of age, was a woman fully developed and yet this man coolly bade me take down my dress."[11]

By refining our sense of this all-embracing patriarchy, we can better understand why women at the bottom of the penarchy were rarely deceived about the interlocking systems of racial and sexual oppression. They did not separate out categories of oppression, as white feminists frequently demanded, and as many black feminists refused as resistance.

Any student of slavery knows it is a waste of effort to play the numbers game. It is even hard to convince some historians that the thousands of slave mulattoes were not all products of mutual consent. Documents, records, and statistics have become tangled issues within our combative field. Memory can provide alternate substantiation. Before turning to memory, I want to outline in brief some theoretical problems.

I am firmly opposed to constructions of models of feminism that fail to include men. Theoretical frameworks of rape which exclude males seems shortsighted at best, but sexist regardless. In *Beloved,* Toni Morrison describes Paul D.'s experience his first day on the chain gang: "Chain-up completed, they knelt down. The dew, more likely than not, was mist by then. Heavy sometimes and if the dogs were quiet and just breathing you could hear doves. Kneeling in the mist they waited for the whim of a guard, or two, or three. Or maybe all of them wanted it. Wanted it from one prisoner in particular or none—or all." A few lines later, the theme of resistance emerges: "Occasionally a kneeling man chose a gunshot in his head as the price, maybe, or taking a bit of foreskin with him to Jesus."[12]

Rape can be viewed as a means of social control for women in both the empowered and subordinate groups within the Old South. In antebellum Virginia, in twenty-seven out of sixty cases wherein a white woman charged a black man with rape, the jury argued for clemency for the convicted rapist due to the extenuating circumstance of the white woman's "familiarity" with blacks. In one particularly chilling case, a black alleged to have attempted rape was to be excused because his victim, a minor, was the *daughter* of a woman who was suspected of sexual congress with blacks. In another case, a ruling specified that "the law was made to preserve the distinction which should exist between our two kinds of populations, and to protect whites in possession of their superiority."[13] White women who defied custom could be stripped of their protection by law and denied consent, reduced in status just as all African-American women were before the bench.

This intersection between black males, white females, and rape affords fascinating data. Looking at the issues in terms of both penarchal imperatives and racial politics, new interpretations emerge. Because the vast majority of the secondary literature on rape deals so exclusively with the rape of white women and this same overwhelming majority applies to the question of historical literature on rape in the South, my focus will not stray. Black women are all but invisible.

The sexual coercion of black women by white men requires massive inquiry and renewed research efforts. Under slavery no legal recourse protected slave women. Whites practiced the schoolteacher's maxim from *Beloved* that "definitions belonged to the definers."

Defining rape was relatively easy as compared with the very complex proposition of publicizing and preserving records of violations. Men and women subjected to slavery quite pointedly discuss sexual coercion in their analysis of the system. They condemned the despicability of masters' attempts at matchmaking, and linked this invasion of privacy with "forcing" a slave by rape or some other form of coercion.[14]

Slaves saw rape as part of a continuum of humiliation, coercion, and abuse. Although each and every slave might not have been subjected to assaults, all slaves were brutalized by indignities and felt the shame and dishonor the system fostered. Women bore the brunt.[15]

The voices of women from the slave narratives call out to us, begging readers to confront the cruel circumstances of slave women's fate. Elizabeth Keckley is again instructive:

> I was regarded as fair-looking for one of my race, and for four years a white man—I spare the world his name—had base designs upon me. I do not care to dwell upon this subject, for it is one that is fraught with pain. Suffice it to say that he persecuted me for four years, and I—I—became a mother. The child of which he was the father was the only child that I ever brought into the world. If my poor boy ever suffered any humiliating pangs on account of the birth, he could not blame his mother, for God knows that she did not wish to give him life; he must blame the edicts of that society which deemed it no crime to undermine the virtue of girls in my then position.[16]

In her compelling autobiography, *Incidents in the Life of a Slave Girl* (1861), Harriet Jacobs depicts the fate of those preyed upon by licentious members of the master class.[17]

Jacobs's personal testimony is extraordinary in the boldness of its confrontation both of slaveholders' sexual brutishness and of the complexity of slaves' responses. In her own difficult case, Jacobs brings alive those coercive forces which dictated women's decisions. A harassing master is counterposed with a white lover. Is the suitor who allows Jacobs to be seduced into thinking she might free herself and any subsequent children any less brutal than her master who relentlessly pursues her? Jacobs's case is echoed in the fate of *Beloved*'s Baby Suggs, who couples "with a straw boss for four months in exchange for keeping her third child, a boy, with her—only to have him traded for lumber in the spring of the next year and to find herself pregnant by the man who promised not to and did."[18] These deals were one-sided, the risks high, the lottery rigged. Yet slave women gambled, driven by desperation.

I remain puzzled. As I read the culture, all liaisons between slave and free were tainted, but especially those bonds between slave women and slave-owning men. By law if a slave woman raised her hand against a white man, even to protect her own body, she was committing a crime. My seeking any evidence of "resistance" makes me feel like the modern prosecutor who exploits cultural sexism to reviolate the rape victim. But if I characterize all relations between white males and slave females as rape, am *I* not denying these women consent? What of those African-American who sought these sexual alternatives as a strategy within slavery? And what of those inspired by motives beyond the realm of "strategy"?

If, as some scholars are prone to paint it, slavery was one big happy family, then it was one which fostered and perhaps even encouraged incest: the father figure (owner) could sexually abuse his female charge (surrogate daughter). The mother (white woman) was much less likely to abuse her male charges (slave men), but she could. More often the mistress was silent accomplice to the abuse of unprotected females within the plantation household. Many theories of interracial sex support the notion of this activity as *preventing* actual incest in the white family, while others claim its "symbolic" incestuous nature because of the alleged maternal role of the Mammy.[19] To suggest that slave women "preferred" the sexual favors of white men is folly. Slave women may have had choices, but the circumscription of slavery denied them "freedom" in any meaningful sense.

Once again, I fear entrapment. Am I infantilizing slave women, victimizing them, stereotyping them—or all three—by "theorizing"? A historian even more than a novelist finds the political impact of her choices, her representations, haunting.

Memory keeps alive those pasts—unmangled by record keepers and schoolteachers. Storytelling defies the dictates of scholars, the assaults of historical methodology. The power of memory, which has handed down stories through generations, outlasts its rivals through centuries of struggle. The past remains contested terrain.

The past comes alive in important documents besides those preserved by the penarchy. Toni Morrison has argued:

> There is not a place you or I can go, to think about, or not think about, to summon the presence of, or recollect the absences of slaves; nothing that reminds us of the ones who made the journey and of those who did not make it. There is no suitable memorial, or plaque or wreath or wall or park or skyscraper lobby. There is no 200-foot tower. There's no small bench by the road. There is not even a tree scored, an initial that I can visit or you can visit in Charleston or Savannah or New York or Providence or better still, on the banks of the Mississippi.[20]

Yet there is a place we can go.

The pages of African-American literature are strong medicine against the whitewash of slavery. Novelists have borne witness and provide scholars with material to rebuild our appreciation of the past—not decorated with images of blacks gleaned solely from white records. These vivid, jarring voices from the black past demand complex and often contradictory renderings.

African-American men have frequently employed the metaphor of southern white male sexual prerogative—penarchal imperative—as a symbol of racial oppression. From W. E. B. Du Bois's rendition in "The Story of John" in *The Souls of Black Folks* (1903) to Alex Haley's family saga in *Queen* (1993), sexual coercion is a recurrent theme. The familiar story is repeated and almost always with similar outcome: interracial sex spells misery, and perhaps death.

In Jean Toomer's *Cane* (1923), Louisa, a black woman, is at the center of a complex triangle. "Blood-Burning Moon" is set in the rural South, a tale fraught with too many overlapping meanings to explore at length. But, in brief, Toomer illuminates the powerful grip of memory on the descendants of slave owners as well as slaves.

Scholars have long used the testimony of whites to "shed light" on black behavior or black experience, and only recently have we begun the painful process of revision which restores black voices to mainstream American folklore. An equally challenging task awaits—to explore black sources as evidence of white perspectives on race. Toomer's "Blood-Burning Moon" is a short story that is ripe with penarchal imperative. Etched in acid, this story from *Cane* highlights an interracial liaison and explosive emotions that lead to lynching and murder. In "Blood-Burning Moon," Tom Burwell, who is black, becomes enraged at the thought that "his gal," Louisa, meets with a white man, Bob Stone, at the canebrake. Bob Stone is equally angered by the rumor of Burwell's involvement with Louisa, and he boasts to himself: "No nigger had ever been with his girl. He'd like to see one try. Some position for him to be in. Him, Bob Stone, of the old Stone family, in a scrap with a nigger over a nigger girl. Beautiful nigger gal. Why nigger? Why not, just gal? No, it was because she was nigger that he went to her. Sweet . . . the scent of boiling cane came to him."[21]

Bob Stone was even more acutely aware of the implications of his sexual arousal as he daydreams. "He passed the house with its huge open hearth which, in the days of slavery was the plantation cookery. He saw Louisa bent over that hearth. He went in as a master should and took her. Direct, honest, bold."[22] Clearly, this act takes place only in Stone's imagination. In this racialized memory, the white man fantasizes his rape of a black woman with whom he is regularly having consensual sex. *The memory of the rape of black women is a part of his historical consciousness*—his Southern tradition, his fantasy life, his lost inheritance.

Stone feels himself dethroned because Louisa gives herself rather than being taken by force. He rages at the new regime. As an emasculated heir of the master class, he complains: "None of this sneaking that he had to go through now. The contrast was repulsive to him. His family had lost ground. Hell no, his family still owned the niggers, practically. Damned if they did or he wouldn't have to duck around so."[23] Shortly thereafter, Stone repeats this theme of disinheritance as he plunges into the canebrake and stumbles upon

Burwell and Louisa together. Infuriated, Stone physically attacks his black rival. In the ensuing battle, Burwell slashes Stone's throat, and Stone dies. Blacks put out their lamps while, once the word spreads, whites, "like ants upon a forage, rushed about." Shortly after, Tom Burwell is burned at the stake.

In *Uncle Tom's Children* (1938), Richard Wright depicts the tragic consequences of an interracial sexual encounter with the story of Sarah and Silas in "Long Black Song." Wright portrays the white man's wooing of Silas's black wife—and the subsequent sexual encounter—as forced sex. However, Wright allows the episode to end ambiguously with the following description: "A liquid metal covered her and she rode on the curve of white bright days and dark black nights and the surge of the long gladness of summer and the ebb of deep dream of sleep in winter till a high red wave of hotness drowned her in a deluge of silver and blue and boiled her blood and blistered her flesh bangbangbang . . ."[24]

Wright's ambiguity raises questions. If I were to characterize Wright as denying Sarah a "rape," by not portraying a "rape scene," my critique is problematic. In fiction, "rape" most often is depicted romantically: a scene of sexual struggle whereby a conquering male melts a woman's resistance, with the conquest ending in mutual rapture. Surveys of either romance fiction or pornographic novels inevitably demonstrate male force as a means of "unlocking" female desire—the male must force the woman into sex for her own good or pleasure. To his credit, Wright does not serve up this sexist convention. He merely blurs Sarah's response to the salesman's sexual advances—and to the sex act itself.

Subsequent to the encounter, Sarah tries to bury the incident, to preserve her marriage and her family. But white men leave their mark—and, in this case, evidence. When Silas discovers a telltale handkerchief in the bed covers (in a brilliant nod to *Othello*), memory is jarred, home life unravels, and violence erupts. Silas chases Sarah from the house. She is able to rescue her child from the hearth side before all hell breaks loose. Her husband turns a gun on a white man. Before his last stand (dying in flames), Silas screams at Sarah, "The white folks ain never gimme a chance! They ain never give no black man a chance. There ain nothin' in yo whole life yuh kin keep from 'em! They take yo land. They take yo freedom. They take yo women. N they take yo life."[25] This speech maps out Wright's broader themes in the book.

In this, as in many other works by black male writers, white men's access to black women becomes the emblem of racial oppression which inevitably spurs violence. And here, as in many other texts of black fiction, the black woman's violation by a white man is seen not as her submission but as a white man's act of aggression against the entire race. It is an individual act, but with a collective impact. In Wright's work a woman suffers wretched violation, but both the character and the reader share the author's appreciation of rape as part of a larger constellation of racial oppression.

In both of these violent, woeful fictional episodes, the authors portray black women as virtual blank slates upon which males inscribe their desires.

Both Sarah and Louisa are painted as vacant sleepwalkers. In the end, they are alone—numbed by the violence that interracial sex (perhaps sexual passivity?) has wrought. The conspicuous absence of the female will is a disquieting feature in both stories.

These vacant, voiceless women have been replaced by a vigorous and varied cast of characters created by African-American women novelists. Many have departed from tradition in breaking the silence surrounding rape and incest. Some have even tackled the thorny questions of the intersections of race, rape, and gender in modern society.[26]

An earlier generation of black women writers had to surmount obstacles that we are now only beginning to understand. As Anna Julia Cooper confessed in her autobiographical writing in 1892, "My mother was a slave and the finest woman I have ever known. . . . Presumably my father was her master, if so, I owe him not a sou and she was always too modest and shamefaced ever to mention him."[27] Cooper went on to complain, "And not many can more sensibly realize and more accurately tell the weight and the fret of the 'long, dull pain' than the open-eyed but hitherto voiceless Black woman of America."[28] Cooper's generation fought to have a voice in the larger society. These strong, articulate women wanted their work to honor the generations silenced before them and pave the way for those who would speak out thereafter.

Pauline Hopkins, in her *Contending Forces* (1900), approaches the subject of rape by describing the brutal attack upon a woman in such a way that, as Hazel Carby suggests, most readers confront sexualized violation. In Hopkins's novel, Mrs. Montfort suffers a metaphoric rape after being branded as a woman with "tainted blood":

> She was bound to the whipping post as the victim to the stake, and lashed with rawhides alternately by the two strong, savage men. Hank Davis drew first blood by reason of his wrongs at Mr. Montfort's hands. With all his mighty strength he brought the lash down upon the frail and shrinking form. O God! was there none to rescue her! The air whistled as the snaky leather thong curled and writhed in its rapid vengeful descent. A shriek from the victim—a spurt of blood that spattered the torturer—a long raw gash across a tender, white back. Hank gazed at the cut with critical satisfaction, as he compared its depth with the skin and blood that encased the long, tapering lash . . . another shriek, a stifled sob, a long-drawn quivering sigh—then the deep stillness of unconsciousness. Again and again, was the outrage repeated. Fainting fit followed fainting fit. The blood stood in a pool about her feet.[29]

By the twentieth century black women writers not only deal explicitly with the consequences of racism and sexism and with slavery's legacy of sexual violation, but they comprehensively approach almost all aspects of the institution. Fiction allows black women to transform their foremothers' stories into truths, into authentic portraits of the past.

One of the most imaginative means of a woman confronting her past is employed by science fiction author Octavia Butler. In her brilliant tapestry of modern America and the antebellum South, *Kindred* (1979), we watch the horror of a twenty-six-year-old African-American woman, Dana, transported from California in the 1970s into slavery in Maryland in the 1820s. On her second encounter with time travel, Dana is attacked by a white patroller. He confides, "I guess you'll do as well as your sister. I came back for her, but you're just like her."[30]

Through her encounter with a rapist, Dana instantly is aligned with her slave sisters. Finding herself reduced to a replaceable sexual commodity within her ancestral home, she is born again. Although interracial rape plays a central role in the book's violent climax, Butler does not dwell on the theme of penarchal imperative. Instead Butler, like numerous black novelists, simply incorporates rape into the formula of slave life. By the tenth page of her novel *Dessa Rose* (1986), Sherley Anne Williams includes this theme. The sexual exploitation of slave women is vivid, explicit—an important subtext within African-American women's portraits of slavery. Women's legacy to their daughters, memories of rape and fears of violation "go with the territory."

Like Morrison, Butler reveals her contempt for conventional historians/record keepers/schoolteachers. When Butler's Dana returns from plantation life in Maryland, she bitterly complains: "I read books about slavery, fiction and nonfiction. I read everything I had in the house that was even distantly related to the subject, even *Gone With the Wind,* or part of it. But its version of happy darkies in tender loving bondage was more than I could stand." Dana finds more authenticity in texts on concentration camp survivors from World War II: "As though the Germans had been trying to do in only a few years what the Americans had worked at for nearly two hundred."[31]

Butler and other African-American novelists weave sexual exploitation into the fabric of slave life. Toni Morrison reveals her heroine's surprise when she discovers at her new plantation home that "the Garners, it seemed to her, ran a special kind of slavery, treating them like paid labor, listening to what they said, teaching what they wanted known. And he didn't stud his boys. Never brought them to her cabin with directions to 'lay down with her,' like they did in Carolina, or rented their sex out on other farms. It surprised and pleased her, but worried her too."[32]

The contemporary novelist who has chosen to portray rape and memory in its fullest horror is Gayl Jones. Her *Corregidora* (1975) is a work which literally demolishes history. Both Ursa's memories of her family and her way of unfolding her tale explode the "truth" of history, the meaning of evidence. Five-year-old Ursa is slapped for questioning her great-grandmother's story, as the old woman informs her:

> When I'm telling you something don't you ever ask if I'm lying. Because they didn't want to leave no evidence of what they done—so it couldn't be held against them. And I'm leaving evidence. And you got to leave evidence too. And your children got to leave evidence. And when it come time to hold up the evidence, we got evidence to hold up. That's why they burned all the papers, so there wouldn't be no evidence to hold up against them.[33]

Ursa bears witness. She remembers that her great-grandmother was sexual prey to the Portuguese slave master. Corregidora impregnated his own daughter—and this next daughter was also his granddaughter: a corruption of flesh and blood. Nor was this practice solely a scene from some powerful novelist's imagination: we have testimony by nineteenth-century observers that concubines in New Orleans might be replaced by younger women, upon occasion by their own daughters.[34] Ursa's family legacy is to keep the rage alive: "They burned all the documents, Ursa, but they didn't burn what they put in their minds. . . . That scar that's left to bear witness. We got to keep it as visible as our blood."[35]

Ursa's own life is filled with more than ancestral memories. It overflows with her own alienation and despair. Ursa's sexual encounters are bound up with the memory of Corregidora, who haunts the women of her family. In a dream she feels "that my belly was swollen and restless, and I lay without feeling." She goes on to feel "the humming and beating of wings and claws in my thighs and I felt a stiff penis inside me. 'Those who have fucked their daughers would not hesitate to fuck their own mothers.' Who are you? Who have I born? His hair was like white wings and we were united at birth."[36]

Ursa fights off this curse of Corregidora, but she remains haunted by her grandmother's words. Jones's studied ambiguity offers opportunity for widely conflicted readings. The answer to her sexual riddles might elude us, but the reader cannot forget the brutal dehumanizing rapes of slave women fore-mothers. This searing memory scorches the pages of Jones's text.

And I propose nothing less for those of us confronted by the task of rewriting history. Slavery continues to haunt. The rituals of domination and submission, the intricate interplay of taboos, especially those involving interracial sexuality, require concentrated scholarly inquiry, not another season of neglect.

The pain of an act of rape is something perhaps each of us must address on an individual or private level. However, collective memory of sexual violation, memories of interracial violence against black women, cannot be relegated to the realm of fiction alone. The power of memory must draw us out of the novel and into the archives. Erasure and silence will not defeat us if we remember—this is a story to pass on.

Notes

The author wishes to thank the W. E. B. Du Bois Institute's Working Group on Afro-American History and Memory for comments and support, especially David Blight, Geneviève Fabre, Robert O'Meally, the late Melvin Dixon, and the late Nathan Huggins.

1. The trial involving William Kennedy Smith in 1991 demonstrated the circus and witch-hunt atmosphere which can pervade celebrated cases.

2. Catherine Clinton, *The Plantation Mistress: Woman's World in the Old South* (New York: Pantheon, 1982).

3. See: Calvin Hernton, *Sex and Racism in America* (New York: Doubleday, 1965); Angela Davis, "Reflections on the Black Woman's Role in the Community of

Slaves," *Black Scholar* 3, no. 4 2–16 (December 1971); bell hooks, *Ain't I a Woman? Black Women and Feminism* (Boston: South End Press, 1981); Dorothy Sterling, *We Are Your Sisters: Black Women in the Nineteenth Century* (New York: Norton, 1984); Paula Giddings, *When and Where I Enter: The Impact of the Black Woman on Race and Sex in America* (New York: Bantam, 1984); Deborah White, *Aren't I a Woman? Female Slaves in the Plantation South* (New York: Norton, 1985); Jacqueline Jones, *Labor of Love, Labor of Sorrow: Black Women, Work and the Family from Slavery to the Present* (New York: Basic Books, 1986); Melton McLaurin, *Celia: A Slave* (Athens: University of Georgia Press, 1991); and Darlene Clark Hine, "Rape and the Inner Lives of Southern Black Women: Thoughts on the Culture of Dissemblance," in *Southern Women: Histories and Identities,* ed. Virginia Berhnard, Betty Brandon, Elizabeth Fox-Genovese, and Theda Perdue (Columbia: University of Missouri Press, 1992), pp. 177–89.

4. Catherine Clinton, "Southern Dishonor, Flesh, Blood, Race, and Bondage," in *In Joy and in Sorrow: Women, Family, and Marriage in the Victorian South,* ed. Carol Bleser (New York: Oxford University Press, 1991), pp. 52–68.

5. Bleser, *In Joy and in Sorrow,* p. 66.

6. See, for example, Patricia Williams, *Alchemy of Race and Rights* (Cambridge, Mass.: Harvard University Press, 1991).

7. Susan Tucker, *Telling Memories Among Southern Women* (Baton Rouge: Louisiana State University Press, 1988), p. 24.

8. For two fine and exceptional works see Adele Logan Alexander, *Ambiguous Lives* (Little Rock: University of Arkansas Press, 1991), and Kent A. Leslie, *Woman of Color, Daughter of Privilege* (Athens: University of Georgia Press, forthcoming).

9. Hazel Carby, *Reconstructing Womanhood: The Emergence of the Afro-American Woman Novelist* (New York: Oxford University Press, 1987).

10. Davis, "Reflections," hooks, *Ain't I a Woman?* Hine, "Rape"; Nell Painter "Of Lily, Linda Brent and Freud: A Non-Exceptionalist Approach to Race, Class and Gender in the Slave South," *Georgia Historical Quarterly* 76, no. 2 (Summer 1992):241–59; and Mary Frances Berry, "Judging Morality: Sexual Behavior and Legal Consequences in the Late Nineteenth-Century South," *Journal of American History* 78, no. 3 (December 1991):835–56.

11. Elizabeth Keckley, *Behind the Scenes; or Thirty Years a Slave and Four Years in the White House* (1868) (New York: Oxford University Press, 1989), p. 33.

12. Toni Morrison, *Beloved* (New York: Knopf, 1987), pp. 107–8. I am indebted to Nathan Huggins for calling this to my attention.

13. See Clinton, "Southern Dishonor," p. 59.

14. See Catherine Clinton, "Caught in the Web of the Big House: Women and Slavery," in *Black Women in United States History,* vol. 1, ed. Darlene Clark Hine (Brooklyn, N.Y.: Carlson Publishing Company, 1990).

15. See Orlando Patterson, *Slavery and Social Death* (Cambridge, Mass.: Harvard University Press, 1982). I am indebted to Patterson's theory of natal alienation.

16. Keckley, *Behind the Scenes,* p. 39.

17. Jacobs also mentions slave men forced into sexual liaisons with white women. See Martha Holdes, "Wartime Dialogues on Illicit Sex," in *Divided Houses: Gender and the Civil War,* ed. Catherine Clinton and Nina Silber (New York: Oxford University Press, 1992).

18. Morrison, *Beloved,* p. 23.

19. See Charles Herbert Stember, *Sexual Racism* (New York: Harper & Row, 1976).

20. Toni Morrison, "A Bench by the Road," *World Journal of the Unitarian Universalist Association* 3 (Jan./Feb. 1989), p. 4.

21. Jean Toomer, *Cane* (New York: Boni & Liveright, 1923), p. 32.

22. Ibid., p. 31.

23. Ibid.

24. Richard Wright, *Uncle Tom's Children* (New York: Harper & Row, 1965), p. 113. Wright's ellipses.

25. Ibid., p. 125.

26. See Nellie McKay, "Alice Walker's 'Advancing Luna'—and Ida B. Wells: A Struggle Toward Sisterhood," in *Rape and Representation,* ed. Lynn Higgins and Brenda Silver (New York: Columbia University Press, 1991). pp. 248–60.

27. Mary Helen Washington, "Introduction," in Anna J. Cooper, *A Voice from the South* (New York: Oxford University Press, 1988), p. xxxi.

28. Ibid., p. ii.

29. Pauline Hopkins, *Contending Forces* (New York: Oxford University Press, 1988), p. 69. Carby provides powerful insight in her introduction to Hopkins's novel in the Schomburg edition; see also her "On the Threshold of Woman's Era," in *Race, Writing and Difference,* ed. Henry Louis Gates, Jr. (Chicago: University of Chicago Press, 1985), pp. 301–16.

30. Octavia Butler, *Kindred* (Boston: Beacon Press, 1988), p. 42.

31. Ibid., p. 116.

32. Morrison, *Beloved,* p. 140.

33. Gayl Jones, *Corregidora* (Boston: Beacon Press, 1986) p. 14.

34. See Clinton, "Caught in the Web of the Big House," pp. 225–40

35. Jones, *Corregidora,* p. 72.

36. Ibid., pp. 76–77.

14

Sherley Anne Williams's *Dessa Rose*: History and the Disruptive Power of Memory

ANDRÉE-ANNE KEKEH

Dessa Rose deals with the delicate issue of the writing of history. The novel restores the missing voice of the black woman slave and simultaneously disrupts the writing of a white male historian. Sherley Anne Williams's novel tells not only the birth of a subversive, seminal voice: a voice belonging to Dessa Rose, a black woman slave, a transgressor, a figure threatening to the "peculiar institution." It clearly addresses the ways in which history can be ideologically constructed, the way memory and voice can be used to create some space in an official and historical discourse that has often negated them.

This essay, however, focuses on the crucial role that memory plays in Dessa Rose's achievement of freedom and voice. With this in mind, I would like to place a special emphasis on two moments in the text that I consider to be pivotal in Dessa Rose's itinerary toward self-expression and self-definition. The first moment deals with Dessa Rose's oral contest with Adam Nehemiah, the historian collecting her tale in the very first part of the novel.[1] The second turning point—in the second section—is Dessa Rose's outburst against Mrs. Rufel, the plantation mistress of Sutton Glen.

My concern is to point out how, in the struggle against the authoritative "historical" discourse that Adam Nehemiah represents, Dessa Rose's memories give her the ability to tell a tale of resistance disrupting the written text of Adam Nehemiah and how, in her further encounter with Mrs. Rufel, "Mammy" serves as a potent repository—*lieu de mémoire*[2]—enabling Dessa Rose to achieve full voice and undermine Mrs. Rufel's paternalistic discourse. *Dessa Rose* exemplifies vividly such a contest between memory and history, and it furthermore points to the centrality of narrative within this contest. It is significant that throughout the novel, almost every character tries either to make up a story or to appropriate one: Adam Nehemiah tries to write a "historical," "scientific" story out of Dessa Rose's tale; Mrs. Rufel's sign of achievement is her ability to tell consistent tales in order to protect herself and the fugitive slaves on their way away from Sutton Glen. Nathan and Harker, the slave leaders, elaborate "lying stories" that enable the fugitive slaves of Sutton Glen to mock and undermine slave merchants and thus gain the money they need to flee to the west. As for Dessa Rose, she is the storyteller who masters the art of controlling and telling the narrative in the course of the novel.

Dessa Rose thus stands out as a polyphonic text in which each participant in turn is allowed to speak up and to assume the responsibility of the making of the story/history. As such, Williams's work may be read as a revisionist comment on slave historiography. Here, in *Dessa Rose,* a black woman and a white woman (representing two groups long overlooked by official history) are provided the ability to speak and to perform acts which go against the chauvinistic and racial assumptions of the venal slave system.

The novel develops in three distinct parts, each centered around a specific geographic locale and a "dominant" point of view. "The Darky" encloses the "master's" text written by Adam Nehemiah. The setting is the prison where Dessa Rose is held captive for killing white men and escaping a slave coffle. In "The Darky" she makes her escape on a July Fourth and reaches Mrs. Rufel's plantation. The narrative now moves into the second part, "The Wench," in which Ms. Rufel's point of view prevails. The last section, "The Negress," reveals Dessa Rose now as a full first-person narrative voice. The open geographic setting "on the road" to the West matches her liberated voice and self.

These three distinct sections also chart the different stages in which memory informs Dessa Rose's narrative. In "The Darky," memory leads Dessa Rose to "signify" upon Adam Nehemiah. Signifying is a verbal activity which is essential in African-American culture.[3] According to Michael Cooke, "signifying always involves questions of power on two levels, the social and the mental, and the signifier is the one who as best he can makes up for a lack of social power with an exercise of intellectual or critical power."[4] By telling the historian a culturally coded tale which he completely misunderstands, Dessa Rose displays such a subversive "critical power." At this point, Dessa Rose resorts to "signifying" as a defensive device; through her verbal performance she inscribes herself in a black oral tradition and symbolically undermines the power of the written word. As such, Dessa Rose is not unlike the signifying monkey of the African-American folktale:[5] she signifies upon the master as the monkey signifies upon king lion. Through orality and the rhetorics of indirection Dessa Rose succeeds in reversing the power relationships. Her ability to tell stories that befuddle the historian is a sign of her mastery.

Let us now turn to the type of history that Adam Nehemiah stands for. He says:

> Though the darky had no scars or marks of punishment except on her rump and the inside of her flanks—places only the most careful buyer was likely to inspect—these bespoke a *history* of misconduct.[6]

> Copious notes seem to be the order of the day and I will cull what information I can from them. I have at present no clear outline for the book—nor yet what I shall do with the darky's story, but I have settled upon *The Roots*

> *of Rebellion in the Slave Population and Some Means of Eradicating Them* as a compelling short title.[7]

Adam Nehemiah's words illustrate how historical writing can be an ideological exercise. In this case, such an exercise allows the historian selectively to use and then to negate his "primary source" (Dessa Rose). Adam Nehemiah wants to place Dessa Rose into a historical text and circumscribe her story before she is executed. Dessa Rose's only value to him is merely to provide scientific validity to his historical research. He does not acknowledge the story of pain that is inscribed on Dessa Rose's private parts and cruelly misreads her scars as a sign of "misconduct."

To Adam Nehemiah's demeaning and reductive written discourse, Dessa Rose opposes the power of oral resistance: " 'I kill white mens,' her voice overrode mine, as though she had not heard me speak, 'I kill white mens cause the same reason Masa kill Kaine. Cause I can."[8] She is able to say this to Nehemiah while in prison awaiting the birth of her child and her execution. Recalling her past empowers her to voice a tale of resistance. And indeed her story overwhelms Adam Nehemiah, the historian in charge of transforming it into a repressive mainstream best-seller and history book. Dessa Rose represents a threat. She has killed white men, and through restating it to Adam Nehemiah's face she literally reenacts the transgressive act. Through her will to remember she rebels against authority and institutional history.

Williams unmistakably makes Adam Nehemiah appear as the embodiment of law, history, and intellectual discourse. His first name, Adam, makes him the Adamic man, founder of the American institutions and of mankind. His last name, Nehemiah, may be a reference to a nineteenth-century preacher called Adam Nehemiah. He was a proslavery clergyman belonging to the Essex Street Church of Boston and published a book in favor of slavery entitled *A South Side View of History: Or, Three Months in the South in 1854.*[9]

In the novel the pen functions as an obvious phallic symbol; Nehemiah wants literally to lay Dessa down on paper. Adam Nehemiah's constant holding of this instrument exemplifies simultaneously the domineering power of male writing over other types of discourse or textuality and the sexual oppression of black women slaves. The Bible from which he reads to Dessa Rose when they sit under the elm (a mocking version of the Tree of Knowledge) is, for example, another compelling sign of Adam Nehemiah's authoritative stance. His status as a historian is not unlike the slave trader's. He does not sell slaves per se: he writes them down and sells them as books. Adam Nehemiah's previous work on slaves—ironically entitled *The Guide*—has brought him intellectual fame and money. For Adam Nehemiah, Dessa Rose represents another opportunity to dispossess a "darky" of "its" tale and to record it in his journal in order to elaborate a "master" text on how to stifle the spirit of slave rebellion. Bringing slaves into the center of his discourse is, in fact, an oblique way to dismiss them and deny them any sense of identity and power.

Undeniably, the history that Adam Nehemiah stands for is linked to the politics of appropriation and control. His purpose is twofold: to construct dominant history and to profit from potential secrets Dessa Rose may expose. Williams makes his purposes clear by emphasizing how Adam Nehemiah is interested simultaneously in writing history and in making money out of Dessa's tale: "He couldn't bring himself to believe that negroes actually had some means of preventing conception, yet he could not keep himself from speculating. The recipe for such a potion could be worth a small fortune—provided of course, that one could hit upon some discreet means of selling it."[10] One could argue that Williams points to the ways in which capitalism may have shaped and limited the course and content of historical discourse. Adam Nehemiah's historical endeavor bears a sense of closure and containment. The sense of limitation is conveyed in the novel through the use of the journal. Dessa Rose's voice is symbolically imprisoned, locked in Adam Nehemiah's journal. Its entries, with all their precise temporal and geographic indications, graphically represent boundaries that constrict Dessa Rose's voice. After Dessa's escape, these boundaries collapse. In this respect it is interesting to note that after Dessa Rose has fled from the prison and from Adam Nehemiah's repressive text the journal entries lose their accuracy. This indicates clearly that Nehemiah has lost his bearings and is symbolically defeated.

> *Somewhere* South and West of Linden. July 4th, 1947. Early morning.[11]

The conflict between Dessa Rose and Adam Nehemiah also discloses a dichotomy between orality and writing, between vernacular and institutional language. A perpetual clash between Dessa Rose's tale, grounded on things recalled, and the "scientific" facts so dear to Adam Nehemiah is conveyed throughout the novel. Dessa Rose manages to weaken Adam Nehemiah's text from within through remembering and naming. Her oral profuse tale overwhelms the historian, making him unable to write it down in his diary:

> He hadn't caught every word; often he had puzzled overlong at some unfamiliar idiom or phrase, now and then losing the tale in the welter of *names* the darky called. . . . Yet the scene was vivid in his mind as he deciphered the darky's account from his hastily scratched notes and he *reconstructed* it in his journal as though he remembered it word for word.[12]

The term *reconstructs* is important here, for it signifies the fallacy in Adam Nehemiah's supposedly "scientific" and "objective" writing stance. Moreover, it points to Williams's self-conscious act of rewriting the history of the black community. The author makes it very clear from the preceding quotation that Adam Nehemiah, the historian, cannot manipulate Dessa Rose or her story. Williams skillfully contrasts Dessa Rose's tendency to think in terms of personal names and Adam Nehemiah's cold categories: darky, she-devil, virago, species, animal. As a result of his system, he cannot fully grasp the meaning of Dessa Rose's intimate tale of remembrance and resistance. His written text stands in strong opposition to Dessa's scarred—written—body. Dessa Rose's memories resist white male appropriation and tell a story unaccommodating to Adam Nehemiah's alleged "historical" truth. In this respect, one could say that Dessa Rose symbolizes a powerful Medusa that annihilates Adam Nehemiah. Mesmerized by the power of Dessa's tale, Nehemiah is kept from writing: "Or, he had sat, fascinated, forgetting to write."[13]

Unlike Sethe in Toni Morrison's *Beloved,*[14] Dessa Rose has a will to remember. In turn, this ability provides her with a narrative that she can use to mislead and control Adam Nehemiah. Dessa Rose can, in many respects, be seen as the African-American trickster figure drawing on words to ensure her survival: "Talking with the white man was a game; it marked time and she dared a little with him playing on words, lightly capping, as though he were no more than some darky bent on bandying words with a likely-looking gal."[15] Dessa Rose deliberately talks Adam Nehemiah into listening to her own story, which, given his limitations of rhetoric and insight, he cannot capture in his diary. This example of "signifying" through remembrance represents one way in which Dessa Rose can defy the authoritative interpretative stance of institutional history. Significantly, after Dessa Rose has heard a coded song which again Adam Nehemiah fails to understand, her voice literally escapes Adam Nehemiah's limiting text:

> Dessa joined in, suddenly jubilant, her voice floating out across the yard.
>
> Good news, Lawd, Lawd, good news.
> My sister got a seat and I so glad;
> I heard from heaven today.
> Good news, Lawd, Lawd, Lawd, good news.
> I don't mind what Satan say
> Cause I heard, yes I heard, well I heard,
> I heard from heaven today.
>
> I (Nehemiah) listened and finally managed to catch the words—something about the suffering of a poor sinner . . . this is the liveliest tune I have heard Odessa sing and I went round to her cellar window—.[16]

After hearing this song, Dessa Rose escapes from the prison house. Only by participating in the singing and understanding the hidden message of the song can she run away from the prison house of institutional history. Thus Dessa Rose's subversive power clearly derives from an oral tradition and a shared black cultural heritage.

The plantation of Mrs. Rufel marks the next space where Dessa Rose is able to express her will to remember. The house stands apart from the slave system. Attempts to grow cotton, a cogent sign of slavery, have failed there. This symbolically tells that Dessa Rose should go to such a place after her escape from the prison. For the first time in her life, Dessa Rose goes into the heart of the "Big House." This gesture can be seen as another subversive act on her part, even though she resents being in the house and having to share a bedroom and a bed with Mrs. Rufel. Although the two women are unaware of it, a mood of solidarity pervades the beginning of "The Wench." Both women are new mothers, and it is interesting to note that Mrs. Rufel, the white woman, nurses Dessa Rose's infant. Obviously, Williams's purpose here is to counter the enduring image of "the black mammy" feeding white babies which has been so popular in American literature and history. At one point Dessa Rose's thoughts literally entwine with Mrs. Rufel's words about a cherished past where Dorcas, "her" black mammy, was still alive. Paradoxically, it is through this semblance of sharing that Dessa Rose is driven to the verbal outburst which represents a turning point in her way to self-definition.

Mammy, a recurring memory in both women's minds, organizes their respective articulations of their past. Dessa Rose's anger breaks out because she refuses to be dispossessed of her repository—Mammy—by Mrs. Rufel. The two women are not talking about the same woman, but Mrs. Rufel's excessive use of the generic name Mammy to designate her dead nurse creates the misunderstanding and brings about the confrontation. Dessa Rose's voice goes unleashed, and she cries Mammy's story and genealogy to Mrs. Rufel: "Wasn't no mammy to it. The words burst from Dessa . . . The words exploded *inside* Dessa. 'Your mammy' . . . You ain't got no mammy . . . Remembering the names now the way mammy used to *tell* them, lest they *forget* she would say; lest her poor children die to *living memory* as they had in her world."[17] Dessa Rose's cathartic crisis connotes giving birth. It is a very painful search within herself to revive Mammy, her ten " 'chi'ren," and the past of her community. Through this naming and telling, Dessa Rose reenacts Mammy's giving birth to her dead children. Only by going back to Mammy and establishing her as a *lieu de mémoire* can Dessa Rose gain power and authority to rebel against Ms. Rufel, who, earlier in the novel, assumes that Mammy is outside history anyway: ". . . the pretty clothes, well, I know Mammy didn't know a thing about history, but I know she was right about clothes."[18]

Dessa Rose's outburst helps her reclaim legitimacy for Mammy and her people, identity and space in a history where slaves have been written off. Another interpretation could be to see it as a tale which deconstructs some of the enduring stereotypes of black mammies that white society has enjoyed imposing on black women. For Dessa Rose, Mammy stands for a cultural repository that must be defended at all costs.

The image of hair care associated with Mammy throughout the novel is essential. Braiding enhances the idea of kinship and linkage, but it may also be read as a way of providing the missing *text* black women slaves needed to write their stories and perpetuate familial and communal ties: "This was one way we told who they peoples was, by how their hair was combed. Mammy cornrowed our hair . . . This is where I learned to listen right between Mammy's thighs, where I first learned how to speak, from listening at grown people talk."[19] Hair care provides an alternative intimate space in which to inscribe cultural identity and memory. Significantly enough, at the end of the novel Dessa Rose is an aged grandmother doing her grandchildren's hair while telling them the story of her life. At the close of the novel, braiding thus becomes the necessary medium through which to tell tales suppressed by dominant discourse. Eventually, Nehemiah's official written text is displaced by this *other* women's text and Dessa Rose can eventually pass on and write her tale of resistance: "This why I [Dessa] have it wrote down, why I has the child say it back. I never will forget Nemi trying to read me, knowing I had put myself in his hands."[20]

The prologue and the epilogue surrounding the novel are told from Dessa Rose's perspective: both focus on her dreams of the past and her expectations of the future. Graphically, then, Dessa Rose encircles the narrative, showing her full control over her tale. Setting Dessa Rose as the main narrator of the prologue and the epilogue shows not only her narrative authority in the novel, it is also Williams's strategy to undermine the conventions ruling traditional slave autobiographies. In this respect, it is interesting to consider Robert Stepto's critical formulation:

> In their most elementary form, slave narratives are, however, full of other voices that are frequently just as responsible for articulating a narrative's tale and strategy. These other voices may be those of various "characters" in the "story," but mainly they are those found in the appended documents written by slaveholders and abolitionists alike. . . . Their primary function is, of course, to authenticate the former's slave account; in doing so, they are at least partially responsible for the narrative being accepted as historical evidence.[21]

By framing her polyphonic novel with Dessa Rose's voice only, Williams goes against such official "voices" that were entitled to legitimize slave narratives. The centrality of Dessa Rose's voice in the prologue and the epilogue shows that Williams grants the slave woman narrative authority over the whole tale. Williams consequently dismisses the legitimizing power of official discourses. First imprisoned in Nehemiah's written text, Dessa Rose manages in the course of the narrative to escape his limiting text and to become, in the last part of the novel, the controlling first-person narrator. At the end of the novel, Dessa Rose has completed her trip. She has journeyed to the West and obtained her freedom and voice. Remembering has helped her to become the author of her own "herstory." At last she is able to tell her whole name: " 'Well, if it come to that,' I told her, 'my name is Dessa, Dessa Rose.' "[22]

Ironically, while in the course of the novel Dessa Rose has expanded, Adam Nehemiah has dramatically shrunk. By the end, his name is reduced to a "Mr. Nemi." Preventing Nemi from completing his book is Dessa Rose's ultimate victory over him. Nemi's last exit is that of a little man wearing worn clothes and gesticulating with a notebook full of "blank" pages. Despite his frightful statement—"I know it's her Nemi say. 'I got her down here in my book"[23]—Nemi's discourse no longer has the capacity to contain Dessa Rose. In defeating Nemi, Dessa Rose not only gains freedom and voice; one could argue that she also gets access to publishing space to tell her story in her own words. It is no coincidence, indeed, that Nemi's publisher is called Browning Norton.[24] Dessa Rose has not only developed as the master of her own tale but she has deconstructed the authoritative power of institutional history. Perhaps even more, she has obtained space and power to tell the missing stories of the United States.

Dessa Rose vividly raises the issue of historical interpretation: it exemplifies the ways in which historical constructions are deeply embedded in dominant ideologies and work as instruments of power. In the final analysis, could not Dessa Rose be seen as the modern historiographer revising and subverting the institutional historical constructs? By inserting in her story the personal memories, names, and stories that have been excluded or misnamed, Dessa Rose manages to break through and to create a space for herself and her people, and it is she who achieves authority.[25]

Notes

1. All references are to Sherley Anne Williams, *Dessa Rose* (New York: William Morrow, 1986).
2. The term *lieu de mémoire* is a concept that I borrow from the French historian Pierre Nora. In his book *Les Lieux de mémoire: La République* (Paris: Gallimard, 1984) Nora is concerned to point out the uncanonized spaces (objects, customs, stories, songs, themes) where the French have been able to inscribe their unofficial memories. The term might be translated loosely as "repository" and seems appropriate in a reading of *Dessa Rose*.
3. See Henry Louis Gates, Jr., *The Signifying Monkey* (New York: Oxford University Press, 1988); Claudia Mitchell-Kernan, "Signifying," in *Mother Wit from the Laughing Barrel,* ed. Alan Dundes (New York: Garland, 1981), 310–28.
4. Michael Cooke, *Afro-American Literature in the Twentieth Century: The Achievement of Intimacy* (New Haven, Ct.: Yale University Press, 1984), 26.
5. See "The Signifying Monkey," in *Book of Negro Folklore,* ed. Langston Hughes and Arna Bontemps (New York: Dodd, Mead, 1958), 365–66.
6. *Dessa Rose,* 21.
7. Ibid., 23.
8. Ibid., 20.
9. Adam Nehemiah, *A South Side View of History: Or, Three Months in the South in 1854* (Boston: Ticknor and Fields, 1854).
10. *Dessa Rose,* 19.
11. Ibid., 68, 69. My italics.
12. Ibid., 18. My italics.
13. Ibid.
14. Toni Morrison, *Beloved* (New York: Knopf, 1987).
15. *Dessa Rose,* 60.
16. Ibid., 67–68.
17. Ibid., 118. My italics.
18. Ibid., 117.
19. Ibid., 234.
20. Ibid., 236.
21. Robert Stepto, "Narration, Authentication, and Authorial Control in Frederick Douglass' *Narrative of 1845,*" in *The Reconstruction of Instruction,* ed. Dexter Fisher and Robert Stepto (New York: Modern Language Association, 1979), 178.
22. *Dessa Rose,* 232.

23. Ibid., 231.

24. Ibid., 24.

25. The relationship that Hayden White sees between narrative and the issue of authority could well apply to Sherley Anne Williams's text: "We cannot but be struck by the frequency with which narrativity, whether of the fictional or factual sort presupposes the existence of a legal system against or on behalf of which the typical agents of narrative account militate. And this raises the suspicion that narrative in general, from the folktale to the novel, from the annals to the fully realized 'history,' has to do with the topics of law, legality, legitimacy, or more generally, *authority.*" Hayden White, "The Value of Narrativity in the Representation of Reality," *Critical Inquiry* 7, no. 1 (Autumn 1980): 5–27.

15

Art History and Black Memory: Toward a "Blues Aesthetic"

RICHARD J. POWELL

Although many African-American artists have been the subjects of general art histories and art biographies, the actual works themselves have more or less been relegated to a position of illustrating that history rather than being central to it. Questions regarding the existence of a unique school or style of "African-American art" and the recognizable traits and relationships of such to African and Western art traditions are frequently addressed, yet to a great extent they are still left unanswered.[1]

Contemporary efforts by scholars and critics to define an "African-American," or "black" aesthetic have resulted in no clear consensus of meaning or value. Many have completely rejected the notion of an African-American aesthetic, and argue that it is impossible to distinguish common characteristics among the works of African-American artists.[2] On the other hand, when preconceived notions about the art of African Americans are shattered by artists working in widely employed modes of Western modernism and postmodernism, confusion among the critical rank and file sets in.[3] Among the many false assumptions implicit in these arguments concerning "African-American" art are the misconceptions that: (1) so-called Western modes of modern and contemporary art making are essentially European in origin, and (2) the term "African-American" art presupposes that all black artists would be creating in that mode. Tripped by these fallacies, those purporting to define "African-American" art offer an empty term; its use as a tool of visual segregation attests to its hollowness.[4]

Not surprisingly, others suggest that the term "African-American" art is largely a by-product of the political climate of the late 1960s and early 1970s, and that it has very little to do with aesthetic issues.[5] Certainly, the countless printed arguments addressing group shows by black artists underscore this point of view. Nevertheless, in the midst of critical impasses, accusations, and counteraccusations, the ultimate question which comes to the surface is the applicability of so-called white European aesthetic standards and alleged "established values" to African-American art. But because of the aroused passions surrounding the notion of the all-black show and the absence of a comprehensive and practical definition for "black" art, one is left with an almost totally ineffectual body of art commentary, deficient in the kind of scholarly depth and analytic breadth that is endemic to the critical genre.[6]

Even when scholars have acknowledged the presence of an "African-American" aesthetic, it is almost always seen as synonymous with a social realist style, or with what is described by some as nationalistic and didactic art.[7] Although this emphasis on an object's "content" and sociopolitical import—seen in the works of both black and white artists—is now receiving a much warmer reception than it did a decade ago, focusing on it alone often obscures the formal issues which concern so many African-American artists. Furthermore, when one sees the "African-American" aesthetic as limited to realistic works which rely strongly upon social and political messages for their appreciation, other works which stretch one's capacity to "read" a meaning are somehow placed outside of this "African-American" sphere, regardless of the attitudes underlying them.[8]

One of the first scholars to grapple with this notion of a racial idiom in art was Alain Locke. In writings as early as 1924, this Rhodes scholar and Howard University professor of philosophy expressed his hopes for an African-American art that would seek visual nourishment from its legacy—both remembered and recollected—of African ancestral arts. Along with the visual impetus from Africa, it was Locke's expectation that "a new technique, enlightening and interpretative revelations of . . . feeling" and a "lessening of that timid imitativeness" would enter into the African-American artist's repertoire, triggering "fresher and bolder forms of artistic expression."[9] These ideas, which seem fundamental to the formulation of an African-American aesthetic, reverberated throughout the remainder of the twentieth century, all the while laying down additional groundwork for future discussions.

In the 1980 exhibition catalogue *Romare Bearden, 1970–1980* published for the Mint Museum in Charlotte, North Carolina, one encounters several critical essays that fulfill Locke's 1924 prescription for fresher, more empathetic inquiries into an African-American cultural psyche.[10] In that catalogue, Albert Murray and Dore Ashton explore Bearden's art in its aesthetic totality, paying particular attention to Bearden's place in modern art history and to his collaged glorification of childhood memories, human rituals, and the African-American landscape. In their descriptions, Murray and Ashton adjust their critical antennae not just to the obvious parallels with Western European art but to the equally apparent, but rarely articulated, connections with black culture. It is in their careful appropriation of a language (which is normally used to describe a fashionably dressed citizen of Harlem, a stirring jazz performance, or a twelve-bar blues composition) that their critical faculties emerge as a possible gauge for subsequent critiques of selected African-American artworks. One finds especially in Albert Murray's essay a plausible and pliant equation in his discussion of Romare Bearden's style and the aesthetic pull of black music. That "blues timbres, downhome onomatopoeia, urban dissonance, and cacophony"[11] can be seen as musical counterparts to the high-affect colors, improvisational patterning, and perspectival distortions of

Aaron Douglas, *Crucifixion,* 1927. Oil on board, 48″ × 36″. Private Collection of Drs. Camille and William Cosby.

Aaron Douglas, *Aspects of Negro Life: Song of the Towers,* 1934. Oil on canvas, 9′ × 9′. Schomburg Center for Research in Black Culture, Art & Artifacts Division, The New York Public Library, Astor, Lenox and Tilden Foundations (Photo: Manu Sassoonian).

Alison Saar, *Blue Boy,* 1986. Tin, copper, and linoleum, 34″ × 18″. Collection of Richard and Jan Baum.

Romare Bearden, *A Walk in Paradise Gardens,* 1955. Oil on canvas, 27″ × 23⅓″. Museum of African-American Art, Tampa, Florida.

Romare Bearden, *Carolina Shout,* 1974. Collage with acrylic and lacquer on board, 37½″ × 51″. Mint Museum of Art, Charlotte, North Carolina. Museum Purchase: National Endowment for the Arts Matching Fund and the Charlotte Debutante Club Fund (Photo: David Ramsey).

Eldzier Cortor, *Room No. 6,* c. 1946–49. Oil on gesso on board, 31½″ × 42″. Private Collection, New York, New York.

Bearden's art suggest ways of seeing other works of art, and may even have the potential of defining the contours of a larger aesthetic. In Bearden's work, in other words, black music functions as a powerful inspiration and *lieu de mémoire.*

The early career of African-American painter Aaron Douglas (1899–1979) illustrates this black art/black music connection. Douglas's aesthetic values consciously shifted from a Western European and academic mode to what he described in the mid-1920s as a mode negotiating the spaces between African-American music, memory, and visual art.[12] After completing his studies at the Universities of Nebraska and Kansas, and after several years of teaching art in an all-black high school in Kansas City, Douglas moved to New York City. Upon his arrival in 1925, Douglas worked for a brief period in the stockrooms of the NAACP's official magazine, *The Crisis.* From 1925 through 1927, Douglas took art lessons from Winold Reiss, a German painter and graphic designer, who himself was a student of American Indian art and Old and New World "racial types."[13] It was primarily through Reiss's encouragement that Douglas embarked on an African-American-influenced painting style that was destined to become his signature style in murals and book designs.

In later years Douglas discussed his initial doubts about Winold Reiss's insistence that in order to explore that "inner thing of blackness," he would have to visit the museums and galleries that had African art on display:

> I clearly recall his [Reiss's] impatience as he sought to urge me beyond my doubts and fears that seemed to loom so large in the presence of the terrifying spectres moving beneath the surface of every African masque and fetish. At last, I began little by little to get the point and to take a few halting, timorous steps towards the unknown. I shall not attempt to describe my feelings as I first tried to objectify with paint and brush what I thought to be the visual emanations or expressions that came into view with the sounds produced by the old black song makers of antebellum days when they first began to put together snatches and bits from Protestant hymns, along with half remembered tribal chants, lullabies and work songs. . . .[14]

As evidenced in this recollection of Douglas's, his search for a particular "style," though initially starting with African sculpture, soon gave way to a reassessment of and a new appreciation for African-American musical arts. The African sculptures that he saw in the downtown museums and galleries became the formal backdrops for the cabaret blues and storefront spirituals that he experienced uptown. Obviously, Douglas realized that if he wanted his art to speak to the masses of black people, then it would have to have the same vitality, spirit, and ability to transfigure as did African-American music.

Douglas's artistic presence was definitely felt during his first five years in New York City. In easel paintings, murals, and book illustrations, Aaron Douglas developed a geometric style that was in sync both with African-American rhythms and with concurrent Art Deco design tenets. The flat and generalized delineation of figures, with an emphasis on precisionistlike color changes were described by Douglas as "suggestive of the uniqueness found in the gestures and bodily movements of Negro dance and [in] the sounds and vocal patterns . . . of Negro song."[15]

Aaron Douglas's *Crucifixion,* a 1927 illustration from James Weldon Johnson's *God's Trombones,* is a good example of how one formal quality of African-American musical expression—a tendency toward polyphonics and polymetrics—is visually achieved.[16] Douglas's depictions of Jesus Christ, the Roman soldiers, and the cross are reduced to a succession of silhouetted shades of purple and lavender, and illusionistically overlaid with diagonal and concentric bands of lighter tones. This composition, with the overlaid circles and diagonal band of contrasting values, creates a complex work in spite the simplicity of the silhouetted forms. Along with Douglas's intentional fragmenting of this biblical scene, an aural quality is evoked by his use of tonal gradations. From the sunlike core containing Christ to the surrounding fragments of "light" which get gradually darker and darker as they emanate from the haloed figure, the multivalenced facets of *Crucifixion* recall the layers of sound in traditional black church services. A turn-of-the-century visitor to "Little St. Johns" in South Carolina gives his musical impressions from a black revival service and, in doing so, expresses some of the same characteristics that Aaron Douglas's *Crucifixion* displays:

> The blending was close, the effect rich and full, the passionate, dramatic melody (with gradations of tone which sharps and flats are inadequate to express . . .) now and then rising in a rush of sound into the harmony of some strange, chromatic, accidental chord. Individual voices were distinguished . . . all feeling, as if without knowledge or intent, for that vibrating sense which attests perfect harmony, or for that unjarring flow of perfect unison; . . . some were singing antiphonally, . . . using indifferently and irrelevantly harmonies of the 3rd, 5th, or 6th, producing odd accidental concords of sound, strange chromatic groups of semitones, and irregular intervals. . . .[17]

This language mixes musical terminology with visual allusions, thus suggesting, at least in the mind of this visiting commentator, a kind of sensory "glide" in the music's effect. The preacher's sermon, the deacon's response, the congregation's vocal acknowledgment, and the simultaneous singing, calling out, screaming, crying, moaning, clapping, and foot patting from various church members are akin to the visual faceting and layering of compositional elements of *Crucifixion* and, as suggested in a survey of other twentieth-century African-American-inspired creations, the works of many other artists as well.[18]

Another painting by Douglas that also takes its cues from a multisensorial, rhythmic, and recollected impulse is *Song of the Towers.* One of the four panel paintings—collectively called *Aspects of Negro Life*—that Douglas created in 1934 for the 135th Street Branch of the New York Public Library, *Song of the Towers* was described by the artist in the following manner:

> A great migration, away from the clutching hand of serfdom in the South to the urban industrialized life in America, began during the First World War. And with it there was born the creative self-expression which quickly grew into the New Negro Movement of the twenties. At its peak, the Depression brought confusion, dejection, and frustration.[19]

Perhaps more than previous works by Douglas, *Song of the Towers* represents a major departure from his more orchestrated, romantic depictions of modern black life.[20] Here, a gigantic cogwheel, skyscrapers, and the burning smokestacks of urban industrialization are shown off kilter, pulling his figural elements and one's perceptions of this scene into a kind of spatial ambiguity. Although Douglas's architectural and human silhouettes in *Song of the Towers* are similar to previous examples, the multiple themes in this latter work—migration, escapism, urban industrialization, creative self-expression, confusion, and dejection—along with the slanting and swaying scenery, bring it into a category entirely unto itself.

Without question, the three core images in Douglas's *Song of the Towers*—a silhouette of a man (on the far right) shown ragged, running on a cogwheel, and carrying a suitcase; another man (in the center) shown standing at the top of the cogwheel and holding up a saxophone; and a third man (in the lower left corner) shown in repose and dazed—are visual representations of the black music and culture of that era. This "pack my bags and make my getaway" theme, although based on the actual black migration experience, can be found as well in 1930s black music (W. C. Handy's "St. Louis Blues," and Robert Johnson's "Dust My Broom"), and in depression-era black literature (Sterling Brown's "Long Track Blues" and Richard Wright's "Big Boy Leaves Home").

The section of the painting that best visualizes Douglas's notion of "creative self-expression" is the silhouette of the man holding a saxophone. As art historian Robert Farris Thompson has pointed out in his study of Kongo-influenced cultures in the black Americas, the ecstatic, arm-raised gesture is an answer "to the challenge of the crossroads, to the presence of death, to the proximity of God."[21] Fusing the metaphysical import of this gesture with the creative connotations of the saxophone, Douglas conveys a shared message here about musical and spiritual upliftment.

The concentric circles in *Song of the Towers,* like those in *Crucifixion* and other works by Douglas, act as a kind of zoom lens, taking the viewer into the center of painted matters, so to speak. From a core which includes the man, his saxophone, and the Statue of Liberty (shown in the implied far distance), one could conclude that one of the painting's primary themes is the musical and cultural contributions of blacks to America.

The "confusion, dejection, and frustration" that Douglas referred to in his written description of *Song of the Towers* is no doubt represented by the figure in the lower left corner of the canvas. Appearing disoriented and somewhat oblivious to all that surrounds him, this figure is a kind of painted incarnation of the Depression, as well as a figural evocation of the lowly blues, that component of the music and culture which is about failure and tragedy. Above his head is a skeletal hand which, like the *Dance of Death* cycles in sixteenth-century European art, is a convoy to the other side of Douglas's cogwheel of life and death.

On a more formal level, *Song of the Towers* can be seen as a blues idiom artwork in terms of Aaron Douglas's overall stylistic approach. The layering of a pure abstraction over a representational scene is not unlike a similar phenomenon in black music, where an improvised solo rides over a fixed melodic composition.[22] In both cases, the artist must be aware of the standard version in order to make nonstandard changes or additions. The key difference, of course, is that in the performed context, several musicians contribute to a final product, whereas in Douglas's painting, *he* is the rhythm section, the chorus, the soloist, the composer, and the conductor. The collection of creative ingredients that constitute the bands of Fletcher Henderson, Duke Ellington, and Count Basie is transposed here to the world of painting through what art historian David C. Driskell has referred to in Douglas's murals as "an intriguing blend of abstract construction with objective perception."[23]

The formal complexities of classic African-American painting and in the sounds flowing from African-American music are also expressed in the multilayered sensibilities of the black folk aesthetic. Writing in the early 1930s, novelist and folklorist Zora Neale Hurston described this design attitude in African-American homes during the early years of the Depression:

> On the walls of the homes of the average Negro one always finds a glut of gaudy calendars, wall pockets and advertising lithography. . . . I saw in Mobile, Alabama a room in which the walls were gaily papered with Sunday supplements of the *Mobile Register.* There were seven calendars and three wall pockets. One of them was decorated with a lace doily. The mantle-shelf was covered with a scarf of deep, homemade lace, looped up with a huge bow of pink crepe paper. Over the door was a huge lithograph showing the Treaty of Versailles being signed with a Waterman fountain pen.
>
> It was grotesque, yes. But it indicated the desire for beauty. And decorating a decoration, as in the case of the doily on the gaudy wall pocket, did not seem out of place to the hostess. The feeling [in] back of such an act is that there can never be enough beauty, let alone too much. . . .[24]

Hurston's description of this African-American "will to adorn," through a kind of *collage sensibility,* bears a striking resemblance to the layered images of Douglas and to a whole world of African-American mixed-media, assemblage, and collage artists. From the assembly of objects found on graves—black and white—in the African-American-influenced southern United States to the newspaper-lined walls in the homes of poor, rural black folk, this persistently rhythmic and unabashedly folkloric impulse cuts across time and through the minds and imaginations of innumerable people who identify with the African-American tradition.[25]

It was this engagement with cultural memory—via the innovations of artists like Aaron Douglas and Hurston's anonymous, Mobile, Alabama, assemblagist—that propelled an artist like Romare Bearden (1914–88) to embrace a style in the early sixties that Albert Murray described as being "conditioned by the blues-idiom in general and jazz musicianship in particular."[26] In a 1964 interview, Bearden spoke about his transition from being a nonfigurative, abstract painter to being a culturally grounded and rhythmically oriented collagist: "I felt that the Negro was becoming too much of an abstraction, rather than the reality that art can give a subject. . . . What I've attempted to do is establish a world in which the validity of my Negro experience could live and make its own logic."[27]

For Romare Bearden this excavating of the "Negro experience" necessitated a departure from the nonfigural and nontextual constructs of his paintings of the fifties and a movement instead toward an art of pieced and patched realities.[28] With an approach that (1) combined cut and torn photographs from illustrated magazines; (2) presented Aaron Douglas's silhouette within a new, vigorous context; and (3) rearranged these odd scraps of colored paper, bits and pieces of human parts, sculptural segments, and slices of nature into a loosely structured narrative, Bearden invested black imagery with a sense of newness and energy which really hadn't been transmitted in American art since the late forties. Appropriately, the public's response to these new, fusion works by Bearden was one which recognized both the dreamy, fictive qualities in his imagery and the real, documentary aspect of his work. Dore Ashton made note of this peculiar dichotomy in perception in 1964:

> Although Bearden's stress is insistently on art, it is in the artlessness of the "real" that the power of these photomontages lies. The times and places he depicts are unmistakable, no matter how much regulated by his plastic manipulations. In this sense, Bearden's photomontages may be compared with the best film documentaries which, through their uncompromising severity, their strict adherence to visual fact, transcend reportage and become art. Depth of feeling and discipline are the keys.[29]

One might add to Ashton's assessment that in works like *Carolina Shout* (from the 1974 *Of the Blues* series), Bearden recognized the artistic potential and validating power of African-American life and music. By donning the mantle of a cultural *rememberer* or, in the parlance of African peoples of the western Sudan, a *griot,* Bearden, like Eldzier Cortor's folk interior in the 1947 painting *Americana,* turned old gazettes and newspapers into something timeless, expressive, and real.

Bearden's career-long search for an African-American reality through art is in some ways echoed in a statement made by artist Aaron Douglas over sixty years ago. Writing to the poet Langston Hughes, Douglas set forth the following strategy for creating an authentic "Negro" art:

> Your problem Langston, my problem, no our problem is to conceive, develop, establish an art era. Not white art painted black. . . . No, let's bare our arms and plunge them deep through laughter, through pain, through sorrow, through hope, through disappointment, into the very depths of the souls of our people and drag forth material crude, rough, neglected. Then

> let's sing it, dance it, write it, paint it. Let's do the impossible. Let's create something transcendentally material, mystically objective. Earthy. Spiritually earthy. Dynamic.[30]

Though couched in the romantically imagistic language of a young artist, Douglas's strategy for establishing his very own "art era" was predicated, like Bearden's aesthetic experiments of forty years later, on a thorough excavation of African-American history and memory. What Douglas sought to tap was a reality that was often raw, unpolished, and marginalized. A reality that was variegated and multifaceted in character. A reality that could be both spiritual and material. A reality that, if we had to come up with a metaphor for all of the above, would be embodied in cultural expression like "the blues." Surely, in an effort to define African-American art and/or culture, scholars should acknowledge this thematic and expressive vein within the production of selected, twentieth-century works which, by virtue of their respective artists, have a predetermined, *conscious* basis in a "mystically objective" African-American reality such as in "the blues."

The riffs in art and time that are created by generation after generation of African-American artists bring to mind the declaration of Amiri Baraka that "all styles are epochs. They come again and again. What is was, and so forth."[31] One might also add to this statement that because styles are cyclical like the seasons, they are ultimately revolutionary and redemptive. The blues, as the delta of twentieth-century African-American culture, spawns inlets of style that color a vast and gray ocean of tradition. From the anonymous songsters of the late nineteenth century who sang about hard labor and unattainable love, to contemporary rappers blasting the airwaves with percussive and danceable testimonies, the blues is an affecting, memory-induced presence that endures in every artistic overture made toward African-American peoples.

Notes

1. Three recent publications have attempted to answer this question and, in doing so, have offered up several intriguing approaches to the concept of "African-American" art: Richard Powell, ed., *The Blues Aesthetic: Black Culture and Modernism* (Washington, D.C.: Washington Project for the Arts, 1989); Alvia Wardlaw, ed., *Black Art/Ancestral Legacy: The African Impulse in African American Art* (Dallas, Tx.: Dallas Museum of Art, 1990), and *New Generation: Southern Black Aesthetic* (Winston-Salem N.C.: Southeastern Center for Contemporary Art, 1990).

2. Barbara Rose, "Black Art in America," *Art in America* 58 (September/October 1970), p. 55; and Hilton Kramer, "Black Art or Merely Social History," *New York Times,* June 26, 1977, p. D25.

3. "Daubings Protest Geneva Show of Paintings by Afro-Americans," *New York Times,* June 12, 1971, p. 25, recounts what happened when Swiss youth protested against an exhibition of eight black American artists. In the eyes of the protesters, the exhibition (which included works by Romare Bearden, Sam Gilliam, and Richard Hunt, among others) was not genuinely "Afro-American," nor did it give an "adequate representation" of the black protest movement in the United States. About

eighteen years later, the vandalizing of artist David Hammons's sixteen-foot-high billboard/painting of a blond and blue-eyed Jesse Jackson (*How Ya Like Me Now,* 1989) by disgruntled black youth in Washington, D.C., is yet another example of censuring the works of African-American artists because of dashed expectations.

4. Elsa Honig Fine, *The Afro-American Artists* (New York: Holt, Rinehart and Winston, 1973), p. 281. Recently art historian and cultural critic Kobena Mercer discussed the inherent problems with the current terminology for artists of the African diaspora in a lecture entitled "Transcultural Icons and Aesthetics in African Diaspora Media Arts," delivered at the College Art Association, on February 21, 1991, in Washington, D.C.

5. Rose, "Black Art,", p. 54

6. Ibid.

7. Edmund B. Gaither, "Introduction," in *Afro-American Artists: New York and Boston* (Boston: National Center of Afro-American Artists, 1970), n.p., and Hilton Kramer, "Trying to Define 'Black Art': Must We Go Back to Social Realism?" *New York Times,* May 31, 1970, p. D17.

8. See Ann Gibson, "Two Worlds: African-American Abstraction in New York at Mid-Century," *The Search for Freedom: African-American Abstract Painting, 1945–1975* (New York: Kenkeleba Gallery, 1991).

9. Alain Locke, "A Note on African Art," *Opportunity* 2 (May 1924), pp. 134–38.

10. *Romare Bearden, 1970–1980* (Charlotte, N.C.: Mint Museum, 1980).

11. Albert Murray, "The Visual Equivalent of the Blues," in *Romare Bearden, 1970–1980,* p. 18.

12. For information on Aaron Douglas see: Mary Schmidt Campbell, *Harlem Renaissance: Art of Black America* (New York: Harry N. Abrams, for the Studio Museum in Harlem, 1987).

13. For information on Winold Reiss see: Jeffrey C. Stewart, *To Color America: Portraits by Winold Reiss* (Washington, D.C.: Smithsonian Institution Press, for the National Portrait Gallery, 1989).

14. Aaron Douglas, "The Harlem Renaissance," unpublished manuscript dated March 18, 1973, Special Collections, Fisk University, Nashville, Tennessee.

15. Aaron Douglas, untitled, unpublished manuscript, n.d. (ca. 1966), Special Collections, Fisk University, Nashville, Tennessee.

16. James Weldon Johnson, *God's Trombones* (New York: Viking, 1927).

17. John Bennett, "A Revival Sermon at Little St. Johns," *Atlantic Monthly* 98 (August 1906), p. 257.

18. For a discussion of how African-American culture informs artists across racial and ethnic lines see: Richard Powell, ed., *The Blues Aesthetic: Black Culture and Modernism* (Washington, D.C.: Washington Project for the Arts, 1989).

19. Aaron Douglas, printed handout on *The Aspects of Negro Life* panels, October 27, 1949, Manuscripts Division, Schomburg Center for Research in Black Culture, New York Public Library, New York, New York.

20. Douglas's decided shift to a more political stance in *The Aspects of Negro Life* murals was noticed by at least one critic of his day: T. R. Poston, "Murals and Marx: Aaron Douglas Moves to the Left with PWA Decorations," *New York Amsterdam News,* November 24, 1934, p. 1.

21. Robert Farris Thompson, *Four Moments of the Sun: Kongo Art of Two Worlds* (Washington, D.C.: National Gallery of Art, 1981), pp. 176–77.

22. Albert Murray's description of Kansas City jazz "stylizations" in *Stomping the Blues* (New York: McGraw-Hill, 1976), p. 170, bears a striking resemblance to Doug-

las's improvisational approach to layering and patterning one set of designs on top of another image.

23. David C. Driskell, *Two Centuries of Black American Art* (Lost Angeles: Los Angeles County Museum of Art, in cooperation with Alfred A. Knopf, 1976), p. 68.

24. Zora Neale Hurston, "Characteristics of Negro Folk Expression," in *Negro Anthology,* ed. Nancy Cunard (London: Wishart, 1934), p. 40.

25. Kongo-influenced grave decorations in Afro-America are discussed in Robert Farris Thompson, *Flash of the Spirit: African and Afro-American Art and Philosophy* (New York: Random House, 1983), pp. 132–42.

26. Albert Murray, "The Visual Equivalent of the Blues," in *Romare Bearden, 1970–1980,* p. 18.

27. Romare Bearden, as quoted in Charles Childs, "Bearden: Identification and Identity," *Artnews* 63 (October 1964), p. 62.

28. Lowery Sims, "The Unknown Romare Bearden," *Artnews* 85 (October 1986), pp. 117–20.

29. Dore Ashton, "Romare Bearden—Projections," *Quandrum* 17 (1964), p. 110.

30. Aaron Douglas, letter to Langston Hughes, December 21, 1925, Langston Hughes papers, James Weldon Johnson Memorial Collection of Negro Arts and Letters, Beinecke Rare Book and Manuscript Library, Yale University, New Haven, Connecticut.

31. Imamu Amiri Baraka, *In Our Terribleness* (Indianapolis, Ind.: Bobbs-Merrill, 1970), n.p.

16

On Burke and the Vernacular: Ralph Ellison's Boomerang of History

ROBERT G. O'MEALLY

> Perhaps if we learn more of what has happened and *why* it happened, we'll learn more of who we really are. And perhaps if we learn more about our unwritten history, we won't be so vulnerable to the capriciousness of events as we are today. And in the process of becoming more aware of ourselves we will recognize that one of the functions of our vernacular culture is that of preparing for the emergence of the unexpected, whether it takes the form of the disastrous or the marvelous.
>
> —Ralph Ellison, *Going to the Territory*

> *Boo'mer-ang,* n. 1 . . . When thrown it may be made to describe remarkable curves, esp. that in which, starting nearly horizontally, it soon curves upward, and returning, falls near the starting point The returning boomerang is regarded as a toy or plaything. The heavier kind, called *war boomerang,* does not return. . . . 2. A means to an end, esp. an unworthy one, which reacts to the damage of its user.
>
> —*Webster's New International Dictionary,* 2nd ed.

History, says Ralph Ellison's Invisible Man, moves not like an arrow but like a boomerang. Anyone who declares history a spiral, he warns, is "preparing a boomerang. Keep a steel helmet handy."[1] The history Invisible Man sees has been thrown down not by God or gods but by human hands: it circles, it rises, it dips and rears, it attacks. It's a sports toy, it's a weapon, it's a metaphor for action that is self-defeating. As the wielder of such a figure of speech, Ellison's critique is not only of a vulgarly Marxian concept of history—one persistent theme of the novel—but of *any* deterministic or easy schematic tracing of history. History swoops. It *boomerangs.*

Here I define the word *history* as Kenneth Burke does, as the flow of experience or even "the world."[2] For both Ellison and Burke, who is an extremely significant intellectual influence on Ellison, the world is too full of unexpectedness to be reduced to a formula, whether arrow-straight or coolly cycling. Erratic in its shiftings, not just upward and downward but "crabways and crossways,"[3] its changes can occur in any time frame or space. One way of reading *Invisible Man* is as a novel in which the boomerangs of history are ever whirling down on the protagonist's naive head. Eventually the encounters with boomeranging history bop him toward deeper personal and cultural awareness. "I have been boomeranged across my head so much," he reports, "that I now can see the darkness of lightness."[4]

My thesis is that more than any other form of human expression, art communicates the excitement as well as the treacherous unpredictability of history's flights. Further, that particularly in an American context, *vernacular* art and artifacts convey this fast-changing and invisible history. They tell aspects of the American experience that do not get told in any other way, and that perhaps cannot be told in any other way. It's Burke who makes the key point that aside from its value as entertainment and escape (both functions he sees as valid and much more complicated than usually judged), art offers people what he says language in general offers, namely, "equipment for living."[5] Through encounters with the vernacular, Americans are steadied for the surprises, either "the disastrous or the marvelous," that life in the United States offers in such abundance—the boomerangs of American history.

It is in this crucial sense that vernacular expression may be described as a *lieu de mémoire:* that which induces a reappraisal of one's place and circumstances, a remaking of the official calendar, a reconsideration of the past, the given histories. That which inspires the conscious, critical rethinking of attitudes toward history and memory. If a *lieu de mémoire* may be defined as a "site of memory," the vernacular is a monumentally significant American *lieu de mémoire.*[6]

Burke's systems suggest useful ways of reading both vernacular art and the part it plays in American life. In the shortest conceivable summary of the aesthetics according to Burke—the leading point to make is that he views both history (as defined) and artistic expression in dramatic or "dramatistic" terms. All the world is not a stage, he says; still, one is hard put to specify precisely *how* it is not a stage. In a watershed essay, he examines Hitler's World War II motives as part of a dark drama involving sexual symbolism and rituals of sacrificial death;[7] in turn he considers "Ode on a Grecian Urn" as an "action" that enables further reenaction.[8] Thus the world of war and politics is an unfolding poetic drama; and the poem (read *poem* here to mean art in general, including vernacular art), too, is a field of action. To make the latter point plain, Burke declares that to make words is to take action in the world, that *language is symbolic action.*[9] More than just a mental and emotional readying for action, literature presents its audience with specific inducements to act in certain ways: it "advertises" a stance toward rottennesses in varied Denmarks. Burke: To make art or to be moved by it = to *act.* No wonder when Ellison's Invisible Man remembers hearing Louis Armstrong's horn he thinks, "This familiar music had demanded action."[10]

For the Burkean observer, evaluating life's or literature's dramatic action means considering not just isolated acts by themselves but acts in the context of five indispensable terms: the *action* itself as well as the *actor, purpose, agency,* and *scene.*[11] In other words, to analyze motive (and of course Burke is fully aware that a *motive* is both an incentive to action and a pattern of images or metaphors in art), the trained observer asks these five questions: *Who?* Did *what? Why? How? Where?* To analyze black *lieux de mémoire* with Burkean fullness is to ask not one question but an interlocking quintet of questions.

Any student of Ralph Ellison quickly learns that these questions have been of continuing importance to his own sense of an action's meaning, either in history or in art. On the question of an action's locale, the key question for those concerned with *lieux de mémoire,* Ellison has often warned sternly that observers typically have held too simplistic an idea of the African American's scene. The impulse has been to reduce it to a spattering of social science numbers without considering the mazy poetics of the spaces themselves as their inhabitants know them.

Take Harlem. It's too easy to forget the general Americanness of the black city within a city (with its networks of subway lines, chain stores, municipal office buildings, and cable TV lines) or, for that matter, its background *Dutchness* and *Indianness.* Too easy to forget the quick-changing history of that place and the varied histories of those who live there: many not just with Afro-Southern but with West Indian, Hispanic, or even Old New York backgrounds. Saying simply, "I know a lot about her, she's from Harlem," one can flippantly underestimate this layered experience. For nearly sixty years, Ellison himself has lived in and near Harlem. So for him Harlem is more than just a place of the present as it now meets the eye; it is a place of history and long memory, a *lieu de mémoire.* He remembers when it was a glistening neighborhood of dreams, "a glamorous place, a place where wonderful music existed and where there was a great tradition of Negro American style and elegance."[12]

He now lives in Washington Heights, in upper Manhattan at the edge of Harlem, in a neighborhood that is predominantly U.S. black but also significantly Latin American as well as Anglo. He also keeps a country home in the Berkshires and retains strong allegiances to Alabama, where he attended college—and, most emphatically, to his birthplace of Oklahoma, to which he regularly returns and of which, he says, he often dreams. To the question Where are you from? "Harlemite" Ellison might most quickly answer, "Oklahoma." Is there any wonder that his sense of place and identity is an intricately involved one? Yet, figured in this way—with this sense that setting mirrors history—scene does tell much of the story. It is in this way that, as Ellison often says, "Geography is fate."

In his essays Ellison often makes the point that black American identity is too often reduced to a simplistic idea of scene; or it is flatly explained *merely* in terms of place, as if the lines and shadows of one's surroundings were everything. "I am invisible," his novel's character says, "understand, simply because people refuse to see me. Like the bodiless heads you see sometimes in circus sideshows, it is as though I have been surrounded by mirrors of hard, distorting glass. When they approach me they see only my surroundings, themselves, or figments of their imagination—indeed, everything and anything except me."[13]

Throughout his work Ellison plays with ironies concerning the who and the where of it all. To know who I am, Invisible Man discovers, I must know *where* I am. But if where is no easy question, it also cannot, as we have warned, be the only significant question. In an example often cited by Ellison, the tubercular slums of Oklahoma City were deadly in their squalor, but from them emerged the brilliant Charlie Christian, "inventor" of modern jazz guitar technique. It is here that the vital fine print of *Who? What? When?* and *How?* assert themselves against a quite unpromising *Where?*

Christian himself, says Ellison, "was from a respectable family." For all its dilapidation, the wooden tenement where Christian lived "was also alive and exciting," Ellison recalls, "and I enjoyed visiting there, for the people both lived and sang the blues." And elsewhere Ellison asks this question about Christian's environs, and about this general issue of scene and self: "How many geniuses do you get *anywhere?*"[14] So let us not overplay this issue of scene—particularly when it is measured in discouraging numerical terms that can disguise the contour of a place's true possibilities. Then, too, lest we wax romantic about the poor black neighborhoods of our society, Ellison the writer of the blues also inserts these words about the place where Christian lived: "Nonetheless, it was doubtless here that he developed the tuberculosis from which he died."[15]

Elaborating Burke's history-as-drama analogy, Ellison observes that such close-up details of the American setting and drama are often too troubling and challenging for Americans to face directly. So while we read and write "official" American histories, unrecorded or invisible histories also unfold. "Perhaps," says Ellison, "we possess two basic versions of American history: one which is written and as neatly stylized as ancient myth, and the other unwritten and chaotic and full of contradictions, changes of pace, and surprises as life itself."[16] And of course who tells the history is as important as the why-where-how-and-when of its telling. "History," Invisible Man muses after Tod Clifton has been shot down,

> records the patterns of men's lives, they say: Who slept with whom and with what results; who fought and who won and who lived to lie about it afterwards. All things, it is said, are duly recorded—all things of importance, that is. But not quite, for actually it is only the known, the seen, the heard and only those events that the recorder regards as important that are put down, those lies their keepers keep their power by.[17]

And then concerning the murder, he wonders: "Where were the historians today? And how would they put it down?"

Much of the history of people like the novel's Tod goes unseen, but that does not mean that the unseen is unreal or ineffectual. According to Ellison:

> There's no denying the fact that Americans can be notoriously selective in the exercise of historical memory. Surely there must be some self-deceptive magic in this, for in spite of what is left out of our recorded history, our

> unwritten history looms as its obscure alter ego, and although repressed from our general knowledge of ourselves, it is always active in the shaping of events. . . . Perhaps it is our need to avoid the discouraging facts of our experience that accounts for the contradiction between those details of our history which we choose to remember and those which we ignore or leave unstated.[18]

Much that goes unstated in printed histories does get expressed in the fluid media of the vernacular. And what do I mean by "the vernacular"?[19] According to *Webster's New International Dictionary* (2nd ed.):

> ver-nac-u-lar [L. *Vernaculus,* born in one's house, native, fr. *verna,* a slave born in his master's house, a native, of uncert. origin.] 1. Belonging to, developed in, and spoken or used by, the people of a particular place, region, or country; native; indigenous. . . . 2. Characteristic of a locality; local. . . .

Relying on Ellison and John Kouwenhoven, by vernacular I also refer to *the dynamic processes and products of cultural interaction* between more established conventions of expression and those which are more improvised and unself-conscious, and thus more unpretentiously American. In Ellison's words, the vernacular is a process

> in which the most refined styles from the past are continually merged with the play-it-by-eye-and-ear improvisations which we invent in our efforts to control our environment and entertain ourselves. And this not only in language and literature, but in architecture and cuisine, in music, costume, and dance, and in tools and technology. In it the styles and techniques of the past are adjusted to the needs of the present, and in its integrative action the high styles of the past are democratized. From this perspective the vernacular is no less than the styles associated with aristocracy, a gesture toward perfection.[20]

For Americans, says Ellison, the vernacular is "our most characteristic style."

By vernacular I do not mean only the unvarnished "texts" of transcribed song lyrics or folk stories. Here, as many students of culture have argued, *performance* is the thing. In this field there's nothing quite so misleading, for example, as a study of the blues—which involves very specific musical structures as well as spare, evocative poetry and complicatedly layered rituals enacted most meaningfully at parties and public dances—as if it consisted of nothing more than denotative words on a page. When I speak of the blues and other vernacular forms I mean all of the vital aspects of the performance, including the interplay between performer and audience as well as the socioeconomic and ritual settings in which performances take place. All are integrally linked to the meaning of vernacular expression. And it is important to know that concentrating on any one aspect of such performances—again, for example, to blues lyrics alone—leads to what Hemingway calls "decadence": the reduction of something as magnificent as a bullfight to something more like butchery. Of something life-affirming like the blues to the sad sacking of a "blue" victim. Which of course can lead to a wretchedly mistaken notion both of who the African American really is and of what his or her history actually has meant.

Television, movie, and now video shows, as well as American barns, bridges, and railroad cars—and the reaching, jagged lines along the improvised Manhattan skyline—exemplify the relation between modern technological savvy and the American's playful hammering together of lines, blocks, and spheres.[21] All of these American vernacular forms have certain traits in common. Like so many American game sports, they may well be described as *jazz shaped:* all involve U.S. changes and rhythmic swing as well as certain playfully improvisational aspects and ideals of spirited coordination.[22]

Surely Kouwenhoven is right to say that New York's definitive skyscrapers rise like jazz solos out of the steady backbeatlike grid of the city's streets.[23] And as in jazz, all of these forms place an insistent emphasis not so much on finished cultural products as on their processes. Witness again the Big Apple skyline, and, to choose unlikely-seeming items from Kouwenhoven's American vernacular list, chewing gum or comic books—all typically refuse to conclude with anything like the grand sense of finality that one gets in classical tragedy, a European sonata, or a Gothic cathedral—or, if you will, in a soup-to-nuts banquet. By contrast, the comics' stories go on and on, book after book, indefinitely. Likewise, a skyscraper could be five or ten stories taller or shorter, and aesthetically it would not matter much; what matters is that endless ascent of lines, the rocketing rise.

A jazz piece usually has no rigidly set number of sections: the vamp may continue until it is virtually a piece unto itself; the choruses, solo breaks, and out-choruses may repeat until the bandleader, on a given night, calls a halt which can come quite suddenly and, for that matter, may meld easily into the piece which comes after it, as if an entire evening's performance were one extended skyscraper with a variety of stories and styles blended into one. Played "live," blues or jazz admits no such thing as a fixed or definitive version of a work.[24] "Sometimes," as Billie Holiday once put it, "I do a song a little bit slower, the next time it's a little bit brighter. It's according to how I feel."[25] Jazz—that incredible American product that ranges from the tragic to the comic, from slapstick to the heroic, but never entirely beyond the danceable—is a tremendously significant form of vernacular expression. I'd go so far as to name it the apotheosis of the American vernacular.[26]

Yet, in part because of Americans' continuing reverence for European culture—and in part because we can't face our history as encoded in its indigenous expressive forms—jazz and other American vernacular forms are still typically put aside as nothing serious.[27] This very mistreatment and indifference have been the vernacular's mixed blessing: we play it and play with it without the thou-shalt-nots that govern more formal or accepted art. Which permits us to enjoy it and to take it in without the heavy self-consciousness sometimes associated with Art.[28] How imposing can the study of jazz music be when even now the touchstone books of classic jazz solos are entitled "fake books"?

Of course the risk of this casually dismissive attitude is that we will ignore vernacular art's deepest significances. Those that spring from the works as aesthetic statements which at their best are dense with individual and group experience, ringing with history. Consider black social dances, quilting, gospel music, rap music, or—especially—jazz. Again, these forms tell a history that is told in no other way. They reflect, symbolically, actions and attitudes as they have evolved through history; at their best, they embody attitudes having to do with resiliency, improvisation, confrontation, and the yearning for technical mastery and teamwork.[29] In this sense, what we put aside when we put aside the vernacular is the least Old Worldly part of ourselves as New World dwellers: precisely that part of our identity that defines us as Americans. As Romare Bearden saw, American experience is a patchwork of forms and colors: it is a collage. It is an improvised "play-it-by-eye-and-by-ear" expression, a jazz work.

It is Bearden, too, who has observed that too often students who complain of too little high-quality American art simply have no idea where to look for it. In the forties he would send such people to the Savoy Ballroom, he said, and ask them to consider the lindy hop, with its elaborate turns and twists, and with its imitation of Lindy's flight, reenacted with cool spirit by the dancers sail-"hopping" over their partners' backs: African-American art in motion.[30] Perhaps, wrote Ellison in 1942, "the symmetrical frenzy of the Lindy-hop conceals clues to great potential power" as an example of the black masses' unexamined "incipient forms of action."[31]

Nor is the vernacular a romanticized or ideological construct. Rather, it is the inversive and inventive edge of African-American culture, constantly in search of newly turned forms. As Cornel West has suggested, it is constantly being co-opted by the culture at large—consider traditional New Orleans music, "swing," or even rap music; thus it is always in search of new forms that have not yet been absorbed. In this sense, U.S. black vernacular forms, as conservative as they can be, also are fueled by an aggressive impulse to change, not only "to make it new" but to make what they do uncopyably different. Classic vernacular forms like jazz music and jazz dance show their roots and also have this impulse to break away: to the tradition as they receive it they boldly turn this creative edge of new discovery.[32] Perhaps in part it is this impulse for survival by means of creating cultural forms that "the white boys can't steal" that accounts for so much of the African American's sustained centuries of creativity on these shores.

Repeatedly in Ellison's fiction, naive protagonists are put in touch with the surging power of American vernacular culture. In "Flying Home" (1944),[33] a brilliant story presaging *Invisible Man,* wise Jefferson tells a tall tale that helps heal the greenhorn Todd's isolation and hubris as it helps provide him with a healthy attitude toward the troubles he must face. Jefferson grants Todd a "vernacular perspective," as it were, teaching him that it's not enough to have mere aeronautical engineering and fly-boy know-how; not enough to have an arrow-line scientific view of the world. To survive, the young flyer learns, he must have something of the pragmatic vernacular training that Jefferson embodies; must have some of Old Jeff's humor, intelligence, and the readiness for disciplined action (including restraint) under pressure. He needs what a blues-trained character in *Invisible Man* calls "shit, grit and mother-wit."[34]

Set during World War II, "Flying Home" depicts Todd, a black American pilot-in-training who is counting on a change in the country's policy that has barred black airmen from flight duty overseas. While on a practice mission over Alabama, Todd is brought down to earth by distractions on the ground and by a collision with an embodiment of racist unpredictability and violence, a "jim-crow bird" (a buzzard). "It had been as though he had flown into a storm of blood and blackness" (259). When Todd regains consciousness on the ground, he realizes that he has had a brush with death. He also sees that his attendant is elderly black Jefferson, who passes the time while help arrives by spinning Todd an old yarn, delivered in terms that are unmistakably African and American. (Of course it is no mistake that old black Jefferson is named for the only American president who was an artistic genius.)

"It's like when I was up in heaven," Jefferson's story begins. It is the much-collected story of the flying fool, the black angel who travels too fast for his own good. Who is caught "flying up to the stars and divin' down and zooming roun' the moon . . . [and] accidentally knocked the tips offa some stars and they tell me I caused a storm and a coupla lynchings down here in Macon County." Not surprisingly, for asserting too much individual power the black angel is ejected from heaven, which turns out to be run less like the heaven of the Bible than like the Alabama of old. Peter does the job himself. "Son," Jefferson tells Todd, "I argued and pleaded with that old white man, but it didn't do a bit of good. They rushed me straight to them pearly gates and gimme a parachute and a map of the state of Alabama. . . ." One of the other angels breaks out laughing, so Jeff takes Peter up on his offer to say a last few words: "Well," he tells him, "you done took my wings. And you puttin' me out. You got charge of things so's I can't do nothin' about it. But you got to admit just this: While I was up here I was the flyinest sonofabitch what ever hit heaven!" (262).

At first, Todd's reaction to the comical tale is to bristle defensively: "Why do you laugh at me this way?" he screams. Jefferson explains that he meant to do no such thing, and then warms up for more talk in the vernacular mode. "What you was doin' flyin' over this section, son? Wasn't you scared they might shoot you for a cow?" Suddenly the crash, the injury, and perhaps most importantly of all, the old man and his "lie"—all release in Todd a constellation of remembrances of things past. The whole experience forces him to retrace the history of his motives for wanting to be a flyer:

> Todd tensed. Was he being laughed at again? But before he could decide, the pain shook him and a part of him was lying calmly behind the screen of pain that had fallen between them, recalling the first time he had ever seen a plane. *It was as though an endless series of hangars had been shaken ajar in the air base of his memory and from each, like a young wasp emerging from its cell, arose the memory* of a plane. (263)

For our purposes, the main point here is that the vernacular tale is a *lieu de mémoire* the helped spark Todd's memory, and that helped provide him with the psychic stance that he will need to survive Alabama of the 1940s and his own ambitions there. The oral literature has provided "equipment for living."

Nor is it insignificant to the Ellison/Burke connection or to the vernacular as *lieux de mémoire* that the solution to Todd's problem turns out to involve, in a central way, *comedy*. Exemplifying the way to stay alive—and still in some sense to be the very "flyingest sonofabitch what ever hit heaven"—Jefferson is a story maker in the comic vernacular mode. As such he has adopted what Burke calls the "comic frame" through which to evaluate his circumstances. The comic, says Burke, "takes up the slack between the momentousness of the situation and the feebleness of those in the situation by dwarfing the situation. It converts downwards, as the heroic converts upwards."[35] For after all, he continues: "Humor specializes in incongruities; but by its trick of 'conversion downwards,' by its stylistic ways of reassuring us by dwarfing the magnitude of obstacles or threats, if provides us relief in laughter." In sum, "The comic frame will appear the most serviceable for the handling of human relationships. . . . By astutely gauging situation and personal resources, it promotes the realistic sense of one's limitations . . . yet the acceptance is not passive."[36] For when it comes to confronting the troubles of life with resiliency and flexibility, says Burke, the comic is the stratagem supreme. According to his idea of the comic perspective, one redefines blunders and disappointments as opportunities to grow. Laughing at one's predicaments, one is better able to confront them, to evaluate them, and to cope with them: "The comic frame should enable people to be observers of themselves, while acting. Its ultimate would not be passiveness, but maximum consciousness. One would 'transcend' himself by noting his own foibles."[37]

Near the end of "Flying Home," Ellison finds an image for this Burkean comic objectivity, self-awareness, and control. Blinded by sweat and bent by the weight of the whole difficult day, Todd looks at Jefferson, who seems to hold in his hand a miniature version of himelf: "It was a little black man, another Jefferson. A little black Jefferson that shook with fits of belly-laughter while the other Jefferson looked on with detachment" (268). When Graves, the ominously named white man who owns the land, finally shows up, it turns out that he has come not to help Todd at all but to have him strapped in a straitjacket: "You cain't let the nigguh git up that high without his going crazy," Graves says (269). Todd at last sees his impossibly nutty predicament from the saving comic angle. He is convulsed with laughter beyond his control: "He thought he would never stop, he would laugh himself to death." The white man decides he won't straitjacket the young man; more than anything he wants this guffawing "black eagle" out of his sight.

To complete the ritualized lesson, Todd is carried bodily from the field and thus is reintegrated in the world where human rates of speed and time are as important as those of airplanes. Taken away by Jefferson and by Jeff's son, Todd felt "as though he had been lifted out of his isolation, back into the world of men. A new current of communication flowed between the man and boy and himself." He's learned to do more than just belly-laugh; he's joined the group of vernacular-trained Americans who can cope with troubles and who can remain optimistic enough, as the expression goes, *to keep on keeping on*. Grounded, the flier encounters comic tale and teller as *lieux de mémoire* that grant him a saving attitude toward the boomerang of history. In this story named for the famous jazz song, "Flying Home," the youngster learns that to be a great solo flyer he must also be connected with others and mindful both of history's imposed limitations and of its invitations to soar.

How are these terms involving vernacular culture, history, and memory evinced in *Invisible Man?* In the novel, there is another Tod, with the name spelled slightly differently but still suggestive of the German noun for "death." Arguing in a Brotherhood meeting over the meaning of the fatal shooting of this Tod (and in this sense over how to read history), Invisible Man responds to a white know-it-all whose harshly authoritative tone is prompted by his having a black wife. What Invisible Man tells him is that there are areas of American experience that he (IM) knows too well to be tricked about—even by those speaking scientese, even by those with primary sources at home. Signifying, Invisible Man tells him that to be in touch with what's happening in Harlem, he would have to spend time in vernacular spaces where the local people are talking as they do when no outsiders are around. Back-talking in the vernacular mode, he says:

> Ask your wife to take you around to the gin mills and the barber shops and the juke joints and the churches, Brother. Yes, and the beauty parlors on Saturdays when they're frying hair. A whole unrecorded history is spoken there, Brother. You wouldn't believe it but it's true. Tell her to take you to stand in the areaway of a cheap tenement at night and listen to what is said. Put her out on the corner, let her tell you what's being put down. You'll learn that a lot of people are angry because we failed to lead them in action. I'll stand on that as I stand on what I see and feel and on what I've heard, and what I know.[38]

This short speech is a measure of the advancement in consciousness achieved by this young man who, like the protagonist of "Flying Home," is undergoing a series of tests in the vernacular (and again, significantly, the comic) mode. Several of his earlier encounters have prepared him for the aggressively ironic attitude of his words, just quoted, for their sharp-edged "comic frame." His encounters with Trueblood and "Peter Wheatstraw," in particular, but also with Brother Tarp and Mary, all have provided him with the stuff of "orientation and survival."[39]

One of *Invisible Man*'s most comprehensive lessons in what might be termed a dramatistic interpretation of the vernacular and its spaces as *lieux de mémoire* comes somewhat before the moment described earlier, when he heads uptown immediately after the attack and death of Tod. Struggling to make meaning out of the Harlem youth leader's loss, Invisible Man notices three young men on the Forty-second Street subway platform. Tod's wretched death and the encounter with the three on the platform trigger Invisible Man's memory; both events cause great shifts in his perspective on the American drama. He wonders what the "historians" would have to say about a "transitory" figure like Tod:

> What did they ever think of us transitory ones? . . . Birds of passage who were too obscure for the learned classification, too silent for the most sensitive recorders of sound; of natures too ambiguous for the most ambiguous words, and too distant from the centers of historical decision to sign or even to applaud the signers of historical documents? We who write no novels, histories or other books. What about us? . . . Yes, I thought, what about those of us who shoot up from the South into the busy city like wild jacks-in-the-box broken loose from our springs—so sudden that our gait becomes like that of deep-sea divers suffering from the bends? (429)

Standing down in that underground railway space—ready to head north—Invisible Man stands on a scene that is ringing with psychological and historical associations. No wonder he finds himself boomeranged into considering the crucial historiologic questions just quoted. That the novel's hero is literally waiting for a subway train associates his situation with that of Underground Railroad riders who traveled mainly by foot as well as with those like Frederick Douglass who managed to head toward freedom by riding the rails. Especially for blacks in America, trains, be they blues trains or gospel trains, have been indelibly associated with escape and ascension—beyond the troubles of the world toward heaven or, if not heaven, then at least another town, maybe Chicago or New York (or, as Bessie Smith proclaims in one song, back to Florida); maybe just anyplace but here.

Then, too, Invisible Man links being on board a train with being part of "history": here to be part of "history" means being conscious or, literally, and also reflects the Malrauxian idea that those who are part of "history" are those who play an assertive role in the tumultuous "world of action" around them.[40] "Why," he wonders, had Tod chosen to "step off the platform and fall beneath the train? Why did he choose to plunge into nothingness, into the void of faceless faces, of soundless voices, lying outside history?" (428). Considering the subway trio and others like them, Invisible Man thinks, "They'd been there all along, but somehow I'd missed them. I'd missed them even when my work had been most successful. They were outside the groove of history, and it was my job to get them in, all of them" (433). It was his job to get them into the groove, onto the train of history. Like Ellison the writer, his character wants to find a way to show how unseen black characters nonetheless play parts in the American scene and story that are utterly integral. Where they are left out, he wants to put them in. "*To get them in,*" he says, "*all of them*" (emphasis added).

It is in this thickly charged underground scene of the novel's twentieth chapter, this *lieu de mémoire,* that Invisible Man first takes the measure of the three black youths who, if they themselves do not constitute a sort of *lieu de mémoire,* certainly complete a deeply resonant *milieu de mémoire.* Invisible Man studies their styles of presentation with Ellisonian attention to details of dress and personal culture. What's clear from the description is that they represent a shared sense not of pathology but of vital culture; it's as if they belonged to a secret society where the signs and symbols were in sight but nonetheless were known to members only:

> Tall and slender, walking stiffly with swing shoulders in their well-pressed, too-hot-for-summer suits, their collars high and tight and about their necks, their identical hats of black cheap felt upon the crowns of their heads with a severe formality above their hard conked hair? It was as thought I'd never seen their like before: Walking slowly their shoulders swaying, their legs swinging from their hips in trousers that ballooned upward from cuffs fitting snug about their ankles; their coats long and hip-tight with shoulders far too broad to be those of natural western men. These fellows whose bodies seemed—what had one of my teachers said of me?—"You're like one of these African sculptures, distorted in the interest of a design." Well, what design and whose? (429–30)

Somehow the mystery of how to get them onto history's "train" is woven into the African-American cultural signs and symbols they display. Waiting for the subway, they "seemed to move like dancers in some kind of funeral ceremony," their "heavy heel-plated shoes making a rhythmical tapping as they moved . . . their shoulders rocking, their heavy heel plates clicking remote, cryptic messages in the brief silence of the train's stop." And if they are some sort of dancers in some sort of ceremony, what can we make of the dance's meanings? Like classic tap dancers of the forties, with their lightning and thunder syncopations, do they signal the end of an era and the beginning of something new, like bebop?[41] Does their "muted" but stylish presentation suggest a young Miles Davis-like coolness and reserve, an early fifties stance of control and expectancy just before the sweeping changes of the civil rights era began to explode? Echoing Shakespeare, the college boy asks, "Do they come to bury the others or to be entombed, to give life or to receive it?" (430). Or is the point that their styles of self-presentation suggest stances against chaos and—like Jefferson's tale which prepared the young man for his meeting with Graves—trouble even unto death?

Funereal though they may be, the youngsters regard their surroundings, their "scene," with a strong does of humor. As they pass around a comic book—that form, recall, that Kouwenhoven names as one of America's quintessentially vernacular ones—they silently communicate with one another with eyes full of irony. They don't just glance at the comic book; they study it, as Invisible Man observes, "*in complete absorption.*" Invisible Man notices a picture in one of the comic books held by one of the heel-plated subway three. It reminds him of Tod Clifton, whose blood, as he would later tell the crowd on the day of Tod's funeral, "ran like blood in a comic-book killing, on a comic-book street in a comic-book town on a comic-book day in a comic-book world" (446).

On this subject of comic books, Ellison later notes in an essay that when it comes to reflecting the thorniness or the funniness of the American briar patch, many highly technical American novels have failed where comic books have succeeded. "The reader who looks here [in such novels] for some acknowledgement of the turbulence he feels around him," says Ellison, "would be better satisfied with a set of comic books."[42] In 1986 Ellison wrote that to understand America, "the United States of Jokeocracy,"[43] one must realize that

> American society contained a built-in joke . . . that the joke was in many ways central in our condition. So we welcomed any play on words or nuance of gesture which gave expression to our secret sense of the way things really were. Usually this took the comic mode, and it is quite possible that one reason the popular arts take on an added dimension in our democracy lies in an unspoken, though no less binding agreement that popular culture is not to be taken seriously. Thus the popular arts have become an agency through which Americans can contemplate those aspects of our experience that are deemed unspeakable.[44]

In "Flying Home" and throughout his career Ellison repeatedly has presented the vernacular's secret wisdom in the form of a joke that is so well turned that it brilliantly sums things up and suggests a way to survive in "a nation of jokers." As a student of American humor, Ellison pays homage to Burke, as we have noted. But he also shows his kinship with Constance Rourke, who says of American comic types:

> Their comedy, their irreverent wisdom, their sudden changes and adroit adaptations, provided emblems for a pioneer people who required resilience as a prime trait. Comic triumph appeared in them all; the sense of triumph seemed a necessary mood in the new country. Laughter produced the illusion of leveling obstacles in a world which was full of unaccustomed obstacles. Laughter created ease, and even more, a sense of unity, among a people who were not yet a nation and who were seldom joined in stable communities.[45]

On *Invisible Man*'s underground platform—this *lieu de mémoire*—the protagonist is stunned into recalling certain heretofore hidden aspects of his past (and thus of the continuing past that is his present). Watching these young men moving silently through the subway crowd—these young guys who, in their cultural styles, "clash" so with those around them—he achieves a jolt in the form of what Burke calls "perspective by incongruity," the heightened awareness that can come from suddenly witnessing people or objects paradoxically juxtaposed.[46] In his state of heightened perceptivity, Invisible Man sees that the three on the subway are figures of transition, latency, unfulfilled potentiality.[47] Not only are they small-town southerners in the North's biggest city and black men in "white America," they are youngsters from the underground world of America's vernacular culture. Their speech, manner, conked hair, tapping shoes, and comic books all associate them with a level of society that history has not adequately recorded. Like the novel's main man, they are "invisible men."

No wonder Invisible Man calls them "men out of time," these characters from the interstices of their culture. Their laughter and speech are "muted," their masklike faces immobile. They speak a "jived-up transitional language full of country glamour, [they] think transitional thoughts, though perhaps they dream the same old ancient dreams" (430). And what was Invisible Man's relation to these in-between figures? "Perhaps an accident," he thinks,

> like Douglass. Perhaps each hundred years or so men like them, like me, appeared in society, drifting through; and yet by all historical logic we, I, should have disappeared round the first part of the nineteenth century,

> rationalized out of existence. Perhaps, like them, I was a throwback, a small distant meteorite that died several hundred years ago and now lived only by virtue of the light that speeds through space at too great a pace to realize that its source has become a piece of lead. (432)

Perhaps they were men for Invisible Man somehow to reclaim for the train of history. Or, as Invisible Man says to himself in a spirited consideration that may comprise, in a novel full of revelations and momentous psychic changes, the most potent epiphany,

> who knew (and now I began to tremble so violently I had to lean against a refuse can)—who knew but that they were the saviors, the true leaders, the bearers of something precious? The stewards of something uncomfortable, burdensome, which they hated because, living outside the realm of history, there was no one to applaud their value and they themselves failed to understand it. What if Brother Jack were wrong? What if history was a gambler, instead of a force in a laboratory experiment, and the boys his ace in the hole? What if history was not a reasonable citizen, but a madman full of paranoid guile and these boys his agents, his big surprise! His own revenge? For they were outside, in the dark with Sambo, the dancing paper doll; taking it on the lambo with my fallen brother, Tod Clifton (Tod, Tod) running and dodging the forces of history instead of making a dominating stand.

What, in other words, if history were not a straight and narrow "groove," suppose it were a boomerang? (431)

As Invisible Man emerges from the subway back onto 125th Street, the narrative's haunting sound track is supplied by the loudspeaker from a record store that was "blaring a languid blues." Having been boomeranged by a headful of new insights, by "perspectives by incongruity," Invisible Man asks a question that is as pertinent for the three on the subway as it is for Tod or for himself: "Was this all that would be recorded? Was this the only true history of the times, a mood blared by trumpets, trombones, saxophones and drums, a song with turgid, inadequate words?" (433). What he must face is that yes, although blues music is not the only history of the United States, it is a very vital one. Perhaps it is the most vital one. It's Ellison, remember, who in essay after essay has insisted that the blues may come closest to expressing Americans' sense of their comic/tragic predicament in a country full of the blues. If the sidewalk blues music seems too incidental or vague, then it is still true that like the cultural signs of the boys on the subway—with their ceremoniousness suggesting a death as well as the hope to prevail even in the face of death; with their sly humor suggesting that they are mockingly insightful as well as poised for action—the recording must be read with the most extreme care. In a sense it *is* the true history of the times, one of America's most dramatic forms of incipient action.

It is obvious that the study of formally written accounts of our experience, of our history, can and do coax and surprise us Americans into a better understanding of the American drama. (Note that Ellison himself turned from music to the disastrously explicit medium of writing as a professional career.) But like Ellison himself, his fiction's heroes are witnesses that we also are wise to study sources that are *not* written down, including *the American drama itself,* the metaphorically charged and layered *scene* through which we pass. And this particularly when we are aware that a scene can be both a forest of symbols and a powerful prompter of remembrance, a maker and shaper of the past (and thus of our perspectives on the present), a *lieu de mémoire.* Any careful study of scene should recognize it as only one element in the Burkean pentad of key terms, each one touching all the others. And any full study of the American scene should take into account the enormity of the importance of the vernacular—those homespun and thus quintessentially American styles and products which thinkers from Emerson to Ellison have warned us to take more seriously.

Both Invisible Man and "Flying Home" 's Todd experience close encounters with the vernacular, and are forever changed. What they learn is not only that unpretentious American people and their well-tested stuff of everyday use—their blues, tales, dances, comics; their styles of dress, and, in the case of our subway boys, their very body language—not only can make them remember their own boomeranging American histories (and their connections, each with the other). They also are reminded of the country's most "flyingest" democratic ideal: "ordinary" women and men are of transcendent value; if national salvation is possible at all, they are the ones to make it happen.

Notes

1. Ralph Ellison, *Invisible Man* (New York: Random House, 1952), p. 6.

2. I refer to the operative definition in Kenneth Burke's *Attitudes Toward History,* 2nd ed. (Boston: Beacon, 1959).

3. Here is part of the marvelous setting for this phrase: "My God [thought Invisible Man], what possibilities existed! And that spiral business, that progress goo! Who knew all the secrets; hadn't I changed my name and never been challenged even once? And that lie that success was a rising *upward.* What a crummy lie they kept us dominated by. Not only could you travel upward toward success but you could travel downward as well; up *and* down, in retreat as well as in advance, crabways and crossways, and around in a circle, meeting your old selves coming and going and perhaps all at the same time. How could I have missed it for so long?" Ellison, *Invisible Man,* pp. 498–99.

4. Ellison, *Invisible Man,* p. 6.

5. See Kenneth Burke, *The Philosophy of Literary Form: Studies in Symbolic Action* (Baton Rouge: Louisiana State University Press, 1941), pp. 293–304. In one of the many instances in which Ellison cites this telling phrase, he glosses it as follows: "Language is equipment for living, to quote Kenneth Burke. One uses the language which helps to preserve one's life, which helps to make one feel at peace in the world, and which screens out the greatest amount of chaos." *Going to the Territory* (New York: Random House, 1986), p. 66.

6. Here, of course, I refer to the seminal article by Pierre Nora, included as the final chapter of this volume.

7. Kenneth Burke, *The Philosophy of Literary Form,* pp. 191–220.

8. Kenneth Burke, *A Grammar of Motives* (New York: Prentice-Hall, 1954), pp. 447–63.

9. See Kenneth Burke's *Language as Symbolic Action: Essays on Life, Literature, and Method* (Berkeley: Univ. of Calif. Press, 1966).

10. Ellison, *Invisible Man,* p. 12.

11. Ibid., pp. x–xvi.

12. Ellison, "Harlem's America," *New Leader,* September 26, 1966, p. 2.

13. Ellison, *Invisible Man,* p. 3.

14. Ellison, *Territory,* p. 72.

15. Ralph Ellison, *Shadow and Act* (New York: Random House, 1964), p. 238; see also "Flying Home," a chapter containing statements from Ellison, in Rudi Blesh, *Combo: U.S.A.* (Philadelphia: Chilton, 1971), pp. 161–86.

16. Ibid., pp. 123–24.

17. Ellison, *Invisible Man,* pp. 428–29.

18. Ellison, *Territory,* p. 124.

19. The idea to look at the word *vernacular* owes something to Henry Louis Gates, Jr. The idea that the vernacular is crucial to American art first was introduced to me by Albert Murray.

20. Ellison, *Territory,* pp. 139–40. On this issue of "gestures toward perfection" see also Kenneth Burke, *The Rhetoric of Religion: Studies in Logology* (Berkeley: Univ. of Calif. Press, 1970; for more on the definition and meaning of the vernacular, see John A. Kouwenhoven, "What Is Vernacular?" in *Made in America, The Arts in Modern Civilization* (Newton Centre: Charles T. Branford, 1948), and idem, *The Beer Can by the Highway, Essays on What's American About America* (Baltimore, Md.: Johns Hopkins University Press, 1961; 1988 ed. includes a foreword by Ralph Ellison).

21. Here my primary reference is Kouwenhoven, *Beer Can,* pp. 37–73.

22. See "What America Would Be Like Without Blacks," in Ellison, *Territory,* pp. 109–10.

23. Kouwenhoven, *Beer Can,* pp. 50–58.

24. Of course, recorded jazz is a special case. Certain records, like Coleman Hawkins's "Body and Soul" (1939) are canonized on record. Every jazz player who plays the song, most certainly every tenor player, refers to the Hawkins masterwork. But even so, both in the record studio and on stage, Hawkins himself freely revised his own famous early version for the rest of his career. His improvisations were open to improvisation.

25. Holiday says this on the CBS television program *The Sound of Jazz,* recorded on December 8, 1957.

26. Speaking in New York on January 14, 1991, August Wilson said that the blues were a major influence on his writing: "It's *all* in the blues," he said.

27. Note, for example, that Duke Ellington never received a Pulitzer. When Ellington was sixty-six, the Pulitzer board almost awarded him a special award but ultimately turned him down (and as a result certain board members resigned). With characteristic suave and signifying humor, Ellington said that it was all right: "Fate doesn't want me to be too famous too young" (Ellison, *Territory,* p. 223).

28. With particular reference to jazz, Ellison makes this point in "Ralph Ellison's Territorial Vantage," *The Grackle,* 4 (1977–78), pp. 5–15.

29. Here I am relying on the work of the novelist and cultural critic Albert Murray; see his *Stomping the Blues* (New York: McGraw-Hill, 1976).

30. Conversation with the writer, May 15, 1981.

31. "Editorial Comment," *The Negro Quarterly: A Review of Negro Life and Culture* 1, no. 4 (Winter–Spring 1943), p. 301.

32. I refer to a lecture given by West at Wesleyan University called "From Bebop to Hip-hop," March 27, 1987.

33. In *Cross Section,* ed. Edwin Seaver (New York: L. B. Fischer), pp. 469–85; my page references are to *Dark Symphony, Negro Literature in America,* ed. James A. Emanuel and Theodore L. Gross (New York: Free Press, 1968), pp. 254–70.

34. Ellison, *Invisible Man,* p. 172.

35. Burke, *Attitudes,* p. 43.

36. Ibid., p. 106.

37. Ibid., p. 171.

38. Ellison, *Invisible Man,* pp. 460–61.

39. Letter from Ellison to the author, March 11, 1988.

40. See R. W. B. Lewis, *Malraux: A Collection of Critical Essays* (Englewood Cliffs, N.J.: Prentice-Hall, 1964), pp. 4–5.

41. According to the dance historian Jacqui Malone, one signal of the new thing in jazz, bebop, was the tap dancers' shifting of rhythms and "dropping bombs" within the big-band era's famous shuffle beat.

42. Ellison, *Territory,* p. 261.

43. This phrase comes from Ellison's short story "It Always Breaks Out," *Partisan Review* 24 (Spring 1963), p. 17.

44. Ellison, *Territory,* pp. 138–39.

45. Constance Rourke, *American Humor: A Study of the National Character* (New York: Harcourt, 1931), p. 99.

46. See Kenneth Burke, *Permanence and Change: An Anatomy of Purpose* (New York: New Republic, 1935), pp. 95–213.

47. Here I am indebted to my colleague at the Ecole Normale Superieure, Professor Pierre-Yves Petillon, who spoke of this issue of latency in *Invisible Man* when he lectured at Wesleyan University in the spring of 1987.

17

The Journals of Charlotte L. Forten-Grimké: *Les Lieux de Mémoire* in African-American Women's Autobiography

NELLIE Y. McKAY

In an interview in *Time* magazine in 1989, Toni Morrison described her then most recent novel, *Beloved,*[1] in this way: "I thought this has got to be the least read of all the books I'd written because it is about something that the characters don't want to remember, I don't want to remember, black people don't want to remember, white people don't want to remember. I mean, it's national amnesia."[2] The object of this wish for forgetfulness that Morrison explodes in her book is, of course, slavery, which she spells with a capital *S*. However, she also noted that *Beloved* was not about the institution of slavery but about those "anonymous people called slaves," those who endured even in the face of unbearable horror, and gained dignity by staying alive; and the others too: the 60 million (the figure has been estimated as high as 200 million by some historians) who died, brutally and wantonly destroyed while in passage to America—the ones to whom she dedicates the novel. *Beloved* charges us that we must never forget to remember all of these people.

In yet another interview Morrison further explained the genesis of her masterpiece:

> There is no place you or I can go, to think about or not think about, to summon the presences of, or recollect the absences of slaves; nothing that reminds us of the ones who made the journey and of those who did not make it. There is no suitable memorial or plaque or wreath or wall or park or skyscraper lobby. There's no 300-foot tower. There's no small bench by the road. There is not even a tree scored, an initial that I can visit in Charleston or Savannah or New York or Providence or better still, on the banks of the Mississippi. And because such a place doesn't exist (that I know of), the book had to."[3]

Beloved, perhaps the most widely read of Toni Morrison's novels, is a "site of history and memory," that phrase used here in a somewhat loose English translation of French historian Pierre Nora's term *lieux de mémoire.*[4]

Freed from a dictatorial history, which considered itself universal but represented only particular segments of memory, Nora tells us we have adopted *lieux de mémoire.* The quest of history and the privilege of authenticating memory now belong to everyone. As Nora describes his term, *lieux de mémoire* occur

> where memory crystallizes and secretes itself at a particular historical moment, a turning point where consciousness of a break with the past is bound up with the sense that memory has been torn—but torn in such a way as to pose the problem of the embodiment of memory in certain sites where a sense of historical continuity persists.[5]

In other words, with the loss of the prior traditional structure of an all-encompassing history (cohabiting with state or monarchical-authorized memory), there is now a wide separation between history and memory. Into this space Nora claims we have inserted *lieux de mémoire,* the result of a conviction that multiple histories and memories exist. For these we "deliberately create archives, maintain anniversaries, organize celebrations, pronounce eulogies . . . [and exercise] commemorative vigilance."[6]

In the context of Nora's argument, as the characters in *Beloved* engage in the deliberate act of remembering (or "rememory," as Sethe, the main character, calls it), Toni Morrison recreates a lost history (writing down their words so that we cannot forget them)—out of their memories of what no longer exists for them or for us: the culture of slavery. Her history is particularly significant for its attempt to probe the psychological meaning of slavery through the experiences of the slave.

Although Morrison was absolutely correct in observing the absence of a single named wall or plaque or building or bench or tower as a national memorial to American slavery, in turning to African-American culture we immediately identify many examples of *lieux de mémoire.* Excluded from the national history for almost two hundred years, the descendants of Africans brought to this country in chains were forced to find other ways to construct an identity and preserve the memory of their lives and sufferings on this continent, and to recall who they were before slavery. These range from the academic, like the novelized versions of slavery,[7] to the communal, like Juneteenth and Kwanza celebrations. Names of places and people have always been among the most popular ways for African Americans to reconstruct their history and perpetuate the memories of who they were and are. For example, during the first seventy years or so following the Emancipation Proclamation, Lincoln's name appeared in many contexts within the black community. More recently, all across the country, street names like Martin Luther King, Jr., or Frederick Douglass, or Malcolm X boulevards are ongoing history lessons in memory for the inhabitants in these communities, while many African Americans have adopted or given African names to their children. W. E. B. Du Bois records one very significant *lieu de mémoire* in *The Autobiography,* in which he tells of his Bantu female ancestor brought to America in the eighteenth century, who never became "reconciled to this strange land." With her hands clasped around her knees, and refusing to be comforted, she rocked herself and crooned her despair. Although the words of her song were unintelligible to her American-born generations, they were never forgotten. Du Bois, too, learned them at his grandfather's fireside and in the tenth decade of his life he included them in his narrative.[8]

African-American autobiography itself provides another important space to which we can turn in this quest for examples of the mechanisms at work in the creation of black history and cultural memory. For, in a nation with as many varied group experiences as our own, history and memory can be rightfully understood only through our willingness to listen to the chorus of its multiple voices. And as Albert Stone so wisely commented: "No . . . mode of American expression seems to have more widely or subtly reflected the diversities of American experience or the richness of American memories and imaginations [than autobiography]."[9]

The contemporary African-American turn toward autobiographies as *lieux de mémoire* began with the demand for black studies programs in the educational curriculum in the 1960s and 1970s. In strident tones, black intellectuals made claims for revisions of the history of American slavery, the remembering (reconstruction) of then accepted history through reexaminations of the "peculiar institution," and in the new history, prominently include the perspectives of those who understood it best: the slaves. Ignored by white scholars for two centuries, the slave narratives of the eighteenth and nineteenth centuries (one of America's two unique forms of autobiography)[10] and the oral histories collected from still-living slaves or their offspring in the early part of this century became primary source material for those revisions. Personal accounts of slavery like those of William Wells Brown, Frederick Douglass, Sylvia Du Bois, and Harriet Jacobs established the dignity and humanity of the slaves and recalled cultural memories of the violations they were made to suffer. With the recuperation of these texts and dozens of others of their kind, chapters in American history that had been deliberately erased and all but forgotten by almost everyone were recalled to memory and reinstated in their rightful place. Toni Morrison (like other contemporary writers) has borrowed from the slave narrative tradition for the creation of *Beloved.*

African-American autobiography, in many forms—the slave and spiritual narratives, memoirs, reminiscences, confessions, case histories, personal journalism, essays, diaries, and journals—like autobiography in other groups, is an "act of memory and imagination." Each text "remodels the past into a narrative shape which necessarily resembles chronicle, fiction, dream, and myth . . . [b]ut is also and simultaneously 'history' [that] recreates a past shared with others, one [that] actually occurred and [was] not simply imagined."[11] Stone argues that, like other historians, the autobiographical "I," as creator and recreator of her or his remembered experiences, presented through the artistry of verbal images and metaphors, "offers an interpretation of the surviving records of his or her own past."[12] Further, he points out, the writing of autobiography, an "originating act of consciousness" in which the self seeks order and meaning in her or his past experiences by telling a story of those experiences, begins as historical consciousness. And, as James Olney notes in a discussion of Richard Wright's *Black Boy,* "Memories [of one's past] and present reality [in the moment of writing] bear a continuing, reciprocal relationship, influencing and determining one another ceaselessly . . . shaped by the present moment and by the specific psychic impress of the remembering individual."[13] If Stone and Olney are correct, as I think they are, then autobiography is a prime site for *lieux de mémoire.*

For the examination of an autobiographical African-American *lieu de mémoire,* in this essay I focus on *The Journals of Charlotte Forten-Grimké,* one of three such extant documents by nineteenth-century African-American women.[14] Charlotte began to keep a record of her life on May 24, 1854, at age sixteen, and continued to do so until July 1892; for unexplained reasons she seems to have skipped the period between 1864 and 1885, and returned to this activity only intermittently between 1885 and 1892. Altogether, in their originals, five journals exist—"slender, leather-bound volumes, each covered with a graceful marble paper [with] delicate, faded black-ink handwriting."[15] In 1953, the first four volumes (ending in 1864), edited by Ray Allen Billington, brought the existence of the journals to public knowledge.[16] Then, in 1988, the full five volumes, in a scholarly edition with an introduction by Brenda Stevenson, were published in the Schomburg Library's Nineteenth-Century Black Women Writers series.

Charlotte Forten was born in Philadelphia in 1837 into a socially prestigious, wealthy, black abolitionist family. Although her ancestors had been slaves, there were four generations of free Fortens before her birth. James Forten, Sr. (1766–1842), her grandfather, who made the family fortune in sail making, served in the revolutionary war when he was a young man and later became a staunch abolitionist who gave considerable time, energy, and monetary support to the antislavery movement. He was a close friend and financial backer of William Lloyd Garrison, the well-known Boston abolitionist and editor of the *Liberator,* the leading antislavery newspaper in the country at that time. Forten's home was a meeting place for black and white reformers. Among his other activities, in 1800, Forten unsuccessfully petitioned Congress to modify the Fugitive Slave Act of 1793; and in 1813 he published a pamphlet against legistlation to ban free blacks from settling in Pennsylvania. He vociferously opposed the American Colonization Society on the relocation of free blacks in Liberia and was a force behind the 1830 National Negro Convention in Philadelphia.[17] James Forten participated in other civic organizations as well, championing the causes of black education, temperance, women's rights, and world peace. When he died in 1842, at age seventy-six, he had one of the largest funerals in the history of Philadelphia.

The most important influences on Charlotte Forten's young life included her father, Robert, also an abolitionist; her grandmother, Charlotte; her three aunts, Margaretta, Sarah, and Harriet; and the husbands of Sarah and Harriet, Joseph and Robert Purvis. Activist abolitionists and feminists, the older Forten women gave young Charlotte Forten her most significant female role models. Charlotte Forten, Sr., her daughters, and Mary Woods Forten (young

Charlotte's mother), were founding members of and active in the Philadelphia Female Anti-Slavery Society (1833). Margaretta taught in a black segregated school in Philadelphia, and Sarah, a writer, contributed poems and essays to the *Liberator.* The three sisters, their mother, and Charlotte's mother (who died when her daughter was three years old) were educated, hardworking women who were part of a group of nineteenth-century black and white women committed to work on race and gender issues.

Robert and Joseph Purvis, sons of a wealthy English cotton broker and his freeborn woman-of-color wife, devoted much of their energies and wealth to the abolitionist movement and the welfare of free blacks. Robert Purvis (1810–98), for several years vice-president of the American Anti-Slavery Society, was a longtime member of the Pennsylvania Society for Promoting the Abolition of Slavery and was its president from 1845 to 1850. His home in Bucks County was a station on the Underground Railroad. By refusing to pay his taxes in 1853 he succeeded in convincing his township to permit black children to attend local public schools.

Charlotte Forten did not attend Philadelphia's segregated schools. She had tutors at home and in 1853 went to Salem, Massachusetts, to complete her education and prepare for a career in teaching. In Salem she lived with close family friends: Charles Lenox and Amy Matilda Remond and their two children. Charles Remond and his sister Sarah Parker Remond, educated, intelligent, and eloquent, were prominent nineteenth-century New England abolitionists and women's rights advocates. He was the first black person to lecture for the Massachusetts Anti-Slavery Society.

In 1855 a hardworking Charlotte Forten graduated from the Higginson Grammar School in Salem. Her poem "A Parting Hymn" was selected from a group submitted by her classmates to be sung by the students during their graduation ceremony. But her relationship with the principal, Mary Shephard, who became her lifelong friend, was the highlight of that experience. Following her completion of the Higginson program, in 1855, Charlotte enrolled in the Salem Normal School and in that year published her first poem, "To W.L.G. on Reading His 'Chosen Queen,' " which appeared in the *Liberator.* For graduation in 1856 she wrote "Poem for Normal School Graduation," also published in the *Liberator,* and she accepted an appointment at the Epes Grammar School, the first person of color to hold such a position in Salem. In keeping with her family's tradition, in 1856 Charlotte became an active member of the Massachusetts Female Anti-Slavery Society.

Charlotte, like many of the people she knew, suffered from an ongoing respiratory ailment, and in November 1856, at the start of her teaching career, she began to have severe headaches. Between then and 1862, she intermittently was too ill to work. Not to be outdone by this problem, she developed a pattern of returning to Philadelphia during her sick times, resting for a while with her family, then resuming her duties in New England. There, in the summer of 1862, the poet John Greenleaf Whittier, a family friend of the Fortens, suggested she take a teaching position in the Union's recently launched "social experiment" on the South Carolina coast, an experiment for the mass education of former slaves. Whittier encouraged this on the basis that it offered Charlotte an opportunity to serve her race. The idea appealed to her as well. She also hoped that a warmer climate might be beneficial to her health.

In October 1862 Charlotte Forten, one of the first black teachers to arrive in the South in the wake of the Civil War, and the only one on St. Helena during her stay there, left Philadelphia for Port Royal, on that island. She remained there until May 1864. In a one-room schoolhouse she tried to teach the basics of elementary education and to instruct children and adults in moral and social behavior. For her it was a physically and emotionally challenging job, and in the early months she faced mixed responses from teachers, military personnel, and even the blacks she wanted to help. Over time she made friends and gained the admiration of many, especially those who like her had gone there to help.

Charlotte wrote to William Lloyd Garrison of her experiences on St. Helena in two letters that were published in the *Liberator* in 1862. Her two-part essay "Life on the Sea Islands" appeared in the *Atlantic Monthly* in 1864. A combination of continued failing health, her ambivalence toward living conditions on the island, and perhaps the death of her father in April 1864 led her to resign her post and return to Philadelphia in May of that year.

A position in Boston with the Teachers Committee of the Freedmen's Union Commission and a year of teaching at the (Robert Gould) Shaw Memorial School in Charleston occupied Charlotte Forten's time between 1865 and 1871. Then she moved to Washington, D.C., where she first taught at the M Street School (later the Paul Laurence Dunbar High School) and subsequently took an appointment with the U.S. Treasury Department through 1878, when she married the Reverend Francis Grimké, minister of the Fifteenth Street Presbyterian Church in Washington. Charlotte Forten spent most of the rest of her life in the nation's capital.

In spite of disparities in their births, ages, and upbringings (he was a former slave and thirteen years younger than she), Francis Grimké and Charlotte Forten were well suited to each other. Like her, he was intelligent, educated (he held degrees from Lincoln University, Howard University, and Princeton Theological Seminary), morally upright, and deeply concerned about matters of race. After the death of their infant child, Charlotte worked with her husband in his mission to the world: speaking out and writing against racism and oppresion.

Although her health was a constant problem for her, except for the last thirteen months of her life, when she was confined to bed, Charlotte Forten-Grimké never gave up her engagement in church work and civic activities. On the personal side, in her journals she claims a good marriage, a niece whom she adored, and many well-loved friends who, like her, were well-educated political activists. She died in her home in Washington, in 1914, at the age of seventy-six. Credit for the preservation of her journals goes to her close friend, the late Anna Julia Cooper, black feminist scholar, to whom Francis Grimké entrusted Charlotte's writings after her death. Cooper painstakingly made typescripts of these documents. Typescripts and originals are housed in the Moorland Spingarn Library of Howard University.

Aside from her work to make better the condition of black life in America, Charlotte Forten nurtured literary aspirations. In the 1850s, while recuperating from one of her frequent bouts with illness, she expressed in her journal the wish that were she ever an invalid she might be able to support herself through her writing. Toward that effort, between 1855 and the 1890s she sought to establish herself in the world of letters. The *Liberator,* which published her earliest poems in 1855 and 1856, also published "The Wind Among the Poplars" in 1859. Other poems appeared in the *National Anti-Slavery Standard,* the *Christian Recorder,* and the *Anglo-African Magazine.* In 1857 Charlotte submitted the only short story she is known to have written, "The Lost Bride," to *Ladies Home Journal.* It was not published, but in 1893 her "Personal Recollections of Whittier" appeared in *New England Magazine.* Her study of foreign languages, which she undertook in Massachusetts for the self-discipline she wanted to cultivate, gave her one success: a translation of Emil Erckmann and Alexandre Chatrian's novel *Madame Thérèse; or The Volunteers of '92,* published by Scribner's in 1869. But for all these efforts, her reputation as a writer rests almost entirely on *The Journals,* private records that have become public documents.

Because of their rarity, the journals and diaries of nineteenth-century black women (none by black men have yet surfaced) are especially valuable documents. From the slave narratives to the contemporary autobiographies of writers like Angela Davis, Maya Angelou, Audre Lorde, and John Widemen, it was inevitable that black writers should deliberately use the form as a forum for public protest against America's race problems. Although a larger number of nineteenth-century black journals and diaries may exist than have come to light so far, it is likely that the urgency felt for public protest discouraged those interested in constructing personal narratives from engaging in private writing. There is also no indication that any of the three women whose journals/diaries we have actually ever intended them for publication. In fact, a penciled inscription in Diary 2 (January 1, 1857–January 27, 1858) of Charlotte's journal reads: "To be burned in case of my death immediately. He who dares read what here is written, Woe be unto him."[18] One of the most significant aspects of these works, then, is the rare view they give us of what may have been the truly private worlds in which the women lived. Another is that since journals and diaries are kept in chronological time and bypass the processes of selection, meditation, mediation, and interpretation employed by the formal autobiographical narrative, they record a more spontaneous response to experience.

Charlotte Forten, we know, grew up in a world that, on one hand, gave her many privileges denied to the vast majority of her racial group—a fine home, travel, and an opportunity to develop social refinements—and on the other, imbued her with a sense of duty toward that vast unfortunate majority. At no time in her adult life did she withdraw from or attempt to deny that responsibility. As a result, her journals, begun when she was sixteen years old, reveal the development of two parallel lines of history: one on which she takes as many opportunities as possible to engage in the intellectual and/or pleasurable activities available to her by dint of her class: reading great European literature, studying, attending lectures, learning foreign languages, nurturing her literary ambitions, and enjoying the company of friends with tastes equally as refined as her own; and the other on which she spent her time engaged in equally energetic performances of the duties she felt to be her civic responsibilities to those less fortunate than herself.

Reading Charlotte Forten's journals as *lieux de mémoire* brings to mind Alice James, sister to William and Henry, and another nineteenth-century American woman diarist. By accidents of birth, in all things but race Forten and James were women from equally privileged backgrounds, and both had many similar sensibilities. Educated and sensitive, they even shared the afflictions of familiar nineteenth-century female ill health for most of their adult years. But the similarities ended there, for differences of race determined vast disparities in the scope of their worlds and the directions of their lives. In the words of one critic, James's diary, kept only during the last three years of her life when she was an invalid in England, gave her the opportunity to exercise her "decorative sense . . . that [she] applied to the wasted rooms of her life."[19] For in the insight it gives into the exhorbitant toll paid for social privilege by some middle-class nineteenth-century white American women, the contents of this diary reveal how embedded it is in a history that calls into memory hundreds of years of the reproduction of patriarchal ideologies of gender that culturally silence women. Interestingly, unlike Forten, James appears to have wanted her diary published after her death. Her achievement in it remains a monument to the individual self, the acquisition of a voice that permitted her to speak beyond the grave in a way that distinguished her from her famous brothers, made her a person in her own right.[20] Sadly for her, what James remembered most in those final years of her life, and she reminded her brother William of this in a letter shortly before her death, was that custom had forced her to be "a creature who might have been something else."[21]

On the other hand, in spite of her social advantages, Charlotte Forten, growing up closely associated with the political passions of energetic abolitionist activities inside and outside of the households of her childhood, was in a different stream of cultural history from James. Doubtless, early in her (Charlotte's) life, she knew of the grave dangers the family faced in harboring fugitive slaves. She also learned from the example of the women in the family that idleness (as it was for James) was not her lot, and she viewed her social privilege as a sacred charge to serve her people. Dutifully, she accepted an active participatory role to leave an imprint of her own on the history of the struggle for human dignity for all people. Nor, had she wanted to, could Charlotte Forten have forgotten that race stamped her as an inferior "other." Privilege of birth and upbringing did not shelter her from that harsh reality of African-American life. Her journal records insults and humiliations of racial prejudice that she suffered from her school peers in New England, and in Philadelphia, where she was sometimes refused service in public establishments such as ice cream parlors. But while these episodes were painful and humiliating, and at times she was disheartened, she never capitulated to despair.

The opening entry in Charlotte's journal, May 24, 1854, makes note of her rising at 5 A.M. and feeling "vexed" because the sun had risen before she did.[22] Her New England school days were marked by early morning risings (sometimes before 4 A.M.) and long hours of study and reading to improve her mind, punctuated by assisting her hostess, sewing, enjoying friends, having uplifting conversations, and taking brisk walks to observe and admire nature. On May 25, the second day in the life of her journal, Charlotte recorded: "Something [has happened] that must ever rouse in the mind of every true friend of liberty and humanity, feelings of the deepest indignation and sorrow."[23] The reference was to the horrible incident with Anthony Burns, a fugitive slave, captured two months after his escape from the South. In describing the event, her notation, "another fugitive," tells us that she had been paying close attention to the effects of the Dred Scott law. For her the memory of the plight of escaping slaves whom her family concealed at great risk to themselves was part of her living black history.

The following day, May 26, Charlotte discussed Burns's capture and the issue of slavery with her teacher, Miss Mary Shepard, who later became her friend. Although she was thrilled to discover that Miss Shepard felt as she did, and was equally as outraged by the atrocity, the two seemingly engaged in a lively discussion in which the teacher disagreed with her pupil that the "churches and ministers [were] generally supporters of the infamous system."[24] Several other incidents of escaped slaves are recorded in Charlotte's early journals. She brooded greatly over the ones who were returned to the South, and rejoiced for those who escaped that injustice. Most of the people in New England whom she knew, admired, and associated with were abolitionists, and a good deal of her time was spent in attending abolitionist meetings and doing what she could to help to relieve the anguish of the victims of the system. It comes as no surprise, except for the frailty of her health, that she volunteered for service on the Sea Islands to work with the newly emancipated slaves.

In contrast, although thirty years later she wrote in her diary in defense of the northern goals of the Civil War, in the middle years of the nineteenth century Alice James and her family moved around Europe (1855–60) outside of the periphery of American politics when the debates over slavery were at their peak. One wonders whether Alice, a teenager at the time of their return to America in 1860, was perplexed by her father's behavior. An early supporter of abolition in principle, he did not wish his sons to fight in the war. Against his wishes, her two younger brothers, with whom she was not close, served in the Union forces. Given the circumstances of her life at the time, it is reasonable to suspect that Alice James was physically and emotionally far removed from the meaning of the conflict to the lives of the slaves. In those years when Charlotte (eleven years older than Alice) worked with former slaves in South Carolina, Alice James was already preparing herself for a "career as a patient." The doors to "whatever else she might have been" were already closed to her.

Unlike James, in spite of her illnesses, there were no "wasted rooms" in Charlotte Forten's life. Her journal keeping was not a "rehabilitative activity . . . a way of [occupying] unusable [rooms]," as Janet Varner Gunn describes Alice's.[25] The epigraph to the journals best describes Charlotte's perceptions of the rich commingling of historical consciousness and the reality of memory in her text:

> A wish to record the passing events of my life, which, even if quite unimportant to others, naturally possess great interest to myself, and to which it will be pleasant to have some remembrance . . . recalling to my mind the memories of other days. . . . Besides this, it will doubtless enable me to judge correctly of the growth and improvement of my mind from year to year.[26]

Charlotte Forten was a precocious sixteen years old when she wrote these words. She lived to be seventy-six, and one imagines that over the years she returned many times to her early pages to recall for herself memories of the history of times long past. For today's scholars of African-American life and culture, the personal history and memory embedded in these journals remind us of many things—black family structures, black and white women's roles in the abolition movement and the Civil War, the problems of Reconstruction, and the development of black education, to name a few of the most obvious ones. But perhaps above all, Charlotte's journals continue to remind us that we can never forget the enormous contributions made to the nation's history by the work and lives of the black men and women who, although they might have done otherwise, chose to place themselves, selflessly, at the moral center of the American tradition of social reform—and while they climbed, to lift with them those less fortunate than themselves. In this record of the meeting of vital moments and actors in the evolution of the group's culture, we experience another important construction of an African-American *lieu de mémoire.*

Notes

1. Toni Morrison, *Beloved* (New York: Knopf, 1987).
2. Toni Morrison, "The Pain of Being Black," *Time,* May 22, 1989, 120.
3. Toni Morrison, "A Bench by the Road," *The World* 3, no. 1 (Jan./Feb. 1989): 4.
4. Pierre Nora, "Between Memory and History: *Les Lieux de Mémoire,*" *Representations,* no. 26 (Spring 1989): 7–25.
5. Nora, "Between Memory and History," 7.
6. Ibid., 12.
7. In recent years there have been several novels, the majority by black women, which use slavery as the centerpiece of their stories. These include Margaret Walker's *Jubilee* (1966), Barbara Chase-Riboud's *Sally Hemmings* (1979), Sherley Anne Williams's *Dessa Rose* (1986), and Gloria Naylor's *Mama Day* (1987).
8. W. E. B. Du Bois, *The Autobiography of W. E. B. Du Bois* (New York: International Publishers, 1975), 62.
9. Albert Stone, *Autobiographical Occasions and Original Acts: Versions of American Identity from Henry Adams to Nate Shaw* (Philadelphia: University of Pennsylvania Press, 1982), 1.

10. The other is the Indian captivity narrative.

11. Stone, *Autobiographical Occasions,* 3.

12. Ibid., 4.

13. James Olney, "The Ontology of Autobiography," in *Autobiography: Essays Theoretical and Critical,* ed. James Olney (Princeton, N.J.: Princeton University Press, 1980), 244.

14. *The Journals of Charlotte Forten-Grimké,* ed. Brenda Stevenson (New York: Oxford University Press, 1988). The others are *Gifts of Power: The Writings of Rebecca Jackson, Black Visionary, Shaker Eldress,* ed. Jean McMahon Humez (Amherst: University of Massachusetts Press, 1981); and *Give Us Each Day: The Diary of Alice Dunbar-Nelson,* ed. Gloria T. Hull (New York: Norton, 1984).

15. Joanne M. Braxton, *Black Women Writing Autobiography: A Tradition Within a Tradition* (Philadelphia: Temple University Press, 1989), 84.

16. *The Journal of Charlotte L. Forten: A young black woman's reactions to the white world of the Civil War era,* ed. Ray Allen Billington (New York: Norton, 1953).

17. The convention condemned colonization, discussed the expansion of rights for free blacks, and advocated the abolition of slavery and equal rights for all black people in the country.

18. Quoted in Braxton, *Black Women Writing Autobiography,* 84.

19. Janet Varner Gunn, "The Autobiographical Occupation: Alice James's Diary and the Decoration of Space," *A/B Auto/Biography Studies,* 4, no.1 (Fall 1988): 38.

20. Jean Strouse, *Alice James: A Biography.* (Boston: Houghton Mifflin), 1980, ix.

21. Ibid., x.

22. *Journals,* ed. Stevenson, 59. All subsequent quotations from the *Journals* refer to this edition.

23. Ibid., 60.

24. Ibid., 60–61.

25. Gunn, "The Autobiographical Occupation," 38.

26. *Journals,* 58.

18

Washington Park

ROBERT STEPTO

After the first summers in Idlewild, I returned to Chicago to live with my parents, and also with Aunt Marge and Uncle Rog and my grandparents, in my grandparents' house: "fifty-seven twenty-*two* Indiana Ave*nue*." The happy bounce of that jingle, so frequently rattled off by family members of any generation, reminds me of what a warm communal arrangement it was. The necessity of housing all seven of us produced the will to make it workable and genial; it was not a setting, in Robert Hayden's words, of "blueblack cold" and "chronic angers."

Grandma and Grandpa Burns lived in a neighborhood officially known as Washington Park, though I never heard anyone who resided there call it that. I myself first discovered that it was named Washington Park when, in a moment of true boredom around the age of ten, I started in reading the telephone book and discovered an "official" map of Chicago's neighborhoods. Finding out that I had lived, and that my grandparents continued to live, in a neighborhood with a *name* completely unknown to me bewildered and unmoored me. It was, I think now, the first moment, the first sensing, of knowing that there could be mammoth discrepancies between the reality certain people lived and the reality of maps and other constructs. And the realities of the constructs were not to be dismissed: people *read* such abstractions, and accordingly make decisions, dole out largesse, and so forth. Down at City Hall, as I imagine it, the Mayor (shall it be Kelly? Kennelly? even Daley?) growls, "Can we count on Washington Park?" and the functionaries from up the neighborhood *better* be able to translate ("Washington Park" that's us!) and answer: "Yes, Mister Mayor, you can count on us; we'll vote early and often!"

While the people in the neighborhood had no particular name for it, I believe other people—other black people—did. The name or names were probably derogatory, for the neighborhood was, in the 1940s, "out south," meaning that it was south of the original, pre-1920, black ghetto. South by a mile or more of the corners of Forty-seventh Street and South Parkway (now Martin Luther King, Jr., Drive)—the crossroads of the district Gwendolyn Brooks and many others called Bronzeville; south enough even to be within the area serviced by an integrated high school, Englewood (my father was class of '38), though that (i.e., the racial composition) was soon to change. The playwright Lorraine Hansberry was a teenager in Washington Park around the time I was a toddler there, and in *To Be Young, Gifted, and Black* she describes an episode of frightening racial tension at Englewood. Matters became more volatile, and then quickly resolved, when cars full of black high schoolers arrived at Englewood from the Bronzeville high schools named for the black priest Jean Baptiste Point Du Sable and for the abolitionist Wendell Phillips. The Du Sable and Phillips students (". . . in their costumes of pegged pants and conked heads and tight skirts and almost knee-length sweaters and—worst of all—*colored* anklets, held up by rubber bands!") charged upon the scene because they were convinced, in Hansberry's words, that "THEM CHICKEN-SHIT NIGGERS OUT THERE AIN'T *ABOUT* TO FIGHT!" If that was what they truly thought, then heaven knows what else they called us—or what they called our neighborhood; surely not "Washington Park."

Of course, what they called us and thought of us had nothing to do with what we didn't have (and there were plenty of "have-nots" in Washington Park), and everything to do with what we had, or seemed to have. We were the black people who had been in Chicago for twenty or thirty years, or maybe had been born there (the case for my parents, for example), and were not necessarily being defeated by it. We were the Negroes "experimenting" with faiths other than Baptist and Methodist and otherwise supporting the churches in which the likes of Du Bois and Weldon Johnson spoke when they came to town. We were the railroad workers and train porters, postal workers and social workers, small businessmen, schoolteachers, ministers, homemakers, and scant few doctors and lawyers insistent upon making of the neighborhood, if only for a moment's time, a ceremonial ground for uplift; we were hunkered down to "strive" for what parents and schools had taught was worth the effort.

According to a map in St. Clair Drake and Horace Cayton's study, *Black Metropolis,* while Washington Park was one of the several Southside neighborhoods into which Negroes were allowed to settle (encroach?) in the 1920s (my mother's family arrived there in 1928), it was virtually the only one in which black settlement, then, was greeted with violence. The reason for this, I believe, had less to do with the expansive, adjacent park, or with the still attractive apartment buildings, than with the presence of houses—single-family dwellings both attached and free-standing. Such houses were the repositories of American dreams—the most desirable sites for special acts of hearthing and nesting—for people of any race. Hence, the attacks, the bricks, the fires: white folks didn't want something as irrational as race to force them to move out; black folks didn't want something as predictable as race to keep them from moving in.

My grandparents' place on Indiana Avenue was indeed a house; a tidy, narrow, two-story brick affair with a limestone face to the street, with a wall in common with the house next door that was a mirror image of our house in terms of stairs, porch, windows, floor plan, and most everything else. Their place was indeed a house because, as my mother tells it, her mother insisted upon it: she was tired of living with her sister at 4545 Vincennes, a common enough arrangement for migrants to any big city—but an arrangement for how long? She was probably thinking, too, that if she was in Chicago to stay, and it was looking more and more that way, then she might as well begin to approximate in Chicago the house and household she had established in St. Joseph, Missouri, twenty years before. Of course, there wouldn't be the chickens, but maybe there could be much of what had been relinquished when Ocie, her husband, realized that even before the age of thirty he had exhausted his prospects in their hometown of St. Joe, despite or maybe *because* of his college degree.

And so they moved to Chicago and later to Washington Park, timing matters, ordering their lives as family, church, Spelman, and Tuskegee had taught them to do, so that it was no mere coincidence that they began to save and plan for a move right after my mother was born (they knew full well that you do not raise *three* children in someone else's house), or that they were poised to move right after Ocie received his pharmacy degree from Illinois and right before Ann (my mother) was to enter elementary school. And when they moved they bought; and what they bought was a house with a garage opening out onto an alley where you could trade with the ice man, the rags 'n' old iron man, the vegetable man; a house with a bare narrow yard that my wife and I later would have strained to cultivate into a restful city garden, but which was for them a functional rectangle, suitable for burning trash at one end and for hanging clothes to dry at the other.

My grandparents bought their home from Germans who were master furniture makers, and who were, as I presently imagine it, slightly confused about why they had to sell and move no sooner than they had attained America—or better, why they had to move in order to maintain a certain citizenship in Chicago and America. At any rate, once the negotiations with the Germans were done, my grandparents finally had a Chicago house of their own, and two fine-crafted chairs in the bargain. I would like to think that the chairs, which are still in our family, were gifts of goodwill and housewarming. That's a good story. But the more significant one is the one my mother tells of the day, fifty years later, when my grandmother's eyes lit upon the chairs—after childrearing and householding, after Idlewild, after the death of Ocie—and said, "The chairs; is this *all* that is left?"

Our immediate neighbors to the north and south were, like Grandpa Burns and most everybody else I knew of that generation, black postal workers, loyal both to the NAACP and to the Republican party. To call their names and ours is like sounding the roster of an NBA basketball team, or like whispering that of a Yale secret society of yore, for we all had names like Collins and Kelly, Brown and Burns, York and Bush. We knew the Kellys best: the parents were kind and jovial, their sons both brilliant and destined for extremes of livelihood well beyond the steady rote of family, church, and modest sinecure. One boy would prove gifted in mathematics and earn advanced degrees in that field despite the major obstacles the University of Chicago and the field itself would put before him. The other son was equally smart but far more social, streetwise, and slick. In other words, he was "into" "politics." When I saw him last he was dapper and clean, wearing a little moustache and a good suit, and looking much too much like a younger version of my father. Last I heard, he was about to do time for some political "impropriety"—unusual but nonetheless possible in Chicago, especially if one has crossed the wrong person in the ward or down at City Hall.

One neighbor whom I cannot name was different from the rest of us. He had a big car, possibly a boat, and when he came home from wherever he worked he paraded around in "sport clothes," which told all that he had *not* come home to fix something or burn trash or stoke a furnace. I know he wasn't a postal worker, and I think maybe he was a milkman: for some reason, they seemed to have a whole lot of style in the early 1950s, probably because they were delivering something in addition to milk. At any rate, this man was bouncy, happy, and possession-laden; that's why he bought a big Doberman pinscher, to help him protect his stash. This was seen in the neighborhood as both a necessary act (hence, on some level, to be forgiven) and an act of enormous hubris. Down at Mr. Harris's barber shop, certain Negroes were probably saying things like: "The next thing that nigger is goin' do is go to *France* and marry hisself the onliest *Chinese* woman he can find."

This neighbor—let us call him Mr. Simms—loved his Doberman and his Doberman loved him back. They would go through all sorts of paramilitary exercises in Simms's version of the spare backyard we all had; grandstanding, really, quaking the neighbors who merely wanted to take down wash or wax a car—or simply sit a bit without a whole lot of foolishness going on. Another thing Simms and the dog did was to prance down Indiana Avenue to the newsstand every waking morning, scattering schoolchildren like leaves before a blower, and some adults, too. On the way back, much was the same, only now the Doberman delicately held the morning paper in his huge jaws while Simms smirked like a circus lion tamer.

This and other things Simms was up to clearly communicated the following: "I got me a Doberman, got him trained, mess with me and you got much Dog up your ass." People respected that; Simms's house was never approached, let alone robbed. But, as I have suggested, they were also incensed: for Simms's notion of the Protecting Dog was really that of the Harassing Dog, and that made Simms resemble a cracker sheriff more than anything else, and more than he, all vibrant in his sport clothes, ever realized. Perhaps that's why the following story was told and softly chuckled over many times in my boyhood.

One morning, Simms was late for work and hadn't time for the prance to and from the corner newsstand. He carefully explained this to the Doberman, in just the way serious dog owners talk to their animals, and then went off to work. When he came home that night to a dark house, Simms turned on a light and called out the dog's name, eager to see his buddy, his best friend. But there was no response, no leaping, licking greeting. Simms went into another room, switched on a light; called. Nothing. Then he went into a third room, called, and before he could flick the light switch, the damn dog leapt from the dark into Simms's face, and bit Simms's ear off.

Just up the avenue from us was Fifty-eighth Street, and the short stretch of Fifty-eighth from Indiana Avenue east to Prairie to Calumet Avenue was an intense commercial district, brimming colorfully with every sort of store, business, and service. This was no doubt a result of the El stop at Fifty-eighth—stores have always sprouted around train stops of any kind—right between Prairie and Calumet. Some of the stores were members of chains: there was a Walgreen's drugstore at Fifty-eighth and Prairie, and the other drugstore a block away at Indiana, Silberman's, was a Rexall. But most of the enterprises were small, family or mom-and-pop affairs, with the usual breakdown of colored folk owning the barber and beauty shops, the rib joints, soul-food cafés, and more than a few of the bars, while the whites ran the pharmacies, the hardware, dry goods, and grocery stores, the meat and fish markets. A few of these places are as memorable to me as are the houses I have lived in.

Silberman's was a dark, narrow place that was rather uninviting. But it is to be remembered because my father had his first office in the warren of rooms on the second floor, and because when Mr. Silberman retired, he sold his business to a black employee—that was a breakthrough and a great and good thing. The Walgreen's was ordinary enough but stood out then as now for me because of its lunch counter. It was there, usually while out on a romp with my mother or Aunt Marge, that I would be treated to a frothy milk shake or to my favorite out-of-the-house sandwich, grilled ham on raisin toast. The counter was run by two or three foxy brown-skin ladies, breathtaking even in uniforms and hairnets. Sisters like that naturally inspired a lot of fast talk—and Lord did they know how to dish it back. The banter at the lunch counter was funny, saucy, memorable; not as dirty as what came down at the barber shop, but still very adult.

When the lunch counter sit-ins began a few short years later in the South, and I watched the news films of the clubbings and draggings, the smearings of mustard and catsup, the burnings with lit cigarettes, my horror was matched only by my shame, the haunting shame of privilege. Nothing my elders ever said about privileges and "being grateful" cut half as deep as what I felt when I recognized that all I knew about lunch counters before 1958 was sweet talk and pretty ladies.

Harris's Barber Shop was on the south side of Fifty-eighth, in the middle of a block not darkened by the girders of the El. It was the first of the several barber shops I've been destined to frequent where the talk is loud and quick and where an elder barber, usually the proprietor, can tell somebody to tone down ("Hey now, hey now, there are youngsters present," or, "Don't be talkin' 'bout *my* God that way!") and make it stick. Harris's was also typical in that the front of the shop displayed for sale shaving powders, pomades, and bacon rinds while the back had a curtain, behind which *something* to do with money was always going on. But what made Harris's a vintage, cut-from-the-true-mold (dare I write "dyed-in-the-wool"?) African-American barber shop was that it always took ten hours to get a haircut because there were always forty Negroes ahead of you, even on a weekday morning.

A measure of my father's rise in the world, I see now, came when he decided he couldn't wait around Mr. Harris's—the amusements no longer offsetting the time lost—and found himself a barber with whom he could make an *appointment.* But I, the child, continued on at Harris's for several years more, perhaps because the family still wanted to give him our trade, perhaps because the few times my mother had taken me to a shop nearer our home someone had been fresh with her (how vividly I recall my mother's rage when a barber on Sixty-fifth Street called her "baby"). No one said this, but of course what was also going on was that my haircuts were a means by which my parents kept in touch with a life and neighborhood they were growing beyond. The same could have been said of my churchgoing, which for stretches of time was the only churchgoing being done.

Mory's Met Music Shop was east of the El, in a shadowed block that may be dark in my mind for other reasons. The Met was in those days (and until its demise) the paragon of record shops, known for its jazz (and written up accordingly in all the jazz magazines) but, frankly, it had everything. My father and I would go in the Met frequently at night, when the shop was something of a hangout for jazz buffs, disc jockeys, and musicians. We'd grab a few sides and then make our way through the smoke and slick talk—trying hard not to jostle the clean dudes in cashmere overcoats and Florsheim's, the hopheads, or the Dizzy Gillespie look-alikes in their berets—to one of the listening booths lining the back wall. Crammed in a cubicle as small as a telephone booth, we'd check out Ella, Sarah, the Duke, the Count. I remember listening to our selections, marveling at how my father could sometimes listen to just one cut and then declare, "I *have* to have this jam!" But I also recall watching other people listening away in their booths. Once I watched a fellow, who looked a lot like Malcolm X, close his eyes and just take off for another world; Monk, I think, was doing that to him. But then he suddenly "woke up" and glared at me. I huddled closer to my father.

It was hard to leave the Met with just a record or two. But I seem to remember our purchases being that modest in the early days. Later, when my father began to make a little money, he would come home with a sack of take-out Chinese food from the Rumpus Room and five, maybe *ten,* records from the Met. What pleasure this brought him: he was playing Provider, and, indeed, what better provisions are there than Chinese food and a new stack of sides?

Though I have mentioned the Rumpus Room in words about my father, I most associate that restaurant with good times with my mother. We would go there together before my sister was born on the Friday evenings when my father had a dinner meeting, perhaps after I had spent the afternoon waiting interminably for a haircut at Mr. Harris's or after we had had a short visit with Grandma and Grandpa around the corner on Indiana. I would invariably order beef and green peppers, my mom would order all those good things in dark oyster sauces which I wouldn't like until I was in high school. The Rumpus Room occupied a floor or two of what had obviously been an apartment building, and so there was a pronounced sense that that booth over there was in a former parlor, while that one there was in a former bedroom, and so forth. Maybe I am completely wrong in this, but it is now I choose to reconcile the space with the sense of intimacy it emoted: soft jazz flowed through the speakers, couples learned into each other, nice smells wafted from the kitchen; it was definitely Friday night. (Later, as a "college poet," I would vainly try to commemorate all this with lines about "colored kitchens with Chinese cooks singing Lady Day.")

After dinner my mother and I sometimes went home and watched TV, which was no letdown for me since "Superman" was on and I was generally up for whatever was on since I could not watch TV during the school week. But other times we went to the "show," the movies, and saw some great stuff: *Shane, The African Queen, High Noon.* To this day, my mother and I talk about these films not in the context of television or videos or VCRS, but in that of strolling down the avenue, safely parking the car, and safely walking to a neighborhood theater to safely watch the film—not to mention safely going to the bathroom, if that was necessary.

The Rumpus Room was the restaurant I most had in mind when I blew up in 1972 at a now distinguished colleague who chose then to suggest that my professed love of Chinese food indicated that my "blackness" was suspect. The Rumpus Room was as a much a part of the neighborhood as was any of the soul-food cafés, as the patronage of it readily attested. That colleague now resides in a northern city, and I hope she now has enough information to change her view.

As I have mentioned before, after I moved with my parents to our own house in the Woodlawn district, I would return to the old neighborhood for haircuts and church. Church in the beginning was Good Shepherd—the Church of the Good Shepherd; later, around the age of nine or ten, I attended St. Edmund's, more formally known as St. Edmund's King & Martyr.

Good Shepherd had formed in the late 1920s right around the corner from my grandparents' home on Indiana Avenue. Grandma and Grandpa Burns had joined Good Shepherd right after moving to the neighborhood, and thus were members of the church from its inception. This always struck me as being curious since Good Shepherd is Congregationalist (now, United Church of Christ) and they were raised as Baptists and had been reinforced in that faith by their experiences at Tuskegee and Spelman. When I finally asked my mother about this, she explained that when her parents had come to Chicago, they had joined one of the famous, established Baptist churches, Olivet (in other words, they were among the five thousand black migrants who, according to James Grossman, joined Olivet between 1916 and 1919). But there had been a "falling out," something to do with "disrespect" at the time of my grandmother's sister's death. There may have been other reasons as well but, at any rate, by the time I was born, Good Shepherd had been our church for almost twenty years. I was baptized there; it is the church to which the family returns to bury its dead, half wondering with no small degree of shame whether we can get home before getting mugged.

St. Edmund's is Episcopal and was my father's family's church. Indeed, my grandfather, Pa Step, had been a member of the original vestry: somewhere I have a photo of him almost glaring at the camera while at a board meeting, as I also have a photo of my father in his acolyte years, replete with cassock, surplice, and a puffy bow at his neck. In its early years in the 1930s, St. Edmund's had no church building; its services and meetings (including the one Pa Step is attending in my photo) were held in rooms at the Wabash YMCA. By the 1950s, however, the parish had grown and prospered: in buildings once occupied by a Greek Orthodox church at Sixty-first and Michigan, we had both a church and elementary school.

St. Edmund's was not just Episcopal but high church, something that was mischievously explained as a trace of Father Martin's former days as a Roman Catholic. We had "bells and smells" in abundance, "exotic" images on the walls and in the architecture left over from the Greek Orthodox days, a choir that knew how to turn everybody on with its mix of Bach and spirituals. We had the usual assemblage of trifling, cigarette-sneaking acolytes who (myself included) nonetheless showed up every Sunday and actually knew the mass. I was confirmed into the Episcopal Church at St. Edmund's in June in 1957; Grandma and Grandpa Burns gave me as a present the Bible I still have. I doubt they would have been so congratulatory if they had known that I had become, not so much through coaching as through sheer self-invention, a "confirmed" Anglo-Catholic, deeply suspicious of Roman Catholics and Protestants alike. My days with them at Good Shepherd were just that far behind me.

How this came about—and why I was abruptly moved from Good Shepherd to St. Edmund's in the first place—is something I have tried to piece together. The family line on this is that I was moved because the Sunday School at Good Shepherd was lousy, nonexistent. There is some truth to this: all I can remember of Good Shepherd's Sunday School is the softball games. Perhaps this is because it was during one of those games that I received the revelation that left-handed people are supposed to bat from the *other* side of the plate. (With that knowledge, and a little practice, my batting average went up a zillion points.) At St. Edmund's, by contrast, those rooms in the elementary school were put to *use* on Sundays: we had Sunday School and homework, too.

The family line makes sense but is too pat an answer: what more were we leaving behind, what else were we moving to? Why would my mother leave the church of her youth and join St. Edmund's? Why did I accept the move so easily—is it possible that I may have even initiated it? Two stories seem to bear on this.

It was late on a wintry Saturday afternoon; Good Shepherd's Cub Scout pack, of which I was a member, was returning to the city after a joyous day of tobogganing out in the western suburbs. Suddenly, the church bus pulled to the side of the road right in front of a hamburger joint. We were going to have a treat! a snack! Visions of milk shakes and french fries danced in my head.

The scoutmaster got off the bus and went in to see if it would be "all right." We all knew that "all right" wasn't simply about whether twenty Cub Scouts could enter the premises; it was truly about whether twenty black boys who claimed to be Scouts should be let in. When the scoutmaster returned, he spoke to us like this: "Now boys, we are going to go in here and have ourselves a sandwich or something. But I can tell you the people in there are none too pleased about all this. Now, I needn't *remind* you that we are *not* on the South Side of Chicago; this is *not* the chicken shack down the street from your house—do you follow me? Good, so I needn't *remind* you of how to BEHAVE, right? Am I right? Ok; ok, now; let's go." With that, we filed off the bus, hitting each other whenever someone thought someone else was talking too loud.

The scene inside the hamburger place was not good. I would say that the white cook and counterman (both of whom looked like they should be sitting outside a filling station in Alabama) had instantly discovered, once deep into serving a bunch of Negroes, how much that disgusted them. They scowled, they muttered, they turned redder and redder by the minute. They half-cooked the food, threw it on a plate, and hurled the plate in almost anyone's direction. They clearly wanted us to leave, but in their fury constantly got the food orders wrong. We stayed, waiting for our food, perhaps out of conviction but more likely out of a kind of politeness (after all, the scoutmaster said, "BEHAVE"); witness probably for the first time in our lives to the spectacle of white men becoming unglued because of race. Then I said, loud enough and to no one—hence, to all: "Gee, this place has lousy service." No one replied; it was as if no one had heard me; but I had been heard.

When we got back on the bus, the scoutmaster started up: "You boys did fine in there. You all were real gentlemen. That is, all of you but one. I *asked* if you all knew how to behave, and you all said you did. Well, one of you *doesn't* know, and it's going to be a long time before I take *any* of you anywhere again." I honestly wondered who this terrible person was; who had brought this down on the whole Scout pack? I tried to recall if someone had been loud in the restaurant, or otherwise cut the fool. Had anybody not used their silverware, their napkin? Had someone forgotten to say "please" or "thank you" or "yes sir"? I knew I hadn't.

But the bad egg was me, and the scoutmaster in effect both listed my sins and had them posted. I was told that I had made a bad situation worse, and that if I had held my tongue the situation might have gotten better. I was told that I had endangered all of us, and had risked bringing violence upon us. I was told in pungent, quite vernacular terms that I knew nothing about "facing adversity with stoic dignity." I wanted to retort "bullshit." I wanted to remind everyone of who took us in that "cracker cafe" in the first place, instead of waiting until we were back in Chicago. I wanted to scream, but I said nothing, and not even a scream came out. I just sat and took it, my cheeks burning, my body seemingly shrinking, tucking itself into the folds of my winter parka, into the darkness enveloping the bus as day so gratefully became night.

Soon the bus cranked up, and we were on our way. No one spoke to me, but I was consoled by the quickening certainty that we were no longer stalled in the suburbs and that being home was somehow going to happen. But we had an accident on the way home—a minor one—but accident enough. I am sure that there were some people on that bus who thought, "This would not have happened if Stepto hadn't queered the whole day for us." My thought was, "This is happening because we were so goddamn servile." We were a long time getting home.

After the episode in the suburbs, I was at best an indifferent Scout. I stopped doing the chores and projects that would earn me merit badges. I began to "play hooky" from Scout meetings, finding great pleasure in inventing places to go and in coercing a Scout or two to go with me. Once we rode to the end of the line of the commuter train I usually used merely to go from one point to another within Chicago; we went to "see what we could see" and were bitterly disappointed to sight nothing of interest. Another time we went downtown to the Loop to have a meal in a coffee shop famous for its hamburgers—I see now that that was a brave attempt to undo or revise what had happened in the suburbs after tobogganing. I continued as a Scout because I had a few friends, liked the uniform, and had no idea of how to act upon the emotions washing over me. So, too, did I value being in a context where I had an identity: at Good Shepherd and even in the Cub Scouts I was "Miss Burns's grandchild." I thought that was my best merit badge, and I thought everybody thought so as well, but that was before the Sunday Grandma was hooted in the large basement room where Sunday School was held, and I had to witness the spectacle.

As best I recall, I was outside the church playing softball. It had been a long time since any adult had suggested that Sunday School ought to foster something other than ball games, and so I was surprised when our game was broken up, and astonished by everything in the manner of the adult corraling us that told us we had been up to no good. When we arrived back inside the Sunday School area, there was much disarray and tension; apparently, the games and crafts which customarily occupied the youngsters not playing softball had been interrupted as well. People were grumbling: "What's going on?" "Who says this ain't a Sunday School?" "Sunday school these days ain't nothing but day care any way." "Somebody better wake up!" "I bet you one of them old-timey sisters from one of the guilds is behind this." "Who's that over there, passing out lessons?" "These children ain't going for none of that." "Who'd you say? Miss Burns? Oh, Lord, she done come back and doing it to us again."

The nut-brown woman with a determined look on her face, who was furiously slapping down lesson books (with Gentle Jesus on the cover) on top of board games and crayon drawings, was indeed "Miss Burns," my grandmother. I was mortified but also confused: I hated the way she was calling attention to herself (and hence, so I thought, to me); I hated what most everyone was saying about her (but knew that I had thought those things, especially those times when she abruptly turned off the television, because the cowboy movie I was watching was "too violent"). Matters did not improve during the excruciating remaining minutes of the Sunday School hour. Most of the youngsters were, I would say, disrespectfully silent; most of the erstwhile

Sunday School teachers remained so, even though it *looked* like they were up to something pedagogical. Meanwhile, my grandmother, from her perch near the upright piano, sternly surveyed the scene, looking ever so much like your worst nightmare of a school principal or a plant manager.

Twenty minutes later, it was over, or almost over; Grandma had another card to play: she insisted that we revive the custom of ending Sunday School with a rousing rendition of "Onward, Christian Soldiers," which would end with all of us youngsters marching single-file out of the church building, gloriously into the sunshine. There was no recourse, especially after Grandma sat down at the upright and blanketed the room with hymnal chordings. The way out was simply the doorway through which we were to march, and march we did, though our clatter was hardly soldierlike. Once out into the sunshine, we wandered about, meandering in circles and half circles, trying to get a compass fix on our whereabouts. What I realized, once I got my bearings, was that I was in a zone of strange contradictions: I was outside the church when I was supposed to be inside; I was outside because my good Christian grandmother had in some real sense marched me outside; moreover, she had marched me outside in order to bring me, among others, inside—to make us true inhabitants of the church. It was all very confusing, wrenchingly so; I recall being quiet and subdued the rest of the day—perhaps I needfully got lost in a book, knowing well enough that this wasn't a good day for testing the limits on *The Lone Ranger.* All this occurred in the spring, in May I think. By the fall I was a regular in the pews at St. Edmund's.

I was last at Good Shepherd a few years ago for my Aunt Marge's funeral. It was blisteringly hot, so much so that when we found out to our great dismay that the air-conditioning in the church had broken down that afternoon, a few family members just stayed in the cool of the rented limousines until the service began. I was exceedingly uncomfortable but too restless to sit in a limo; I needed to explore what I could of the church, revisiting, for example, the vast basement room where the Cub Scouts had met, and from which I had marched to the strains of "Onward Christian Soldiers" into another boyhood. I also needed to get a closer look at the children across the street, playing in the spray of an opened fire hydrant. Would they mind? Would they let me get close enough to see if I could see my child self in them? The heat bore in, I needed to get back in one of the limos, but I wanted more to walk around to the Fifty-seventh Street side of the church to scrutinize the lot (really, the church's backyard) where I had played so many outdoor games, and learned to hit a softball, too. It was much as I thought it would be: narrow, spare, scruffy; I must have been a little tyke indeed to have once considered it a suitable space for serious ball games.

Then it occurred to me: you're already on Fifty-seventh Street, maybe a quarter of the way to Grandma's house, why don't you walk down the street and around the corner and have a look? The appropriateness of this could not be disputed. To see the Burns house would be to see where our Washington Park life had begun sixty years before, and where my life had begun just after World War II. Even from across the street, I would be able to examine the little side entrance to the basement apartment where Marge and Rog had lived, and to watch the fading August sun burnish the second-floor window of what had been my parents' room, and later my room whenever I overnighted with my grandparents. I though that all I was trying to pull together by roaming around instead of being in the limo would instantly coalesce once on Indiana Avenue, once reading the house numbers, "5722."

But I didn't go around the corner, even though I ventured seven or eight steps toward it. This was not because I thought I might miss the beginning of the service or simply because it was too hot to amble the streets. I didn't go because I was too well dressed and too light skinned; because I had a little money in my pocket and because I was wearing the nice watch my wife gave me for our twentieth anniversary. One side of my brain said, "Hey, my man, you're a brother—go on down to your grandmother's house and check it out." The other side said, "Don't fall for that romantic shit; this neighborhood has *changed;* walk two blocks and you're a dead man; the next funeral at Good Shepherd will be yours." Perhaps because a woman had been mugged at the wake the night before—she came running back into the church screaming, "My purse's been taken, he took my purse!" as if any of us could do anything about it—I listened to the second voice in my head. But I was angered by what was preventing me, a former child of those streets, from doing anything I wanted. So, too, was I angry about not being able to make the connection, which I thought to be the best possible connection, with the people, sites, and images that would put my life in order.

But I was wrong, for when I finally quit gazing down the street I wouldn't walk and entered the church, I found a feast for my eyes: the much older but still quite recognizable visage of the scoutmaster who had taken us tobogganing and later pilloried me some thirty-five years before. Family and friends from the year one broached conversation, and I believe I engaged them. But my eye was on Mr. B. Later I approached him, reminded him of how we knew each other, asked him how he had been, asked after his son, whom I remembered to be the Willie Mays of Cub Scouts. Mr. B. was very good at assisting the minister with the service, very short on everything else. He didn't remember me, and I almost got the feeling that he didn't remember the son of whom I had inquired.

This and the fact that, when it was time for me to speak, I was actually introduced as a *friend* of the family, and not as family, not as the firstborn nephew of the woman we were burying, made me aware not just of the corrosive forces of time, but also of what the young put in place to create chasms between the generations. I had wanted to be shut of Good Shepherd, and thirty-five years later I was faced with the evidence of how well I had succeeded.

19

Between Memory and History: *Les Lieux de Mémoire*

PIERRE NORA

The acceleration of history: let us try to gauge the significance, beyond metaphor, of this phrase. An increasingly rapid slippage of the present into a historical past that is gone for good, a general perception that anything and everything may disappear—these indicate a rupture of equilibrium. The remnants of experience still lived in the warmth of tradition, in the silence of custom, in the repetition of the ancestral, have been displaced under the pressure of a fundamentally historical sensibility. Self-consciousness emerges under the sign of that which has already happened, as the fulfillment of something always already begun. We speak so much of memory because there is so little of it left.

Our interest in *lieux de mémoire* where memory crystallizes and secretes itself has occurred at a particular historical moment, a turning point where consciousness of a break with the past is bound up with the sense that memory has been torn—but torn in such a way as to pose the problem of the embodiment of memory in certain sites where a sense of historical continuity persists. There are *lieux de mémoire,* sites of memory, because there are no longer *milieux de mémoire,* real environments of memory.

Consider, for example, the irrevocable break marked by the disappearance of peasant culture, that quintessential repository of collective memory whose recent vogue as an object of historical study coincided with the apogee of industrial growth. Such a fundamental collapse of memory is but one familiar example of a movement toward democratization and mass culture on a global scale. Among the new nations, independence has swept into history societies newly awakened from their ethnological slumbers by colonial violation. Similarly, a process of interior decolonization has affected ethnic minorities, families, and groups that until now have possessed reserves of memory but little or no historical capital. We have seen the end of societies that had long assured the transmission and conservation of collectively remembered values, whether through churches or schools, the family or the state; the end

Translated by Marc Roudebush

too of ideologies that prepared a smooth passage from the past to the future or that had indicated that the future should keep from the past—whether for reaction, progress, or even revolution. Indeed, we have seen the tremendous dilation of our very mode of historical perception, which, with the help of the media, has substituted for a memory entwined in the intimacy of a collective heritage the ephemeral film of current events.

The "acceleration of history," then, confronts us with the brutal realization of the difference between real memory—social and unviolated, exemplified in but also retained as the secret of so-called primitive or archaic societies—and history, which is how our hopelessly forgetful modern societies, propelled by change, organize the past. On the one hand, we find an integrated, dictatorial memory—unself-conscious, commanding, all-powerful, spontaneously actualizing, a memory without a past that ceaselessly reinvents tradition, linking the history of its ancestors to the undifferentiated time of heroes, origins, and myth—and on the other hand, our memory, nothing more in fact than sifted and sorted historical traces. The gulf between the two has deepened in modern times with the growing belief in a right, a capacity, and even a duty to change. Today, this distance has been stretched to its convulsive limit.

This conquest and eradication of memory by history has had the effect of a revelation, as if an ancient bond of identity had been broken and something had ended that we had experienced as self-evident—the equation of memory and history. The fact that only one word exists in French to designate both lived history and the intellectual operation that renders it intelligible (distinguished in German by *Geschichte* and *Historie*) is a weakness of the language that has often been remarked; still, it delivers a profound truth: the process that is carrying us forward and our representation of that process are of the same kind. If we were able to live within memory, we would not have needed to consecrate *lieux de mémoire* in its name. Each gesture, down to the most everyday, would be experienced as the ritual repetition of a timeless practice in a primordial identification of act and meaning. With the appearance of the trace, of mediation, of distance, we are not in the realm of true memory but of history. We can think, for an example, of the Jews of the Diaspora, bound in daily devotion to the rituals of tradition, who as "peoples of memory" found little use for historians until their forced exposure to the modern world.

Memory and history, far from being synonymous, appear now to be in fundamental opposition. Memory is life, borne by living societies founded in its name. It remains in permanent evolution, open to the dialectic of remembering and forgetting, unconscious of its successive deformations, vulnerable to manipulation and appropriation, susceptible to being long dormant and periodically revived. History, on the other hand, is the reconstruction, always problematic and incomplete, of what is no longer. Memory is a perpetually actual phenomenon, a bond tying us to the eternal present; history is a representation of the past. Memory, insofar as it is affective and magical, only accommodates those facts that suit it; it nourishes recollections that may be out of focus or telescopic, global or detached, particular or symbolic—responsive to each avenue of conveyance or phenomenal screen, to every censorship or projection. History, because it is an intellectual and secular production, calls for analysis and criticism. Memory installs remembrance within the sacred; history, always prosaic, releases it again. Memory is blind to all but the group it binds—which is to say, as Maurice Halbwachs has said, that there are as many memories as there are groups, that memory is by nature multiple and yet specific; collective, plural, and yet individual. History, on the other hand, belongs to everyone and to no one, whence its claim to universal authority. Memory takes root in the concrete, in spaces, gestures, images, and objects; history binds itself strictly to temporal continuities, to progressions and to relations between things. Memory is absolute, while history can only conceive the relative.

At the heart of history is a critical discourse that is antithetical to spontaneous memory. History is perpetually suspicious of memory, and its true mission is to suppress and destroy it. At the horizon of historical societies, at the limits of the completely historicized world, there would occur a permanent secularization. History's goal and ambition is not to exalt but to annihilate what has in reality taken place. A generalized critical history would no doubt preserve some museums, some medallions and monuments—that is to say, the materials necessary for its work—but it would empty them of what, to us, would make them *lieux de mémoire*. In the end, a society living wholly under the sign of history could not, any more than could a traditional society, conceive such sites for anchoring its memory.

Perhaps the most tangible sign of the split between history and memory has been the emergence of a history of history, the awakening, quite recent in France, of a historiographical consciousness. History, especially the history of national development, has constituted the oldest of our collective traditions: our quintessential *milieu de mémoire*. From the chroniclers of the Middle Ages to today's practitioners of "total" history, the entire tradition has developed as the controlled exercise and automatic deepening of memory, the reconstitution of a past without lacunae or faults. No doubt, none of the great historians, since Froissart, had the sense that he was representing only a particular memory. Commynes did not think he was fashioning a merely dynastic memory, La Popelinière merely a French memory, Bossuet a Christian and monarchical memory, Voltaire the memory of the progress of humankind, Michelet exclusively the "people's" memory, and Lavisse solely the memory of the nation. On the contrary, each historian was convinced that his task consisted in establishing a more positive, all-encompassing, and explicative memory. History's procurement, in the last century, of scientific methodology has only intensified the effort to establish critically a "true" memory. Every great historical revision has sought to enlarge the basis for collective memory.

In a country such as France the history of history cannot be an innocent operation; it amounts to the internal subversion of memory-history by critical history. Every history is by nature critical, and all historians have sought to denounce the hypocritical mythologies of their predecessors. But something fundamentally unsettling happens when history begins to write its own history. A historiographical anxiety arises when history assigns itself the task of tracing alien impulses within itself and discovers that it is the victim of memories which it has sought to master. Where history has not taken on the strong formative and didactic role that it has assumed in France, the history of history is less laden with polemical content. In the United States, for example, a country of plural memories and diverse traditions, historiography is more pragmatic. Different interpretations of the Revolution or of the Civil War do not threaten the American tradition because, in some sense, no such thing exists—or if it does, it is not primarily a historical construction. In France, on the other hand, historiography is iconoclastic and irreverent. It seizes upon the most clearly defined objects of tradition—a key battle, like Bouvines; a canonical manual, like the *Petit Lavisse*—in order to dismantle their mechanisms and analyze the conditions of their development. It operates primarily by introducing doubt, by running a knife between the tree of memory and the bark of history. That we study the historiography of the French Revolution, that we reconstitute its myths and interpretations, implies that we no longer unquestioningly identify with its heritage. To interrogate a tradition, venerable though it may be, is no longer to pass it on intact. Moreover, the history of history does not restrict itself to addressing the most sacred objects of our national tradition. By questioning its own traditional structure, its own conceptual and material resources, its operating procedures and social means of distribution, the engine discipline of history has entered its historiographical age, consummating its dissociation from memory—which in turn has become a possible object of history.

It once seemed as though a tradition of memory, through the concepts of history and the nation, had crystallized in the synthesis of the Third Republic. Adopting a broad chronology, between Augustin Thierry's *Lettres sur l'histoire de France* (1827) and Charles Seignobos's *Histoire sincère de la nation française* (1933), the relationships between history, memory, and the nation were characterized as more than natural currency: they were shown to involve a reciprocal circularity, a symbiosis at every level—scientific and pedagogical, theoretical and practical. This national definition of the present imperiously demanded justification through the illumination of the past. It was, however, a present that had been weakened by revolutionary trauma and the call for a general reevaluation of the monarchical past, and it was weakened further by the defeat of 1870, which rendered only more urgent, in the belated competition with German science and pedagogy—the real victors at Sadowa—the development of a severe documentary erudition for the scholarly transmission of memory. The tone of national responsibility assigned to the historian—half preacher, half soldier—is unequalled, for example, in the first editorial of the *Revue historique* (1876) in which Gabriel Monod foresaw a "slow scientific, methodical, and collective investigation" conducted in a "secret and secure manner for the greatness of the fatherland as well as for mankind." Reading this text, and a hundred others like it, one wonders how the notion that positivist history was not cumulative could ever have gained credibility. On the contrary, in the teleological perspective of the nation the political, the military, the biographical, and the diplomatic all were to be considered pillars of continuity. The defeat of Agincourt, the dagger of Ravaillac, the day of the Dupes, the additional clauses of the treaty of Westphalia—each required scrupulous accounting. The most incisive erudition thus served to add or take away some detail from the monumental edifice that was the nation. The nation's memory was held to be powerfully unified; no more discontinuity existed between our Greco-Roman cradle and the colonies of the Third Republic than between the high erudition that annexed new territories to the nation's heritage and the schoolbooks that professed its dogma. The holy nation thus acquired a holy history; through the nation our memory continued to rest upon a sacred foundation.

To see how this particular synthesis came apart under the pressure of a new secularizing force would be to show how, during the crisis of the 1930s in France, the coupling of state and nation was gradually replaced by the coupling of state and society—and how, at the same time and for the same reasons, history was transformed, spectacularly, from the tradition of memory it had become into the self-knowledge of society. As such, history was able to highlight many kinds of memory, even turn itself into a laboratory of past mentalities; but in disclaiming its national identity, it also abandoned its claim to bearing coherent meaning and consequently lost its pedagogical authority to transmit values. The definition of the nation was no longer the issue, and peace, prosperity, and the reduction of its power have since accomplished the rest. With the advent of society in place of the nation, legitimation by the past and therefore by history yields to legitimation by the future. One can only acknowledge and venerate the past and serve the nation; the future, however, can be prepared for: thus the three terms regain their autonomy. No longer a cause, the nation has become a given; history is now a social science, memory a purely private phenomenon. The memory-nation was thus the last incarnation of the unification of memory and history.

The study of *lieux de mémoires,* then, lies at the intersection of two developments that in France today gave it meaning: one a purely historiographical movement, the reflexive turning of history upon itself, the other a movement that is, properly speaking, historical: the end of a tradition of memory. The moment of *lieux de mémoire* occurs at the same time that an immense and intimate fund of memory disappears, surviving only as a reconstituted object beneath the gaze of critical history. This period sees, on the one hand, the decisive deepening of historical study and, on the other hand, a heritage consolidated. The critical principle follows an internal dynamic: our intellectual, political, historical frameworks are exhausted but remain powerful enough not to leave us indifferent; whatever vitality they retain impresses us only in their most spectacular symbols. Combined, these two movements send us at once to history's most elementary tools and to the most symbolic objects of our memory: to the archives as well as to the tricolor; to the libraries, dictionaries, and museums as well as to commemorations, celebrations, the

Pantheon, and the Arc de Triomphe; to the *Dictionnaire Larousse* as well as to the Wall of the Fédérés, where the last defenders of the Paris commune were massacred in 1870.

These *lieux de mémoire* are fundamentally remains, the ultimate embodiments of a memorial consciousness that has barely survived in a historical age that calls out for memory because it has abandoned it. They make their appearance by virtue of the deritualization of our world—producing, manifesting, establishing, constructing, decreeing, and maintaining by artifice and by will a society deeply absorbed in its own transformation and renewal, one that inherently values the new over the ancient, the young over the old, the future over the past. Museums, archives, cemeteries, festivals, anniversaries, treaties, depositions, monuments, sanctuaries, fraternal orders—these are the boundary stones of another age, illusions of eternity. It is the nostalgic dimension of these devotional institutions that makes them seem beleaguered and cold—they mark the rituals of a society without ritual; integral particularities in a society that levels particularity; signs of distinction and of group membership in a society that tends to recognize individuals only as identical and equal.

Lieux de mémoire originate with the sense that there is no spontaneous memory, that we must deliberately create archives, maintain anniversaries, organize celebrations, pronounce eulogies, and notarize bills because such activities no longer occur naturally. The defense, by certain minorities, of a privileged memory that has retreated to jealously protected enclaves in this sense intensely illuminates the truth of *lieux de mémoire*—that without commemorative vigilance, history would soon sweep them away. We buttress our identities upon such bastions, but if what they defeated were not threatened, there would be no need to build them. Conversely, if the memories that they enclosed were to be set free they would be useless; if history did not besiege memory, deforming and transforming it, penetrating and petrifying it, there would be no *lieux de mémoire.* Indeed, it is this very push and pull that produces *lieux de mémoire*—moments of history torn away from the movement of history, then returned; no longer quite life, not yet death, like shells on the shore when the sea of living memory has receded.

Memory Seized by History

What we call memory today is therefore not memory but already history. What we take to be flare-ups of memory are in fact its final consumption in the flames of history. The quest for memory is the search for one's history.

Of course, we still cannot do without the word, but we should be aware of the difference between true memory, which has taken refuge in gestures and habits, in skills passed down by unspoken traditions, in the body's inherent self-knowledge, in unstudied reflexes and ingrained memories, and memory transformed by its passage through history, which is nearly the opposite: voluntary and deliberate, experienced as a duty, no longer spontaneous; psychological, individual, and subjective; but never social, collective, or all encompassing. How did we move from the first memory, which is immediate, to the second, which is indirect? We may approach the question of this contemporary metamorphosis from the perspective of its outcome.

Modern memory is, above all, archival. It relies entirely on the materiality of the trace, the immediacy of the recording, the visibility of the image. What began as writing ends as high fidelity and tape recording. The less memory is experienced from the inside the more it exists only through its exterior scaffolding and outward signs—hence the obsession with the archive that marks our age, attempting at once the complete conservation of the present as well as the total preservation of the past. Fear of a rapid and final disappearance combines with anxiety about the meaning of the present and uncertainty about the future to give even the most humble testimony, the most modest vestige, the potential dignity of the memorable. Have we not sufficiently regretted and deplored the loss or destruction, by our predecessors, of potentially informative sources to avoid opening ourselves to the same reproach from our successors? Memory has been wholly absorbed by its meticulous reconstitution. Its new vocation is to record; delegating to the archive the responsibility of remembering, it sheds its signs upon depositing them there, as a snake sheds its skin.

What we call memory is in fact the gigantic and breathtaking storehouse of a material stock of what it would be impossible for us to remember, an unlimited repertoire of what might need to be recalled. Leibnitz's "paper memory" has become an autonomous institution of museums, libraries, depositories, centers of documentation, and data banks. Specialists estimate that in the public archives alone, in just a few decades, the quantitative revolution has multiplied the number of records by one thousand. No society has ever produced archives as deliberately as our own, not only volume, not only by new technical means of reproduction and preservation, but also by its superstitious esteem, by its veneration of the trace. Even as traditional memory disappears, we feel obliged assiduously to collect remains, testimonies, documents, images, speeches, any visible signs of what has been, as if this burgeoning dossier were to be called upon to furnish some proof to who knows what tribunal of history. The sacred is invested in the trace that is at the same time its negation. It becomes impossible to predict what should be remembered—whence the disinclination to destroy anything that leads to the corresponding reinforcement of all the institutions of memory. A strange role reversal has occurred between the professional, once reproached for an obsession with conservation, and the amateur producer of archives. Today, private enterprise and public administration keep everything, while professional archivists have learned that the essence of their trade is the art of controlled destruction.

In just a few years, then, the materialization of memory has been tremendously dilated, multiplied, decentralized, democratized. In the classical period, the three main producers of archives were the great families, the church, and the state. But who, today, does not feel compelled to record his feelings, to write his memoirs—not only the most minor historical actor but also his witnesses, his spouse, and his doctor. The less extraordinary the testimony, the more aptly it seems to illustrate the average mentality.

The imperative of our epoch is not only to keep everything, to preserve every indicator of memory—even when we are not sure which memory is being indicated—but also to produce archives. The French Social Security archives are a troubling example: an unparalleled quantity of documents, they represent today three hundred linear kilometers. Ideally, the computerized evaluation of this mass of raw memory would provide a reading of the sum total of the normal and the pathological in society, from diets to life-styles, by region and by profession; yet even its preservation and plausible implementation call for drastic and impossible choices. Record as much as you can, something will remain. This is, to take another telling example, the conclusion implied by the proliferation of oral histories. There are currently in France more than three hundred teams employed in gathering "the voices that come to us from the past" (Philippe Joutard). But these are not ordinary archives, if we consider that to produce them requires thirty-six hours for each hour of recording time and that they can never be used piecemeal, because they only have meaning when heard in their entirety. Whose will to remember do they ultimately reflect, that of the interviewer or that of the interviewed? No longer living memory's more or less intended remainder, the archive has become the deliberate and calculated secretion of lost memory. It adds to life—itself often a function of its own recording—a secondary memory, a prosthesis-memory. The indiscriminate production of archives is the acute effect of a new consciousness, the clearest expression of the terrorism of historicized memory.

This form of memory comes to us from the outside; because it is no longer a social practice, we interiorize it as an individual constraint.

The passage from memory to history has required every social group to redefine its identity through the revitalization of its own history. The task of remembering makes everyone his own historian. The demand for history has thus largely overflowed the circle of professional historians. Those who have long been marginalized in traditional history are not the only ones haunted by the need to recover their buried pasts. Following the example of ethnic groups and social minorities, every established group, intellectual or not, learned or not, has felt the need to go in search of its own origins and identity. Indeed, there is hardly a family today in which some member has not recently sought to document as accurately as possible his or her ancestors' furtive existences. The increase in genealogical research is a massive new phenomenon: the national archives reports that 43 percent of those doing archival research in 1982 were working on genealogical history, as compared with the 38 percent who were university researchers. It is striking that we owe the most significant histories of biology, physics, medicine, and music not to professional historians but to biologists, physicists, doctors, and musicians. Educators themselves have taken charge of the history of education, from physical education to instruction in educational philosophy. In the wake of attacks on established domains of knowledge, each discipline has sought validation in the retrospective perusal of its own origins. Sociology goes in search of its founding fathers;

anthropology undertakes to explore its own past, from the sixteenth-century chroniclers to the colonial administrators. Even literary criticism occupies itself in retracing the genesis of its categories and tradition. As for history, positivism, long since abandoned by professional historians, has found in this urgent need a popularity and necessity it never knew before. The decomposition of memory-history has multiplied the number of private memories demanding their individual histories.

An order is given to remember, but the responsibility is mine and it is I who must remember. One of the costs of the historical metamorphosis of memory has been a wholesale preoccupation with the individual psychology of remembering. Indeed, the two phenomena are so intimately linked that one can hardly avoid comparing them, down to their exact chronological coincidence. At the end of the last century, when the decisive blow to traditional balances was felt—in particular the disintegration of the rural world—memory appeared at the center of philosophical thought, with Bergson; at the core of the psychological personality, with Freud; at the heart of literary autobiography, with Proust. We owe to Freud and to Proust those two intimate and yet universal sites of memory, the primal scene and the celebrated *petite madeleine*. The transformation of memory implies a decisive shift from the historical to the psychological, from the social to the individual, from the objective message to its subjective reception, from repetition to rememoration. The total psychologization of contemporary memory entails a completely new economy of the identity of the self, the mechanics of memory, and the relevance of the past.

In the last analysis, it is upon the individual and upon the individual alone that the constraint of memory weighs insistently as well as imperceptibly. The atomization of a general memory into a private one has given the obligation to remember a power of internal coercion. It gives everyone the necessity to remember and to protect the trappings of identity; when memory is no longer everywhere, it will not be anywhere unless one takes the responsibility to recapture it through individual means. The less memory is experienced collectively, the more it will require individuals to undertake to become themselves memory-individuals, as if an inner voice were to tell each Corsican "You must be Corsican" and each Breton "You must be Breton." To understand the force and appeal of this sense of obligation, perhaps we should think of Jewish memory, which has recently been revived among many nonpracticing Jews. In this tradition, which has no other history than its own memory, to be Jewish is to remember that one is such; but once this incontestable memory has been interiorized, it eventually demands full recognition. What is being remembered? In a sense, it is memory itself. The psychologization of memory has thus given every individual the sense that his or her salvation ultimately depends on the repayment of an impossible debt.

In addition to archive-memory and duty-memory, a third aspect is needed to complete the picture of this modern metamorphosis: distance-memory.

This is because our relation to the past, at least as it reveals itself in major historical studies, is something entirely different from what we would expect from a memory: no longer a retrospective continuity but the illumination of discontinuity. In the history-memory of old, accurate perceptions of the past were characterized by the assumption that the past could be retrieved. The past could always be resuscitated by an effort of rememoration; indeed, the present itself became a sort of recycled, updated past, realized as the present through such welding and anchoring. True, for there to be a sense of the past there had to be a "before" and an "after," a chasm had to intervene between the present and the past. But this was not so much a separation experienced as radical difference as it was a lapse experienced as a filiation to be restored. Progress and decadence, the two great themes of historical intelligibility at least since modern times, both aptly express the cult of continuity, the confident assumption of knowing to whom and to what we owe our existence—whence the importance of the idea of "origins," an already profane version of the mythological narrative, but one that contributed to giving meaning and a sense of the sacred to a society engaged in a nationwide process of secularization. The greater the origins, the more they magnified our greatness. Through the past we venerated above all ourselves.

It is this relation which has been broken. Just as the future—formerly a visible, predictable, manipulable, well-marked extension of the present—has come to seem invisible, unpredictable, uncontrollable, so have we gone from the idea of a visible past to an invisible one; from a solid and steady past to our fractured past; from a history sought in the continuity of memory to a memory cast in the discontinuity of history. We speak no longer of "origins" but of "births." Given to us as radically other, the past has become a world apart. Ironically, modern memory reveals itself most genuinely when it shows how far we have come away from it.

We should not believe, however, that this sense of discontinuity finds only unfocused and vague expression. Paradoxically, distance demands the *rapprochement* that negates it while giving it resonance. Never have we longed in a more physical manner to evoke the weight of the land at our feet, the hand of the devil in the year 1000, or the stench of eighteenth-century cities. Yet only in a regime of discontinuity are such hallucinations of the past conceivable. Our relation to the past is now formed in a subtle play between its intractability and its disappearance, a question of a representation—in the original sense of the word—radically different from the old ideal of resurrecting the past. As comprehensive as it may have wished to be, in practice such a resurrection implied a hierarchy of memory, ordering the perspective of the past beneath the gaze of a static present by the skillful manipulation of light and shadow. But the loss of a single explanatory principle, while casting us into a fragmented universe, has promoted every object—even the most humble, the most improbable, the most inaccessible—to the dignitary of a historical mystery. Since no one knows what the past will be made of next, anxiety turns everything into a trace, a possible indication, a hint of history that contaminates the innocence of all things.

Representation proceeds by strategic highlighting, selecting samples and multiplying examples. Ours is an intensely retinal and powerfully televisual memory. We can link the acclaimed "return of the narrative" evident in recent historical writing and the omnipotence of imagery and cinema in contemporary culture—even if, to be sure, this narrative is very different from traditional narrative, with its syncopated parts and formal closure. How can we not connect our scrupulous respect for archival documents, themselves fragments put before our eyes, and the unique frame we give to oral literature, quoting informants to render intelligible their voices—are they not clearly connected to the sense of directness that we have become accustomed to elsewhere? How can we but see in our taste for everyday life in the past a resort to the only remaining means for restoring the flavor of things, the slow rhythms of past times—and in the anonymous biographies of ordinary people the understanding that the masses do not allow themselves to be measured as a mass? How can we fail to read, in the shards of the past delivered to us by so many microhistories, the will to make the history we are reconstructing equal to the history we have lived? We could speak of mirror-memory if all mirrors did not reflect the same—for it is difference that we are seeking, and in the image of this difference, the ephemeral spectacle of an unrecoverable identity. It is no longer genesis that we seek but instead the decipherment of what we are in the light of what we are no longer.

Strangely, this alchemy of essentials contributes to making the practice of history—from which the relentless drive toward the future ought to have excused us—a repository for the secrets of the present. This thaumaturgical operation is accomplished more by the historian than by history. The historian's is a strange fate; his role and place in society were once simple and clearly defined: to be the spokesman of the past and the herald of the future. In this capacity his person counted less than his services; his role was that of an erudite transparency, a vehicle of transmission, a bridge stretched as lightly as possible between the raw materiality of the document and its inscription in memory—ultimately, an absence obsessed with objectivity. But with the disintegration of history-memory, a new type of historian emerges who, unlike his precursors, is ready to confess the intimate relation he maintains to his subject. Better still, he is ready to proclaim it, deepen it, make of it not the obstacle but the means of his understanding.

Imagine a society entirely absorbed in its own historicity. It would be incapable of producing historians. Living entirely under the sign of the future, it would satisfy itself with automatic self-recording processes and auto-inventory machines, postponing indefinitely the task of understanding itself. By contrast, our society—torn from its memory by the scale of its transformations but all the more obsessed with understanding itself historically—is forced to give an increasingly central role to the operations that take place within the historian. This historian is one who prevents history from becoming *merely* history.

In the same way that we owe our historical overview to a panoramic distance, and our artificial hyper-realization of the past to a definitive estrangement, a changing mode of perception returns the historian, almost against his will, to the traditional objects from which he had turned away, the common knowledge of our national memory. Returning across the threshold of one's natal home, one finds oneself in the old abode, now uninhabited and practically unrecognizable—with the same family heirlooms, but under another light; before the same *atelier,* but for another task; in the same rooms, but with another role. As historiography has entered its epistemological age, with memory ineluctably engulfed by history, the historian has become no longer a memory-individual but, in himself, a *lieu de mémoire.*

Les Lieux de Mémoire: Another History

Lieux de mémoire are simple and ambiguous, natural and artificial, at once immediately available in concrete sensual experience and susceptible to the most abstract elaboration. Indeed, they are *lieux* in three senses of the word—material, symbolic, and functional. Even an apparently purely material site, like an archive, becomes a *lieu de mémoire* only if the imagination invests it with a symbolic aura. A purely functional site, like a classroom manual, a testament, or a veterans' reunion belongs to the category only inasmuch as it is also the object of a ritual. And the observance of a commemorative minute silence, an extreme example of a strictly symbolic action, serves as a concentrated appeal to memory by literally breaking a temporal continuity. Moreover, the three aspects always coexist. Take, for example, the notion of a historical generation: it is material by its demographic content and supposedly functional—since memories are crystallized and transmitted from one generation to the next—but it is also symbolic, since it characterizes, by referring to events or experiences shared by a small minority, a larger group that may not have participated in them.

Lieux de mémoire are created by a play of memory and history, an interaction of two factors that results in their reciprocal overdetermination. To begin with, there must be a will to remember. If we were to abandon this criterion, we would quickly drift into admitting virtually everything as worthy of remembrance. One is reminded of the prudent rules of old-fashioned historical criticism, which distinguished between "direct sources," intentionally produced by society with a view to their future reproduction—a law or a work of art, for example—and the indiscriminate mass of "indirect sources," comprising all the testimony an epoch inadvertently leaves to historians. Without the intention to remember, *lieux de mémoire* would be indistinguishable from *lieux d'histoire.*

On the other hand, it is clear that without the intervention of history, time, and change, we would content ourselves with simply a schematic outline of the objects of memory. The *lieux* we speak of, then, are mixed, hybrid, mutant, bound intimately with life and death, with time and eternity; enveloped in a Möbius strip of the collective and the individual, the sacred and the profane, the immutable and the mobile. For if we accept that the most fundamental purpose of the *lieu de mémoire* is to stop time, to block the work of forgetting, to establish a state of things, to immortalize death, to materialize the immaterial—just as if gold were the only memory of money—all of this in order to capture a maximum of meaning in the fewest of signs, it is also clear that *lieux de mémoire* only exist because of their capacity for metamorphosis, an endless recycling of their meaning and an unpredictable proliferation of their ramifications.

Let us take two very different examples. First, the revolutionary calendar, which was very much a *lieu de mémoire* since, as a calendar, it was designed to provide the a priori frame of reference for all possible memory while, as a revolutionary document, through its nomenclature and symbolism, it was supposed to "open a new book to history," as its principal author ambitiously put it, or to "return Frenchmen entirely to themselves," according to another of its advocates. The function of the calendar, it was thought, would be to halt history at the hour of the Revolution by indexing future months, days, centuries, and years to the revolutionary epic. Yet, to our eyes, what further qualifies the revolutionary calendar as a *lieu de mémoire* is its apparently inevitable failure to have become what its founders hoped. If we still lived today according to its rhythm, it would have become as familiar to us as the Gregorian calendar and would consequently have lost its interest as a *lieu de mémoire.* It would have melted into our memorial landscape, serving only to date every other conceivable memorial site. As it turns out, its failure has not been complete; key dates still emerge from it to which it will always remain attached: Vendémiaire, Thermidor, Brumaire. Just so, the *lieu de mémoire* turns in on itself—an arabesque in the deforming mirror that is its truth.

Let us consider too the celebrated *Tour de la France par deux enfants,* also incontestably a *lieu de mémoire;* like the *Petit Lavisse,* it trained the memory of millions of French boys and girls. Thanks to it, the Minister of Public Instruction could draw his pocket watch at 8:05 A.M. and declare, "All of our children are crossing the Alps." Moreover, the *Tour* was an inventory of what one ought to know about France, an exercise in identification and a voyage of initiation. But here things get more complicated: a close reading shows that as of its publication in 1877, the *Tour* portrayed a France that no longer existed, and that in this year, when May 16 saw the consolidation of the Third Republic, it drew its seductive power from a subtle enchantment with the past. As is so often the case with books for children, the *Tour* owed its initial success to the memory of adults. And later? Thirty-five years after publication, on the eve of the war of 1914 when it was still a sovereign text, it seemed already a nostalgic institution: despite revisions, the older edition sold more than the new. Then the *Tour* became rare, employed only in marginal areas in the remote countryside. Slipping out of collective memory, it entered historical memory, then pedagogical memory. For its centennial, in 1977, however, just as the sales of an autobiography from the provinces, Pierre Hélias's *Le Cheval d'orgueil,* reached a million copies and when an industrial France stricken by economic crisis discovered its oral memory and peasant roots, the *Tour* was reprinted, and once again entered the collective memory, a different one this time, but still subject to being forgotten and revived in the future. What is the essence of this quintessential *lieu de mémoire*—its original intention or its return in the cycles of memory? Clearly both: all *lieux de mémoire* are objects *mises en abîme.*

It is this principle of double identity that enables us to map, within the indefinite multiplicity of sites, a hierarchy, a set of limits, a repertoire of ranges. This principle is crucial because, if one keeps in mind the broad categories of the genre—anything pertaining to the cult of the dead, anything relating to the patrimony, anything administering the presence of the past within the present—it is clear that some seemingly improbable objects can be legitimately considered *lieux de mémoire* while, conversely, many that seem to fit by definition should in fact be excluded. What makes certain prehistoric, geographical, archaeological locations important as sites is often precisely what ought to exclude them from being *lieux de mémoire:* the absolute absence of a will to remember and, by way of compensation, the crushing weight imposed on them by time, science, and the dreams of men. On the other hand, not every border marking has the credentials of the Rhine or the Finistère, that "Land's End" at the tip of Brittany ennobled in the pages of Michelet. Every constitution, every diplomatic treaty is a *lieu de mémoire,* although the constitution of 1793 lays a different claim than that of 1791, given the foundational status of the Declaration of the Rights of Man; and the peace of Nimwegen has a different status than, at both ends of the history of Europe, the Verdun compromise and the Yalta conference.

Amid these complexities, it is memory that dictates while history writes; this is why both history books and historical events merit special attention. As memory's ideal historical instruments, rather than as permutations of history and memory, they inscribe a neat border around a domain of memory. Are not every great historical work and the historical genre itself, every great event and the notion of event itself, in some sense by definition *lieux de mémoire?* The question calls for a precise answer.

Among history books, only those founded on a revision of memory or serving as its pedagogical breviaries are *lieux de mémoire.* In France, there have been relatively few moments that have established a new historical memory. The thirteenth-century *Grandes Chroniques de France* condensed dynastic memory and established the model for several centuries of historiography. In the sixteenth century, during the Wars of Religion, the school of so-called "perfect history" destroyed the legend of the monarchy's Trojan origins and restored Gaulish antiquity: Etienne Pasquier's *Recherches de la France* (1599), by the very modernity of its title (referring to "research" and "France" rather than to chronicling and dynastic rule), is an emblematic example. The historiography of the late Restoration abruptly introduced the modern conception of history: Thierry's *Lettres sur l'histoire de France* (1820) provided the inaugural impulse, and their publication as a volume in 1827 coincided, within a few months, with an illustrious beginner's first book, Michelet's *Précis d'histoire moderne* and with Guizot's first lectures on "the history of European civilization and of France." Next came the advent of national positivist history, whose manifesto was the *Revue historique* (1876) and whose monument is still Lavisse's twenty-seven-volume *Histoire de France.* One could also cite the rise of memoirs, as well as autobiographies and diaries. Chateaubriand's *Mémoires d'outre-tombe,* Stendhal's *Vie de Henry Brulard,* and the *Journal d'Amiel* are *lieux de mémoire* not because they are bigger or better examples but because they complicate the simple exercise of memory with a set of questions directed to memory itself. As much can be said for the memoirs of statesmen. From Sully to de Gaulle, from Richelieu's *Testament* to the *Mémorial de Sainte-Hélène* or Poincaré's *Journal,* the genre has its constants and specificities, independent of the uneven value of the texts. It implies an awareness of other memoirs, a superimposition of the man of letters and the man of action, the identification of individual discourse with collective discourse, the insertion of individual rationality into *raison d'état:* all motifs that, in the broad perspective of national memory, compel us to think of them as *lieux de mémoire.*

As for "great events," only two types are especially pertinent, and not in any way as a function of their "greatness." On the one hand, there are those minuscule events, barely remarked at the time, on which posterity retrospectively confers the greatness of origins, the solemnity of inaugural ruptures. On the other hand, there are those nonevents that are immediately charged with heavy symbolic meaning and that, at the moment of their occurrence, seem like anticipated commemorations of themselves; contemporary history, by means of the media, has seen a proliferation of stillborn attempts to create such events. Thus, on one side, the election of Hugh Capet, an unremarkable incident but one to which ten centuries of posterity, ending on the scaffold, have given a weight it did not possess at the start; on the other side, the wagon of Rethondes, the handshake of Montoire, or the Liberation parade down the Champs-Elysées. The founding event or the spectacular event, but in neither case the event itself: indeed, it is the exclusion of the event that defines the *lieu de mémoire.* Memory attaches itself to sites, whereas history attaches itself to events.

Within the category, however, nothing prevents us from imagining every possible distribution and necessary classification, from such natural, concretely experienced *lieux de mémoire* as cemeteries, museums, and anniversaries; to the most intellectually elaborate ones—not only notions such as generation, lineage, local memory, but also those of the formal divisions of inherited property (*partages*), on which every perception of French space is founded, or of the "landscape as a painting" that comes to mind when one thinks of Corot or of Cézanne's *Mont Sainte-Victoire.* Should we stress the *lieu de mémoire*'s material aspects, they would readily display themselves in a vast gradation. There are portable *lieux,* of which the people of memory, the Jews, have given a major example in the Tablets of the Law; there are the topographical ones, which owe everything to the specificity of their location and to being rooted in the ground—so, for example, the conjunction of sites of tourism and centers of historical scholarship, the Bibliothèque nationale on the site of the Hôtel

Mazarin, the Archives nationales in the Hôtel Soubise. Then there are the monumental memory-sites, not to be confused with architectural sites alone. Statues or monuments to the dead, for instance, owe their meaning to their intrinsic existence; even though their location is far from arbitrary, one could justify relocating them without altering their meaning. Such is not the case with ensembles constructed over time, which draw their meaning from the complex relations between their elements: such are mirrors of a world or a period, like the cathedral of Chartres or the palace of Versailles.

If, on the other hand, we were to stress the functional element, an array of *lieux de mémoire* would display themselves, ranging from those dedicated to preserving an incommunicable experience that would disappear along with those who shared it—such as the veterans' associations—to those whose purpose is pedagogical, as the manuals, dictionaries, testaments, and memoranda drafted by heads of families in the early modern period for the edification of their descendants.

If, finally, we were most concerned with the symbolic element, we might oppose, for example, dominant and dominated *lieux de mémoire.* The first, spectacular and triumphant, imposing and, generally, imposed—either by a national authority or by an established interest, but always from above—characteristically have the coldness and solemnity of official ceremonies. One attends them rather than visits them. The second are places of refuge, sanctuaries of spontaneous devotion and silent pilgrimage, where one finds the living heart of memory. On the one hand, the Sacré-Coeur or the national *obsèques* of Paul Valéry; on the other, the popular pilgrimage of Lourdes or the burial of Jean-Paul Sartre; here de Gaulle's funeral at Notre-Dame, there the cemetery of Colombey.

These classifications could be refined ad infinitum. One could oppose public sites of memory and private ones; pure sites, exhaustive of their commemorative function—such as funeral eulogies, the battlefield of Douaumont or the Wall of the Fédérés—and those composite sites in which the commemorative element is only one amid many symbolic meanings, such as the national flag, festival itineraries, pilgrimages, and so on. The value of a first attempt at a typology would lie not in its rigor or comprehensiveness, not even in its evocative power, but in the fact that it is possible. For the very possibility of a history of *lieux de mémoire* demonstrates the existence of an invisible thread linking apparently unconnected objects. It suggests that the comparison of the cemetery of Père-Lachaise and the Statistique générale de la France is not the same as the surrealist encounter of the umbrella and the sewing machine. There is a differentiated network to which all of these separate identities belong, an unconscious organization of collective memory that is our responsibility to bring to consciousness. The national history of France today traverses this network.

One simple but decisive trait of *lieux de mémoire* sets them apart from every type of history to which we have become accustomed, ancient or modern. Every previous historical or scientific approach to memory, whether national or social, has concerned itself with *realia,* with things in themselves and in their immediate reality. Contrary to historical objects, however, *lieux de mémoire* have no referent in reality; or, rather, they are their own referent: pure, exclusively self-referential signs. This is not to say that they are without content, physical presence, or history; it is to suggest that what makes them *lieux de mémoire* is precisely that by which they escape from history. In this sense, the *lieu de mémoire* is double: a site of excess closed upon itself, concentrated in its own name, but also forever open to the full range of its possible significations.

This is what makes the history of *lieux de mémoire* at once banal and extraordinary. Obvious topics, classic material, sources ready at hand, the least sophisticated methods: one would think we were returning to long outmoded historical methods. But such is not the case. Although these objects must be grasped in empirical detail, the issues at stake are ill suited to expression in the categories of traditional historiography. Reflecting on *lieux de mémoire* transforms historical criticism into critical history—and not only in its methods; it allows history a secondary, purely transferential existence, even a kind of reawakening. Like war, the history of *lieux de mémoire* is an art of implementation, practiced in the fragile happiness derived from relating to rehabilitated objects and from the involvement of the historian in his or her subject. It is a history that, in the last analysis, rests upon what it mobilizes: an impalpable, barely expressible, self-imposed bond; what remains of our ineradicable, carnal attachment to these faded symbols; the reincarnation of history as it was practiced by Michelet, irrestibly putting to mind the recovery from lost love of which Proust spoke so well—that moment when the obsessive grasp of passion finally loosens but whose true sadness is no longer to suffer from what one has so long suffered, henceforth to understand only with the mind's reason, no longer with the unreason of the heart.

This is a very literary reference. Should we regret it or, on the contrary, suggest its full justification? Once again, the answer derives from our present historical situation. In fact, memory has never known more than two forms of legitimacy: historical and literary. These have run parallel to each other but until now always separately. At present the boundary between the two is blurring: following closely upon the successive deaths of memory-history and memory-fiction, a new kind of history has been born, which owes its prestige and legitimacy to the new relation it maintains to the past. History has become our replaceable imagination—hence the last stand of faltering fiction in the renaissance of the historical novel, the vogue for personalized documents, the literary revitalization of historical drama, the success of the oral historical tale. Our interest in these *lieux de mémoire* that anchor, condense, and express the exhausted capital of our collective memory derives from this new sensibility. History has become the deep reference of a period that has been wrenched from its depths, a realistic novel in a period in which there are no real novels. Memory has been promoted to the center of history: such is the spectacular bereavement of literature.

Contributors

David W. Blight is associate professor of history and black studies at Amherst College. He is the author of *Frederick Douglass' Civil War; Keeping Faith in Jubilee* (1989) and editor of *Narrative of the Life of Frederick Douglass: An American Slave* (1993). He is currently writing a book tentatively titled "Race and Reunion: The Memory of the Civil War in American Culture."

Hazel V. Carby is professor of English, African-American, and American studies at Yale University. She is the author of *Reconstructing Womanhood: The Emergence of the Afro-American Woman Novelist* (1987). She is presently completing *Race Men: Geneologies of Race, Nation and Manhood* (forthcoming, Harvard University Press) and *Women, Migration and the Formation of a Blues Culture* (forthcoming, Verso).

VèVè A. Clark is associate professor of African and Caribbean literature in the African American Studies Department at the University of California, Berkeley. She is coeditor of the multivolume biography *The Legend of Maya Deren* (1984—) and has published widely on African and Caribbean literatures, Haitian theater, and Katherine Dunham's contributions to American dance.

Melvin Dixon was professor of English at Queens College and the Graduate Center of the City University of New York. He was the author of several books, including *Vanishing Rooms* (1991), *Trouble the Water* (1989), *Ride Out the Wilderness: Geography and Identity in Afro-American Literature* (1987), and *Change of Territory* (1985). He was also the translator of *Leopold Senghor: The Collected Poetry* (1991).

Geneviève Fabre is professor at the University of Paris. She is the author of *Le Théâtre noir aux Etats-Unis* (1982), revised and translated as *Drumbeats, Masks and Metaphor: Contemporary Afro-American Theater* (1983), and is the editor of several volumes of essays, including ones on Toni Morrison (*Profils Américains,* 1993; *Beloved She's Mine,* 1993) and on ethnic identity (*Configurations of Ethnicity,* 1993; *Parcours Identitaires,* 1994). She has also recently written on Zora Neale Hurston, the blues culture in the 1920s, and the Harlem Renaissance. Her current projects include two books on ethnic celebrations in the United States (coedited with Ramón Guttérez, forthcoming from the University of New Mexico Press) and on celebrative and commemorative events in African-American culture.

Michel Fabre is the director of the Center for African-American Studies and New Literatures in English at the Université de la Sorbonne Nouvelle (Paris III). His latest publications are *From Harlem to Paris: Black Americans in France, 1840–1980* (1981); with Robert Skinner and Lester Sullivan, *Chester Himes: An Annotated Primary and Secondary Bibliography* (1992); a new edition of *The Unfinished Quest of Richard Wright* (1993), and *Conversations with Richard Wright* (1993).

Karen Fields was a founding director of the Frederick Douglass Institute for African and African-American Studies (1986–92) at the University of Rochester and remains on the faculty. She is the author of *Revival and Rebellion in Colonial Central Africa* (1983) and coauthor with Mamie Garvin Fields of *Lemon Swamp and Other Places: A Carolina Memoir* (NY: Free Press 1983).

Andrée-Anne Kekeh teaches American studies and translation at the Université du Maine (Le Mans, France). Her dissertation was on African-American women writers, and she has published two articles: "Corps singuliers: Les Corps féminins dans l'oeuvre de Toni Morrison" (*Profils Américains*) and "Au pays des couleurs: Voyage dans les imaginaires de Toni Morrison et Ntozake Shange" (forthcoming, in *Parcours Identitaires*. Presses de La Sorbonne Nouvelle, 1994).

Angelika Krüger-Kahloula teaches English, French, and Spanish at a high school near Frankfurt am Main, while working on a postdoctoral thesis on "Social and Cultural Aspects of Death and Dying in African-American Culture." She is the author of *Die List des Schwächeren: Motivgeschichte und Anthropologie der afroamerikanischen Erzähltradition* (1984) and "Homage and Hegemony: African-American Grave Inscription and Decoration," in *Slavery in the Americas* (1993).

Nellie Y. McKay teaches American and African-American literature at the University of Wisconsin, Madison. She is the author of *Jean Toomer, Artist: A Study of His Literary Life and Work* (1984) and editor of *Critical Essays on Toni Morrison* (1987). She has published many essays on black American women writers and on issues in contemporary literary black and/or feminist studies. She is currently working on a study of black women's autobiographies and is coeditor of the forthcoming Norton Anthology of African-American Literature.

Robert G. O'Meally is Zora Neale Hurston Professor of American Literature at Columbia University. He is the author of *The Craft of Ralph Ellison* (1979) and *Lady Day: The Many Faces of Billie Holiday* (1991). He is currently working on a book-length study of Sarah Vaughan.

Alessandro Portelli is professor American literature at the University of Rome ("La Sapienza"). He is the author of *The Death of Luigi Trastulli: Form and Meaning in Oral History* (1991) and *The Text and the Voice: Orality, Writing, and Democracy in American Literature* (forthcoming, Columbia University Press).

Richard J. Powell, associate professor of art history at Duke University, has written extensively on African-American art and culture, including essays in edited collections, journal articles, and exhibition catalogs. His major publications include *Jacob Lawrence, Homecoming: The Art and Life of William H. Johnson* (1991) and *The Blues Aesthetic: Black Culture and Modernism* (1989).

Werner Sollors teaches English and African-American studies at Harvard University and is currently completing *Neither Black Nor White and Yet Both* (forthcoming, Oxford University Press), a thematic study of interracial literature. Most recently he has edited *The Return of Thematic Criticism* (1993) and a bilingual version of Jean Toomer's *Cane* (1993); he is also the coeditor of *Blacks at Harvard: A Documentary History of African American Experience at Harvard and Radcliffe* (1993).

Robert Stepto, a professor of American literature at Yale University, is the author of *From Behind the Veil: A Study of Afro-American Narrative* (1979) and an editor of *The Harper American Literature.* "Washington Park" is taken from a forthcoming collection of essays entitled *Idlewild and Other Seasons.*

Index

N.B.: Page numbers in italics refer to illustrations.